Alexandra Grey
Language Rights in a Changing China

Contributions to the Sociology of Language

Edited by
Ofelia García
Francis M. Hult

Founding editor
Joshua A. Fishman

Volume 113

Alexandra Grey

Language Rights in a Changing China

—

A National Overview and Zhuang Case Study

ISBN 978-1-5015-2100-3
e-ISBN (PDF) 978-1-5015-1255-1
e-ISBN (EPUB) 978-1-5015-1240-7
ISSN 1861-0676

Library of Congress Control Number: 2020952711

Bibliographic information published by the Deutsche Nationalbibliothek
The Deutsche Nationalbibliothek lists this publication in the Deutsche Nationalbibliografie;
detailed bibliographic data are available on the Internet at http://dnb.dnb.de.

© 2022 Walter de Gruyter Inc., Boston/Berlin
This volume is text- and page-identical with the hardback published in 2021.
Cover image: sculpies/shutterstock
Typesetting: Integra Software Services Pvt. Ltd.
Printing and binding: CPI books GmbH, Leck

www.degruyter.com

In memory of Hannah Yiu.

Preface

In my journey to a research problem centered on languages in the South of China, I gathered many photographs of places and people. The small selection in Figures 1 to 3, all from cities in the Guangxi Zhuangzu Autonomous Region (GZAR) in South China, indicate how everyday urban streetscapes and associated language practices in China have changed since the middle of the twentieth century. Moreover, the obvious changes in public, urban life revealed in these photographs hint at potentially significant changes in linguistic, social and cultural spheres of life that photographs cannot capture. What language varieties did the photographed soldiers, pedestrians and cyclists use? How did their language practices, and views about them, change along with the enormous transformations in Chinese society during this time?

Figure 1: Urban main street, unspecified city in GZAR, circa 1940s from (Li and GZAR Areal Annals Compilation Committee 2010: 308, with thanks to participant "Mr S").

One of the transformations evident in these photographs is the addition of English on signage by the twenty-first century, while written Mandarin is a fixture across

Figure 2: Photographs captioned "Main street of Kweilin [Guilin]", GZAR, 1976, photographed by the author's mother, reprinted with permission.

Figure 3: A main street of Guilin, GZAR, 2015, photographed by the author during fieldwork.

the span of these photographs. However, the photographs show a striking absence of *Zhuang* language. Zhuang language is a Tai language – not a Mandarin language – and it was considered so widely spoken and defining of ethnicity that the Zhuangzu minority group was recognized by the People's Republic of China (PRC) government and named after the language in the early 1950s. Then the Guangxi Zhuangzu Autonomous Region was named after – and for – this group in 1958. (NB. I use 'the PRC' instead of China only when I need to disambiguate the current nation from its forebears.) Moreover, this area was where the Zhuang dialects originated. Yet Zhuang does not appear on any of the signs in these photographs. Rather, in the pre-communist era shown in Figure 1, public texts are prevalent in the urban streetscape, mostly commercial slogans in Mandarin exclusively using traditional characters. In the 1970s (Figure 2), by contrast, large signage seems absent from a streetscape designed for pedestrians, cyclists and minimal commerce. The small signs that are visible on the right in this photograph are written in simplified Mandarin characters; many are indistinct but on close inspection, one says 拉链 (zipper) i.e. a repair shop. Nowadays, as Figure 3 shows, a mixture of large commercial and orientation texts, designed to be visible to motorists, dominate the urban streetscape. In addition to the Mandarin in simplified characters on this contemporary signage, the Roman alphabet now also has a visible presence, used both for English and as the official auxiliary *Pinyin* script for the national language, *Putonghua* (officially standardized Mandarin).

These simple observations point to an intriguing interplay between language practices and political and economic transformations. Moreover, as noted by the renowned contemporary sociolinguist, Monica Heller (2003: 473), changes relating to economic globalization in the late twentieth century are inseparable from transformations to languages and identities. Economic globalization reached China – or rather, China launched itself into economic globalization – after 1978. This globalized and still globalizing context ought therefore be an inseparable part of my research into language and identity in China.

Heller goes on to make the point that processes of economic, linguistic and identity change can be viewed with particular clarity through the "window" of ethnolinguistic minority groups. That is, groups like the Zhuangzu offer a way to re-focus an examination into China's processes of change under conditions of globalization from its more visible, mainstream aspects to the marginal experiences. Looking again at my selection of photographs, which are another kind of window, we may wonder especially how China's opening-up has transformed languages and identities in GZAR.

This question struck me and gradually clarified into a research project, after I moved to China in 2010. China's ethnolinguistic diversity often came up in conversations as both a source of pride and a problem, but – as in the photographs – this diversity was invisible to me within everyday linguistic landscapes. Walking the streets of Beijing, where I then lived, I saw mainly Putonghua and some English, much like in Figure 3. Ethnolinguistic minorities seemed to exist more in rhetoric than reality in Beijing; while I knew minority people continued to live and speak various languages in peripheral parts of China, they were not obvious in the nation's urban centers. I travelled through China as much as work and studies allowed me, finding both high levels of sameness and high levels of difference. In the northern and southern reaches of the nation, ethnolinguistic diversity became more obvious to me.

When I first travelled to the southern periphery, visiting a rice-growing village and small cities in Guizhou in 2011 and then hiking a tea field route near the Myanmar border in Yunnan in 2012, I found myself in landscapes and linguistic soundscapes more different to Beijing than anything I had so far encountered in China. Although I was also familiar with the rocky Great Wall and the gilded elegance of Imperial Chinese art, it was this 'other' China that resonated with me. And yet, at the same time, Guizhou and Yunnan were as similar to Beijing as they were different: there were still Putonghua street signs in simplified characters naming a People's Street and a People's Square in every city, and there were the same hotpot eateries, China Mobile stores, advertisements for private English tuition, supermarket chains and China Central Television (CCTV) soap operas playing on small televisions in guard posts and tobacconists. People wore the same casual and colorful Western-inspired clothing (but with less luxury branding outside of Beijing) and the new airport in Jinhong, in southern Yunnan, looked to be a miniature version of Beijing's Capital International Airport. I became ever more intrigued: how was diversity, especially linguistic diversity, continuing, and when and where was it *not* continuing, given high levels of internal migration and the apparent reach of cultural homogeneity and the unified market?

Wherever I went, I found that locals were, like me, interested in talking about linguistic diversity. That, and my observations of the way linguistic diversity was foregrounded and backgrounded in different contexts, motivated me to study China's sociolinguistic minorities as my window into China's fast-paced political, social and economic transformations. And so I began doctoral research in 2013. The endeavor eventually culminated in this book, which I dedicate to all the colleagues, teachers, students, friends and strangers who have helped me better know, see and hear China.

Contents

Preface —— VII

List of Figures —— XV

List of Tables —— XVII

Part I: Foundations

1 **An ethnographic study of contemporary Chinese language rights** —— 3
1.1 What is this book about? —— 3
1.2 How have researchers responded to a changing China? —— 7
1.3 Extending Bourdieusian critical sociolinguistic theory into language rights and policy studies —— 14
1.4 Why focus on Zhuang language and linguistic landscapes? —— 19
1.5 What did I find? (A chapter outline) —— 23
1.6 How did I do this study? —— 26
1.6.1 Multi-sited and multi-modal data collection —— 27
1.6.2 Anchor site selection —— 28
1.6.3 Purposive participant selection —— 29

2 **What is Zhuang? A critical sociolinguistic profile** —— 34
2.1 Introducing the sociolinguistic profile of Zhuang —— 34
2.2 A Zhuang language —— 35
2.3 A Zhuang polity —— 38
2.4 A Zhuang territory —— 45
2.5 A Zhuang speaker —— 49
2.6 A Zhuang reader —— 57
2.7 A Zhuang disadvantage —— 59
2.8 Concluding discussion: Naturalizing and denaturalizing Zhuang —— 62

Part II: Laws and Governance Structures

3   **The foundational language rights: Legal provisions about minority languages and minority peoples —— 67**
3.1   The minority language right —— 68
3.2   Language rights in education —— 73
3.3   Language rights in courts —— 76
3.4   Criminalization as a form of language right —— 79
3.5   Concluding discussion: Legally weak minority language rights —— 79

4   **Beliefs about law and language —— 83**
4.1   Participants' views as discourse about linguistic justice —— 85
4.2   Case law as discourse about linguistic justice —— 89
4.3   Laws and policies as discourse about linguistic justice —— 93
4.4   Concluding discussion: Linguistic developmentalism further constrains minority language rights —— 102

5   **The structural distribution of language governance powers —— 107**
5.1   Geographic boundaries in Zhuang language governance —— 109
5.2   Institutional boundaries in Zhuang language governance —— 114
5.2.1   Representation through the participation of minority minzu within organs of governance —— 115
5.2.2   Representation through using minority languages within organs of governance —— 124
5.2.3   Perceptions of the structure of Zhuang language governance —— 126
5.3   A close up: The constrained governance of Zhuang in education in GZAR —— 128
5.4   Concluding discussion: The structures of territory, authority and representation struggle to respond to Zhuang interests —— 137

Part III: Lived Linguistic Landscapes

6   **Visual ideologies of Zhuang in linguistic landscapes —— 141**
6.1   Introducing the linguistic landscape study of visual ideologies —— 141
6.2   The choice of landscapes —— 143

6.3	An empirical analysis of patterns in language display —— 144	
6.3.1	Monolingual use of Putonghua or Zhuang —— 144	
6.3.2	Bilingual signage —— 151	
6.3.3	Multilingual signage —— 168	
6.4	Analyzing the linguistic order produced by patterned multilingualism —— 174	
6.4.1	Spatialized linguistic orders —— 176	
6.4.2	Commercial ideologies —— 181	
6.4.3	Grassroots language practices and state ideologies of polyvocality —— 183	
6.5	Concluding discussion: Normatively displacing Zhuang —— 184	

7 New semiotic displays of old "Zhuangness" —— 187
7.1 Introducing multi-modal representations of Zhuangness —— 187
7.2 Explicit references to "Zhuang" or "Zhuang language" —— 188
7.3 Non-linguistic references to Zhuangness —— 195
7.4 Referencing Zhuangness in the "Zhuang" magazine, *Third of the Third* —— 204
7.5 Concluding discussion: Temporal and cultural otherness is made visible in the landscape —— 213

8 The multiple meanings of Zhuang displays in lived landscapes —— 218
8.1 Introducing the lived landscape approach —— 218
8.2 Misrecognition of Zhuang displays —— 222
8.3 Overlooking Zhuang displays —— 228
8.4 Zhuang displays as tokenistic —— 230
8.5 Zhuang displays as contributions to heritage and language maintenance —— 235
8.6 Perceptions of learning to read Zhuang displays —— 243
8.7 Concluding discussion: Mobilizing signage as an identity resource —— 247

9 Linguascaping through language policy —— 251
9.1 Introduction —— 251
9.2 Laws intervening directly to regulate linguascapes —— 255
9.3 Laws about linguistic landscapes as dynamic discourses —— 260
9.3.1 Under-application of language laws —— 261

| 9.3.2 | Over-application of language laws —— 263 |
| 9.4 | Concluding discussion: What this linguascaping analysis implies for the new *GZAR Regulations* —— 266 |

Part IV: Conclusions

10 Summary and conclusions regarding language rights in a changing China —— 275
10.1 Conclusions regarding language rights in a changing China —— 275
10.1.1 The findings, overall —— 277
10.1.2 Recapitulating Part One —— 278
10.1.3 Recapitulating Part Two —— 279
10.1.4 Recapitulating Part Three —— 282
10.2 Looking ahead for Zhuang and other Chinese minority languages —— 286
10.2.1 A letter to twenty-first century Zhuang policy-makers —— 287

11 General implications for language rights and policy research and practice —— 294
11.1 Linguistic justice —— 295
11.2 The nationalization of heritage —— 300
11.3 Implications for policies of minority language display —— 302

Appendix —— 305

Acknowledgements —— 313

References —— 315

Index —— 337

List of Figures

Figure 1   Urban main street, unspecified city in GZAR, circa 1940s from (Li and GZAR Areal Annals Compilation Committee 2010: 308, with thanks to participant "Mr S") —— VII
Figure 2   Photographs captioned "Main street of Kweilin [Guilin]", GZAR, 1976, photographed by the author's mother, reprinted with permission —— VIII
Figure 3   A main street of Guilin, GZAR, 2015, photographed by the author during fieldwork —— VIII
Figure 4   Map highlighting GZAR in South China; map adapted from OpenStreetMap (openstreetmap.org) and OpenStreetMap Foundation (opendatacommons.org) —— 20
Figure 5   Anchor fieldwork sites, adapted from Maps Open Source (n. d.) —— 28
Figure 6   Illustration of script diversity: Zhuang scripts adapted from Ager (2016), other data my own —— 37
Figure 7   "Province de Quang-Si" (d'Anville 1785), with thanks to the National Library of Australia —— 40
Figure 8   Territories with titular Zhuangzu governments, adapted from Chinafolio (2016) —— 47
Figure 9   "A Zhuang girl" (China Encyclopedia Compilation Group 2008: 42) —— 49
Figure 10 Annotation showing Zhuang-speaking "Zh" areas on CASS Institute of Linguistics et al.'s (2012) map entitled 广西壮族自治区语言分布 ('GZAR Language Distribution') —— 53
Figure 11 Educational attainment as at 2005, by minzu, based on Guo (2013: 25–33) —— 61
Figure 12 Cartoon from the 'Guangxi News web', 2014 —— 92
Figure 13 Zhuang language governance organization chart —— 112
Figure 14 Billboard, curb outside GZAR Library; Nanning: Putonghua —— 145
Figure 15 Entrance, GU campus; Nanning: Putonghua —— 146
Figure 16 GZAR Library; Nanning: Putonghua-only —— 146
Figure 17 Billboard; Nanning: Putonghua —— 147
Figure 18 Street-name signs with advertising panes; Nanning: Street-name: dual-script Putonghua/Zhuang, poster: Putonghua —— 148
Figure 19 Cafeteria tabletop, GUN; Nanning: Putonghua —— 149
Figure 20 Street-name sign; Nanning: Putonghua —— 149
Figure 21 Road sign; Nanning: Putonghua —— 150
Figure 22 Foyer, GZAR Library; Nanning: Zhuang —— 151
Figure 23 Road sign; highway between Nanning and Wuming: Putonghua/English —— 152
Figure 24 Bins; Nanning: Putonghua/English —— 153
Figure 25 GZAR Library entrance; Nanning: Putonghua/English —— 153
Figure 26 On-campus street-name sign, YMU; Kunming: Putonghua/English —— 155
Figure 27 Commercial signage; Nanning: some English, mainly Putonghua —— 156
Figure 28 Billboard; Nanning: Putonghua/English —— 156
Figure 29 Billboards; Nanning: Putonghua/English —— 157
Figure 30 Street-name; Nanning: Zhuang/dual-script Putonghua —— 158

List of Figures

Figure 31 Screenshot of baidu.com map of GZAR Library environs: Putonghua —— 159
Figure 32 Street-name; Wuming: Zhuang/dual-script Putonghua. (Background: commercial signage; dual-script Putonghua.) —— 160
Figure 33 GZAR Museum entrance; Nanning: façade: Zhuang/Putonghua characters, banner: Putonghua, assorted signage: mainly Putonghua —— 160
Figure 34 Government agency entrance; Guilin: Putonghua/Zhuang —— 161
Figure 35 Entrance stone, GZAR Library; Nanning: traditional Chinese characters/Zhuang —— 162
Figure 36 Dining area, Zhuang Home-style Restaurant; Wuming: Putonghua/Sawndip —— 163
Figure 37 Billboard; Guilin: Putonghua/Zhuang —— 165
Figure 38 Screenshot of Zhuang Language News 31 March 2014 —— 167
Figure 39 Main entrance, Guangxi University of Nationalities; Nanning: gateway sign: Zhuang/Putonghua/English. Bank sign: Putonghua/English —— 169
Figure 40 Departures entrance; Nanning Airport: Putonghua/English/Vietnamese —— 171
Figure 41 Office of Zhuang Studies academics, MUC; Beijing: Zhuang/Putonghua/Dong —— 173
Figure 42 Campus notices, YMU; Kunming: banner and LHS poster in Putonghua, RHS poster in eleven minority languages including Zhuang, and Putonghua —— 173
Figure 43 Department store stall; Nanning: Putonghua/English —— 190
Figure 44 Curation, Zhuang Culture Exhibition, Guangxi Museum of Nationalities; Nanning: Putonghua/Zhuang/English —— 191
Figure 45 Guangxi Museum of Nationalities; Nanning: Zhuang/Putonghua —— 196
Figure 46 Cover of first *Third of the Third* magazine —— 197
Figure 47 A section of Plate 13 from Tapp and Cohn (2003) —— 198
Figure 48 Map of GZAR with Putonghua toponyms and images of Zhuang costumes, Guangxi Museum of Nationalities; Nanning —— 199
Figure 49 Postcard purchased at GZAR Museum gift shop; Nanning —— 200
Figure 50 Images in the Zhuangzu Cultural Exhibition Hall, Guangxi Museum of Nationalities, 2014 —— 201
Figure 51 Minority peoples on billboard, Guangxi Museum of Nationalities' forecourt, 2014 —— 202
Figure 52 Billboard on a road in Urumqi, 2013 —— 203
Figure 53 1990 *Third of the Third* cover —— 206
Figure 54 1987 magazine covers —— 207
Figure 55 1998 *Third of the Third* covers —— 208
Figure 56 2014–2 *Third of the Third* front and back covers —— 209
Figure 57 Pages from 2018(3) edition of *Third of the Third* —— 211
Figure 58 Embroidered shoes and dolls on sale at the Guangxi Museum of Nationalities Ethnic Park's Black-Clothes Zhuang House, 2014 —— 212
Figure 59 Mr E gives an impromptu lesson in reading Zhuang to staff-member at GZAR Museum —— 247

List of Tables

Table 1 Relative Zhuangzu poverty. Source: (Guo et al. 2015: 37–38, 46,174–175; Guo 2013: 125–127, 141–142, 160–161) —— **60**
Table 2 Student participants' profiles —— **305**
Table 3 Language leader participants' profiles —— **310**
Table 4 Student participants' places of origins and of university —— **312**

Part I: **Foundations**

1 An ethnographic study of contemporary Chinese language rights

1.1 What is this book about?

This book is an investigation of how language rights now affect *Zhuang*, the most-spoken official minority language in China. The book asks how language rights and attendant policies are practiced and are made socially meaningful in relation to Zhuang, its speakers and its "notional inheritor[s]" (Rampton and Charalambous 2010: 4), that is, the people who might once have grown up as Zhuang speakers but no longer do. Unlike some countries, China sees linguistic diversity and language use as matters to be governed. It therefore enacted laws and promulgated official policies about certain non-Mandarin languages, national standardized Mandarin (*Putonghua*), and Mandarin topolects, over the course of the twentieth century. This has included having a minority language right regarding non-Mandarin languages in constitutional form since 1949 and a national majority language right regarding Putonghua in legislation since 2000. China has updated its official language policies this century but its laws about minority language have remained virtually unchanged. And yet the linguistic and socio-economic contexts in which those laws operate has changed markedly.

China opened itself to global economic and political interactions in the late 1970s in a top-down transitional phase of liberalization known as "Opening and Reform", steering the nation towards an internationally connected, capitalist-socialist hybrid political economy. Opening and Reform paved the way for an ongoing drive towards what the state still calls "modernization" e.g. in its recent *Communiqué on the Fifth Plenum* (quoted in Bishop 2020), which is an important national policy document. In the 1980s, modernization entailed a degree of de-centralization of policy-making. This included de-centralizing language policy (Adamson and Feng 2009: 322). This modernization also included the beginning of gradual and still ongoing reform to the structures of social organisation, specifically, no longer binding people as tightly to place through the *hukou* rural and urban household residency system and developing structures through which employment and welfare could be organized other than through *danwei* (workplace units). Migration – mainly migration to the quickly-growing cities of East China – resulted from this structural modernization and from relaxing the central control over both university placements and the job market.

Opening and Reform built upon almost a century of dramatic transformation, including the mid-century transition from a young republic enduring a civil war to a stable, communist, industrialized and centrally-planned state, the

People's Republic. The social significance of linguistic diversity changed with these changes, and continued to evolve once the PRC was established, as the politics of diverse languages – by the 1950s dominantly constructed as diverse *minority* languages – fell prey to the perception that ethno-linguistic difference was threatening and bourgeois during the Cultural Revolution. Perceptions changed again with Opening and Reform and modernization, particularly as these transformations merged with globalization.

As the modernization progressed, the current era of globalization emerged, further catalyzing change within China. Globalization manifested in China in many ways, including the state-backed but also highly commercial spread of English language teaching and learning. This has prompted significant changes in beliefs about and practices of English. Gao (2015: 4) notes that historically English was considered "barbarian". State-led discourses have reframed English as a useful language, but as inherently separate from the language of cultural essence, Mandarin: this is called the *yong-ti* dichotomy. More recently, however, there is some indication that younger Chinese people are also starting to value English language for other reasons, including identifying with English language practices.

English was not the only language to spread as modernization and globalization fused in China, Putonghua did too. Of a piece with the introduction in 2000 of the law containing the right to learn and use Putonghua, Putonghua has increasingly been deployed by the government but also by commentators, academics and individuals as a "rallying point" (adopting the phrase of Heller et al. 2014: 542; also Coupland 2001: 18; Fishman 1999: 364) for national cohesion and Chinese identity (see e.g. Simpson 2016). By the turn of this century, Zhou and Ross (2004: 16) observed that "coupled with globalization and the forces of market economy, China's modernization drive appears to favor only two dominant languages, [Putonghua] Chinese as the national commonly-used language and English as the world language." Moreover, as the twenty-first century began, China was preoccupied with harmonizing a nation-wide society. 2020's *Communiqué on the Fifth Plenum* makes clear that China remains focused on national security and civic harmony (Bishop 2020). In this context, the old fear of ethno-linguistic difference as a threat to the nation has re-emerged, hardening into securitized language policy, especially in areas of unrest in the North-West.

A recent language policy change which implies the scale of language shift that the other transformations are creating is China's new, national *Yubao* ('Language Protection') project. Shen and Gao (2019: 7) explain that Yubao explicitly and officially frames linguistic diversity as a resource and "is supposed to address the problems that may be generated by [the state's] commitment to unity, such as disappearing diversity". While Yubao considers some languages as resources worth maintaining for international economic exchange (but not many minority languages), it considers all language as cultural resources. To operationalize this belief, it focuses on documenting minority languages as they disappear. It has "limited effects on bringing these varieties to life" (Shen and Gao 2019: 7). This is another change to be investigated in this book. Will the resulting, disembodied records of minority languages – historic language artefacts – remain meaningful as cultural and identity resources in the future, if people do not also still speak those languages?

Even from this overview of how China is changing, a reader may also be starting to consider such questions as:
- Are these newer circumstances causing existing language rights to engender new practices and norms, or to become obsolete?
- How are linguistic toleration, promotion, marginalization or oppression changing as China changes?
- How is society now linguistically and socially organized, and what roles are laws about language playing in that?

These are pressing questions because they are relevant not only within China but also to language policy-makers, advocates and scholars in other nations. Many aspects of China's transformation, and some of its law and policy approaches, are not unique to China. Nevertheless, the research literature has largely focused on liberal democracies of the "Global North"; it stands to benefit from a widening of the array of studies, especially studies of China as that nation's global influence grows.

Although these questions are pressing, the official texts of laws and policies, by themselves, cannot fully answer these questions. This is because they cannot tell us about the actual experiences and practices of language governance in specific, real contexts. To better answer the questions I have therefore combined legal analysis and sociolinguistic ethnography: a research approach entailing empirical fieldwork on people's uses of, and beliefs about, language. This combination required methodological innovation. The rich data-sets it produced are the foundation for this unusually comprehensive addition to the relatively new academic field of language policy ethnography, a field so far comprised mainly of journal-article-length studies. I have therefore provided a brief methodological overview at the end of this chapter. Before we get to that, and before even proceeding to further examine the relevance of recent changes in China as well as the theoretical motivations for this study, let me introduce the language rights in question.

First, a fundamental minority language protection is enshrined in the current *PRC Constitution* (National People's Congress 1982: "*Constitution*"). It is expressed as a "freedom to use and develop" officially-recognized minority languages, of which Zhuang is one. This current protection follows the inclusion of more or less the same provision in each of the three preceding constitutions (National People's Congress 1954: Article 3, 1975: Article 4, and 1978: Article 4) and in the *Common Program* (Communist Party of China 1949, Article 53), which served as the constitution from the throes of the PRC's founding in 1949 until 1954. A minority language freedom is one of the various species of language right found in laws around the world, a form sometimes called a liberty or a negative right. This form of language right has its own legal limitations which I examine in depth later in this book, but expressing such a language right in the Chinese constitution is nevertheless part of a commitment by the state to protecting the interests of China's 55 official minority groups or *minzu*.

Second, from the turn of this century onwards, there has been an important piece of national legislation in force concerning Putonghua: the 中华人民共和国国家通用语言文字法 '*Law of The PRC on the Standard Spoken and Written Chinese Language*' (Standing Committee of the National People's Congress 2000: "*Putonghua Law*"). This legislation underpins the current suite of protective and promotional policies relating to Putonghua. As a piece of legal drafting, it is extensive and detailed, and it mobilizes legal authority to monopolize certain domains of language use for Putonghua. Moreover, this legislation expresses another language right, a positive right to learn and use Putonghua. This legislation enshrines what was already developing in practice in the late twentieth century: the lingua franca usage of Putonghua across the nation (Rohsenow 2004: 35; Blachford 2004: 121). Putonghua became the official, national "common language" in 1956 (Guo, 2004: 45) and while only widely spoken amongst Han peoples or *Hanzu* in North China in the early PRC, it became the "common language of all Han [Mandarin] dialect speakers by the end of the 1970s" (Blachford 2004: 121). That is, Standard Mandarin came to be spoken by increasing numbers of people across the country who were from the ethnic Hanzu majority and from other minzu who were already speakers of the many Mandarin topolects in China.

The legislation: from 2000 and the early PRC government's legal recognition of Putonghua as the national, common language both built on historic state practices of language standardization: the Imperial and Republican Chinese states also prescribed varieties of Mandarin as their official, national language. These origins are why even the Putonghua variety of Mandarin is sometimes still called 汉语 *hànyǔ* 'Han language' in Mandarin by participants in this study, and more broadly. Instead of using the conventional translation "Mandarin" or "Chinese", I have retained "Hanyu" in translations of participants' words to reflect their emphasis on the Hanzu association of this language. Note that this law protects only the Putonghua variety of Mandarin, not other Mandarin topolects such as Cantonese (see eg Qian et al. 2012, Qian 2014 on political rather than legal disputes to protect Cantonese).

Finally, there are a number of more specific, derivative language rights in various national laws. These include a right to have court proceedings translated and interpreted into local languages if necessary, criminal penalties for state employees who seriously encroach on minority cultural customs, a legal permission for schools in minority areas to use a minority language for instruction in the early years, and a legal obligation on schools to popularize Putonghua. These derivative language rights are explained in detail in Part Two.

There is a tension between China's minority and majority language rights. They exist in different legal forms and have different levels of technical specificity: the newer, Putonghua rights are legally stronger. Yet the minority language freedom has been around over the 70 years of the PRC's existence, while the right to learn and use the national language is just 20 years old, potentially shifting the balance of power between them. Both now underpin China's state practice in regards to language. The minority language freedom, itself, also contains a potential tension between an egalitarian language order and a hierarchic, instrumentalist language order. The friction between the minority and majority language rights, and between the recognition of the inherent or the utilitarian value of minority languages, sparked this research problem.

Another important motivation came from my studies of the existing scholarship. Within it, I found both theoretical inspiration and a significant gap in our knowledge in regards to up-to-date, empirical and people-centered data on how language rights in China are working. The inspiration was Bourdieusian critical sociolinguistics. I will expand on the significance of this theoretical outlook for research about language rights and policies, below, after explaining how China's transformations have not yet been fully addressed by sociolinguistic, language policy or language rights researchers.

1.2 How have researchers responded to a changing China?

The modernization drive and globalization of China, introduced above, raise many of the social, political and economic changes that sociolinguistic theory predicts will change the value, use and intergenerational transmission of languages. Although China has committed itself to a convergence toward certain global norms and systems, the "globalized new economy" (Heller 2003: 473) is not uniform, and has been experienced in China with so-called "Chinese characteristics". Foremost amongst them is the Chinese Party-State structure, and its focus on balancing international connectedness against a strong national interconnectedness, both for reasons of domestic political strength and because national interconnectedness is integral to China optimizing its economic growth in the globalized economy. National interconnectedness has had many fronts. These include infrastructural and economic linkages, as exemplified by the "Open up the West" campaign; the promotion of cultural 熔合 *rónghé* 'melding or assimilation' and a neo-Confucian national identity; 和谐 *héxié* 'social harmony' campaign and its correlate, the coercive containment of social instability and diversity. Another facet of China's interconnectedness is the movement of people within the nation, including the movement of people from the majority Hanzu ethnic group into minority areas. The result of these social, economic and political changes is therefore both top-down homogenization *and* the kind of bottom-up complexification that some sociolinguists call "superdiversity": "Superdiversity [...] denot[es] the new dimensions of social, cultural and linguistic diversity emerging out of post-Cold War migration and mobility patterns" (Blommaert and Backus 2013: 13; see further Vertovec 2007). This has spurred an increase in sociolinguistic studies of China.

However, sociolinguistics "was developed relatively late" (Sun and Coulmas 1992: 5) in China, and later still in relation to minority languages. The sociolinguistic research into experiences of modernization and globalization in China still tends to focus on the impacts of English on mainstream Chinese language and identities. For example, Zhang (2011: 221) argues that the belief that "a unified Chinese language is regarded as the foundation of a unified Chinese national identity" is galvanizing in reaction to English's spread into China, and on the adoption of this view by individuals, see e.g. (Gao 2015; Yang 2012: 102–103). The identities of minority language speakers, and the effect of the changing sociolinguistic economy on minority languages in China has been a side-issue, although this is being remedied by recent research (e.g. Baioud 2018; Roche 2017). There has been a related delay in building up socially-situated language policy studies which do not accept the 56 minzu groupings as natural facts, although the origins of enumerating minorities in ideologies of European modernity and the nation-state are well known in the wider literature (e.g. Costa et al. 2018: 8, following Appadurai 2006 and Anderson 2006) and these ideologies have been carefully traced into the PRC by Mullaney (2006, 2011).

Tam's (2020a) new book focuses on Mandarin topolects and their place in social and political organization, and in so doing decentralizes the 56 minzu. These topolects still do not count as officially recognized minority languages, with the consequence that their speakers are not polities. Her book examines the changing social and political uses and beliefs about Mandarin topolects and their position vis-à-vis the national language between 1860 and 1960. However, Tam does not then examine where the non-Mandarin languages and their speakers fit into the early twentieth century shifts in language policy that, by her account (Tam 2020b: 2), then strongly influenced PRC language policy. Tam's (2020b: 4) observations that there has been a long-running "tension between two visions of the nation – one that saw the Chinese nation as represented by a singular, standardized language, and the other that saw the nation as more flexible and heterogenous, spoken in many voices instead of just one" and that topolects came to be framed as "backwards" nevertheless resonate with this book's inquiry into later twentieth century and twenty-first century language policies and ideologies in relation to non-Mandarin languages in China.

Further, the responsiveness of the minority language governance framework to the incoming of English, or to other aspects of modernization and globalization, has been little studied, although there are some notable exceptions including (G. Hu 2012; G. Hu and Alsagoff 2010; Li and Lundberg 2008; Lin and Luk 2005; Wang 2016). Of these, I have found Lin and Luk's (2005) sociolinguistic study from Hong Kong particularly useful for this study. It is one of the few studies to focus on language policy in relation to two major, international languages, English and Mandarin, together dominating a marginalized language, in this case Cantonese. Lin and Luk (2005: 80) dub this linguistic order "double domination". Double domination describes the linguistic order in which English and Mandarin are, jointly, dominant over Cantonese. Lin and Luk (2005: 80) show how this linguistic hierarchy is entrenched through official language policy. Adamson and Feng (2009: 321) use the term "tripolar complexity" to describe a similar Mandarin-English-Minority Language order which they find to be reproduced in language policy within mainland China, but that term does not convey the hierarchic nature of a doubly dominated linguistic order.

Beyond China, sociolinguistic and language rights/policy studies have addressed globalization by examining the spread of English, and examined the dominance of regional/national languages over minority languages, but very few studies do both. That is, few consider the mutual reinforcement of the language de Swaan (2001) calls "hyper-central" in the global system, English, and a "super-central" language to jointly marginalize smaller "peripheral" languages, rather than considering the competition between English and a (super-)central regional or national language.

Moreover, this possibility for double domination, created by the globalization of English, is not what China's mid-twentieth century language law- and policy-makers envisaged. Given this, as well as the marketization and migration phenomena now changing where minority minzu people live in China, and what these people speak in their daily lives, we may wonder what sort of sociolinguistic orders the language governance framework is aspiring to, reproducing or resisting today, and whether it needs updating.

To further introduce the socio-linguistic order, let me outline the system of minzu categorization; ethnolinguistic diversity is still rarely discussed in China without reference to this official organization of diversity. The current Chinese state (i.e. the PRC) was built around 56 officially recognized categories of ethnicity, now usually called *minzu* in English, loaning the Mandarin term, but translated more often as "nationalities" during the twentieth century (and in 2017's *Chinese Nationalities Encyclopedia*: State Council Information Office 2017). These 56 minzu continue to exist as fundamental administrative categories in China and every adult is allocated to one. The 56 minzu comprise one official majority, the Hanzu (the *-zu* suffix abbreviates *minzu*), and 55 "small number" minority minzu (see list in Ramsey 1987: 164–165) who together accounted for 8.49 percent of the national population by 2013 (Zhou 2013: 4). This ethnolinguistic classification was one of the highest-priority undertakings of the new Party-State when the PRC was established in late 1949 (Blachford 2004: 101; Chaisingkananont 2014; Kaup 2000: 65–91), and followed the general modernist trend, identified by Scott (1998), of making the subjects of a state "legible" by arranging them into rigid and predictable categories. This minzu system thus created a nation of compartmentalized multiculturalism, or that which Benhabib (2002: 8) has elsewhere called "mosaic multiculturalism" i.e. "human groups and cultures are clearly delineated as identifiable entities that coexist, while maintaining firm boundaries". These 56 minzu categories are socially accepted and reproduced discursive constructions. They are a hegemonic state construction. The state often refers to itself as a 统一多民族国家 *tǒng yī duō mínzú guó* 'unified multi-minzu country' and these social structures are "internalized [...and] evoked and performed across China on a daily basis: from the filling-in of official paperwork to the singing and dancing of ethnic performers on television" (Leibold 2015: 274).

This minzu classification system built over widespread discrimination against minority peoples. Most of China's current official minority languages were, like English, considered to be languages of foreign "barbarians" in the past. The historic foreignness of China's southern minorities, in particular, is explicated and illustrated in watercolor in Tapp and Cohn (2003: see Figure 47 in Chapter Seven). The minzu classification was a deliberate response, attempting to raise the status of minority peoples through official inclusion and thereby address "Han chauvinism" head-on; however, this book will show that the vestiges of a Han-centric social hierarchy were not entirely supplanted. In fact, given the nationalization processes which mobilize Putonghua and other cultural practices associated with the Hanzu majority, and given the wealth accruing in China from modernization and globalization has been concentrated in the largely Hanzu-populated East, the processes of cultural reproduction radiate especially powerfully from Hanzu-centric areas these days.

Moreover, despite substantial structural changes in relation to marketization of the economy and liberalization of property ownership, labor and education, older state systems continue to play influential roles in structuring society. For example, the economic consequences of the previous collectivization of landholding and labor mean that there is now limited capital accumulation amongst rural households and households in lower-tier cities, and with rural household residency it remains hard to settle, access social security, or enroll children in school in cities. This legacy of disadvantage disproportionately affected minority peoples, although there were and are many rural Hanzu, too. This means that ethnolinguistic minoritization still tends to intersect with poverty, even as China's overall wealth has vastly increased.

The current patterns of residency also mean more change is coming for most minority peoples. Adamson and Feng (2009: 322) report that the minority minzu are mainly "living in 155 largely resource-rich but economically under-developed ethnic autonomous areas, many of which are located near the country's frontiers". Change is afoot within these very areas and in terms of their centrality to the nation. In this era of international trade and international security concerns, these areas' borderland locations make them strategically important, plus they now have greater potential for extractive industries and urban settlement than the already industrialized, densely-populated East.

Moreover, urbanization is affecting minority peoples, even the many who stay within autonomous regions; those regions' cities are also growing. The competition introduced by China's overall move from a planned economy to a market economy has created not only the possibility but also the need to move to find work and to access the opportunities that have emerged. The consequent movement of people within China's borders is known as 流动 liudong (lit. 'movement/flow', i.e. a flow of people) and translated into English as "internal migration". Animated by the quest for work and upward economic mobility, this widespread internal migration of people has especially sapped China's poorer areas but it has also included the movement of the Hanzu majority to every corner of the nation (Iredale et al. 2003). This migration is, in particular, migration to urban centers. This "volume of rural–urban migration in such a short period [1979–2010] is likely the largest in human history" (Chan 2013). In addition, more foreigners are permitted to live in China these days compared to any previous time (Leibold and Chen 2014: 8). As a consequence, cities across China have increasingly diverse ethnic populations and are increasingly home to people with rural residency status or rural backgrounds. But this does not mean that Chinese cities are diversifying linguistically: in fact, they seem to be homogenizing. People are changing their language practices when they move to cities, as this book will explore.

And of course in China's cities as well as its rural areas, there are now global communication systems of the kind Blommaert and Backus (2013: 13) note as sociolinguistically significant elsewhere. There is also Sinosphere-specific new media. These are capable of feeding processes of diversification as well as capable of being mobilized to forge a unified, pan-Chinese identity (Leibold 2015). However, under these combined conditions of change, more than ever, "Standard Chinese is viewed by many sectors of society, including many leaders in ethnic minority regions, as a facilitator for economic development through commercial interaction with the rest of the PRC" (Adamson and Feng 2009: 323). There is therefore still much grist for the mill of critical sociolinguistic studies of power and ideology as they relate to China's non-Mandarin languages.

These socio-political and economic changes in China are surely disrupting the late twentieth century language governance framework. That framework has been described in the literature as promoting a "balance of bilingualism" since 1991 (Adamson and Feng 2009: 323), having reached a "pluralistic" stage (Zhou 2000: 126), or as having been a period of "recovery and development" (Feng and Sunuodula 2009: 685). Similarly, Beckett and Postiglione (2012: 4) summarized the late twentieth century phase of Chinese language policy as forming a "parallel language order" in which minority languages were positioned as local lingua francas with Putonghua only a supplement. But these interpretations of Chinese language policy are contested: Zhou (2012b: 4) argues that since the USSR collapsed, "China has been gradually replacing its Soviet model with a native model of an inclusive Chinese nation with diversity [...] This model attempts to establish a language order where Putonghua functions as the dominant language while minority languages serve as the supplementary ones". Zhou (2012b: 4) calls this "ordered multilingualism". Harrell's (1993, 1995, 1996; Harrell and Ma 1999) pioneering work on Han-centric linguistic hegemony meanwhile offers a more critical, late twentieth century counterpoint. Harrell (1993: 108) argues that, in demanding one standard(ized) written dialect for each minority, despite many minority languages having mutually unintelligible dialects, the state has coerced minorities into learning Putonghua or other Mandarin varieties as their local lingua franca. To Harrell (1993: 108), Chinese language policy therefore "subverts as well as fulfils the policy principle of linguistic equality". Similarly, and more recently, Roche (2017: 15, following Hirsch 2000) applies the concept of "double assimilation" to minority language policy in China. In a recent study of the Tibetan regions, he argues that language policy is part of "the assimilation of diverse peoples into nationality categories and the assimilation of [these] nationally categorized groups into mainstream society". And He's (2014) critical history of China's minority language-in-education policies emphasizes the long tradition of linguistic "imperialism", especially in regards to Chinese written characters (called *Hanzi*, lit. 'Han characters').

These studies suggest to me that even as the pluralistic phase was being named as such by scholars around the end of last century, a new and more minoritizing phase of language policy was emerging. However, the application of these conflicting terms, and the analytic chronologies of Chinese language policy from which they come, have not been tested against data from the twenty-first century. They need to be. Given the changes I have canvassed so far in this chapter, can we still describe modernized China as having balanced, pluralistic language policy with ordered multilingualism, just because some of the key legal texts remain the same? Or do China's language rights now produce, or at least allow, "aspiring monolingualism", to borrow the apt phrase that Hult (2014: 209) uses in the context of another massive nation, the USA?

An additional reason for the study is to contribute to the global literature examining how language rights and official policies about language work to naturalize certain social constructions, particularly of an "ineluctable connection between language and (ethnic) identity" (May 2005: 327; see also Jaffe 2004: 273, 2007: 63). Although Chinese linguists recognize more languages than minority minzu (Sun 1992: 9), the Chinese state does not. Each minority minzu is officially considered to correspond to just one language (except the *Huizu*, the minzu ascribed to Muslim traders who were seen to have no language of their own). State practice continually reinforces this, for example the bulk of mid-to-late twentieth century minority language policy was directed at developing one standard variety and one script for each minority group (see e.g. State Council Information Office of the PRC 2005b; Nanning Municipal Minority Language Works Commission 2019: §1). However, there is a recent (re)emergence of variation in unofficial social groupings in China, especially socio-economic classes (Tomba 2014) and ethnic identities other than the recognized 56 (e.g. Lickorish 2008).

Thus, Chinese state practice concerning multilingualism might be seen to display the "over-determined sense of linguistic fixity" which Pennycook (2004: 2) argues sociolinguistics should call into question. This is a globally-relevant concern: Schiffman (1996: 30) cites Fasold in arguing language policies "always [...] force binary distinctions on to variable, gradient phenomena". The tension between social constructions of groups, and the Chinese state's rigid classifications of majority and minority "ethnies" (Smith 2005), thus sets up a fundamental dynamic suited to sociolinguistic research. Realizing this, newer sociolinguistics studies of China take denaturalizing China's official ethno-linguistic groupings as their starting point. Nevertheless, such studies are not numerous in the overall scheme of things. The bulk of twentieth century Chinese linguistic literature concerned "describing merely the structure and historical evolution of languages"

(Sun and Coulmas 1992: 7). In particular, twentieth century Chinese "ethnosociolinguistics" (Zhou 1992: 59) reconstructed an essential connection between abstractions of ethnicity and language, intending to map language variation onto officially ascribed social categories. Moreover, Zhou (1992: 64) reports that the dominant understanding amongst Chinese ethnosociolinguists was that whenever minority and Hanzu majority groups lived in contact, the minority language speakers would shift to Hanyu. It followed, then, that minority bilingualism and the role of minority language rights and policy in response to the spread of Hanyu were not deeply studied.

A final rationale for studying language rights in China today is that China's combination of formal minority language rights and political economy offers a contrast to the language policies in liberal democracies of the Global North that overpopulate sociolinguistic literature. The social and governmental challenges of linguistic diversity and globalization may well be akin, despite the divergent systems. And any divergences may also enrich our understanding. Spolsky and Shohamy (2004: xvi), Wee (2011: 73) and Zhou (2001: 59) have made these arguments specifically in relation to China's language rights and policy. The scholarship within which this is just one book fits is therefore on a journey to the "South". With this broader relevance in mind, I will now explain this book's relationship with established, internationally-applied Bourdieusian critical sociolinguistic theory.

1.3 Extending Bourdieusian critical sociolinguistic theory into language rights and policy studies

Many readers will be familiar with Bourdieu's (1977a, 1977b, 1991) conceptualization of symbolic power arising from the exchange of linguistic and other capital, and the broader social constructionist theory within which this fits. To recapitulate, he theorized that societies will ascribe to some language practices, and to those who use them, not only value for their communicative utility but also other values. For example some types of speech are lauded for their cultural prestige (or cultural "capital"). By contrast, using language practices which the society treats as culturally impoverished or lacking in other value may also be understood as an indication of the language users' lack of economic, cultural or social capital. Indeed, having symbolic power from the linguistic and other capital associated with language can affect how a person's other language practices are evaluated, and vice versa. Xu (2019) illustrates this in an atypically Bourdieusian sociolinguistic analysis of minority multilingualism in China, arguing that Putonghua is the "admission ticket": if a speaker does not garner the symbolic power of socially-accepted Putonghua practices, the other languages in their repertoire will be valued far less also. Because of the relationship between forms of capital, a Bourdieusian critical sociolinguistic approach acknowledges that "struggles over language are not centrally about language at all" (Heller 2004: 285). Rather, by analyzing the "linguistic order" (originally Bourdieu 1977a: 665) we can examine the role of language practices in organizing social categories and hierarchies, i.e. the "social order" (Jaworski and Thurlow 2010: 6).

Less often cited in Sociolinguistics is Bourdieu's (1987) essay *The force of law: toward a sociology of the juridical field*, but it struck me as especially relevant to a project on language rights. In that essay, Bourdieu (1987: 816, 839) specifically theorizes law as a dialectically structured and structuring common belief, or *doxa*, to use the Greek nomenclature preferred by Bourdieu. In this way, Bourdieu theorizes, law has a special and powerful role in "the process by which power relations come to be perceived not for what they objectively are, but in a form which renders them legitimate in the eyes of those subject to the power" (Terdiman 1987: 813). In Bourdieusian theory, this process is called *méconnaissance* 'misrecognition'. As such, law is examined as a discourse strengthening and naturalizing power relations, not only as a system of legal entitlements or mechanisms. This foregrounds the role of law in influencing common beliefs, particularly beliefs about how an individual or a society *should* be or what standards they *should* meet. Beliefs about what should be are called norms. In Bourdieusian critical sociolinguistic theory, common beliefs and norms are greatly influenced by the symbolically empowered discourses and the structures of social organization which each person lives amongst, and we in turn use those common beliefs and norms to organize our individual expectations and our knowledge about our world and ourselves. Specifically, the doxa around us provides a hierarchical structure into which a person is socialized, which creates their dispositions (in Latin, *habitus*) and their internal version of the apparent dominant order of the world.

In relation to language, our habitus shapes how we each evaluate our own language practices and those of others, as well as how we link those language practices' to social identities. A habitus is likely to reflect dominant beliefs about language, and what the state says and does in regards to language is a key component of dominant beliefs. This is because expressing a belief, implicitly or explicitly, in official rules and policies amplifies that belief and makes it more enduring: i.e. laws and policies about language, and state practices with regards to languages, are invested with significant symbolic power. Because language policy "can exist at all levels of decision making about languages", from individuals' and families' decisions up to schools', regions' and nations' decisions, only some language policies are "expressed in terms of language laws" (Shohamy 2006: 48, 50). Following this understanding of language rights as just one type of "policy device" (Shohamy 2006: 57), this book treats China's constitutional and legislative language rights as part of a framework of legislative and policy devices at central, regional and local levels of government. What makes this framework important as a whole, and therefore subject to far greater examination in this book than I have seen elsewhere, is not only the legal weaknesses or pathways relevant to language that we can then see systematically across laws and policies, but that the symbolic power of the state vests in these laws and policies as one discourse. This is very important if we theorize a dialectic relationship between society and law: people are not responding to, or being influenced by, each piece of legislation in isolation but as part of their experiences of a discursive (and legal) governance framework.

This study is therefore designed to include an inquiry into the normative impacts of language laws as an "active discourse" (Bourdieu 1987: 839). Otherwise, we would miss the important role of law as symbolically empowered discourse in mediating the relationship between social structures and the individual's habitus. We might also overlook the potential agency of individuals to reflect upon, reinterpret or resist law, i.e. the dialectic aspect of law.

In a work foundational to this one in its linking of a dynamic view of language policy to Bourdieusian sociolinguistics, Wee (2011, following Bonham 1999), extends the central Bourdieusian notion of habitus as it relates to agency. Wee argues: "Bourdieu's 'pre-reflective habitus' is too 'one-dimensional' and makes no place for 'deliberate processes and practices' [...] Mitigating this determinism requires a conception of agency that is both reflective and transformative, one that recognizes 'the capacities of socially and culturally situated agents to reflect upon their social conditions, criticize them, and articulate new interpretations of them'" (citations omitted). That is, individuals are animated by a habitus reflecting language governance structures, their own experiences, and common beliefs but also by reflexive, potentially critical evaluations of law, their own dispositions and their beliefs. Theoretically, then, this conceptualization of agency anticipates dynamism, even resistance and counter-hegemony, in language governance. This analytic view has informed my situated and ethnographic method of language governance research and is why I foreground agency in this book's "lived landscape" and "linguascaping" extensions to the research literature.

Moreover, Bourdieu (1987) argues that it is not only the rights and procedures set out in laws that create legal entitlement. A subject must also have a habitus within which she represents herself as entitled to justice and constructs particular experiences of disequilibria as unjust, or as failing to meet an expectation to which she believed she was entitled. Linguistic justice thus arises in a dialectic relationship with law and policy, and this is oftentimes under-examined in language policy research. Laws make some languages "hard edged" such that these languages may have "considerable symbolic power as part of the dominant discourse, and [this] is strategically useful to minorities in their struggle for language rights" (Freeland and Patrick 2004: 8), but they also exclude certain constructions of languages, their indices and their values, imposing an ideational "regime" (Costa 2013; Irvine and Gal 2000) onto that which can be imagined, articulated and claimed. We must therefore ask what China's constitutional minority language right entitles people to claim of the state, both in a strictly legal sense of what it legitimates and in a broader, discursive and ideological sense. Moreover, this study adopts the general critical sociolinguistic conceptualization of language as resources, following Heller's (2010) extension of Bourdieu. Language resources – whether resources for communication, identity-building, place-making, socio-economic mobility etc. – are in unequal distribution, because symbolic power is unequally distributed and agents are unequally empowered (Bourdieu 1991: 238; see also Bourdieu 1977a, 1984[1979]). Within this framework, language rights and the attendant language policy framework can be seen as structures mediating and regulating the availability and value of language resources.

With this Bourdieusian critical sociolinguistic theoretical orientation, I therefore took language rights as positing an authorized distribution of power, without assuming that they worked as posited. To investigate language rights this way, I turned to ethnographically-oriented methods, including an ethnographically-oriented investigation of minority language governance in public spaces through an extended linguistic landscape study, because ethnography "takes the concrete functioning of [established] norms and expectations [...] as problems rather than as facts" (Blommaert and Dong 2010: 10). We need to examine beliefs and practices, as well. Beliefs about languages, i.e. language ideologies, together with socially-situated practices, are objects of inquiry in ethnographies of language policy because they facilitate the investigation of the theoretically and empirically anticipated "cleavages" between "overt" and "covert" language policy (Schiffman 1996: 27; Shohamy 2006: 51–52); or between posited and practiced language governance, in my terminology.

Language rights and policy research has been insufficiently attendant to the socially-situated practice or discursive nature of language rights and policy, or even to the difference between the formal and actual locus of power. Thus, established language policy and language rights scholars have been calling for more situated studies, rather than typological analyses. Ricento (2000) encouraged language policy scholars to examine individual agency. Before that, Ricento, with Hornberger (1996: 419–420), had "hint[ed] at the roles played by ideology, culture, and ethnicity" while Paulston (1997: 79) called for "situated" language rights. Even earlier, McRae (1975: 52) argued that "group value systems" affect what language policy alternatives are available and how they operate so language policy types should not be analyzed, assessed, or predicted in the abstract. The literature has begun to respond. Freeland and Patrick's (2004: 2, 8) edited compilation explicitly attempts to advance the study of "emic" perspectives and ideologies within critical language rights research. While I was writing this book, Pia Lane, James Costa and Hayley De Korne (Lane et al. 2018) contributed an edited compilation of emic studies of language standardization policies from the critical sociolinguistics perspective that "standardization is [...] an ideological phenomenon" (Gal: 2018 222). Within that compilation, the editors provided a useful intellectual history of language policy about standardization (Costa et al. 2018). Advances are also being made through the emergence of ethnographies of language policy, a sub-field which so far centers on language-in-education policy (see further Johnson and Ricento 2013). A pioneering language policy ethnographer, Katherine Mortimer (2016: 350), argues in her Paraguayan study of language-in-education policy that "ethnographic approaches dovetail with increasing attention to the role of local norms, practices, and epistemologies in various aspects of language policy activity [...] demonstrat[ing] that when we look at language policy text, we have but a partial understanding of its meaning". This book takes Mortimer's idea and the growing body of emic and ethnographic language rights and policy research forward. It thus shares the momentum of the (slow) shift in language policy research observed by Hult (2018: 341) from "centralized government policies and a linear path to their implementation to [a focus on] governmentality, whereby certain linguistic regulations emerge through iterative choices mediated by values about language that permeate multiple domains of society".

Other than this book, the only Chinese language policy ethnography that I know of is Li Jia's (2017) thoroughgoing Bourdieusian high school study in South China. It reveals a contrast between China's international education policy support for immigrant Burmese students, and their lived experiences. Despite having learnt and spoken Mandarin before coming to China, identifying with China and mostly being of Chinese heritage, Li Jia finds that the students do not count as legitimate learners or speakers in the school environment.

Having identified my theoretical bases, there remained an issue of scope. China is too big for one study, even for a study motivated by such big actual and theoretical issues. I therefore developed a case study of particular types of language governance, especially governance of public language practices, and of one minzu, the Zhuang minzu, or Zhuangzu.

1.4 Why focus on Zhuang language and linguistic landscapes?

I determined that I would begin by tracing China's constitutional language rights through their overarching legal context, then through to Zhuang-specific local laws implementing them, and thence to their reception by and effect on social actors with a relationship to Zhuang. A major reason for selecting the Zhuangzu as my "window" is that it is the most populous minority minzu in China, comprising almost 1 percent of the national population and about as populous as the Uyghurs and Tibetans combined. In 2011, the Zhuangzu population was 17.283 million (Guo et al. 2015: 68). The Zhuangzu is associated with – and indeed named after – the Zhuang language (Kaup 2000: 127; Mullaney 2011). There are varying reports of Zhuang speaker numbers, between 10 million (Ager 2016) and 14 million (Liu 2005: 4, 6; Li 2005: 10). I tend to accept the lower figure (Grey 2019: 444) but even on that figure, Zhuang has many speakers compared to other minoritized languages in China and around the world. Another reason for selecting Zhuang is that, despite the number of Zhuang speakers and size of the Zhuangzu polity, Zhuang language is not examined in much sociolinguistic literature, even recent Chinese language policy studies (e.g. Leibold and Chen 2014; Lo Bianco et al. 2009; Postiglione and Beckett 2012; Shen and Gao 2019).

Moreover, unlike most of China's official minority groups, the Zhuangzu have nominal self-government over a large, provincial-level region. I wanted to select a minzu with nominal self-government of an autonomous region to test out whether this structure empowers language policy-makers or minority language speakers. The Zhuangzu are the titular autonomous minzu of Guangxi Zhuangzu Autonomous Region (GZAR). GZAR is located on China's southern border with Vietnam (shown in Figure 4).

GZAR is something of a Chinese everywhere, and a nowhere, making Zhuang an attractive case study. Positioned in the central South, it straddles East and West China, i.e. the richer and the poorer halves. GZAR has received targeted poverty alleviation measures since the 1980s (State Council Information Office of the PRC 2005b: IV(6)) but it is still the poorest region in East China (Anon. 2016a). Its poverty and its ethnic autonomous government structure (rather than its location) caused it to be included in the national "Open up the West" policy (Moody et al. 2011: 1), which evened out China's economic growth by investing 850 billion yuan in less economically developed areas between 2000 and 2005 (State Council Information Office of the PRC 2005b: IV(1)). Now catching up with the nation, GZAR's integration into national and global economies has begun in earnest. Moreover, the Region has long been a national borderland and was not fully integrated into the imperial Chinese state, but it is now a central government-

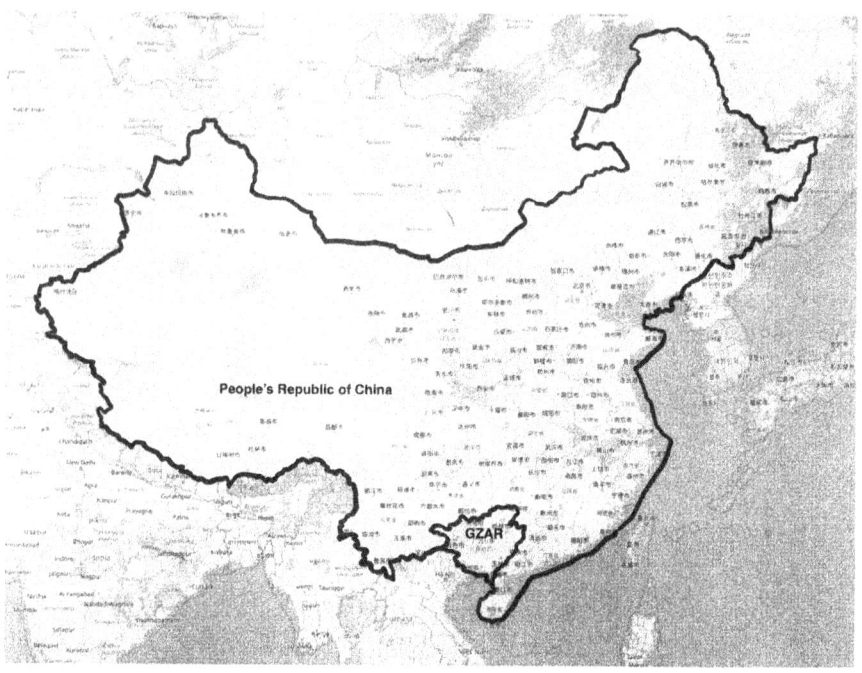

Figure 4: Map highlighting GZAR in South China; map adapted from OpenStreetMap (openstreetmap.org) and OpenStreetMap Foundation (opendatacommons.org).

designated hub for China's engagement with its ASEAN neighbors (see Grey 2021a: 20). Finally, while GZAR is positioned as the Zhuang language homeland, it has also long been home to speakers of major Mandarin dialects. GZAR's historic and current multilingualism, and the long process of a Zhuangzu polity emerging from social constructions of diversity in South China, are explored in Chapter Two.

It struck me as especially interesting to study the sociolinguistics of a group that appeared to be blending in but at the same time reputedly maintaining a non-Mandarin language, Zhuang. I was further intrigued by this group that was large and, at least symbolically, powerful in that they had an autonomous region, but which seemed not to leverage this power politically or economically. I wondered what role the Zhuang language was playing in organizing South China's multi-ethnic communities which enjoy a desirably placid state of affairs compared to the violence ratcheting up in other autonomous regions, such as the Xinjiang Uyghur Autonomous Region in North-West China.

Moreover, I believed it was worthwhile studying something other than extreme cases of violently oppressive language policy. Studying those extreme cases also remains important morally and scholastically, even as it becomes almost impossible to do, but it was too difficult to undertake a PhD study on this topic in those North-Western contexts. By contrast, the capital city of the Zhuangzu autonomous region, where I undertook significant fieldwork, has recently become a "demonstration city of minzu unity and progress" (Nanning Municipal Minority Language Works Commission 2019), although the region is not entirely without civil unrest and violence (Grey 2015a, b). Studying Zhuang language policy can tell us about how China operates towards minorities and linguistic diversity most of the time in most of the country. This is not to assume that the South is free from the underlying ideologies about languages and ethnicities. Given the same system can produce both a relatively peaceful but apparently multilingual South and an aggressive aspiration to monolingualism in the North, it is important to understand the ideologies and structures of the system overall, and how they operate in the South. The state's linguistic insecurity is a national paranoia, not a regional one, as we can see for instance in Chinese linguistic scholarship about English or in the recent moves to reduce bilingual schooling even for the "model" Mongolian minority in the Central North (Baioud 2020). This linguistic paranoia is the flip-side of a nationalist one-nation one-language ideology. How does nationalist ideology emerge and play out in ways other than Uyghur reeducation camps? Is GZAR a success story of linguistic diversity, a place of hegemonic minority marginalization, or both?

Banality is beguiling. In this context which is not as openly conflictual and otherwise as closed-off as the North-West, we will see through the minority window the many more subtle and interlacing vines of oppression and inequality, and perhaps also of opportunity and desire, which are rooted in the structures and ideologies of language policy, of the market, of the division of the state into administrative units, and of the construction of social groups. These and other fault-lines, problems or even successes that become clear through the Zhuang case study will resonate with other nations which have not gone to extremes.

In using the Zhuang case study to respond to questions which speak to global changes, I believe the book will be relevant to people interested in minority groups other than the Zhuangzu, and regions other than GZAR, and indeed language politics beyond China or minority politics beyond language. But I hope readers will also become increasingly interested in Zhuang along this journey, as I have become.

In examining how national, regional and local laws relate to Zhuang language, I have been influenced by Shohamy's (2006: 57) influential typology of four key types of language policy mechanism. These are: "laws, rules and regulations, standardization and officiality"; "language education policies"; "language tests"; and "language in the public space". In fact, legal mechanisms (i.e. the first group) intervene in all the others. My ethnography of contemporary Zhuang language governance therefore covered all four types of language policy mechanism. I was most interested, however, in how legal mechanisms supported or inhibited Zhuang in the urban and mobile contexts of public space and education. "[T]he presence (or absence) of language displays in the public space communicates a message, intentional or not [...] that affects, manipulates, or imposes *de facto* language policy and practice" writes Shohamy (2006: 110), and Dal Negro (2009: 206) astutely observes that written language in the public space is an "instrument through which a new course in language policy is made immediately apparent". Yet despite this recognized importance, language policy about, and materialized through, public space is less well examined in the language rights and policy literature than language-in-education policy. The extended theoretical and empirical treatment of language policy in public space in this book is therefore, I hope, a welcome contribution. This book focuses on public space as a context of instantiation of and interaction with language policy, rather than on education contexts, in its empirical examination of Zhuang language governance in Part Three (after providing a detailed examination of representation and responsibility in minority language governance, both generally and for Zhuang, in Part Two).

This book's concentration on language policy in public space adopts (and extends) an approach called the "linguistic landscape approach". Writing contemporaneously with me, Hult (2018) highlights a connection right from the beginning between language policy studies and linguistic landscape research. Shohamy and Dal Negro, both just quoted, and four of their co-contributors in Shohamy and Gorter's (2009) edited book investigate language policy through linguistic landscapes, while Hult (2018) reviews other linguistic landscape policy research. But none of these studies is from China.

Taking a linguistic landscape approach as part of my investigation into language policy in and about public space has allowed me to deepen an emplaced and multi-perspective analysis of the Chinese language rights framework as socially situated and spatialized practices. I focus particularly on the linguistic landscapes of public urban spaces (including public transport, roads and shopfronts), public cultural institutions and publicly accessible areas of public universities. The reader will find that my research into standardization, language education policies and language tests (i.e. other key language policy mechanisms) is interwoven where relevant; my separate works on those aspects of Zhuang language governance are summarized at the end of the following Chapter Outline.

1.5 What did I find? (A chapter outline)

This book presents an interdisciplinary study of minority language governance in China which combined legal analysis with an ethnographically-orientated social science, sociolinguistics. This research into language rights in a much-changed and still changing China, presented an opportunity to knit together multiple strands in contemporary sociolinguistic research. These include the emergence of Bourdieusian and ethnographic studies of language planning, policy and rights; the expanded linguistic/semiotic landscape approach; the mobilities paradigm; the expansion of language rights studies to diverse political economies; and the increased interest in multilingualism in the Sinosphere.

This introductory chapter sets China's language rights and minority languages in a context of contemporary change. The Critical Sociolinguistic Profile of Zhuang in **Chapter Two** pulls together my own and others' research into who the Zhuangzu are today and what speaking Zhuang encompasses, including by tracing how official recognition of the Zhuangzu and Zhuang language arose. These chapters together form **Part One** and provide the context of the study.

Next, the three chapters which form **Part Two** analyze China's legislation about language, the language ideological and formal decision-making framework within which this legislation operates, and the limitations that these laws, the ideologies and the organizational structures embed into the minority language governance framework. These limitations pertain to the entire language governance framework, not only to Zhuang, however, **Part Two** uses Zhuang as a case study, particularly in illustrating the language governance framework's fractured nature in the close-up of GZAR's language-in-education laws and structures. I cover recent constitutional amendments and use Bourdieusian critical sociolinguistics, specifically the theorization of law as symbolically powerful discourse and the prediction of multiple, socially-situated constructions of linguistic justice, as well as the critical sociolinguistic concept of language ideologies, to critique these laws. **Part Two** begins in **Chapter Three** with my legal analysis of the nature and the limitations of the fundamental constitutional and legislative provisions relating to languages in China today. **Chapter Four** then illuminates the language ideologies expressed within the official law and policy discourses of the language governance framework, identifying the predominance of a developmentalist language ideology. The voices of the participants start to enter the book at this point. **Part Two's** suite of law-oriented analyses of Chinese minority language governance is rounded out with **Chapter Five's** critique of the distribution of authority to govern Zhuang and of the representation of those with an interest in Zhuang through the division of the territories and organs of governance.

Overall, **Part Two** argues that the language governance framework neither empowers Zhuang speakers nor the institutions tasked with governing Zhuang, despite the existence of a nominally autonomous Zhuangzu region. Furthermore, the Zhuang language governance framework entrenches the normative position of a developmentalist ideology under which Zhuang is constructed as underdeveloped and of low value. The legal, ideological and institutional limitations of the Chinese minority language governance framework have not been studied in detail elsewhere. Thus, **Part Two** provides a useful stand-alone critical analysis of the system of minority language governance, not only of Zhuang language governance, as well as providing a foundation for **Part Three's** investigations into the "sociolinguistic realities 'on the ground'" (Freeland and Patrick 2004: 1).

Note that my use of the term "language governance" is an effort to foreground processual and dialectic practices of law rather than the posited texts. Language governance captures more than the more instrument-specific terms "language policy" or "language right" or the goal-specific term, "language planning", although readers are likely to be more familiar with those terms. It also avoids the uncritical, managerialist re-framing of state actions through another popular term, "language management".

Part Three then empirically explores the Zhuang language governance framework in its situated practice and social reception, in an innovatively layered investigation of public linguistic landscapes through four chapters from four theoretical perspectives. Ben-Rafael et al. (2006: 10) treat the linguistic landscape as "the symbolic structuring of the public space"; public texts and other semiotics of the built environment are not décor but "decorum". I share this view of public spaces as constitutive elements of the doxa through which we learn to self-regulate linguistic and other practices in order to be "in place". Thus, **Part Three** begins with a detailed examination of the linguistic and other visual ideologies of public landscapes which participate in place-making. Specifically, **Chapter Six** examines the participation of urban places, universities, and GZAR as a Zhuangzu territory in structuring people's expectations of where certain language practices and identities are in place. This includes empirically examining the patterns of dominance and marginalization revealed, reproduced and resisted by language display choices in "the aggregate of all visible linguistic forms on the surface of a geographic area" (Lou 2016: 5, citing Landry and Bourhis 1997). **Chapter Seven** then widens the scope to analyze the use of non-linguistic emblems of "Zhuangness" in the same landscapes and the development of these emblematic conventions in other media, as well as examining these landscapes' explicit references to Zhuang language and representations of diverse Zhuang language practices. Overall, these two chapters examine public linguistic landscapes as materialized discourses constructing and emplacing linguistic and social norms – *de facto* language policies – that largely marginalize and even exclude Zhuang.

The influential linguistic landscape scholars, Adam Jaworski and Crispin Thurlow (2010: 6), explain that "[c]ultural geography [...] calls for a decoding of landscape imagery, a reading of the environmental 'maps of meaning' [...] which reveal and reproduce – and sometimes resist – social order". Taking this idea further, my "lived landscape" analysis in **Chapter Eight** draws on ethnographically-oriented data in a way that has not been typical of linguistic landscape studies, in order to reveal the participants' various socially-situated and agentive decodings of landscape text and imagery, and to examine how they take up the linguistic landscapes' affordances in identity construction. **Chapter Eight** thus deepens our insight into the subjective aspects of the operation of language policy and of how "the social is spatially constituted, and people make sense of their social identity in terms of their environment" (Jaworski and Thurlow 2010: 6).

Closing **Part Three**, **Chapter Nine** turns the attention back to the role of *de jure* language policy, now adding local laws and regulations about public texts into the data. It analyzes "the government" as an array of heterogeneous agents shaping – or rather "linguascaping" – these public landscapes, with power to reproduce but also to resist linguo-social orders through legal intervention. This chapter advances Ben-Rafael et al.'s (2006: 10) observation that each public linguistic landscape "is shaped – most often uncoordinatedly – by a myriad of actors operating under the influence of a myriad of motives". It does so by revealing how this study's linguistic landscapes are intentionally produced by the state through legal regulation, but still without coordination or complete control, echoing the dis-organisation of language governance revealed in **Part Two**. Second, it argues that linguascaping is not only achieved by explicit language rules directly shaping the built environment but also by the norms of law-as-discourse. This chapter thus draws the discussion back to the structural and legal limitations, and ideological tensions, identified within **Part Two** as embedded in the language governance framework.

Part Four concludes the book. Within it, **Chapter Ten** recapituates the study then sets out where I think twenty-first century Chinese minority language policy is headed, and in which respects I would like to alter its course. **Chapter Eleven** provides a reflection on the study's general, global implications for theory, methodology and language policy-making.

This book's focus on public linguistic landscapes as sites of dynamic language governance represents much but not all of my broader examination of Zhuang language policy in practice. My analysis of tertiary education policy argues that language-in-education policy does not destabilize the institutional processes which foster a habitus within which Zhuang is dissociated from education (Grey

2017: 358-441). Nor does language-in-education policy redress the absence of economic capital for Zhuang, even as the central government's desire to increase people-to-people connectivity across its ASEAN borders (UNDP 2020; Xinhua 2019) presents a context in which Zhuang language skills could become valued human resources giving Zhuang speakers an edge in mastering a neighboring national language, Thai (Thai and Zhuang both being Tai languages) or the *Nung*, *Tay* and *Caolan* official minority languages of Vietnam. Luo (2015: 3) confirms that these are Zhuang varieties. Rather, language-in-education policy constructs a new way of 'doing' Zhuang language as an objectified research commodity consistent with the latest Yubao language policy focus on heritage as distinct from lived language practices.

Further, I have examined the sociolinguistic effects of the material discourses of South China's new high-speed rail network, a key initiative of the region's economic development policy, in Grey (2021a). I there conclude that these symbolically powerful material and policy discourses are contributing to cultural urbanization across GZAR, emplacing urban norms outside the city limits in pursuit of profitable sameness in the tourism industry, and thus erasing local multilingualism and ideologically displacing Zhuang. The marketability of Standard Zhuang, specifically, is my focus in Grey (in press), which hones in on script policy to rearticulate an argument of this book: that minority language rights have done little to protect against the economic, social and linguistic devaluation of minority languages as China has marketized. Finally, I compare aspects of my Zhuang case study with Gegentuul Baioud's contemporaneous linguistic anthropological study of Mongolian in China's Inner Mongolia Autonomous Region in Grey and Baioud (in press), furthering another argument in this book: that Mandarin and English are being socially constructed as on the same side of a dichotomous and hierarchic linguistic and social order, in contradistinction to minority languages. That article advances a theory of recursive Orientalism to describe the changing social significance of multilingualism in China, drawing on Irvine and Gal's (2000: 38) foundational theory of "recursive" language ideology. These other components of my research program all informed this book's analysis of minority language rights and policies without being the subject of their own chapters.

1.6 How did I do this study?

Taking a critical sociolinguistic approach following Bourdieu, the study traced language rights through their elaboration in legislation and policies, into implementation and social reception. That is, in addition to examining the legal nature and limitations of the constitutional freedom to use and develop minority languages, the study examined the understandings and uses made of language rights and the associated framework of laws and policies, as well as the laws and policies' interaction with beliefs about languages' value, appropriateness and association with certain social categories. I designed a fused legal and ethnographic research project to allow me to investigate the meanings made of law and policy about minority languages (primarily, Zhuang) by heterogeneous agents *within* the state as well as by individuals in society. It required a program of multi-sited and multi-modal data collection anchored in specifically selected urban and university sites, and purposive participant selection.

1.6.1 Multi-sited and multi-modal data collection

I undertook an "itinerant ethnography" across multiple sites in GZAR and in three other parts of China (following Schein 2000: 26–28 and Chaisingkananont 2014: 18). GZAR was the focus, because of its connections to Zhuang and the Zhuangzu polity, but it was important to include sites outside GZAR to illuminate, by comparison, the results of Zhuang-self-government. I undertook fieldwork in and between GZAR, Yunnan Province, Beijing and Inner Mongolia Autonomous Region in 2014 and 2015.

Because of the centrality of university student participants in this study (see 1.6.3 Purposive Participant Selection, below), my fieldwork focused on the university campus anchor sites mapped in Figure 5, as well as the downtown areas of the cities where the universities were located, and tourism and cultural centers both in those cities and outside urban areas in GZAR. I had two cohorts of participants located across the anchor sites. I undertook interviews, activities and participant observations at these sites in 2014. Where possible, interviews used a small-group or individual commented walk method based on Qian (2014; see also Qian et al. 2012; Stroud and Jegels 2014). I followed up via online communications and, in 2015, with additional in-person interactions. That year I also undertook additional linguistic landscape documentation, having begun that side of data collection during the 2014 fieldwork. I photographed, documented and collected samples of language practices in these sites, including public signage, circulating texts and other language displays. From 2013 to 2019, I collected law and policy texts in hard copy and from online repositories, as well as online discussions about them.

Figure 5: Anchor fieldwork sites, adapted from Maps Open Source (n. d.).

1.6.2 Anchor site selection

There are what I call "Zhuang Studies" degrees at a small number of minzu-specialist, public universities, namely *Guangxi University for Nationalities* (GUN) in Nanning City, GZAR, *Yunnan Minzu University* (YMU) in Kunming City, Yunnan Province and *Minzu University of China* (MUC) in Beijing. Consequently, these university were three of my six anchor sites. At each of these universities, undergraduate Zhuang Studies is a similar, four-year mix of literature, language and anthropological studies of South-West China's minority groups, and postgraduate Zhuang Studies extends on these subjects. Zhuang language is but one component. For example, at MUC, the undergraduate degree is called 南方少数民族语言文学 'Southern Minority Language and Literature'. One of its teachers, language leader Mr L, explained that students may select other minority languages – Bouyei, Yi or Miao – instead of Zhuang. YMU students in the equivalent degree program reported taking two compulsory Mandarin subjects and a compulsory foreign language, in addition to Zhuang. Even in Zhuang language classes within Zhuang Studies degrees, Zhuang is not the medium of instruction unless a specific teacher chooses to make it so, as YMU students reported that one of their

Zhuang language teachers did. One language leader participant, Mr C, went so far as to say that nobody *could* use Zhuang to teach a whole university subject, although Mr D retorted that nobody had really tried (field notes 17 June 2014.) Zhuang language does, however, become an instrument to gain preferential entry to these minzu-specialist universities through oral examinations undertaken in addition to the standard high school leavers' examination.

Based on figures reported by language leaders, Messrs L, F and B, and by Zhuang Studies students, each Zhuang Studies department has around one hundred students: 10 to 30 undergraduates per year choose Zhuang Studies at each of GUN, MUC and YMU, and a smaller number of postgraduates. YMU commenced its Zhuang Studies program in 2012, so it did not yet have final-year Zhuang Studies undergraduates, or postgraduates, during my fieldwork. The programs at GUN and MUC both commenced in 1983, according to Mr F, and had students up to PhD level during my study.

In addition, Mr F, reported that Zhuang language is taught to students in the bilingual teaching training program at Guangxi Teachers College. Graduates from Guangxi Teachers College are tied to government postings but Zhuang Studies university students have no employment guarantee.

China's comprehensive public universities do not offer Zhuang Studies. To diversify my fieldwork and recruitment, I also chose three comprehensive universities as anchor sites. Two were in the same cities as anchoring minzu-specialist universities (namely Nanning and Beijing) and one in another autonomous region, Inner Mongolia. In GZAR, the major comprehensive university is *Guangxi University* (GU), situated in downtown Nanning. In Beijing, there are many prominent, comprehensive universities; I recruited students at *Renmin University of China* (RUC), which is in a busy urban center although not right downtown. Recruitment in Inner Mongolia was limited by network and time constraints, but also because I had sufficient participants at the other universities; I recruited only through the comprehensive *Inner Mongolia University of Science and Technology* (IMUST) in Baotou City. Thus, my fieldwork sites came to be chosen in relation to six anchoring universities: GU, GUN, YMU, MUC, RUC and IMUST, which I have indicated on the map in Figure 5.

1.6.3 Purposive participant selection

The study's participants comprised 43 university students who were either Zhuang speakers or Zhuangzu members, and 20 Zhuang language leaders. Eighteen of the 43 students were Zhuang Studies undergraduates and postgraduates. They included students from all three universities offering Zhuang Studies:

GUN in Nanning City, YMU in Kunming City and MUC in Beijing. Twenty-three students were from the anchoring comprehensive universities, GU in Nanning, RUC in Beijing and IMUST in Baotou. They included one student from the comprehensive Yunnan University (YU) in Kunming, who was recruited by the YMU participants. One other of the 23 comprehensive students came from the Peking University (PKU) in Beijing; he was recruited by MUC participants. The 20 language leaders were people doing Zhuang language work, and were envisaged as representatives of those producing and controlling Zhuang language expertise or popularizing or restricting the use of Zhuang language in: cultural heritage; Zhuang policy; education; popular culture and media; language professions; and law (e.g. specialists in researching language rights).

The participants lived and worked in or near the anchor sites. Their profiles are in the Appendix, which also provides a table of the student participants' places of origins and their universities. I have assigned all participants identity-protecting pseudonyms. The students have been given personal names in English to assist the flow of reading this English-medium book. The language leaders are named Mr [Letter], e.g. Mr A. Not all language leaders were men, but most were, and using Mr for all helps obscure their individual identities.

To recruit the 63 participants, I used the "snowball sampling" method (Noy 2007: 331). This was a purposeful sampling method; I chose to build up networks where "'what goes on there' is critical to understanding some process" (Schwandt 1997: 128). In particular, I selected networks connected to universities and to language work, both of which had the potential to illuminate processes of change in Zhuang language usage and Zhuang identities, and the roles of language governance in these processes. I sought to study people who possessed social, cultural and educational capital. They were likely to be more powerful than others in constructing the social meaning of Zhuang-ness and the social value of Zhuang language resources, and in accessing, reproducing or challenging the language rights framework. These people allowed me to tap into vectors of change for Zhuang, building on Han's (2013: 86) framing of participants' lived experience as a type of systematic rather than purely subjective data. In addition, studying how language rights affect people under conditions of social change necessitates studying those close to social change, not those removed from it.

Students' mobility was therefore an important part of choosing to recruit through university networks. As Fan argues, China's university students are relatively geographically mobile. Fan (2008: 60) notes China's "study/training" internal migrants come from either rural or urban locales but "their destinations are overwhelmingly urban areas where advanced education institutes concentrate". Across China, many university students remain in their city of university after graduating; it is a common step in internal migration. The household registration system structures internal migration such that students are "first circuit" state-sponsored migrants because universities are collective units providing urban registration to students (Fan 2008: 41) and university studies count towards applications for permanent urban registration once students graduate (pp. 42, 57). Based on these structures, university education is widely understood in China as a resource for urban-oriented geographic mobility but also upward socio-economic mobility, as well as for career mobility. My purposive sampling of Zhuang-background university students therefore targets "the fast lane [...] of social life" as per the "mobilities paradigm" (originating with Sheller and Urry 2006: 213). As minority group issues are increasingly politicized and problematic in China; universities had the additional advantage of being places I could legitimately access.

The snowball method is particularly useful for accessing "hidden" (Noy 2007: 330) groups. University students with Zhuangzu ethnic status are not numerous at any university but they are not entirely hidden, as this detail is made salient by universities' administrative systems. Thus, one of my fieldwork facilitators could go so far as to highlight every Zhuangzu student on her class rolls as potential participants. Nevertheless, I wanted to keep recruitment open to students without Zhuangzu status who were Zhuang speakers. They are a hidden group because this is *not* an administrative category. The "double marginality" (Roche 2017: 18, following Tenzin 2013) of being a Zhuang speaker who is not also Zhuangzu and therefore not officially recognized as associated to Zhuang language presents an especially interesting context for the interplay of subjective and institutionalized language ideologies. Overall, four student participants were not officially classed as Zhuangzu: one was *Dongzu* and one was *Yaozu* (which are also official minority minzu in China), and two were Hanzu (the majority minzu). One of them was neither Zhuangzu nor a Zhuang speaker but had a Zhuang-speaking parent and grew up in a Zhuang-speaking community in GZAR.

This research was not designed to test or rank the students' Zhuang proficiency. Thirty-seven of the 43 students self-reported being Zhuang speakers, one (Gina) self-reported as a partial speaker and another (Tom) self-reported having listening but not speaking proficiency (i.e. receptive competency). By the time they reached university – indeed, integral to reaching university given their Putonghua-medium university entrance examinations – all the students had Putonghua in their language repertoires and used it for our interviews and correspondence. This accords with the literature; Zhou (2012b: 4–5) shows that across China, "the more education one has, the more likely one speaks Putonghua". Most of the student participants therefore had some choice in whether or not to use Zhuang. Over the course of this book, you will see the multiple direct and indirect influences, including from language rights and from socio-economic change, which constrain that choice.

The language leaders were selected to investigate varied networks of language maintenance, protection and advocacy. They were recruited using criteria in addition (sometimes in the alternative) to being Zhuangzu or speaking Zhuang language. They were introduced to me, and selected, one by one. The language leaders were even more hidden as a social unit because they are not organized, or socially understood, as one group. Snowball sampling was therefore an especially effective method.

To incorporate reflexivity, I arranged fieldwork facilitators who were "insiders" with whom I engaged in some reflexive dialogue, in addition to engaging in reflexive dialogue with language leaders about points emerging from the students' interviews. I ate and/or taught with these facilitators, met their families, friends and colleagues, visited their and their relatives' homes, travelled across cities and counties with them, and had conversations about language and language rights. I maintained contact after fieldwork. My fieldwork facilitators in Yunnan Province and in Inner Mongolia Autonomous Region (IMAR) were both teachers with many years' experience working at universities where I undertook interviewing and observational research. In addition, the former is a minority language speaker, and the latter grew up in a minority autonomous region, and both have studied sociolinguistics. I did not have a facilitator in Beijing, the fieldwork city I knew best, but a contact in GZAR became my third facilitator. As a Zhuangzu and Zhuang speaker, as well as a university educator, he was an informed discussant about Zhuang language and language policy. He also became a language leader participant so he remains anonymous. In many ways, these informal partnerships accelerated my ethnographic understanding of the sociolinguistic context, similar to the advantage a formal rapid ethnography partner could have provided.

Indeed, this accelerated, multi-sited ethnography was adapted from a "rapid ethnography" (Baines and Cunningham 2013: 74) method used in other disciplines. Rapid ethnography "involves at least two researchers in all aspects of data collection" (Baines and Cunningham 2013: 75) so that the two can join in paired reflexivity and thus rapidly derive ethnographic insight, whereas I could not involve data collection partners as my research had to be undertaken independently to qualify for a PhD.

This chapter has introduced the language rights framework in China and the rapid, widespread social, economic and political transformations within which it now operates (or ceases to operate). It has provided an overview of the relevant literature, theory and methods as well as making the case for the book's journey through the overarching structures and laws of minority language governance down to a case study of Zhuang language governance in public linguistic landscapes. To supplement the technical but non-critical and oftentimes static profiles of Zhuang language in the literature and to provide the reader a temporal wide angle before proceeding into the detail of this study, the remainder of Part One offers a critical sociolinguistic profile of Zhuang.

2 What is Zhuang? A critical sociolinguistic profile

Social categories need to be continually replicated to endure. (Goebel 2015)

2.1 Introducing the sociolinguistic profile of Zhuang

Through Chapter One, you have retraced my research journey to South China and towards a Zhuang case study. I have introduced Zhuang language so far as the most-spoken official minority language of the PRC, and connected it to an official minority minzu called the Zhuangzu and a place in the PRC called Guangxi Zhuangzu Autonomous Region. But what is Zhuang language? Why is it associated with this group and this place? As I undertook this research, it became apparent that information about Zhuang language, and its history, speakers and current conditions of practice, was dispersed. In response, the purpose of this chapter is to draw the information together as one coherent body of work, both as a foundation for the rest of this book and as a stand-alone resource for others studying Zhuang. A few years ago, the journal *Current Issues in Language Planning* asked me to describe the Zhuangzu and Zhuang language for a "polity study" of Zhuang language in their series of the same name (Grey 2019: 450–459). This chapter is an extended version of that work which draws as well from more recent research and from my critique of the standardization of Zhuang language in the context of marketization, in *Language standards, norms, and variation in Asia* (McLelland and Zhao in press).

What makes this account of Zhuang cohere, and makes it different from my polity study on Zhuang, is that a critical sociological perspective weaves through it. This is a portrait of Zhuang that does not take for granted what Zhuang is. "Social categories need to be continually replicated to endure" as Goebel (2015) has observed, and during my research I found that Zhuang *is* now an enduring social category, not least as a category of linguistic practices: a language. A theme throughout this book will be how the adjective "Zhuang" and noun "Zhuangzu" continue to be made socially meaningful in changing circumstances; they have been made socially meaningful in changing ways for centuries and that history informs the contemporary discourses and identities which the book will examine.

So how has the category Zhuang been replicated, and how has it been adapted? Goebel (2015) goes on to explain that "[w]hat drives replication are commentaries about others' social practices. In contemporary nation-states mass education, bureaucratic processes, and mass media create large participation frameworks that facilitate replication." My research and many of the studies drawn together in this chapter are themselves commentaries about others' social practices that replicate Zhuang as a meaningful category. The research literature also helps us see how Zhuang has been replicated as a social category in other ways, particularly in this case by bureaucratic processes and state discourses, including formal laws and rules. The chapter updates Kaup's (2000: 1) provocative but partial account of the state "creating the Zhuang[zu]" in the mid to late twentieth century, but also reaches back further, and it illuminates that the state is not the only agent creating the social meaning of Zhuang, nor is the creation necessarily nefarious. Moreover, even a social category initiated by the state can become meaningful to others: in his extensive work on Muslim minorities in the PRC, Dru Gladney (2004: 165) has found that official "ethnic labels [...] have taken on a life of their own."

The chapter is therefore organized around differing meanings of Zhuang, as a historic tribe transformed by state recognition into a polity, as a territory, and what it means to be a Zhuang(zu) person today. Does it mean speaking Zhuang and reading Zhuang, and how does the minority status of the language coincide with the disadvantage of people who might speak it? That Zhuang is made meaningful as a language threads through all these social categories, and I will begin with an overview of what linguists consider Zhuang language to be.

2.2 A Zhuang language

Linguists consider Zhuang to be a language with multiple dialects. Features of contemporary Zhuang varieties have been analyzed in a rich collection of linguistic studies (Chen and Li 2005; Diller et al. 2008; Luo 2008b; Qin and Tian 2011; Zhang 1999). The debate begins over what kind of language it is. Zhuang is placed in the Chinese linguistic literature within the "Zhuang-Dai branch of the Zhuang-Dong language group of the Chinese-Tibetan language family" (China Encyclopedia Compilation Group 2008: 41; similarly Lu and Li 2012: 19). Outside China, linguists use slightly different taxonomies, with some placing Zhuang in the Zhuang-Tai branch of the Kam-Tai group of Sino-Tibetan (Bodomo 2010: 180; Li and Huang 2004: 239; Luo 2008a; Wurm 1988; Zhou 2000: 142) and others proposing "Tai-Kadai" or "Kra-Dai" umbrella groupings that are independent from the Sino-Tibetan family (Diller et al. 2008; Ostapirat 2000). Harrell (1993: 104–105) argues that Chinese linguists' assertion that Tai languages are Sino/Chinese-Tibetan, and the branch name "Zhuang-Dong", are both discursive means of claiming that Zhuang and other Tai languages are rooted within China's borders. Nevertheless, and despite debates about whether Tai languages are Sino-Tibetan, the literature largely agrees that Zhuang language did originate in an area which is now within the PRC's borders (Li and Huang 2004: 239) and that the Tai language family emerged in South-Central China about 2500 years ago (Luo 2008a: 9). Zhuang is similar to the national, Tai language of China's neighbor, Thailand, and to certain language varieties recognized by the Vietnamese government as minority languages spoken within Vietnam. Bodomo (2010: 179) describes Zhuang as "an endangered language" because of the widespread "language shift" towards children becoming proficient in Putonghua rather than Zhuang. However, Zhuang is not included amongst the languages in the PRC listed and mapped as "endangered" by Moseley (2010).

Luo (2015: 3) treats "Zhuang" as "a cover term for the Tai language spoken in Guangxi and adjacent areas in Yunnan, Guangdong in south China with some spill-over in North Vietnam, and which comprises a group of diverse dialects." As this quotations suggests, considerable dialectal variation is recognized in Zhuang. These dialects are classed into the Northern and Southern dialectal groups (Holm 2013: 27; Li and Huang 2004: 239; Lu and Li 2012: 19) but there is debate about whether certain language varieties known to linguists as dialects of Bouyei language are (also) Northern Zhuang dialects and part of a dialect "continuum" (Luo 2008b: 319; see also Harrell 1993: 106; Population Reference Bureau 2011; Ramsey 1987: 243).

This variety is important in that it prompted the government to develop a new, spoken dialect to serve as the standard for Zhuang grammar and pronunciation. The variety between Zhuang dialects is also important because written forms varied, not only oral forms, leading the PRC government to treat Zhuang as a previously unwritten language. That prompted the development of a standardized script and orthography corresponding to the standardized spoken dialect (Li and Huang 2004: 240–243). This standardized variety was developed between the 1950s and 1980s (with interruptions) by Zhuang speakers and the PRC government (Li and Huang 2004: 242), resulting in at least one grammar: Guangxi Language Reform Commission (1989). Literature aimed at teaching Zhuang language is limited, but that which exists offers additional detail on pronunciation, grammar and orthography of the standardized variety. This literature includes: Putonghua-Zhuang texts (Wang 1979, 1983); one English-medium Zhuang proficiency course (Bodomo and Pan 2007); a primer of Zhuang literature (Guangxi Zhuang Literary History Newsroom and Guangxi Teachers College 1961); a Zhuang-Putonghua dictionary (Sinj and Loz 2008); and a government promotion for learning Zhuang script (Wang 1990).

The newly developed writing system was called *Zhuàngwén* 'Zhuang writing' in Putonghua (Holm 2008: 415), and I will call it Romanized Zhuang for clarity. Li and Huang (2004: 240–243) show that developing Romanized Zhuang formed the bulk of the early PRC government's Zhuang language work, in the 1950s. This is consistent with the emphasis on writing that develops with standardization generally (Costa et al. 2018: 6). Romanized Zhuang was revisited by state planners, and reformed, in the 1980s. It had initially included Cyrillic and International Phonetic Alphabet (IPA) graphemes as well as the Roman alphabet, but the Cyrillic and IPA letters were now replaced with Roman letters (see Figure 6, and see further Ager 2016; GZAR Minority Language Working Group Research Team 1984; Li and Huang 2004; Sinj and Loz 2008; Wang 1983).

Script	Example	Meaning in English
Simplified Putonghua characters	壮语	"Zhuang language"
Putonghua pinyin	Zhuàngyǔ	"Zhuang language"
Modern Zhuang pinyin	Vahcuengh	"Zhuang language"
Early Zhuang pinyin	Vabcueŋb	"Zhuang language"
Sawndip	畩㖀	"Sawndip"

Figure 6: Illustration of script diversity: Zhuang scripts adapted from Ager (2016), other data my own.

However, there is controversy within the research literature about whether Zhuang was actually a previously unwritten language. One view sees historic Zhuang writing as "a farrago of nonce creations" (Ramsey 1987: 235). I put within this camp Li and Huang's (2004: 240) account that "for most periods of history, the Zhuang did not have their own writing system" but "often tried to create a native writing system". Zhou (2000: 129, 2001: 56) more modestly claims that there were no "fully functional writing systems before 1949" for Zhuang. Nevertheless, Holm's (2013) thoroughgoing history of Zhuang logographic writing provides copious evidence of written Zhuang texts – primarily religious texts – and writing systems, albeit without one unifying standard orthography (see also Tsung 2014: 161; Tai 2005). Arguably, this was fully functional within a social context where writing was a specialist task not an everyday, mass skill. The historic Zhuang script is known, amongst other names, as 方块字 *fāngkuàizì* 'Square Characters' in Mandarin and *Sawndip*, literally meaning 'uncooked characters' in Zhuang (Sinj and Loz 2008). It adapted many of the traditional characters used to write Mandarin and added indigenous characters (Holm 2008; 2013). By contrast, imperial policies first standardized a Mandarin script and banned non-standard Mandarin scripts in the third century B.C.E. (He 2014: 6).

The PRC's twentieth century development of a standard dialect, a Romanized script and an orthography for Zhuang was not unique. Rather, this was integral in what it meant to the state for Zhuang to be *a language*. Almost all the other official minority languages underwent parallel developments, with a few classified as having their own pre-existing script, while none of the areal Mandarin dialects received this regulation or investment by the state. Treating Zhuang as a language in these ways was politically important because it was part of the newly-formed PRC administration's standard approach to treating people who had been seen to be ethno-linguistically diverse and "backwards" as equally recognized minority polities who were being equally included in the betterment which motivated and legitimized this new nation.

2.3 A Zhuang polity

In the early PRC years, because it was an ideologically important "responsibility of the Communist vanguard to protect and promote the independent development of 'backward,' 'minority' groups" (Leibold and Chen 2014: 5), the PRC studied the people within its borders and then formally recognized and constituted them into 56 polities as one of the earliest state programs. These polities are called *minzu,* to borrow the more precise Putonghua term. This approach to nation-building is encapsulated in the PRC's common, self-given epitaph, 多元一体 *Duoyuan Yiti* 'multiple cultures, one body' i.e. diversity within the unified whole. Of the minority minzu recognized by the PRC, the largest has always been the Zhuangzu. Its members comprise 1.27% of the national population on recent figures (Guo et al. 2015:xv), the relative enormity of which is clear if we recall that the Zhuangzu and other minorities together only comprise about 8% of the population. Guo et al. (2015: 68) report that, in 2011, the Zhuangzu population was 17.283 million.

State recognition of the Zhuangzu has been a naturalizing and symbolically powerful discourse, but who was included and who excluded from the Zhuangzu and from the majority Hanzu were not objective, natural facts. The state classifications relied, in many cases, on government researchers' perceptions of linguistic similarities. For the Zhuangzu, linguistic practices were significant, and taken as more important than local self-identification, as the relevant classification team's leader recounted: "There are also [people] who call themselves Han, and yet recognize that they are different than Han from outside [Guangxi …] Since the language they speak is generally called Zhuang, we recommend calling them Zhuang" (Xiaotong Fei quoted in Kaup 2000: 127 and in Chaisingkananont 2014: 59).

By contrast, the literature suggests that, historically, speaking one Zhuang language variety was not generally understood as indexing a pan-Zhuang group of all the speakers of other Zhuang varieties. Pre-PRC political rhetoric, likewise, did not imagine this large Zhuang community: the Zhuang were not counted in the "five nations" concept of a multi-ethnic China which underpinned the Republic of China (1912–1949). Rather, a Zhuang nation (i.e. a people, not a nation-state) was not consistently "imagined" (Anderson 1991) or taken as "plausible" (Mullaney 2011: 69–91) by either speakers of Zhuang dialects or by the state until the mid-twentieth century. Why then? It was reputedly not only linguistic commonality that was determinative at that time, nor only the genuine communist desire to raise the status of oppressed peoples through state recognition, but a political tactic to carve up the peoples of South China to avoid a Cantonese power-block that would rival the power-block centered in the north and running the new nation. It was also arguably motivated by a communist re-entextualization of the Confucian beliefs that the ruling group (often Han but not always) ought be "responsible for retaining order and stability, and determining what is best for the [non-Han peoples], whether it be exclusion and autonomy or inclusion and assimilation" and that they are "responsible for policing the barrier" (Leibold and Chen 2014: 5) between the Han and everyone else. That is, recognizing 55 minority minzu achieved the constitutional division between the majority Hanzu and the minorities as a foundation of PRC nation building just as much as it distinguished the Zhuangzu from other minorities.

While the Tai language from which the Zhuang dialects descend originated in the southern stretch of well-watered plains and karst mountains which now comprise GZAR (Li and Huang 2004: 239; Luo 2008a: 9), if we look back before PRC times, this area was not associated exclusively or even primarily with Zhuang language or Zhuang people. In the eighteenth century, a European cartographer, Jean Baptiste Bourguignon d'Anville, along with Imperial Chinese guides, produced two esteemed sets of maps of China which were printed in Amsterdam and written in French. D'Anville's (1785) map #15, *Province de Quang-si* 'Province of Guangxi', offers a close-up of Guangxi, spelt using an older Romanization as *Quang-si* (Figure 7). The three biggest cities of GZAR today are marked even then as "*fou*", which d'Anville (1737) defines on another map as *ville du premièr ordre* 'first tier city'. They are NANNING FOU 'Nanning', LIEOUTCHEOU FOU 'Liuzhou' and KOUEI LING FOU 'Guilin'. The same cities (with spelling variations) are marked on his 1737 Guangxi map.

The 1785 map places certain *peuples sauvages* 'wild peoples' in northern Guangxi and in its northern neighboring province *Koei-Tcheou* (now Guizhou Province). These are named as SENG MIAO TSE and TCHOANG KOLAO. The former are located on the map near the Guizhou border in north-central Guangxi,

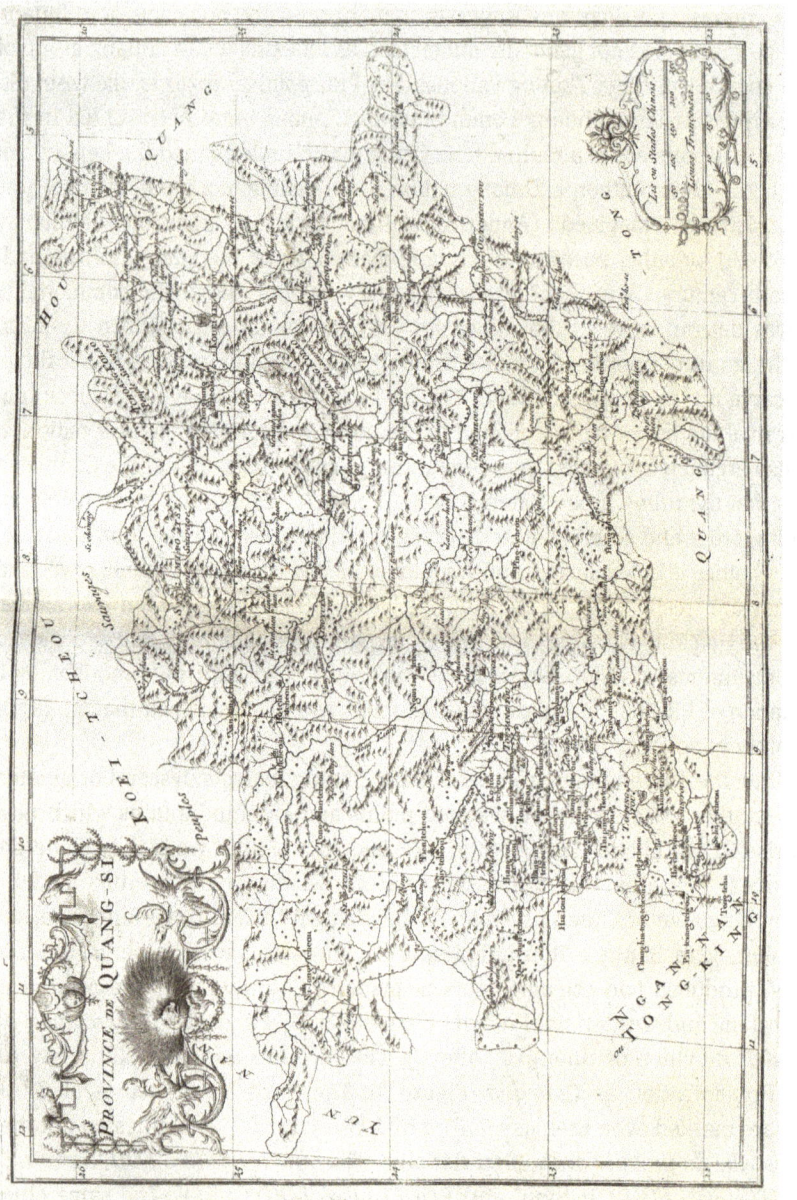

Figure 7: "Province de Quang-Si" (d'Anville 1785), with thanks to the National Library of Australia.

and the latter to their East, above Guilin at the Guizhou border, and between Guilin and Liuzhou in North-East Guangxi. The name *SENG MIAO TSE* sounds like *Miaozu*, a minority minzu recognized today, but "Miao" used to be a general term for China's south-western tribal peoples. Tapp and Cohn (2003: 1, 2, 5) begin their annotated reproduction of Qing Dynasty "Miao albums" by explaining that Miao were "the strange varieties of non-Chinese people within the borders of the empire" and that their sources depict many different Miao of the South-West. Earlier than d'Anville, the cartographer Martino Martini (1659: 175) simply grouped the people of western Guangxi as *una gente ruda* 'a crude race' distinct from *los Sinas* 'the Chinese' and *los pueblos subditos al imperio* 'people subject to the emperor' in Guangxi.

The latter of d'Anville's two named groups, *TCHOANG KOLAO*, sounds like the Zhuang i.e. Tchoang is Zhuang, but these Tchoang "wild people" did not necessarily share the language, culture or bloodlines of today's Zhuangzu polity. At very least, their location on the 1785 map suggests they were a much smaller group than the people recognized as the non-Han Zhuangzu polity in the mid twentieth century, and settled much further to the East of Guangxi than today's Zhuangzu. Contemporary studies show more Zhuang speakers live in South and West GZAR, near Wenshan, than in East GZAR (CASS Institute of Linguistics et al. 2012; H. Chen 2005: 17). In d'Anville's (1785) map #1 of the whole of China, a slightly different spelling is used to label *Tchoangcolao//Sauvages* 'Tchoangcolao//Wild people' above and below Guilin City. Yet in d'Anville's earlier 1737 map of China, while the Seng Miao Tse are again marked and described as *sauvages* 'wild', the Tchoang (using any spelling) are not marked. Further, d'Anville's 1737 map of *Koan si* 'Guangxi' is ambiguous about whether Tchoang (Zhuang) is a social group at all: he writes "*Tchoancolao*" once to the north of Guilin but in the small, cursive script he otherwise uses for place names, not the capitalized style he uses on this map for peoples such as the "*SEN-MIAO-SE*".

The second part of d'Aville's possible term for Zhuang, *kolao/colao*, is a variation of the term *kelao*, and this term was used to name small, autochthonous groups in a way that linked them to the ancient "Lao" population of South China (Tapp and Cohn 2003: 4). Tapp and Cohn (2003: 4) report that the "*kelao*" A.K.A. "*kolao*" were/are speakers of Kam-Sui languages, which also includes the PRC's contemporary, official minority language, Dong. Kam-Sui languages are classed by linguists into the same language group as Zhuang, the Zhuang-Dong/Kam-Tai language group. So, d'Anville's mapping of *TCHOANG KOLAO* is best interpreted as representing a combined grouping of speakers of Zhuang and Kelao varieties living in North-East Guangxi in the eighteenth century.

Tapp and Cohn (2003) reproduce many eighteenth and nineteenth century watercolor-and-text depictions of South-West tribes made for imperial Chinese audiences, and while some depicted tribal customs match customs ascribed to the Zhuangzu today, the name *Zhuang/Tchoang* is not among the many group names in their sources. This reaffirms the irrelevance of Zhuang as a meaningful social group to the Chinese state in pre-PRC times. Moreover, researchers argue that it was not a meaningful social group label for Zhuang speakers, either. The Zhuang-language word now used for "Zhuang" (*cuengh*) was not previously a common autonym (Barlow 1989: 33–34; Chaisingkananont 2014: 32–40; Kaup 2000: 53, 96; Leibold 2007; Mullaney 2011; Zhang 1997: 1128). It was introduced by fourteenth century Yuan Dynasty administrators to name just a certain group of southern barbarian soldiers (Chaisingkananont 2014: 1). Hmong specialist, the late Nicholas Tapp, describes a similar group, the *Kayou-Zhongjia*, based on an eighteenth century Miao album, describing them thus: "[a]ccording to legend [...their king] the Chu King Ma Yin moved (to this location) from Yongguan". Quoting Lin, Tapp and Cohn (2003: 73) write,

> Ma Yin [...] Prince of Chu sent soldiers to garrison in Nanning [in modern day GZAR] in the Five Dynasties period (907–960) whose soldiers took their commanders' name Chung to distinguish themselves from the more general Miao [...] hence the Chung Chia (the old spelling of Zhongjia). [...] Although the Zhongjia were clearly a separate ethnic group, speaking a Tai language, there may have been some intermarriage with Chinese military colonialists, and this attempt to trace their ancestry to Chinese soldiers who had settled down among the natives and become almost indistinguishable from them [...] may be seen as representing the important sense in which the Zhongjia were recognized as unlike other minorities in the region, and closer to the Chinese in their degree of culture.

It seems that speaking Tai but being Chinese-like in other respects was not construed as assimilation at that time, and indeed having some Chinese lineage was seminal to distinct group identity rather than a factor which negated it. Given the dynamism over centuries in conceptions of what makes for a distinct group and what groups are called, it is not surprising that *Zhuang/cuengh* appears not to have been a widely meaningful ethnic category for self-identification in the early twentieth century: Iredale and Guo (2003: 8; also Harrell 1993: 102; Kaup 2000: 73) report that in the 1949 pre-census, people nominated themselves as falling into over four hundred ethnic groups with Zhuang not among them. Some people at the time of the PRC's founding were still reporting themselves as "讲壮语的汉人" [Zhuang-speaking Han peoples] (Zhang 1997: 1128; see also Kaup 2000: 87). Rather, the now-naturalized connection of Zhuang language to Zhuang ethnicity to a Zhuangzu polity developed as state discourses replicated the Zhuangzu category after Zhuangzu was introduced by the state as a category on the 1954 Yunnan census (Mullaney 2006: 142).

The instability of Zhuang as a named social group over time illustrates what Mullaney (2006: 61–62) has called the "taxonomically unstable" organization of ethnic and language groups in historic South China. One of the reasons the correspondences between labels, groups and languages kept shifting was that the state did not need them to be fixed, because the South was not fully incorporated but rather governed by local chieftains paying tribute to the suzerain North. By contrast, consistent bureaucratic discourses about polities is a political and administrative imperative of the PRC today. This is perhaps why some contemporary writers anachronistically write the "Zhuangzu" – i.e. the official PRC polity constructed to recognize the speakers of (non-Bouyei) varieties of Zhuang – into historic accounts. For example, Zhang first reports the "Zhuangzu" in 1007 CE in his three-volume *General History of the Zhuangzu*: "宜州陈进，卢成均率领壮、汉族人民起义" [Chen Jing and Lu Chengjun of Yizhou [in GZAR] led the peoples of the Zhuangzu and Hanzu in an uprising] (Zhang 1997: 1187, emphasis mine).

That quotation also exemplifies an author distinguishing the Hanzu from other historic peoples in a manner consistent with today's official division. Even before fixing Zhuangzu as a category of people emerged as a political imperative, this Hanzu/non-Hanzu division was being replicated throughout discourses and representations, and continues now in the form of the Hanzu majority and 55 minority minzu. Most historians suggest that the dominant social organization in South China in imperial times was likewise the dichotomy between civilized 华 'Chinese' and 夷 'barbarians' (e.g. Harrell 1993: 101; Mullaney 2011: 1).

For the official classification of people into minzu today, the linguistic commonalities which were made central to the initial ethnic classifications are no longer relevant. Rather, minzu classification is now administratively reproduced. The Zhuangzu classification is assigned to a child if her parents' official classification is Zhuangzu. In "two-minzu couples" (Mullaney 2011: 123), the parents nominate one of their minzu classifications for the child at birth but, when aged between 18 and 20 years of age, the child may formally switch to the other parent's minzu. There is no other possibility for reclassification (Zhou 2013: 5). A person's minzu status is constantly re-articulated in bureaucratic processes and on ID cards, where it serves as a basic identifying feature. Thus nowadays, "bureaucratic apparatuses possess a virtual monopoly on ethnocultural identity articulation" (Leibold 2015: 274) and maintain the official frontiers of the Zhuangzu polity. These are frontiers that are both produced by and productive of difference, after all "a legal act of delimitation produces cultural difference as much as it is produced by it" (Bourdieu 1991: 222).

This delimitation of a Zhuangzu category, voiced by the symbolically empowered state, has the capacity to promote a hegemonic belief in this social categorization over other possible categorizations. The Zhuangzu polity now has a meaningful social reality as that which Bourdieu (1987: 844) called a "legitimized discourse", as my data affirms. It is therefore significant that these legal processes, and discourses, elide the transformations from loose groupings of peoples into ethnically distinct minorities including the Zhuangzu, as well as the state's agency in that transformation. Rather, the minzu classification processes which formed the Zhuangzu and other polities were (and are) largely presented as processes of systematically identifying naturally existing ethno-linguistic groups. For example, if people nominate a minzu other than their officially assigned polity on a census, then this is treated as "wrong" and "misreporting" (Zhou 2013: 5–7). Indeed, Zhou (2013: 2) comments that providing a definition of each minzu on the census "seems redundant since its meaning should be as natural as categories of name, age or place of residence". The language ideologies and the linguistic and social orders produced in the Zhuang language governance framework are thus naturalized by it, creating hegemony. This hegemony is important in evaluating what language policies actually do or do not do and the expectations people have of them, a theme to which I return in the Conclusions (Chapters Ten and Eleven).

However, it is important to note that the recognition of polities as naturally distinct ethno-linguistic groups has recently been challenged within central government circles in a wave of political discourse known as 第二代民族政策 'second generation minzu policy' (A. Hu 2012). Second generation policy would dissolve the Zhuangzu and other official minority minzu. Second generation minzu discourse proposes a new paradigm of social organization, removing the symbolic and legal recognition of 56 ethno-linguistic minzu and the minorities' special treatment, and fostering the decline of minzu identities while strengthening a Chinese national identity (Leibold 2012: 7). Prominent proponent, Ma Rong, believes the "systematic segregation of ethnic groups and institutions in China has rendered the Chinese nation (中华民族) an empty concept" and that the "Hanification" of the Zhuangzu and other minority polities is an "inevitable process of modernization" (quoted in Leibold 2012: 7). Second generation policy advocates propose the "death" of minority languages as the only way for all Chinese people to gain equal access to educational and economic opportunities (a comment from Ma Rong cited in He 2014: 3). Another prominent proponent of a second generation minzu policy shift, Hu Angang, has proposed multiple other policy reforms which the PRC government has accepted (Leibold 2012: 7) but so far it has not supported this drastic reform. Nevertheless, these debates remind us that the minzu are dynamic constructions that may not always be replicated in the future, particularly if the social meanings of minority languages and of the national language become very different to their social meanings in the mid-twentieth century when the PRC established the minority minzu polities.

Both the current official grouping of people into ethno-linguistic minority polities and the second generation paradigm promulgate the belief that there is a one-to-one correspondence between polity, ethnicity, language and culture. No one but the minorities speaks minority languages as a first language under either paradigm. Polities and languages have an inextricably linked existence in the former view, and must therefore die inextricably linked on the latter view. Both views relate this ideology not only to polities within the nation but to the national polity. That is, Chinese nationality, ethnicity, language and culture are made essential to one another in the second generation paradigm. Although dismantling the minzu framework is not on the official agenda, this essentialization is also promulgated through discourses other than the second generation minzu policy debates. Indeed, as Roche and Leibold (2020) argue, in the removal of preferential policy for minorities in family planning or university entrance, and in the recent expansion of Putonghua-medium education, "China's second-generation ethnic policies are already here" in all but name.

Yet aligned with the remnant "first generation" Duoyuan Yiti multiple cultures, one body paradigm, conventionalized kinds of emblems are still regularly deployed by the state for each polity: hats, costumes, dances and songs for each. Language – namely the official standardized variety of each minority language – is another such emblem (see, e.g. Harrell 1993: 104) and therefore the official grammars for each, the officially recognized scripts of each, and the official translations of key government documents and speeches for each language can also be emblematic representatives of the minority minzu. Chapters Six and Seven examine, empirically, the key Zhuangzu emblems. Another correspondence still constructed by powerful and official state discourses is that between language, polity and place: many minority minzu are seen to have homelands and some of these homelands are recognized as territories under autonomous minority minzu government.

2.4 A Zhuang territory

Because Zhuang is seen by linguists as a Tai language, and Tai languages developed in the area long known as Guangxi and now as Guangxi Zhuangzu Autonomous Region (GZAR), it is easy for researchers to construct GZAR as a Zhuang language homeland. But research and popular discourses regularly construct Australia, my home nation, as an English-speaking place, and English certainly did not originate there. Where a language is in place, or out of place, is an ideological mediation between linguistic practices and locations. To represent GZAR as a Zhuang homeland is part of making Zhuang a meaningful social category. It is a chicken-and-egg construction: GZAR is represented by the state now as the Zhuang homeland because the people classed as Zhuangzu were the people in this area. Yet historically, South-Central and South-West China was a "language corridor" (Edmondson and Li 1996) or a linguistic "shatter zone" (Holm

2013: 13), because of repeated migrations and resettlements. Speakers sharing a variety of the language now called Zhuang likely migrated together (Holm 2013: 13). Wang et al.'s (2011) toponymal analysis indicates that there were concentrations of Zhuang speakers in South and West Guangxi historically, contrasting with d'Anville's placement of the *Tchoang*/Zhuang people in North and East Guangxi, as discussed above. But Wang et al. (2011: 331) also claim "an increasingly integrated settlement pattern" of Zhuang and non-Zhuang speakers over the *longue durée*. So, older varieties of Zhuang were spoken in various parts of the GZAR area at various times but they were not the only language varieties in the area, and not necessarily even dominant.

Regardless of where Zhuang was mostly spoken or who was identified as Zhuang historically, at the point that the Zhuangzu polity was officially recognized its members lived in higher numbers in Guangxi than in any other province. Guangxi was then officially a province. Guangxi Province was therefore re-designated as the autonomous region for the Zhuangzu in 1958. The PRC has five autonomous regions including GZAR. These autonomous regions have the equivalent rank to provinces within the PRC, making GZAR is the highest ranking, most populous and largest territory officially under Zhuangzu government. Unfortunately, GZAR has also been known to have high levels of government corruption and inefficiency (Cole et al. 2009; Grey 2015a). Yan (2004: 122) nominated GZAR as the "best example of multilayered, top-down chains of local corruption" in China. In Chapter Five, I examine the autonomous government structure of GZAR; a spoiler, I find the autonomy is curtailed.

Moreover, while the Zhuangzu are the most numerous minority minzu in GZAR, they are not the only one: they have constituted about one third of GZAR's population since GZAR was established. For example, I used data from 2000 reported in Liu (2005: 3) to calculate that the Zhuangzu comprised 32.4% of GZAR's total population that year. Including other minority minzu, minority peoples together comprised 38.17% of GZAR's population at roughly that time (State Council Information Office of the PRC 2005a, using 2003 data). The Zhuangzu are clearly a much bigger group in GZAR than any other minority minzu. Nevertheless, by far the most populous minzu in GZAR is the Hanzu – the national majority minzu – who comprise 62.07% of GZAR's population on recent figures (Guo 2013: 225).

In the early PRC, Zhuangzu people also lived in high concentrations in small areas adjacent to GZAR within neighboring provinces. These areas were therefore also designated as Zhuangzu autonomous territories, but sub-provincial ones. They are called Wenshan Zhuangzu-Miaozu Autonomous Prefecture (Wenshan) and Lianshan Zhuangzu-Yaozu Autonomous County (Lianshan). Wenshan is within Yunnan Province to the West of GZAR and Lianshan is within Guangdong Province to the East of GZAR. (D'Anville's 1737 map records a "*Lien-shan*" roughly where Lianshan is today.) In these smaller territories, the Zhuangzu share titular autonomy with other officially recognized minority minzu: the Miaozu in Wenshan and the Yaozu in Lianshan. The locations of these three autonomous Zhuangzu territories, GZAR, Wenshan and Lianshan, are indicated in Figure 8.

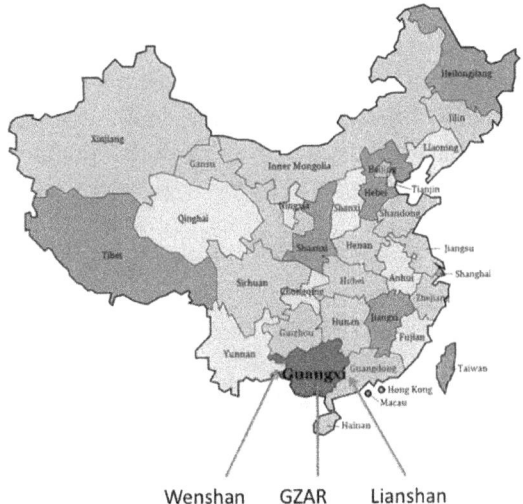

Figure 8: Territories with titular Zhuangzu governments, adapted from Chinafolio (2016).

I calculate that 87.06% of the Zhuangzu lived in GZAR as at 2016. I arrive at this estimate by aggregating reported percentages of the Zhuangzu populating counties outside GZAR in China, and subtracting the aggregate from 100%. This percentage is slightly below Zhou's (2000: 142) approximation of 90% of the Zhuangzu living in GZAR, but either figure shows that the vast majority of the Zhuangzu still live in GZAR (or at least have their residence registered there). This is despite GZAR having had relatively high rates of in- and out-migration since the 1980s compared to other Chinese regions and provinces (Iredale and Guo 2003), indicating that the people who are willing and able to move away from GZAR are likely not to be Zhuangzu. However, Zhuangzu people in GZAR no longer live in such concentrated communities as they did in the mid-twentieth century. Many of them have now moved to GZAR's cities. Urbanization is dispersing formerly Zhuang-speaking communities across GZAR. In 1999, only 10% of the Zhuangzu lived in cities (Stites 1999: 112). By comparison, six years later in 2005's National One Percent Sample Survey data (China's inter-census survey), 34% of the Zhuangzu were registered as urban residents (Guo 2013: 5). From 2000 to 2010, the proportion of the national population who were urban residents rose by 13.46 percentage points (National Bureau of Statistics of China 2011). This period's urbanization rate exceeded the UN's expectation of a 47% urbanization rate in the PRC for 2010 (Cox 2011). The increase included the temporary urban residents who were migrant workers with rural household registration (Cox 2011), but by 2015, *permanent* urban residents, i.e. those with urban household registration, were 56.1% of the national population (Lifang 2018). In peri-urban areas, there may still be communities of concentrated Zhuang speakers. For example, Shanglin County, Yongning County and Long'An County, respectively on the northern, eastern and western margins of Nanning Municipality in GZAR, are reported to house relatively high concentrations of Zhuang speakers (Nanning Municipal Minority Language Works Commission 2019: §1.9). However, urban counties typically do not.

Urbanization in GZAR, where most Zhuangzu are still resident, has been a little slower than the nation's extreme pace. Nevertheless, urbanization in GZAR is growing and the regional urbanization rate was a sizable 47.1% in 2015, while the average urbanization rate for the nation was 56.1 % (Lifang 2018), so many more Zhuangzu than 2005's rate of 34% will now be urban residents. Moreover, data do not show the rate at which Zhuangzu people temporarily or permanently migrated out of GZAR to the urbanized employment hubs of the East Coast, especially the nearby Pearl River Delta in Guangdong Province. We can assume that many did, following the strong national trend, and given that GZAR has remained relatively poor. However, since GZAR's GDP growth rate exceeded the national average in 2015 (State Council Information Office of the PRC 2016) and the regional economy is finally taking off, those leaving rural GZAR may trend towards urban GZAR rather than necessarily migrating outside GZAR to find opportunity in coming years.

Whether it is urban migration into GZAR's cities or into the mega-poleis of the Eastern provinces, the large-scale population relocation underway in China not only means that many Zhuangzu people now live in cities, unlike before, but that the urban Zhuangzu live alongside increasing numbers of Mandarin speakers, as the Hanzu majority are also moving to urban centers in GZAR (Iredale, Bilik and Guo 2003).

The Zhuangzu people in Yunnan Province still live primarily in Wenshan and comprise 6.44% of the whole Zhuangzu polity. The Zhuangzu were 2.64 % of Yunnan's total population of 47,368,000 people in 2015 (Scally 2016). Zhuangzu population data by prefecture is hard to find, but Wenshan itself was reported to have had 1,031,851 Zhuangzu within a prefectural population of 3,517,946 in 2010 (National Bureau of Statistics & Yunnan Bureau of Statistics 2016 [2010]). That is, around a third of Wenshan's population are officially counted as having Zhuang ethnicity. By comparison, in Guangdong Province, where

Lianshan is, the Zhuangzu comprise a smaller proportion of both the Zhuangzu population and the provincial population: Guangdong Province has just 1.54% of the Zhuangzu polity. The Guangdong Zhuangzu population is also less concentrated than in GZAR or Yunnan, with under one fifth of the Guangdong Zhuangzu living in Lianshan. Another 0.13% of the Zhuangzu live in Guizhou Province, to the north of GZAR, while 4.83% of the Zhuangzu live outside of GZAR in unspecified places. As with the Zhuangzu population, Zhuang speakers live in their largest numbers in GZAR and Yunnan Province (Chen and Li 2005). Now let us turn to profiling Zhuang speakers and disambiguating them from the contemporary Zhuangzu polity.

2.5 A Zhuang speaker

I have found that the Zhuangzu people today are often represented as essentially and eternally exotic, as in this photograph of "a Zhuang girl" (Figure 9) gracing the 2008 edition of the "Ethnic Minorities" chapter of the *China Encyclopedia (English Version)*, an official publication produced by the China Encyclopedia Compilation Group and PRC State Council. Here, we meet the gaze of a young woman photographed wearing an embroidered red robe and striking, traditionally-inspired hat

Figure 9: "A Zhuang girl" (China Encyclopedia Compilation Group 2008: 42).

while talking on a mobile phone. This picture may speak the proverbial thousand words, but which words would this girl speak? Would a Zhuang girl talk on her phone in Zhuang, Putonghua, English, Cantonese, or the Mandarin topolect of Nanning, *Baihua* (lit. 'Vernacular')? Zhuang-speaking areas have traditionally been areas of societal multilingualism and moreover, as this section develops, individual multilingualism is common these days.

Representations such as this photograph suggest that the Zhuangzu people, even the young Zhuangzu, maintain distinct cultural traditions while adapting to the lifestyle and technology of the modern era. Speaking Zhuang language may be represented or expected as part of this purported traditionalism. And yet, I have also encountered a common view that Zhuangzu people are culturally indistinct and "well assimilated [people who] can communicate perfectly well in Chinese and are more than happy to do so", as Ramsey (1987: 167) put it. World authority on Zhuang scripts, David Holm, has likewise encountered this view, noting the Zhuangzu's "reputation for being one of the most docile and Sinicized of China's ethnic minorities" (Holm 2013: 799), and Feng and Sunuodula (2009: 692) claim that "Zhuang is rarely taken seriously as the linguistic identity of this largest minority nationality group". The disuse of Zhuang language seems to be expected as part of this purported assimilation. Yet Li and Huang (2004: 239) claim that Zhuang is used for communication "because of the Zhuang's deep emotional attachment to it" and Lu and Li (2012: 36) argue that "the Zhuang people still need a linguistic representation of their ethnic identity." Are Zhuangzu people expected, then, both by other Zhuangzu and by the rest of China, to speak Zhuang? Is the practice of Zhuang language an overt marker of distinct culture and ethnicity, like the young model's anachronistically bright hat, or is Zhuang language a communication technology being replaced, akin to the landlines and telegraphs which her mobile phone has superseded?

To some researchers, at least, the Zhuangzu must be Zhuang speakers, and so census data about the Zhuangzu population suffices as a proxy for Zhuang speaker numbers (Bodomo and Pan 2007; Liang et al. 1988:n5; Luo 2015: 3). However, the Zhuangzu and Zhuang speakers are not coextensive groups. Chapter One cited counts of Zhuang speakers between 10 and 14 million, while the Zhuangzu population is around 17 million. Thus, millions of Zhuangzu people *do not* speak Zhuang. Moreover, some non-Zhuangzu people *do* speak Zhuang, even having Zhuang as their first language. These are typically people raised in Zhuang-speaking locales but who are officially part of other ethnic groups. Language leader participant, Mr G, for example, noted that Hanzu people (from the majority minzu) and Yaozu people (from another minority minzu) in his hometown in GZAR are Zhuang speakers, and other participants gave similar accounts or were themselves non-Zhuangzu Zhuang speakers. Yet because languages are made emblematic of ethnicities by the state, and ethnicities are structured into polities, being from another ethnic polity yet speaking Zhuang goes largely unrecognized and unmeasured. A survey conducted by the Guangxi Language Committee in 2000 contains the only count of non-Zhuangzu Zhuang speakers that I have found, counting 430,830 Zhuang speakers in GZAR who were not Zhuangzu (Chen 2005: 19–20). Nevertheless, the same survey shows Zhuang is GZAR's third most-spoken language variety, after Southwest Guiliuhua and Putonghua, both of which are varieties of Mandarin (the latter is the national language). Chen (2005: 17) reports the survey's finding that Southwest Guiliuhua and Putonghua were each spoken by about 49% of the GZAR population and that 35.518% of people in GZAR spoke Zhuang, which is slightly higher than the percentage of GZAR's population who are Zhuangzu. Thus, there is still a good chance that a Zhuangzu person will be a Zhuang speaker, but Zhuangzu people will not be the only Zhuang speakers.

The number of Zhuang speakers who are not Zhuangzu increases further if we add in the speakers of Bouyei, the language officially associated with the Bouyeizu minority group. I explained in Section 2.2 that some linguists count Bouyei as Zhuang. If we take that approach, the number of Zhuang speakers increases by the estimated 2.6–2.9 million Bouyei speakers (Ager 2018; Asher and Moseley 2007: cxxxix). Including the Bouyei speakers, there are thus somewhere between 14 million and 17 million people who speak some variety of Zhuang in the PRC.

How often and alongside which other language varieties these people speak Zhuang are different matters. Research about those matters usually investigates only Zhuangzu people rather than other Zhuang speakers. It shows that Zhuangzu Zhuang speakers are now often bilinguals who also speak varieties of Mandarin and who organize their multilingual repertoires in similar ways to each other. Let us begin with 1980s data, from the time when the PRC was commencing its Opening and Reform. Li and Huang (2004: 240) report that 42.29% of the Zhuangzu population were monolingual in Zhuang in the 1980s, but even at that time 54.72% were bilingual "Zhuang-Chinese" speakers, i.e. speaking some Zhuang variety as well as some Mandarin variety. By 1990, 57% of the Zhuangzu were "Chinese" speakers (Zhou 2000: 142), and from the surrounding data we can infer this figure represents those speaking Chinese *in addition to* Zhuang rather than instead of Zhuang. At this point, Zhuang speakers' shift to bilingualism started to accelerate. Zhou (2012b: 6, 10), revisiting this topic a decade later, calculated that by the early 2000s 66.15–77.99% of the Zhuangzu population were Zhuang-Chinese bilinguals. The data shows that speaking Mandarin had, to that point, not *necessarily* meant ceasing to speak Zhuang, because Zhuang had remained a relatively widely-spoken language (Chen 2005; Li 2005: 10; Liu 2005: 4–6). Reputedly, at the turn of the millennia, of those people who could speak Zhuang as a 母语 *mǔyǔ* 'mother tongue', 85% were using it in their everyday lives (Chen and Wang 2005: 52).

These studies do not specify if the "Chinese" was Putonghua or another Mandarin dialect. There are many possibilities: Chen (2005: 17) reports that forty-eight Mandarin dialects – including Putonghua – are spoken in GZAR. Chen also reports that seventeen minority languages apart from Zhuang, English, and three other foreign languages are spoken in GZAR, but whether Zhuang speakers' repertoires also include these is not well studied. The language atlas map of GZAR shown in Figure 10 is derived from a different study but it likewise represents societal multilingualism and multidialectism across GZAR. It maps two separate groups of languages. The top-left legend lists 26 languages under a heading translating as Minority Minzu Languages; this list includes Zhuang, indicated on the map as "Zh". The bottom-left legend lists varieties under a heading translating as Hanyu [Mandarin] Topolects. The mapped Mandarin varieties do not include Putonghua. I have annotated the map to indicate the large area of GZAR within which Zhuang language is recorded, which includes the capital city, Nanning. I have also indicated the smaller, isolated Eastern tip of GZAR where Zhuang is recorded. Any transborder usage of Zhuang is elided as the mapping stops at GZAR's borders, but it clearly shows that wherever Zhuang is spoken within GZAR, Mandarin topolects are also spoken, especially 西南官话 *xīnán guānhuà* 'Southwestern Mandarin', 粤语 *yuéyǔ* 'Cantonese', 客家话 *kèjiā huà* 'Hakka', and 平话 *pínghuà* 'Pinghua'. As such, these are likely to be amongst the "Chinese" varieties that "Zhuang-Chinese" bilinguals speak.

Chen provides additional data specifically about Putonghua being common in "Zhuang-Chinese" bilingual repertoires. He (Chen 2005: 19–20) shows that while many members of the minority groups in GZAR are Putonghua speakers, the rate is highest within the Zhuangzu, as 52.56% of the Zhuangzu in GZAR are Putonghua speakers. This is not far off the proportion of the majority Hanzu group in GZAR who speak Putonghua: of the Hanzu in GZAR, 60.72% are Putonghua speakers (Chen 2005: 19–20).

By contrast, for the other minority groups in GZAR, Putonghua speaker rates are at or below 30% (Chen 2005: 19–20) but individual bi-/multilingualism is nevertheless normal across minzu in GZAR. Using 1998 data rather than the 2000 survey, Li reports that only 20.04% of the GZAR population were then monolingual in any language, while nearly half the GZAR population were bilingual in any combination, and that nearly another third were trilingual, with a small percentage speaking four or more languages (Li 2005: 13). This aligns with a trend of increasing proficiency in Mandarin varieties amongst all of China's minority peoples: by the early 1990s, most of the 55 minority minzu had a population that was half or more than half bilingual (Zhou 1992: 60). That Zhuang speakers are

2.5 A Zhuang speaker — 53

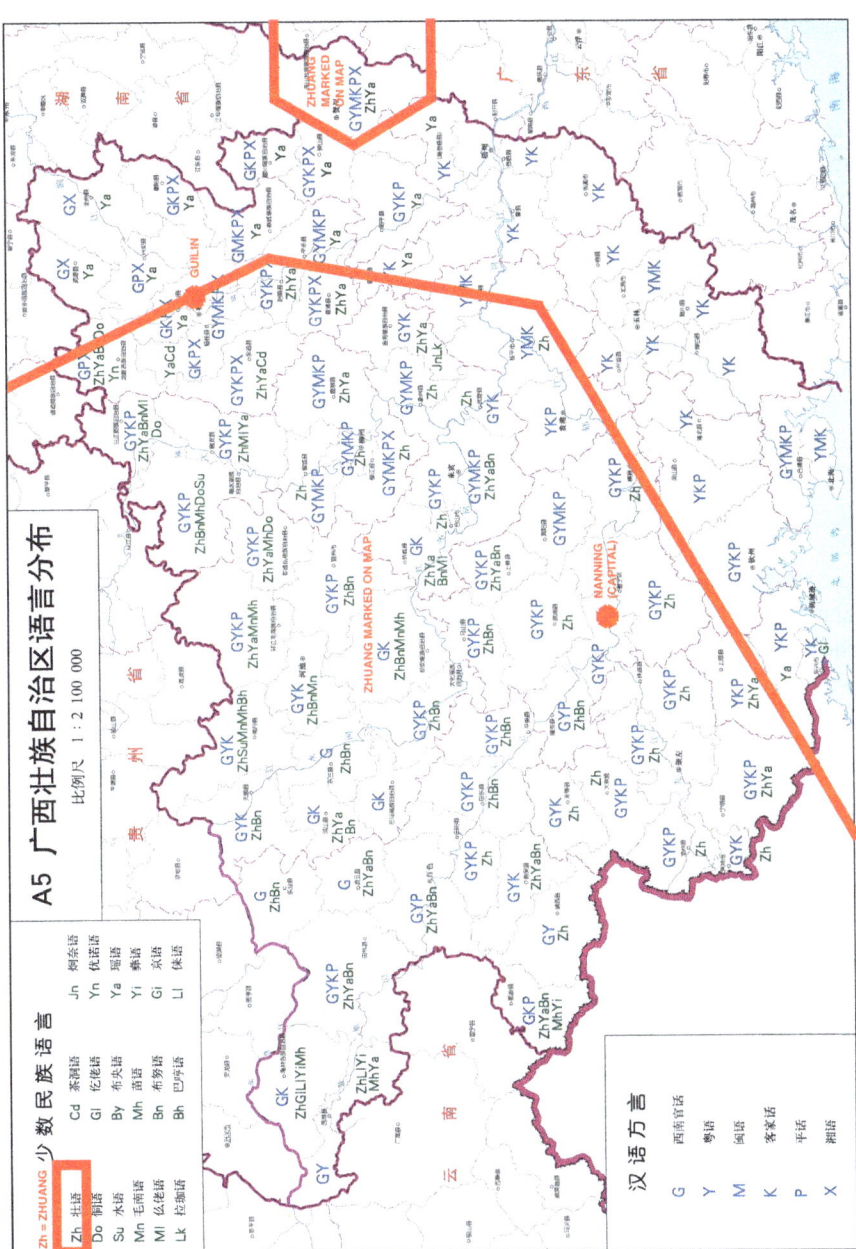

Figure 10: Annotation showing Zhuang-speaking "Zh" areas on CASS Institute of Linguistics et al.'s (2012) map entitled 广西壮族自治区语言分布 ('GZAR Language Distribution').

often bilingual is therefore not remarkable compared to other minority groups, but the Zhuangzu are markedly more likely to be bilinguals who speak the national standard language, Putonghua, than people from other minority groups in GZAR. Further, Zhou (2012a: 4) argues that the proportion of secondary and tertiary school-aged minority people who speak Putonghua is higher than the proportion of all-ages minority people: over 70%. Because the Zhuangzu has population growth skewed towards younger age brackets (Guo 2013: 2–3), we can assume that an increasing proportion of the Zhuangzu are school students and therefore Putonghua speakers.

The 2000 GZAR Language Committee survey provides further detail on how bilingual Zhuang speakers organize their linguistic repertoires, offering insights into Zhuang's disuse in certain domains and functions within Zhuang-speaking areas, but also its vitality. Compared to the 17 other minority languages which the survey records as spoken in GZAR, the usage of Zhuang at home and beyond the home was strong. For instance, across all GZAR's minority groups, 61.47% of those capable of speaking a minority language as their mother tongue reportedly used it *both* inside *and* outside the home, and this was even higher amongst Zhuang speakers: 70.14% of Zhuang speakers in GZAR used it inside and outside the home (Chen and Wang 2005: 52–53). Chen's (2005: 21) study of a sample of 3495 Zhuangzu people found a corroborating result, with 72.38% speaking some Zhuang at home. Moreover, while 23.54% of people across all of GZAR's minority polities used minority language *only* at home, just 11.8% of the Zhuangzu did this (Chen and Wang 2005: 52–53). Li (2005: 14) reports that 50% of bilingual Mandarin-minority language speakers in GZAR divided their repertoire by domain, using the minority language at home and Mandarin away from home. That is, a public/private boundary appears generally salient in the bilingual habitus of people in GZAR. By contrast, Zhuang was not a home-bound minority language in GZAR in 2000.

Further, the literature provides detail – albeit with some ambiguity – on other common domain divisions between Zhuang bilinguals' languages, and on the divisions made by other bilinguals in GZAR. The 2000 GZAR Language Committee survey shows Zhuang and other minority languages are used less than Putonghua as well as less than other Mandarin dialects across the domains of home, shopping, visiting hospitals, visiting government offices and at work (Zhou 2012b: 5). For example, minority languages were used by only 2.30% of respondents at work, Putonghua by 41.97% and other Mandarin dialects by 70.09% (Zhou 2012b: 5). (The total is >100 because some respondents used two or three languages at work.) Referring to the same survey, Chen and Wang (2005: 54) report that, of those who could speak Zhuang as a mother tongue, 81% did so to an unspecified extent at markets, 65% at hospitals, 62% at government offices, and 69%

in the work-unit. These respondents might *also* speak Putonghua or another Mandarin dialect in these places.

Although these indices convey Zhuang's vitality, the number of Zhuang speakers who chose *not* to use Zhuang *either* at home *or* outside home was also higher than the average number of minority language speakers making this choice in GZAR: 15.05% of the Zhuangzu chose not to use Zhuang either at home or outside, compared to 12.43% on average (Chen and Wang 2005: 52–53). Furthermore, the data show that Zhuang was not constructed as appropriate for official functions in recent decades. For instance, Li and Huang (2004: 240) analyze statistics from the early 1990s, reporting that "[i]n the nine counties [of GZAR] where the Zhuang [polity] comprise 90% of the total local population, Zhuang is spoken on most occasions except official occasions and in many classrooms." These official occasions were usually conducted in Putonghua, while "Chinese" (whether Putonghua or another Mandarin dialect) and Zhuang were both used in non-official domains. In addition to this exclusion of Zhuang from official domains, by 2000, only 29.46% of all people in GZAR spoke Zhuang in social communications, while 48.76% spoke the Mandarin dialect Southwest Guiliuhua, and 19.46% spoke Putonghua in social communications (Chen 2005: 21). Overall, while these data suggest Zhuang language has not become home-bound in GZAR, they *do* suggest that Zhuang is a less common choice in many public and prestigious domains than Putonghua and other Mandarin varieties.

Moreover, Chen and Wang (2005: 52) note that even amongst those who can find other speakers of their minority language in outside-of-home environments in GZAR, some will use it only in restricted circles because they feel that speaking a minority language has "降低身份" 'lowered status', especially in cities. This is an important warning, because urbanization rates have rapidly increased amongst the Zhuangzu and all people in China since this 2000 survey, as the preceding section explained. The most recent survey of attitudes to Zhuang language, made in Nanning City while this book was being written, found similar negative attitudes and pressures on using Zhuang:

（三）"壮文无用"等功利性思想观念和壮语文负面评价长期存在，给壮文推行工作带来阻力。受全球化和地区经济社会快速发展及国家通用语言强势推行和互联网发展的影响，本就处于劣势的壮文对外交流功能呈现弱化趋势，社会上对壮文负面评价较为普遍。调查显示，我市不少壮族群众对壮语的前景较为悲观，在壮语传承问题上存在一定的矛盾心理，即从整体角度考虑时，认为壮族人应该学习壮语，但从家庭自身角度考虑时，觉得当前应试教育、通用语言文字更加重要。

[(3) **Utilitarian ideas such as "Zhuang writing is useless" and negative evaluations of Zhuang language have long existed, which have brought resistance to the promotion of Zhuangwen [Romanized Zhuang].** Affected by the rapid development of globalization and regional economic and social development, the strong implementation of the national common language [Putonghua] and the development of the Internet, the already-disadvantaged Zhuang language has shown a weakening trend in its external communication function, and the negative evaluation of Zhuang language has become more common in society. The survey shows that many Zhuangzu people in our city [Nanning] are pessimistic about the prospects of Zhuang language, and there is a certain ambivalence in the inheritance of Zhuang language. That is, when considering the overall perspective, they believe that Zhuangzu people should learn Zhuang language, but from the perspective of the family itself they feel that in the current exam-oriented education system, the common language is more important.]

(Nanning Municipal Minority Language Works Commission 2019: §2.3, emphasis in original)

Finally, it is important to note that research suggests the Zhuang speakers appearing in these counts do not speak Standard Zhuang, but rather areal Zhuang dialects and an emerging contact variety, although most of the linguistic literature describes the Zhuang language in "the eternal present tense" (Lickorish 2008: 3). Lu and Li (2012) challenge the dominant presentation in the literature of Zhuang as static by proposing a contact variety which they call Zhuang-Putonghua. They (Lu and Li 2012: 24–34) describe Zhuang-Putonghua's phonetic, tonal and grammatical differences from Zhuang. Recent research, albeit limited, suggests Zhuang-Putonghua is more widely spoken than any Zhuang areal dialect: Lu and Li (2012: 35) re-analyze survey findings originally from Yang (2006) which show that Zhuang-Putonghua was heard and used by over 80% of respondents across 50 Zhuang communities in 2004. Their own data likewise indicate widespread, consistent usage of Zhuang-Putonghua. Indicating that there is usage across classes, rather than only geographically spread usage, Lu and Li (2012: 23) observe that "[i]n Guangxi, teachers, students, officials, regular employees, and migrant peasant-workers all speak Zhuang-Putonghua to a certain extent." This suggests that Zhuang-Putonghua is emerging as a regional lingua franca, a role for which the Standard Zhuang dialect was previously created but which it never achieved (Grey in press).

Standard Zhuang was based on the Northern Zhuang dialect of Wuming (Luo 2008b: 321; Ramsey 1987: 236). Wuming is a town near Nanning City, the capital of GZAR. (Wuming became a county and then, in 2015, a district of Nanning Municipality). Li and Huang (2004: 241) suggest that Wuming's Zhuang variety was chosen as a model for Standard Zhuang because of Wuming's proximity to Nanning. Others suggest it was because the pronunciation of this areal dialect spanned the breadth of the many Zhuang dialects and was thereby accessible to most speakers. Nevertheless, Standard Zhuang was new to everyone. It was therefore not able to become a lingua franca without exposure and opportunities to learn, but these have been limited, and Standard Zhuang remains unlikely to be learnt informally in homes. Using the most recent data available (from

2004–2005), I calculated that not quite 1% of school-aged Zhuangzu children were enrolled at bilingual Zhuang-Putonghua schools in GZAR in the early 2000s (Grey 2017: 90). The state has, however, trained and employed some speakers of Standard Zhuang for a small number of television and radio broadcasting jobs and for the public simultaneous interpreting of certain government meetings. Further, my own project brought to light contractions in the availability of Zhuang-medium media and interpreting work.

The bilingual schooling data reflect limited access to written Standard Zhuang. What are the typical practices of Zhuang speakers in relation to reading and writing Zhuang?

2.6 A Zhuang reader

Above, I explained that there is a state-sponsored Romanized writing system for Zhuang. This system's planners' objective was an orthography that would be transparent to Zhuang speakers and thus "easy to learn" (Li and Huang 2004: 244) with basic instruction. That would thereby enable rapid mass literacy, which was the PRC's policy goal behind all the minority languages' Romanization (Premaratne 2015; Rohsenow 2004; Zhou 2001: 56). This accords with hopes for standardization elsewhere in the world (Costa et al. 2018: 5) and is one of the indications that language standardization in China drew on the standardization traditions of Europe along with those of Imperial China. The transmission of relevant beliefs in the European tradition about languages, modernity and nation-building from nineteenth century visitors to China and from the Soviet Union are traced in Mullaney (2006, 2011) and Kaup (2000), and circulated internationally through diplomatic and education discourses in which Chinese people participated (see further Section 2.3 on the origins of enumerating national minorities).

With mass literacy being the goal, learning Romanized, Standard Zhuang was therefore initially supported through government campaigns directed at *adults*, and *not* learning it attracted government penalties (Kaup 2000: 141). This literacy campaign was abandoned in the Cultural Revolution but then revived, albeit with significant under-funding (Kaup 2000: 142–143). It was at that point that the second wave of script reform took place and Zhuang came to be officially written only in the same twenty-six letters as English. This enabled Zhuang to be typed and printed using standard technologies but it meant removing Romanized Zhuang's distinguishing graphemes, a tilt at globalization which, as we will see in Chapters Six and Seven, has become a vulnerability. Initially (from 1957), tones in Zhuang had been represented by non-Latin letters which resembled the form of the digits 2–6 and thus the language's 2nd to 6th tones (the first tone was unmarked). These were -Ƨ (2nd); -3 (3rd); -Ч (4th); -5 (5th); -Ƅ (6th). From 1982, these tone-markers were replaced by -Z, -J, -X, -Q, -H and their lower case forms while additional tone-marking letters were added: -P/T/K and -B/G/D. These 1982 reforms mean that Romanized Zhuang is now written using all of the 25 letters used to write Putonghua in its standard, Romanized auxiliary script, Putonghua Pinyin, which does not use *v*, and all 26 letters of the English alphabet, and no others.

As expert on the history of PRC language policy, Zhou Minglang (2001: 56) notes, the result of chop-and-change literacy campaigns was that Romanized Zhuang literacy training and Zhuang bilingual education were not often available in the twentieth century. Zhuang literacy policy is now subsumed within policies about children's bilingual schooling, however, bilingual Zhuang schooling is not widespread, as has been noted above. Nevertheless, Romanized Zhuang is still used, particularly for the translation of government texts including some signage which I analyze in Chapters Six to Nine, for a limited range of state-funded Zhuang-medium print media, and in government-published anthologies of Zhuang literature.

I introduced the traditional Square Character or Sawndip way of writing Zhuang, above. This is not a widespread method of writing today but nor has it disappeared. At the end of Chapter Eight, we will encounter some middle-aged Zhuang revivalists deliberately adding Sawndip to their Zhuang literacy practices and a one interviewee, an editor of the bilingual *Third of the Third* magazine (ie the third day of the third month), described an older group who have kept up Sawndip literacy:

Excerpt 2-1

Mr H: 再有一个的话，就是那帮在那个民族里唱歌的，那帮的话呢他们一般那帮年纪就比较稍微大一点，他会这个壮文，他会用那个壮族方块字。

[Mr H: There is another [kind of contributor to *Third of the Third* magazine], it's the group that sings in that ethnic group. For that group, they are generally a little older. They know this Zhuangwen [Romanized Zhuang], [and] they can use those Zhuang Square Characters.]

By contrast, the major language of literacy in China is Putonghua. It is the written medium of most schooling. Given English has now been taught throughout compulsory primary schooling in China for two decades – and with an emphasis on reading and writing – English could also be considered a language of literacy in China today. Earlier in this chapter, I explained that many Zhuang speakers today are bilingual speakers of Putonghua or other Mandarin varieties, but this does not mean they are necessarily literate in Putonghua. Rather, Zhou (2001: 56) reported high rates of illiteracy amongst the Zhuangzu, compared to both the Hanzu majority and other minority minzu. In communications with me on 13 December 2017, he clarified that he was reporting illiteracy *in Putonghua*. It seems, therefore, that a significant portion of Zhuang speakers are neither literate in Zhuang nor in Putonghua.

Data throughout this study have borne out the following overview of the state of Zhuang literacy provided to me in an early interview with another of the editors at *Third of the Third*.

Excerpt 2-2

Mr G: 我们壮文，它实际上原来也比较热，但是现在随着这个社会各个方面都在变化，那么原来文盲很多的学壮文的，现在很多人会汉文化……在偏远的农村里，那些人不会汉文化，通过壮文先学，然后再带动他学那个汉语，学汉语以后就可以学英语，他是这么来的。但是农村是老人还有小孩基本上是还讲那个母语，就是讲壮语，那么青年人一般他读书，他都会汉语……会讲的人逐渐减少，但是有一些地方他为了保护民族文化，他又在这方面加强，像我们，为什么我们要讲壮语？我是为了要跟我的民族兄弟找回一种真实的感情。那为什么我要学汉语啊？因为汉语是国家通用语言，那我们要工作，要抢饭吃，要谋生，那必须要学汉语……那为什么还要学英语呢？那我们的壮族走向国外，要介绍我们的文化，你不会英语你怎么去介绍啊？

[Mr G: Our Zhuangwen [Romanized Zhuang], it was actually quite popular at first, but now with all aspects of society changing; originally so many illiterate people would learn Zhuangwen [Romanized Zhuang], and now many people are Han-acculturated .... In remote rural areas, those people do not know Han culture. They learn Hanyu [Mandarin] through Zhuang language first, then after they learn Hanyu they can learn English, that's how they do it. However, in rural areas, the elderly and children basically still speak their mother tongue, that is, Zhuang language. The young people normally read books and can all speak Hanyu. ...The number of people who can speak [Zhuang] is gradually decreasing, but in some places they have strengthened this aspect in order to preserve the minzu culture; like us, why do we speak Zhuang? I do it to find a true feeling [shared] with my minzu brethren. Then why should I learn Hanyu, eh? Because Hanyu is the national lingua franca, and we've got to work, have money to eat, make a living, so we must learn Hanyu. ...Then why learn English as well? If our Zhuangzu people go abroad they will introduce our culture. If you don't know English, how will you introduce it?]

While the data indicates that Zhuang literacy is rare, Zhuang literacy turned out to be significant to constructions of Zhuang(zu) identity, as Chapter Eight explores. Illiteracy in one's first language and in the national language are indicia of forms of disadvantage that intersect with minority minzu membership and with speaking Zhuang.

2.7 A Zhuang disadvantage

The Zhuangzu and residents of GZAR and Yunnan Province, especially rural residents, are demographic categories which are relatively badly off on a number of socio-economic measures canvassed below. Most Zhuang speakers fall into one or more of these demographic categories. First, GZAR and Yunnan Province, where the largest numbers of Zhuang speakers (regardless of minzu) live, remain amongst the poorest regions of China. CEIC Data and the World Bank's data show that the GDP per person in both GZAR and Yunnan was under $6000 in 2015, putting them in the poorest bracket of China's regions and provinces, while it was above $14000 in the richest provinces, including Beijing (Anon. 2016a: 42). GZAR's economic growth is variable across counties, higher in its most urbanized areas Nanning, Liuzhou and Guilin, but lower elsewhere, with 5.38 million people still living below the official poverty line in 2015 (Zhang et al. 2018).

Furthermore, recent economic indices collected in Table 1 show not only relative Zhuangzu poverty compared with the Hanzu majority, but also that rural poverty is higher than urban poverty for both the Zhuangzu and the Hanzu. (Because the Hanzu comprise over 90% of the national population, it is unsurprising that the national figures mirror the Hanzu figures.) Table 1 includes comparative Engel coefficients; this coefficient measures food expenditure as a percentage of total consumption expenditure. On this measure, Zhuangzu households are clearly struggling more with everyday food costs than Hanzu households. General rural disadvantage compounds the specific Zhuangzu disadvantage because a greater proportion of the Zhuangzu are rural residents (66%) compared to the proportions of the Hanzu (56%) and the national population (57%) who are rural residents (Guo 2013: 5).

Table 1: Relative Zhuangzu poverty. Source: (Guo et al. 2015: 37–38, 46,174–175; Guo 2013: 125–127, 141–142, 160–161).

	National	Hanzu	Zhuangzu
Urban unemployment rate (2005)	–	3.8	4.1
Urban unemployment rate (2011)	–	3.5	3.5
Per capita GDP (2011)	–	38923RMB	25952RMB
Urban average per capita annual income (2005)	11320.77RMB	11080.44RMB	10248.49RMB
Rural average per capita annual income (2005)	3254.93RMB	3590.78RMB	2555.24RMB
Engel coefficient for urban households (2005)	36.69%	36.71%	41.08%
Engel coefficient for rural households (2005)	45.48%	44.81%	50.52%

In addition, Guo's (2013: 25–33) educational attainment statistics from 2005 show significant attrition amongst the Zhuangzu. I converted these data into percentages of each minzu population, to compare Zhuangzu and Hanzu attrition rates (Figure 11). The National and Hanzu student bodies decreased significantly at the transition to senior secondary school, where compulsory public education stops, and only 32.4% and 32.6%, respectively, of senior school students continued to college (i.e. tertiary education). However, the Zhuangzu student body decreased more: only 26.6% of Zhuangzu senior secondary students continued to college. The high school leavers' examination, called the *Gaokao*, controls entry to universities in the PRC. Government data indicating whether these exams systematically restrict Zhuangzu students' access to tertiary education are not available. However, both Adamson and Feng (2009) and Feng and Sunuodula (2009) accept other studies which show that "Zhuang people are somewhat disadvantaged in learning English when compared to mainstream (Han) counterparts" (Adamson and Feng 2009: 326); because passing the Gaokao has required passing an English examination, this could be a systematic barrier to tertiary education for Zhuang people.

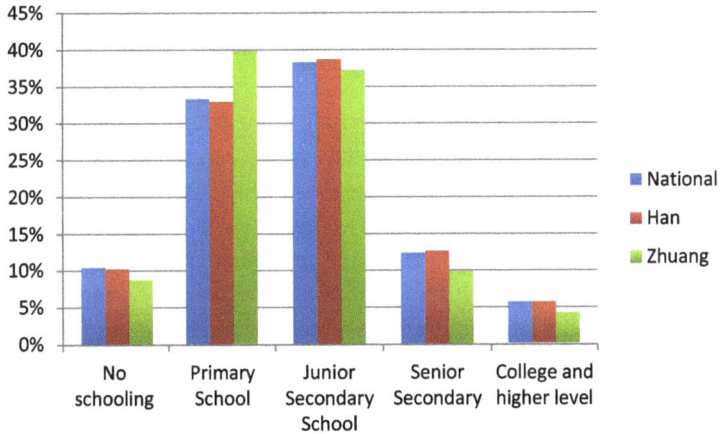

Figure 11: Educational attainment as at 2005, by minzu, based on Guo (2013: 25–33).

We can inquire further into Zhuang speakers' likely disadvantage using Zhuangzu illiteracy rates as a proxy. The 2010 Census includes detailed data on illiteracy in Putonghua by minzu and by place. In GZAR, 3.46% of the population 15 years of age or older were illiterate (GZAR Bureau of Statistics and Office for the Sixth Population Census of GZAR 2010). The illiteracy rate amongst Hanzu people in GZAR was lower than this (2.57%) but the illiteracy rate amongst Zhuangzu people in GZAR was higher (4.54%). Nevertheless, the illiteracy rate of another minority group in GZAR, the Dongzu, was twice the Zhuangzu rate: 8.92% (p. 642). Again, there was a rural disadvantage showing in the statistics: the illiteracy rate for people 15 years old and above in GZAR's cities was only 1.2%, and much lower in the capital, Nanning, where it was just 0.62% (pp. 465, 475). The illiteracy rates got higher with age (pp. 727–728). Therefore, it appears that younger people in cities in GZAR have had more opportunity to acquire literacy in Putonghua.

The government has not been unresponsive. A long-standing preferential policy awards bonus points to the Gaokao results of students from various minority groups and from rural or poor areas, but as the data show this has not yet resulted in equal educational attainment. Moreover, the government is currently implementing reforms to reduce the weighting of the English examination within the Gaokao, which may help Zhuang speakers, but at the same time it is increasing the weighting of the Putonghua language examination (Yang 2014: 13). The reforms were piloted in some provinces from 2014, but nationwide implementation – due for 2020 – has faced delays (Bian 2019).

2.8 Concluding discussion: Naturalizing and denaturalizing Zhuang

This chapter has denaturalized Zhuang as a language or a people. It highlighted the role of recognition by researchers and officials in the acceptance of Zhuang language and Zhuang people as meaningful categories while also providing technical knowledge about Zhuang language and as to the intersection of urbanization and economic disadvantage with Zhuang language and Zhuangzu people. The sociolinguist, Ingrid de Saint-Georges (2013: 7), reminds us that such recognition is an evaluation, drawing on the late Gunther Kress: "recognition integrates the idea of 'value' and 'valuation'. When diverse practices come into contact [...] which practices get recognized? And by whom? [...] Which practices are 'devalued' or 'delegitimized' and for what purposes?" The recognition of an imagined community of Zhuang speakers as an ethnicity and a polity has been important to the PRC government, who named this polity the Zhuangzu. Actual Zhuang language practices are not, however, made relevant to minzu classification today, as this chapter noted. Moreover, the state's investment in Zhuang language has valued standardized spoken and written forms although Standard Zhuang is not widely learnt or used amongst the Zhuangzu.

Yet the Zhuangzu is still a meaningful category to the state, not least because the PRC's territorial divisions and autonomous government structures hinge on the recognition of the Zhuangzu and the historic locations of Zhuang speakers informed the choice of location of these territories. Thus, officially connected to Zhuang language are an autonomous region (GZAR), an autonomous prefecture in Yunnan Province (Wenshan) and an autonomous county in Guangdong Province (Lianshan).

The Zhuangzu label has also come to be widely accepted and used in everyday speech. However, whether Zhuangzu people are meaningfully different from other people is subject to various interpretations, particularly in terms of whether the Zhuangzu are now imagined to have distinctive language practices, and those interpretations were canvassed in this chapter. Specifically, while this chapter has highlighted commentaries constructing the Zhuangzu today as a traditional people essentially tied to Zhuang language, there are also many academic and social commentaries constructing the Zhuangzu as an empty category of people who are no different from the Mandarin-speaking, Han ethnicity majority. I quoted a twentieth century scholar, Ramsey (1987: 167), above to illustrate this view. A normative version of this commentary – that the Zhuangzu *should be* no different from the Mandarin-speaking, Han ethnicity majority – has become prominent recently in proposals for "second generation minzu policy", as outlined in Section 2.3. These competing commentaries help us see that Zhuang language, and Zhuang social categories such as Zhuangzu or Zhuang Speakers, are replicated and made socially meaningful in different ways over time; these differing meanings work in the interests of differing groups and follow differing rationales.

So how and for whom are the Zhuangzu made out to be different, traditional and Zhuang-speaking, and for whom are they indistinguishable from the mainstream? Having raised this question here, the book will now explore it empirically from many angles. As a general starting point, consider Gladney's (2004: 51) argument that a majority/minority binary rather than a 56-way distinction is integral to social categorization in the PRC today. Gladney (2004: 51,58) argues that although the Zhuangzu and other minorities are legitimized as official minzu, "[t]he widespread definition and representation of the minority as exotic, colorful, and primitive homogenizes the undefined majority as united, mono-ethnic, and modern." That is, constructing the Zhuangzu as different and traditional is part of maintaining a necessary Other to replicate self-interested boundaries of a majority identity (see also Stites 1999 and Piller 2011: 18–28, following Said 1978).

Another thread of inquiry running from this chapter through the remainder of the book is the disconnection between the state's construction of language and people, and the people's construction of themselves, others, and language. Together, the data in the latter sections of this chapter indicated a disconnection between the state's expectation that Zhuang speakers will speak Standard Zhuang and the continuing, widespread oral practice of non-standard Zhuang dialects, including a Zhuang-Putonghua contact variety which blurs the minority language-Mandarin divide. Similarly, the state's use of written Romanized Zhuang seems to anticipate a level of Zhuang literacy that data suggest does not exist. These data also indicate a disconnection between the outsiders' view of the Zhuangzu as Han-assimilated, in part because of high rates of Mandarin proficiency, and the reality that most of these Mandarin speakers are bilinguals who still also speak Zhuang. Intergenerational bilingualism is erased in the assimilation narrative. On the other hand, those bilingual Zhuang speakers' level of fluency or proficiency in each language is not reported and their usage of Zhuang may have been over-represented if some of the studies cited here were aiming to present the Zhuangzu as linguistically different and therefore continually meaningful.

A tension appears in the reports of Zhuang language's vitality, with clear patterns of Zhuang's usage in some domains and Zhuang's exclusion from other, symbolically powerful ones. A language in this situation is *minoritized* in the sense of "remaining restricted in its use in higher-status functions" (Deumert and Mabandla 2018: 201) despite speaker numbers. This exclusion from high status functions is likely to be destabilizing intergenerational bilingualism and encouraging shift to the language used for those functions, whether Putonghua or another Mandarin variety or English. Moreover, Kaup (2000) linked a trend of language shift / non-transmission of Zhuang that she saw emerging in the 1990s to urban households. Twenty years later, urbanization is apace amongst the Zhuangzu (and people from other minzu who speak Zhuang) so this book begins without any expectation that intergenerational Zhuang language transmission is guaranteed despite the still relatively high speaker numbers.

This book explores aspects of these disconnections that the existing literature could not tell us about: how are people making the writing of Romanized Zhuang, the speaking of Zhuang dialects, the non-speaking of Standard Zhuang and perhaps the non-speaking of Zhuang at all relevant to being a Zhuang person? How is language policy adapted or reimagined in response to these disconnections, and these questions? To begin my answers, the next chapter takes us to the fundament of PRC language policy, the constitutional freedom to use and develop minority languages.

Part II: Laws and Governance Structures

3 The foundational language rights: Legal provisions about minority languages and minority peoples

> Law [...] confers upon the reality which arises from its classificatory operations the maximum permanence that any social entity has the power to confer upon another [...] It would not be excessive to say that it creates the social world, but only if we remember that it is this world which first creates the law.
> (Bourdieu 1987: 838–839)

The *Constitution* of the PRC is the most enduring and empowered articulation of how speaker groups are constituted in the nation, and which rights as well as legitimate expectations of the state speaker groups can have. It enshrines the many minority minzu and the majority minzu as together constitutive of the nation, officially recognizes and offers a certain level of protection to minority minzu languages, and names a national language. "The fact that status given to official languages is frequently enshrined constitutionally around the world" – as it is in China – "attests to the observation that language still lies at the heart of national narratives" concludes Janny Leung (2019: 259) in her recent, global analysis of official language policies. Leung focus is not China, but her finding rings true for the Chinese constitution and nation. Language has a long history at the heart of the Chinese national narrative; imperial policies first standardized Mandarin script and banned non-standard Mandarin scripts in the third-century B.C.E. (He 2014: 6). The current *Constitution* sets up a national, standard Mandarin language variety and official minority languages as constitutive elements of China today, as have all the constitutional documents since the founding of the PRC at the end of a revolutionary civil war in 1949.

Fundamentally, this *Constitution* both reflects and reproduces the social world in which it was created, as Bourdieu's epigraph anticipates. The current *Constitution* has been in place for almost 40 years (since 1982). It is largely consistent, at least in terms of provisions about minority peoples and languages, with the earlier PRC constitutions. At first, these constitutions aimed to reflect a desired social world different to the actual social world, and over time they have contributed to actualizing at least some elements of that aspiration. Part of the project of New China (the PRC) was the inclusion and equality of peoples of different ethnicities, but this came alongside a desire to improve and modernize them, their culture, language and living conditions (and everybody's). The early PRC's legal recognition and framing of multilingualism in relation to 56 minzu was a deliberate reconstitution of the people into a newly inclusive, multi-ethnic nation after laws in the Republic and Imperial eras had excluded or marginalized many speakers of non-Mandarin varieties, including speakers of Zhuang varieties.

However, the social world created is one in which – as in many countries – "there is always a gap between a constitutional guarantee [about minority language usage] and the right that people actually enjoy", as Zhou (2000: 130) has observed. Pioneers in the study of language policy have observed similar "cleavages" (Schiffman 1996: 27; Shohamy 2006: 51–52) in other contexts.

In China, does this gap exist only because of a failure to follow the *Constitution*? In my view, no; the underlying fissures are there in the *Constitution* itself. This chapter explains how this is in part because of the types of legal mechanism the *Constitution* and related national legislation include, and also because of the ideologies which the *Constitution* encodes. It is also, I argue in the following chapters, because of the legal structures for the representation of diverse interests in government decision-making and the language ideologies amplified by the governance framework. These legal mechanisms, structures and ideologies all reflect particular philosophies for how the social world should be reformed. Now, with their legal durability, they confer the permanence of which Bourdieu's quotation speaks, and in so doing, they naturalize this way of constituting languages, peoples and a nation.

Specifically, this chapter analyzes the constitutional provisions relating to Zhuang language, particularly the "minority language right", explaining in Section 3.1 how this right is limited in its own legal nature as a freedom rather than a positive right, and by the lack of other rights and rules in the national language governance framework to make the constitutional minority language freedom enforceable. This is contrasted with newer and legally stronger Putonghua language rights. I then analyze other forms of minority and Putonghua language rights, specifically looking at the legal regulation and protection of languages in national legislation about education, courts and crime, in Sections 3.2–3.4. In the chapter's concluding discussion, I argue that the constitutional minority language freedom reflects China's law-making at a time when laws were treated as declamations of general policy principles, foregrounding the normative and discursive role of law, and set out the implications of this for the next layer of my legal analysis.

3.1 The minority language right

A minority language protection is enshrined in Article 4 of the *Constitution*, in this phrase in the Putonghua text: "各民族都有使用和发展自己的语言文字的自由，都有保持或者改革自己的风俗习惯的自由" (中华人民共和国中央人民政府 1982);

in the official English translation it reads, "The people of all nationalities have the freedom to use and develop their own spoken and written languages, and to preserve or reform their own ways and customs" (*1982 Constitution*). Variations on this language right date back to the 1949 *Common Program's* Article 53, which stood in for a constitution, and in Article 3 of the PRC's first official *Constitution* in 1954. (I recommend readers to http://www.lawinfochina.com for legislation and metadata in English.)

Some experts call this constitutional language protection a "right" (e.g. Zhou 2000: 130), and so do I. It is also described as a "right" by the state itself when it is re-entextualized within the national education policy (see Section 3.2 below). But I dispute scholars such as Zhu (2014: 696) who interpret this language right as positive in nature, i.e. placing legal obligations upon the state. Let us look a little closer at the wording of the right. The original, Putonghua provision refers to a 自由 'freedom' and, likewise, the official English translation uses "freedom". A freedom is a specific kind of legal right. The nature of legal freedoms is that they do not require state action for their vindication, obliging the state only to refrain from actively infringing on the right, and so freedoms are also called negative rights. By contrast, a more empowering form of legal right obliges a state to take action to protect the right-holder, which is called a positive right. The specific use of 自由/freedom in Article 4 of the Chinese *Constitution* appears to be intended as a legally meaningful distinction between types of constitutional rights, because elsewhere the *Constitution* uses 权利/right instead, e.g. in Article 45's "right to material assistance from the state" for elderly and disabled people.

The same contrast of terms recurs within another foundational law in the language governance framework, the *Putonghua Law*. Its Article 8 repeats the same expression that we see in the *Constitution*: "freedom to use and develop" minority languages. By contrast, the *Putonghua Law's* Article 4 grants that "[a]ll citizens shall have the *right* to learn and use the standard spoken and written Chinese language" [my emphasis]; using 权利 'right' in the Putonghua original. From 2000, this *Putonghua Law* extended upon the pre-existing recognition of Putonghua in Article 19 of the *Constitution*, which declares that "国家推广全国通用的普通话" [The state promotes the nationwide use of Putonghua]. Thus, Article 4 of the *Constitution* constructs minority language diversity as a matter of free personal and group choice and responsibility, rather than constructing the state as having any responsibility to promote or protect minority languages. The Zhuangzu are free to use Zhuang language if they so choose. If they do not, the constitutional framing suggests it is because they – or at least those legally empowered to make decisions on their behalf – choose not to, rather than because of any state failure to take active steps to protect or sustain Zhuang language.

The theoretical extent of state obligations due to a constitutional language freedom can be considered with reference to language rights in international law, because they are also in the nature of freedoms, although these international rights do not legally change how the PRC's constitutional minority language freedom operates legally. The two most relevant international treaties are the *International Covenant on Civil and Political Rights* (*ICCPR*), which was signed by China in 1998 but never ratified (UN Office of Legal Affairs 2016:IV.4), and 1992's *Declaration on the Rights of Persons Belonging to National or Ethnic, Religious and Linguistic Minorities*. That declaration was adopted unanimously by UN General Assembly member states, including China, but is not binding; it provides "essential standards" and "offers guidance" (United Nations Office of the High Commission for Human Rights 2010: 3).

The leading chronicler of language rights in international laws, Fernand de Varennes (1996: 150), has analyzed the twentieth century's debates over the theoretical extent of state obligations due to a legal language freedom, and concluded that the "prevailing view" about language rights in international law was that they provide a guarantee of state non-interference. Specifically, this is the prevailing view about the "right" in Article 27 of the *ICCPR* of minority individuals "in community with other members of their group" not to be denied the practice of their own language, culture or religion. This right is a mid-century codification of a pre-existing minority language right expressed in international law "since the time of the minorities treaties under the League of Nations supervision" (de Varennes 1996: 172). Despite this view of international language rights as language freedoms providing merely a guarantee of state non-interference, de Varennes (1996: 173) points out that even a freedom requires some positive action in that a state cannot "stand by and assist or permit other parties to intervene in the use of a minority's language by members of the group".

De Varennes (1996: 157) comments that it is one thing to agree that linguistic minorities are free to use their language, but the question then becomes: free to do what exactly. What the Zhuangzu and other linguistic minorities are free to do in the PRC is one of the animating questions of this book, and of this chapter. First, I ask here, are they free to invoke the constitutional minority language right in legal proceedings to protect against other individuals, entities or the state?

In short, no. Zhuang and other minority languages have weak legal protection relative to Putonghua because no legal procedure exists by which parties could enforce the freedom in Article 4 of the *Constitution* to use and develop Zhuang. That is, even where people are *not* free to use Zhuang, there is no legal power for individuals or groups to use Article 4 to seek a correction to the situation. A stark illustration is provided by the current, active suppression of other Chinese minority language speakers' freedom to use Uyghur and Kazak, in the face of which the freedom in Article 4 of the *Constitution* has not been empowering. There is a general mechanism for investigation established in Article 5 of the *Constitution* for times when an action appears to contravene any constitutional provision, but there are no constitutional structures entitling minority persons (or anyone) to call for such investigations, besides which the power of such investigations to change the law is unclear. This vulnerability is consistent with other constitutional freedoms in the PRC, which may likewise be infringed upon or limited by subordinate laws.

Although the *Constitution* functions as the legal system's underlying norm this does not increase its enforceability. As its Preamble states, "The people of all nationalities, all state organs, the armed forces, all political parties and public organizations and all enterprises and undertakings in the country must take the *Constitution* as the basic norm of conduct, and they have the duty to uphold the dignity of the *Constitution* and ensure its implementation" (from the official English version). Despite this, none of the key, national law-making bodies are legally compelled to consider Article 4's minority language freedom when making other laws, and nor are they obliged to make laws translating this very general language freedom into concrete rules or actions. While Article 5 of the *Constitution* sets out the legal pre-eminence of the *Constitution*, stating: "no law [...] shall contravene the *Constitution*", there is no procedure to hold to account or invalidate any national law-making that contravenes the *Constitution*, nor to force the legislature to consider Article 4 each time they make new legislation. Moreover, while the Constitution and Law Committee of the National People's Congress (NPC), simply called the Law Committee before 2018, may seem like an institution established to scrutinize the constitutionality of laws, its role is to scrutinize the constitutionality of law made within the subordinate tier of the legal system, specifically the regulations made by major cities (Chung 2018). This committee does not systematically review or pursue the conformity of new national laws with the minority language freedom in the *Constitution*, nor with any other provision of the *Constitution*.

By contrast, the legislative right to learn and use Putonghua comes with specific legal means of enforcement, set out in Articles 26–27 of the *Putonghua Law*. These include a power for administrative departments of the state to discipline and deal with those who infringe another's right to learn and use Putonghua, expressed in Article 27 as "有关单位应当对直接责任人员进行批评教育:拒不改正的，由有关单位作出处理" [The relevant units shall criticize and educate the directly responsible personnel: if they refuse to make corrections, they shall be dealt with by the relevant units]. This mechanism seems to envisage that infringers will be acting in the course of work, rather than private individuals infringing other individuals' rights, by describing them as 人员 'personnel' who will be dealt with by a work unit. (A *danwei* or 'work unit' was a key workplace organizational feature across the PRC when all labour was centrally planned, and continues to be an important part of management structures today.) This mechanism of the *Putonghua Law* creates a legal check against conduct, even conduct by officials. This legally-endorsed response to infringement of a language right – the right to learn and use Putonghua – has no equivalent in the *Constitution*.

Nevertheless, minority minzu languages are afforded official, albeit sub-national, status. They are the only languages to which Article 4 of the *Constitution* is taken to refer. As a result, sub-national legislation and administrative rules in support minority languages can exist and provide a legal backbone to minority language polices. Later in this chapter I will introduce examples of the policies and rules which derive from this constitutional minority language freedom. They cover many topics of minority language policy familiar the world over: language in education; language in access to courts, civic participation and government services; and this book's focal topic, language in public space. Relating to that topic, the book will later consider regulations on public bilingualism both from GZAR's regional government and from the government of its capital city, Nanning. A 2019 government report on those Nanning regulations notes that the capitals of three of the other four autonomous minzu regions (Urumqi, Hohhot and Lhasa) have similar municipal regulations about the public usage of minority languages (Nanning Municipal Minority Language Works Commission 2019: §4). Moreover, these other regional capital's regulations require more use of minority languages than Nanning's and have greater legal status, being laws enacted by municipal congressional standing committees, while Nanning's public language regulations are administrative rules made by a department and approved by the government. In contrast to this framework for support, the many dialects of Mandarin are not officially recognized as corresponding to a particular minzu (Guo 2004) and therefore not provided with organized state support in national laws or, in most cases, at more local levels. These Mandarin dialects include Cantonese, Nanning Baihua and Guiliuhua, all of which are spoken by vast numbers of people in Zhuang-speaking areas in South Central China. Indeed, they are often spoken by multilingual Zhuang speakers, as Chapter Two has pointed out. That is, the *Constitution* does not offer any freedom, no matter how weak, to use or develop Cantonese, Nanning Baihua or Guiliuhua. Some wealthy sub-national governments have nevertheless been able to initiate their own protections for Mandarin topolects in recent years, e.g. Shanghai Municipal Government's promotion of Shanghainese (Shanghaiist 2014; Zhou 2016), but Shanghai's level of funding and political will for Mandarin topolect policy initiatives are absent in the South.

While official minority group members have no legal mechanisms at their disposal to enforce their constitutional minority language freedom, other national laws provide further permissions, and further restrictions, on what individuals and institutions are free to do with minority languages, particularly in education.

3.2 Language rights in education

Education is a field in which advocates for a minority language often wish to see language rights implemented. In the context of the PRC, however, there are two types of language rights emanating from the *Constitution* and other national laws that could be relevant to education: the freedom to use and develop minority languages and the right to learn and use Putonghua. The right to Putonghua is implemented in a two-part obligation, for schools are legally obliged to popularize Putonghua and to teach in "Chinese", as stipulated in Article 12 of the *Education Law of the PRC* (National People's Congress 1995: "*Education Law*") and also Article 10 of the *Putonghua Law*. This is reconciled with the minority language freedom in education by providing, in the *Education Law*, that bilingual schooling is permissible:

> Article 12. The Chinese language, both oral and written, shall be the basic oral and written language for education in schools and other educational institutions. Schools or other educational institutions which mainly consist of students from minority nationalities may use in education the language of the respective nationality or the native language commonly adopted in that region. Schools and other educational institutions shall in their educational activities popularize the nationally common spoken Chinese [i.e. Putonghua] and the standard written characters.

The comparatively robust right to learn and use Putonghua, enacted in 2000, builds on the legal mandates here in Article 12 of the *Education Law* that "Chinese" be the medium of instruction at schools and that schools popularize the official national variety of Chinese, Putonghua. This is a provision that anticipates the reality that many schools operate in non-standard varieties of Mandarin, by referring generally to "the Chinese language" as the obligatory medium of instruction. Article 10 of the *Putonghua Law* continues to allow rather than forbid this use of non-standard Mandarin but it concurrently obliges schools to strive to bring their students up to standard in Mandarin through its obligations to popularize the nationally common language.

The *Education Law's* obligations regarding Chinese-medium instruction and popularizing Putonghua are not displaced by the allowance, in the middle of its Article 12 above, that schools whose students mainly comprise minority minzu members may use the respective minority language or the region's common native language. Using a minority language in education this way may not completely replace Chinese as the basic language of education, but supplement it. However,

Article 10 of the *Putonghua Law* seems to allow an exception whereby minority languages can replace Chinese-medium instruction. The *Putonghua Law* uses almost identical wording to the *Education Law* to stipulate Chinese as the main medium of schooling and to oblige schools to popularize Putonghua yet states: "Putonghua and the standardized Chinese characters shall be used as the basic language in education and teaching in schools and other institutions of education, *except where otherwise provided for in laws*" (my emphasis). However, on closer inspection is is not a legal permission to replace Chinese with a minority language in education. The most important provision otherwise found in the law, i.e. providing an exception, is a permission for minority languages to be used in early primary school years at transitional bilingual schools in designated area of concentrated minority minzu populations in autonomous territories like GZAR, in accordance with Article 27 of the *Law of the People's Republic of China on Regional National Autonomy* (Standing Committee of the National People's Congress 1984: "*Regional Autonomy Law*"):

> Article 27. In schools which mainly recruit students of minority nationalities, textbooks in languages of minority nationalities concerned should be used where conditions exist. Languages for instruction should also be the languages of the minority nationalities concerned. Primary school students of higher grades and secondary school students should learn Chinese language. Putonghua, which is commonly used throughout the country, should be popularized among them.

Furthermore, despite this allowance, the empirical side of this project revealed that using textbooks in the medium of Zhuang was largely not possible, or at least they were not available, and even having school lessons orally in Zhuang was rare. (Part Three takes this point further.)

The combined effect of these laws is that schools *may* use a minority language in addition to Chinese, but they *may not* use a minority language *instead of Chinese* except in places within autonomous territories that meet certain criteria, and even then schools cannot exclude Chinese entirely. Rather, even those schools must ensure that higher-grade primary school and secondary school students learn Mandarin Chinese and that Putonghua is popularized. Nevertheless, this provides a legal foothold for bilingual schools to exist. Offering bilingual schooling is not any government institution's legal obligation. Rather, the *Education Law* provides in Article 10: "The state shall help all minority nationality regions develop educational undertakings in light of the characteristics and requirements of different minority nationalities."

Whether certain characteristics and requirements should be met with more/better bilingual schooling or with more/better Chinese monolingual schooling is a question of policy and politics, and not a decision that can easily be scrutinized or challenged, as Chapter Five will show. The way this is envisaged to work as a policy is described in a 2005 government *White Paper*, which makes clear that Chinese will still be taught from early years in any school where it is not the medium of instruction:

> Schools (classes) and other educational institutions whose students are predominantly from ethnic minority families should, **if possible**, use textbooks printed in their own languages, and lessons should be taught in those languages. Chinese language courses shall be offered at different times of the primary school period depending on the particular situation, to propagate the use of Putonghua (standard Chinese).
> (State Council Information Office of the PRC 2005b: IV(7)) [my emphasis]

This interpretation of the *Education Law* as not allowing monolingual minority language education is consistent with the *National Outline for Medium and Long-term Educational Reform and Development (2010–2020)* (Ministry of Education of the PRC 2010: "*Education Policy*"). This official *Education Policy* supports bilingual education but officially endorses Putonghua as the normative language of education. Chapter Nine of the *Education Policy* is entitled *Education for Ethnic Minorities* and it announces: "No effort shall be spared to advance bilingual teaching, open Chinese language classes in every school, and popularize the national common language and writing system. Minority peoples' right to be educated in native languages shall be respected and ensured. Bilingual preschool education shall be promoted" (Ministry of Education of the PRC 2010: 23).

Thus, minority language-medium schooling has a place within the education policy framework but cannot be demanded in fulfillment of a legal right or obligation. The law cannot be used to prevent the use and promotion of the majority language in schools. That is, a right to education in one's native minority language is satisfied if only the early years of primary schooling are partially in that language. The weakness of legal protections for bilingual schooling is becoming clearer as the policies which will soon replace this 2010–2020 *Education Policy* become public. In the Inner Mongolia Autonomous Region, it has been announced that the Chinese language and literature syllabus will be expanded and that history and morality subjects will be taught in Chinese instead of Mongolian in bilingual secondary schools from 2021 (Education Department of Inner Mongolia Autonomous Region 2020). Neither the *Education Law*, *Regional Autonomy Law* nor *Constitution* can be invoked to challenge that in legal proceedings, and there are fears that further changes in bilingual schooling will follow.

3.3 Language rights in courts

Also in the *Constitution* is a provision permitting commonly used local languages in courts. Unlike the minority language "freedom", this is expressed as a "right": Article 139 offers a "权利" [right] to use minority languages in court and provides that courts and public prosecutors "应当" [should] provide those who do not understand local languages with translations and, if needed, use local languages that are common in minority areas. This language right is not a new expansion of what the freedom to use a minority language means in concrete terms. Rather, even the 1954 *Constitution* included rights to use minority languages in courts and rights to interpreters. Although these were removed in 1975 (Zhou 2004: 77), they were reinstituted in 1982 as part of the current *Constitution* and are now as follows:

> Article 139: Citizens of all China's [minzu] nationalities have the right to use their native spoken and written languages in court proceedings. The people's courts and people's procuratorates should provide translation for any party to the court proceedings who is not familiar with the spoken or written languages commonly used in the locality.
>
> In an area where people of a minority nationality live in a concentrated community or where a number of nationalities live together, court hearings should be conducted in the language or languages commonly used in the locality; indictments, judgments, notices and other instruments should use one or more of the local languages according to actual needs.

I did not collect data specifically about language policy and practice in courtrooms. It was addressed by some participants, with differing views as to whether Zhuang was provided or not in GZAR's courts. Speaking of his legal aid organization's work in rural and minority communities across China, Mr O reported that "we did have a lot of instances where the interpreters, even if they are provided, don't actually speak the language, they speak a similar language." Compounding this problem with access to justice, Mr O explained that "most people don't have a lawyer, right. ... And in the rural provinces, it was only recently that 20% of people are getting a lawyer ... people don't even know what the legal system is." In such circumstances, people are unlikely to even know that the court *should* conduct proceedings in a language that they understand.

Moreover, just as with Article 4, a key weakness with this constitutional mandate for linguistic access to courts is that there are no legal mechanisms to enforce Article 139 if language needs are not met. Even with a lawyer, if a court refuses to make litigation linguistically accessible or provides an interpreter who speaks a language unintelligible to the client, all the lawyer can do is to seek to bring an appeal afterwards. In my investigation of case law, reported fully in Chapter Four, I found just one such appeal, adjudicated in 2017 by the Dalian Intermediate People's Court (Liaoning Province Criminal Ruling 02, Xing Zhong

No. 86). Dalian is a port city in China near the Korean Peninsula. Three illiterate men and one man with primary schooling all from the Yi minzu jointly appealed separate criminal convictions arising in Mandarin-medium trials. The four argued that they "不通晓汉语并要求使用少数民族语言进行诉讼" [did not know Hanyu [Mandarin] well and needed the use of minority languages for litigation]. The injustice of not having had trial proceedings accessible in their language – the decision does not say which language – was accepted as a ground of appeal for two of the illiterate Yi men, named 阿苏尔且 and 吉达达果. Their convictions were revoked and the court ordered that these two men's cases be re-tried. Perhaps the man with primary schooling and the third illiterate man were considered proficient enough in Mandarin to not have been disadvantaged by their Mandarin-medium trials, but the judgment does not explain why they were not successful in their appeal.

In any case, these appellants did not rely on the constitutional right to have court proceedings in a local minority language (Article 139), but on Article 9 of the *Criminal Procedure Law of the People's Republic of China* (National People's Congress 1979: "*Criminal Procedure Law*"):

> Article 9. Citizens of all nationalities shall have the right to use their native spoken and written languages in court proceedings. The People's Courts, the People's Procuratorates and the public security organs shall provide translations for any party to the court proceedings who is not familiar with the spoken or written language commonly used in the locality.
>
> Where people of a minority nationality live in a concentrated community or where a number of nationalities live together in one area, court hearings shall be conducted in the spoken language commonly used in the locality, and judgments, notices and other documents shall be issued in the written language commonly used in the locality.

This Article 9 of the *Criminal Procedure Law* obviously re-entextualizes the words of Article 139 of the *Constitution*, quoted above. Yet it remains unclear how this right to litigation in a local language can be exercised. When analyzing the similar Article 139 of the *Constitution*, above, I noted that if the prosecutor or the court refuses to provide minority-language medium proceedings for those who claim they need them, all a party can do is appeal afterwards. This is likewise the case for Article 9 of the *Criminal Procedure Law*. That there is only one judgment in the China Judgments Online database where a court decision has been challenged on this basis suggests either that Chinese courts are extremely obliging in arranging minority-language medium proceedings, or that very few parties are resourceful enough to push for their right to litigation in a language that they understand. Furthermore, this right to have court proceedings in a local minority language found in both Article 139 of the *Constitution* and Article 9 of the *Criminal Procedure Law* does not create any legal obligation on the state to provide support for individuals or groups who wish to commence legal proceedings about infringements of their freedom to use minority languages.

Moreover, while Article 139 may appear flexible enough to support the use of any Zhuang dialect in court proceedings where the "actual need" is for a non-standard Zhuang variety, the application of Article 139 allows for a standard language ideology to come into play. That is, court officials may assume that all Zhuang speakers can, even should, speak and write Standard Zhuang, although almost no Zhuang speakers have been taught to read or write it (see further Chapter Two and Chapter Eight). Article 9 of the *Criminal Procedure Law* is ambiguous but similarly liable to being implemented through translation and interpretation only into the standard variety of a minority language. If Standard Zhuang is used instead of the Zhuang variety the litigation party actually understands, it will likely be of little use to anyone and will not equalize access to the courts. It may even create a feedback loop of institutional frustration and unwillingness to expend time or resources to translate courts documents or interpret proceedings into Zhuang the next time round. And neither provision protects those who cannot understand a Mandarin variety used in a court, which might be Putonghua, but who could use another Mandarin dialect, as those do not count as "languages".

Finally, it appears that minority language usage in courts is not within national or regional policy-makers' sights as a means of improving access to justice, as it has not been addressed in the *Third Five-Year Reform Outline for the People's Courts (2009–2013)* (reproduced in Sapio 2009), *Fourth Five-Year Reform Outline for the People's Courts (2014–2019)* (Finder 2013) or current reforms (Finder 2020). Minority language use in courts has, however, been addressed by the national 《关于进一步加强和改进民族地区民汉双语法官培养及培训工作的意见》 (*Opinions on Further Strengthening and Improving the Training and Training of Bilingual Judges in Ethnic Areas*) issued jointly by the Supreme People's Court and the National Ethnic Affairs Commissions (a body which Chapter Five will situate within the governance framework). It has also been addressed by the government at the level of Nanning Municipality, within GZAR. A recent evaluation of municipal rules about Zhuang reports that an assessment was being run of the capacity of 12 judges in six counties within the municipality to hear bilingual Zhuang-Mandarin trials. These were the pilot cohort of judges trained in Nanning following a requirement in those national *Opinions on Further Strengthening and Improving the Training and Training of Bilingual Judges in Ethnic Areas*. This pilot was to be evaluated for possible expansion in 2020 (Nanning Municipal Minority Language Works Commission 2019: §1.8). The report on municipal rules about Zhuang also notes that "镇的基层司法所在调解工作中根据调解对象需求灵活使用当地壮语方言" [the local Zhuang dialects are used flexibly in the mediation work of the first-instance judicial office in the towns according to the needs of the mediation] in

Long'An County. (Long'An is on the western outskirts of Nanning Municipality. This suggests that it is not only Standard Zhuang which is used when Zhuang is used in local courts, somewhat allaying the concern raised on the preceding page that the language right in Article 139 of the Constitution only supports standardized varieties of minority languages.

3.4 Criminalization as a form of language right

A more unusual form of language right found in China, compared to real and theoretical rights examined in the research literature, is the criminalization of certain interferences with cultural practice. This criminal law is a means by which the state could be seen to be satisfying an obligation to create the conditions in which there *is* a freedom of language, even though the constitutional minority language freedom is not a positive right. However, my legal analysis concludes that this cultural protection offers limited assistance in protecting the freedom to use and develop Zhuang or other minority languages. The *Criminal Law of the PRC* (National People's Congress 1979: "*Criminal Law*"), Article 251, provides for imprisonment of "workers of state organs who illegally [...] encroach on minority nationalities' customs or habits". First, similarly to the foundational language right in Article 4 of the *Constitution*, this is hard to action. There is no official guidance or jurisprudence on whether Zhuang language practices count as customs that may be encroached, thereby triggering this provision, nor on what type of encroachment would satisfy the standard of "serious" encroachment set elsewhere in the provision. Moreover, even if customs practiced by the Zhuangzu were seriously encroached, the agent having the authority to commence criminal legal proceedings is the state – i.e. the police or a prosecutor – not a Zhuangzu individual or representative. Likewise, Article 250 of the *Criminal Law* protects a minzu not an individual and gives the state the agency to prosecute when it criminalizes the activity of "publishing materials that discriminate or insult minority nationalities". Moreover, whether this provision extends to criminalizing the publishing of *linguistic* discrimination or insults about a minority minzu's language is untested.

3.5 Concluding discussion: Legally weak minority language rights

This chapter has introduced the root of Zhuang language governance, the freedom to use and develop all China's official minority languages in Article 4 of the *Constitution*. The chapter has also introduced the other provisions of the

Constitution and national legislation which, together with the *Basic Principles* to be introduced in the next chapter, create the national governance framework in which this language freedom must operate. My legal analysis concludes that the negative nature of Article 4, as well as the lack of legal enforcement mechanisms, make this a weak legal resource for those with an interest in how Zhuang language is (or is not) governed. This language freedom, by itself, does not legally empower Zhuang speakers or groups, and the related provisions of the national governance framework do not either. By contrast, the newer, positive right to learn and use Putonghua in the national *Putonghua Law* is more robust in its legal nature and its enforceability. Nevertheless, that Putonghua right, like the minority language freedom, is beset by some ambiguity as to who can use it against whom and against which kind of infringement. The next chapter investigates whether official case records and participants' experiences of the legal system can clarify these ambiguities. Readers will therefore start to hear from my university student and language leader participants in that chapter.

This chapter has also highlighted some of the limitations of the legislation about education and regional autonomy in relation to minority language. This is explored further in Chapter Five's analysis of the national and regional structures and institutions of Zhuang language governance, and in Chapter Nine's analysis of recent, local legislative interventions in public linguistic landscapes in GZAR. Finally, this chapter examined the utility of specific minority language rights, namely the constitutional right to accessible language in courts and a national legislative provision that re-enacts it, as well as the unusual use of criminal law to create language rights that are derivative of the constitutional minority language freedom. I concluded that these, like the other language rights canvassed but for different reasons, are largely unenforceable by Zhuang speakers or groups with an interest in Zhuang, for whom they create no legal agency.

Because the constitutional minority language right is freedom from interference rather than positive obligation on the state, I initially classed China's minority language governance within the "tolerance policy" type rather than "promotive policy" in Schiffman's (1996: 28–29) fundamental typology. A tolerance policy provides no state guarantees and reserves no domains for minority language usage. However, in certain sub-national, implementation-oriented laws, such as the 南宁市壮文社会使用管理办法 '*Management Measures for Social Usage of Zhuangwen in Nanning*' (Nanning Municipal People's Government 2013: "*Nanning Measures*") on public bilingualism that will be examined in Chapter Nine, there is some state investment in Zhuang usage. These *Nanning Measures*, with a remit over GZAR's capital city, were "广西第一部少数民族语言文字工作政府规章" [Guangxi's first government regulations about minority language and writing work] (Nanning Municipal Minority Language Works Commission 2019). The *Nanning Measures*, and the similar regional-level *GZAR Regulations* enacted in 2018, which Chapter Nine will also analyze, recall Schiffman's third type, "mixed policy", as they go beyond a tolerance policy. I nevertheless question the extent of the state promotion of Zhuang. The *Nanning Measures* do not contain language rights, for example, and a 2019 government review found problems with their enforcement, recommended that they be strengthened by being upgraded to legislation enacted by the Nanning People's Congress, and recommended including stronger penalties (Nanning Municipal Minority Language Works Commission 2019). Moreover, one of the major changes that the *Nanning Measures* have caused is an increase in bilingual signage in Nanning, which the linguistic landscape analysis in Chapter Six will examine. Schiffman uses the inclusion of multiple languages on some state-authored public signage – i.e. exactly what has happened in Nanning – to illustrate the "mixed" language policy type.

Moreover, the Nanning Government sees its Zhuang language policy as promotive, causing me to reflect further on my application of Schiffman's typology. . The same government review of the *Nanning Measures* and previous city-level policies describes these as 推广 'promoting' Zhuang language, its standardization and the exchange of knowledge between and integration of all ethnic groups including learning each other's languages (Nanning Municipal Minority Language Works Commission 2019). To give a specific example from the report's first section, which sets out the 基本情况 'basic situation' i.e. context and background to the report, "作为首府城市，我市率先在全区用立法的方式来**推广**和规范壮文的使用" [As the capital city [of GZAR], our city takes the lead in **promoting** and regulating the use of Zhuang language in the region by legislation] (my emphasis). In contrast to the local scale of possibly promotive *minority* language policy, this chapter concludes that China's *majority* language policy is unquestionably promotive even on the national scale given its legal nature and the resourcing put into implementing the *Putonghua Law*. This chapter's analysis leads to the conclusion that minority language laws are best classed as mere tolerance policy on the national scale, with other types of minority language policy possibly in play at sub-national scales. This is further explored, and affirmed, in the following chapters.

Further, this chapter's analysis leads me to argue that the constitutional minority language freedom reflects China's law-making at a time when laws were treated as declamations of general policy principles. A trend towards using laws to create specific, actionable and individual legal rights has since developed in newer fields of Chinese legislative activity, such as property and international trade. The trend has merged with the policy goal of governing the nation in accordance with law, which is one of the current leadership's core goals, known as the "Four Comprehensives". The general trend towards creating actionable legal rights did not bypass language governance, although it did not result in reform to the constitutional minority language freedom. Rohsenow (2004: 35), amongst others, notes that the 1990s saw a turn towards using laws to strengthen language policies as well as other policies and social order in China generally and Zhou (2004: 77) argues that, since the 1980s, the practice of implementing constitutional language rights through legislation on education and minority autonomy has largely replaced an earlier practice of implementing constitutional language rights through executive directives and regulations, despite the constitutional minority language right itself not having been updated. By contrast, the newer language right, i.e. the Putonghua language right, reflects the changed approach.

In my view, the older style of open drafting and/or drafting that expounds principles rather than specific rules which we see in the constitutional minority language freedom and in other laws' references to minority languages may have been retained as part of an intentional strategy of using laws to provide normative guidance through changing times. But while this approach could allow laws to remain flexible enough to respond to changing circumstances, it could also render those laws irrelevant to changed circumstances and thus hasten their obsolescence. Taking the constitutional minority language right on its own terms as normative discourse, rather than as a legally enforceable entitlement, the next chapter analyzes the language ideologies that are (re)produced in the language governance framework.

4 Beliefs about law and language

> [T]he feeling of injustice or the ability to perceive an experience as unjust is not distributed in a uniform way; it depends closely upon the position one occupies in the social space [...] The discovery of injustice as such depends upon the feeling that one has rights.
> (Bourdieu 1987: 833)

"If there's no way to enforce the right, is it a right?" mused Mr O, a senior staff member at an access-to-justice training organization, in our 2014 interview. It's a perplexing question that China's minority language governance framework begs. As Chapter Three explained, the foundational minority language freedom found in the *Constitution* is a principle rather than an operative, enforceable mechanism of language protection. If it is supposed to be an ideological guide rather than a legal resource, how is it understood from people in diverse social positions and in the many discourses which shape perceptions of linguistic justice? This chapter investigates that question, looking first to participants' experiences of the legal system and official records of language rights litigation. The participants' experiences and the scarce case law show that the minority language freedom and other laws that would seem to protect linguistic diversity are discourses without much legal or symbolic power. The chapter then looks to policy documents to identify the main language ideologies within this discourse that shape or undermine the power of language rights.

Finally, in the concluding discussion, the chapter argues that despite the varied and imprecise understandings of the constitutional minority language freedom, and although laws about language are not legally or symbolically powerful discursive resources, there is nevertheless a meaningful sense of a right to Zhuang. This, as the epigraph states, is a starting point for the discovery of linguistic justice or injustice. However, a sense of linguistic justice is molded by the language ideologies reproduced in these powerful policy discourses, namely an ideology which I will call "developmentalism".

The book has so far touched on language ideologies, but they now come to the fore as an analytic construct for studying norms of language practice and the linguistic and social orders that they construct. Language ideologies are "presuppositions about types of speakers, their relations and interests, values and authority" (Gal 2018: 222). The idea of a language ideology allows a researcher to "systematically link language and society" (Piller 2015: 920, following Voloshinov) because "language ideology [...] relates the microculture of communicative action to political and economic considerations of power and social inequality, confronting macrosocial constraints on language behavior" (Woolard 1994: 72). Language ideologies are theorized as a structure of habitus which may be instantiated on a societal level as norms (*doxa*) (see particularly Bourdieu 1977a; Bourdieu 1991); unfamiliar readers may wish to refer back to the introduction to Bourdieusian critical sociolinguistics in Chapter 1.3. Thus, a language ideology is a belief about language that has an existence beyond an individual, being produced and reproduced in discourses like laws and policies, and social structures, and informing value systems.

Some of the language ideologies I discuss in this chapter will be familiar from sociolinguistic or language policy studies in other contexts, such as ideologies of formal linguistic equality and of multilingualism as a threat to national unity, the latter being a common component of monolingual nationalism. We will encounter versions of language ideologies that have been identified in the literature in multiple situated instantiations and named, e.g. "standard language ideology" (see e.g. Piller 2015: 920), the "monolingual mindset" (Clyne 2005) and a recursive "language-nation-state nexus" ideology (Heller 2004: 284). Building on beliefs that emerge about languages in nation building, in the next chapter I will delve into a language ideology known as "territorialization" (see e.g. Blommaert 2004: 58) and its interplay with the way that institutions of governance and forms of political representation for minority minzu are organized in the PRC.

What this chapter highlights is the predominance in the discourses of a "developmentalist" language ideology: the belief that languages can be instruments of cultural and economic progress, but also that some languages, or at least some language practices, are *undeveloped* and thus not instrumental for cultural and economic progress. This language ideology has a normative component in regards to the role of the state: because languages can be instruments of economic or cultural development, they *should* be harnessed and developed by the state.

The preceding chapter concluded that the bedrocks of China's language governance framework are statements of principle more than operative rules. They are thus open to being expanded or constrained by language ideologies and other beliefs about what a particular law or the legal system overall is for. It is therefore important to understand the normative cues that are already encoded in the legal system which can shape how, or even whether, legal provisions are made to apply to Zhuang and other minority languages. It is also important, for the same reason, to understand the social significance of the legal system in China (an enormous puzzle to which this study can contribute a few pieces) and of the particular minority language provisions within it (a smaller puzzle to which this study has more to contribute, but which no single study can complete). While accepting in theory that locally situated individual and institutional beliefs about language and about law play important roles, these understandings can be difficult to pin down; investigating them requires data in addition to the legal instruments themselves. This is the motivation behind my integration, in this chapter and from here on throughout the book, of data obtained through ethnographic approaches. Each participant has but a partial account, but by drawing them together a clearer picture of China's language rights and of what linguistic justice means – within or beyond the frame of these rights – starts to emerge.

4.1 Participants' views as discourse about linguistic justice

More of the language leaders than the university student participants were aware that there are laws about minority language, or what I referred to in interviews as "民族语言在法律上的权利" [minzu language rights in law]. One language leader, Mr L, an academic specializing in Zhuang language, spoke from within a milieu in which minority language rights were commonplace knowledge: "壮族把壮语做好用好……这是我的权利，是法律给我的权利，所以不敢来说" [the Zhuangzu [already] use Zhuang and speak Zhuang well … this is my right, the right given to me by law, so it goes without saying]. By contrast, only a few participants amongst the Zhuang-speaking and/or Zhuangzu university students were aware of the *Constitution*'s provision about minority languages. As Morris, a Zhuang-speaking finance undergraduate up north at IMUST said, language rights were a topic of which he had heard "比较少" [relatively little]. Lloyd, a Zhuangzu law student also at IMUST, saw this lack of legal awareness as culturally and historically situated, relating it in Excerpt 4-1 to the historically limited role of law in Zhuang-speaking areas and comparing the situation in the Inner Mongolia Autonomous Region, where he now lives:

Excerpt 4-1

Lloyd: 壮族这方面法律知识的话我应该是还有一些 ……因为现代的话……法学知识在壮文壮族地区的话是很少的，因为比较落后。像蒙族的这些法律知识的话，起码说蒙族还是形成了一个统治过一段时间，所以说还是流传下来了，但是壮族的话，他就是没有统治过，所以说没形成一个统治一定地域的……至于说壮族地区的人民对法律方面，法律权利这些，其实是有接触的，但是没能用自己的，形成所谓的地方特色或者说用自己的地方言语说表达，比较有一些呼声之类的，会有这些方面的进展。

[Lloyd: The Zhuangzu, knowledge of that aspect of law, I must say I only know a bit … because nowadays … legal knowledge in Zhuang writing and Zhuangzu areas is slight, because they're pretty backwards. Regarding the Mengzu's [Mongolian minzu's] legal knowledge, at least the Mengzu formulated uniform rules over a period of time and they are still handed down, but the Zhuangzu, they were not uniformly ruled, so they didn't form a unitary territory … Regarding the views about law of the people in Zhuangzu areas, legal rights etc, in fact there were contracts, but they did not use their own [laws], forming so-called laws with local characteristics or express them in their local language [However,] there are some [upraised] voices, there will be progress in this regard.]

(On historic Zhuang contracts see a contemporaneous description reproduced in Tapp and Cohn 2003: 45.) Lloyd's comment speaks to the social significance of the legal system and its interrelation with popular knowledge.

There were wide-ranging understandings of what language varieties or practices the laws covered or entailed. To illustrate, the same student as above, Lloyd, thought that language rights protected *Baihua*, Nanning's Mandarin vernacular. Lloyd had earlier explained to me that "粤语的分支在广西叫白话" [the branch of Cantonese in Guangxi is called Baihua]; scholars also call Baihua "Nanning Cantonese" (Qin and Wu 2009: 29). Actually, a legal distinction is made between the varieties recognized as distinct languages like Zhuang corresponding to particular official minority groups, on one hand, and dialects of Mandarin such as Cantonese and Nanning Baihua on the other. Non-Mandarin languages that are neither official minority languages are likewise excluded from protection (see e.g. Sonam et al [2019] and Roche's [2019] analyses of the effects of this legal division in Tibetan areas). Article 4 is a freedom to use and development minority *languages*, i.e. the former category. Nevertheless, and because of this misunderstanding, Lloyd saw the *Constitution* as protecting his interests as a Baihua speaker; thus he believed that in Nanning his use of Baihua would be acceptable whereas it would elsewhere disadvantage him in becoming a professional:

Excerpt 4-2

Lloyd: 以后我想当律师的话我说，像我们语言权利，我们那边是，在法律上肯定是尊重少数民族地方的语言特色，尤其是像南宁这样基本都是清一色白话，所以说尤其是老南宁这些人都是讲白话的，所以说人家就感觉我这普通话不太过关。但是我们那边只要能讲白话就行。

[Lloyd: Later, I want to become a lawyer, I'd say, like our language rights: in our laws we there [in GZAR] certainly respect the language characteristics of minority minzu areas, especially places like Nanning [where] basically everyone speaks the same vernacular, so especially old Nanningers all speak Baihua, so people feel my Putonghua isn't very passable. But down there we only need to speak Baihua and it's okay.]

Lloyd's life experience thus far had shaped a view that Baihua was an acceptable language variety for professional work in Nanning. This may have been an impact of the *Constitution* in a normative sense, in so far as the law's expression of support for minority languages had been generalized as an investment of symbolic power in other non-standard language varieties. However, the widespread use and acceptance of Nanning Baihua is not as direct an effect of language rights as Lloyd suggested: the *Constitution* does not provide any legal protection for Baihua or other regional varieties of Mandarin and, as the following chapters will show, nor does the language governance framework task any state institutions with making or implementing language policy about Baihua.

While the understanding of language rights varied across all participants, the language leaders tended to be more precise. Language leaders also addressed legal culture and its role in limiting the impact of laws about minority language. Mr B, one of the few participants with lived experience of Zhuang communities in both GZAR and Yunnan, considered that the limited implementation of Zhuang protections in law resulted from a lack of a culture of people and institutions mobilizing to use the existing laws, rather than resulting from limitations of the legal framework itself:

Excerpt 4-3

Mr B：怎么样才能使他的地位提高？……一方面呢需要本民族的不断地宣传，争取法律给我们赋予的权利，用够，用完。
Author：你觉得这个宪法有用吗
Mr B：这个宪法是有用的，但是我们现在用的好像不够。比如说它规定我们都有使用发展我们自己本民族语言文字的权利，但是我们现在就是很多时候没有用够这些方面的权利。我们自己很多时候也没有一种自觉的意识去为这个事情做很多事情。一个是靠我们自己，我们自己呼吁。

[Mr B: How can one make [Zhuang's] status improve? ... one aspect is you must have the minzu itself consistently promoting it; the law gives us the gift of a right; use it enough, use it entirely.
Author: Do you think the *Constitution* is useful?
Mr B: The *Constitution* is useful, but it seems like nowadays we don't use it enough. For example, it directs we all have the right to use and develop our own minzu language and script, but now we don't make use of these rights most of the time. Also, often we ourselves don't have a consciousness about doing more and more of these things. First, it really relies on us, we ourselves invoking it.]

Mr B and other language leaders therefore saw the need to raise minzu consciousness rather than change language policy texts and structures. Mr B (and other participants) believe that "我们要自己多去培养一些自己本民族的孩子。靠他们起来了，这样影响力才大一点" [We must do more to train our own minzu children. Relying on them, [only] this way can the influence grow]. Similarly, Mr L, just after commenting that language rights go without saying, emphasized that "现在主要的问题是壮族内部" [Nowadays, the important problem is within the Zhuangzu people], rather than in the legal texts.

Moreover, language leaders who were experienced in language activism, like Mr N in Excerpt 4-4, believe firmly that the *Constitution* does not found legal actions, as my analysis in Chapter Three also concluded

Excerpt 4-4

Mr N: ［在国外］只要违反宪法我就可以起诉你，但广西没有这种环境，法院不会给立案，法官不会接手这个案子。

[Mr N: [Overseas] you need only contravene the *Constitution* and I can sue you, but Guangxi doesn't have that environment, the courts will not register your claim, judges won't accept that case.]

Mr N here explains the lack of legal action as a problem of the legal culture (which we could think of as the courts' *de facto* language policy), not necessarily of the legal nature of the rights. This reflects a lived experience of the lack of any formal legal process for commencing litigation to enforce the freedom to use and develop minority languages.

Others saw the problem as the culture of their governing institutions, not the local lack of a culture of seeking to implement of language laws or a lack of legal knowledge. This is expressed in Excerpt 4-5, from a discussion with a language activist and postgraduate student, Hoz, about grassroots script development work.

Excerpt 4-5

Hoz: 然后这几年虽然有些就是广西的青年、壮族人他们就呼吁保护起来做这些方面的工作……所以这几年是有所恢复的。但是总体上方案那个被官方僵化了，已经僵硬了这种感觉，然后他在我们不管怎样去呼吁好像得到官方的回应很少，所以我们就自己想，文件自己另辟一个途径。我们不希望被那个官方僵化的，不符合我们自己壮族人那种习惯的。

[Hoz: Then a few years ago some young Zhuangzu people from Guangxi, they instigated [a campaign] for protection of Zhuang and did some work in that regard ... So recently there's been some recovery. But overall the program became ossified by the officials; they had long ossified their feelings [towards Zhuang], and there rarely seems to be an official response whenever we appeal, so we ourselves think, the document [a new script proposal] opens up another path. We do not want to be officially ossified, [because] we won't conform to habits incompatible with that of our minzu.]

In addition, financial inequalities may limit access to legal recourse for disputes about Zhuang or other languages: Mr P commented that the cost of litigating to protect minority language rights was prohibitively high. Mr N, Mr P and others' perceptions of a lack of legal action over the minority language freedom are borne out empirically when we look at the records of case law.

4.2 Case law as discourse about linguistic justice

The overall finding from the case law data is that the minority language freedom in Article 4 of the *Constitution*, and the more specific right for minority language users in courts, are not widely taken up as legal resources. The absence of any case law expressly relying on Article 4 bears out my legal conclusion, in Chapter Three, that this is not an actionable right, but the case law also shows the limited impact of Article 4 as a principle or normative resource in articulating expectations of justice and/or of government. To provide some context to legal cases in China, the Chinese legal system is not one that treats judges' decisions on the application of laws to specific cases as legal rules that guide or even bind future court judgments. Systems that do are typically called common law, whereas the Chinese system is a version of another major type, civil law. As such, I did not expect to find many published decisions on specific cases nor lengthy reasoning within them. Likewise, I did not expect to find many participants with news or views about language rights litigation. I nevertheless investigated whether *any* relevant judgments might exist to provide a different source of information on the meaning and use being made of the relevant laws in protecting the interests of speakers of minority languages. To this end, I searched online court judgment databases and other Chinese-language law databases; interviewed a law professor in Beijing who researches minority entitlements (Mr P) and a lawyer at an access-to-justice NGO in China who was running training on minority rights (Mr O); searched databases of newspaper articles in both Chinese and English; ran online searches; and asked my participants if they knew of any such cases. The paucity of results confirmed my expectation that, overall, case law is not contributing rules to minority language governance and that the constitutional language freedom does not found claims to legal redress. However, a few interesting concluded and potential cases did come to light.

Some came from a new database of recent court judgments. China instituted its "instructional case system" in 2010, to publish a limited number of "guiding cases" from the Supreme People's Court as national precedents for future disputes (Deng 2016; Li and Deng 2016: 90). In a similar spirit of openness, but not to provide precedents, the government began offering access to a variety of judgments from a variety of courts from 2013, while this study was underway, via two online databases: China Judgments Online (http://wenshu.court.gov.cn/) and China Trials Online (http://tingshen.court.gov.cn/). These databases do not provide a back-catalogue of judgments, only those given since 2013. Before that, judgments were not systematically reported nor available to researchers or people like my participants.

Like my other attempts to search for relevant case records, my searches of China Judgments Online suggested that there were very few disputes about minority language rights being litigated, or at least very few such cases being recorded. China Judgments Online contained millions of records when I last checked in 2019, but a search of 《中华人民共和国宪法》第四条 '《The PRC Constitution》 Article 4' returned a result of 暂无数据！ 'no data!', despite following the site's search bar template. A search of 中华人民共和国宪法 'The PRC Constitution' with 民族 'minzu' and 语言 'language' returned five decisions, none of which appeared to be about minority language disputes from their headnotes (i.e. legal summaries). A search of 少数民族 'minority minzu' and 语言 'language' and 权利 'right' returned 11 pages of results. These also turned out to be about a great many matters not on topic.

I searched again with the phrase 少数民族语言 'minority minzu language'. This returned seven pages of results (105 decisions). I reviewed the headnotes of the first and last 15. Of these 30 headnotes, most were about cases that had taken place in a minority region, for example Wenshan-Zhuang Miao Autonomous Prefecture, or with a party to the dispute whose name included "minority minzu", for example Xinjiang Minority Languages Editorial Department (in a construction dispute). This is why the cases had come up in the search results, rather than because of a connection to minority language rights. I also reviewed the full, published judgments of all the results within these 105 where the case name included my complete search term. This gave me a total of nine judgments. Eight dated from 2019 and one from 2017, i.e. all after my fieldwork. Unfortunately, eight were intellectual property disputes involving Sichuan Provincial Radio, Film and Television Minority Language Translation and Broadcasting Center, with no relevance to this research.

Just one result was relevant: the 2017 judgment in an appeal over four Yi men's restricted access to their own Mandarin-medium criminal trials, which I discussed in Chapter Three when explaining that appeals are one of the few ways to make legal use of laws about minority languages. As I noted in Chapter Three, the successful appellants did not rely on the constitutional minority language freedom (Article 4) or even the constitutional right to have court proceedings in a local minority language (Article 139), but on an article of the *Criminal Procedure Law*. The question to ask about this case at this point is: why not rely on the *Constitution* itself? This case suggests that the *Constitution* was not seen by these litigants or this court as actionable. Rather, the more recent and more topic-specific national legislation on criminal procedure, which embeds the constitutional principle of linguistic equality in courts into a more mechanical legislative framework, is seen as providing a right with the legal authority to found a legal action (the appeal). This indicates that the *Constitution* is constructed as a normative discourse that needs to be translated into other legislation in order to be applied to specific situations. We will see over the course of this book affirmations from different data sources of this pattern in language governance in the PRC.

The interview data about legal cases goes some way to affirming this model. The interviews, like the database research, also affirmed that there are very few cases about minority language rights being litigated. Knowledge of only three cases emerged through the interviews. The first two were disputes claiming a Putonghua entitlement when English was used in safety manuals and for emergency call lines, as described to me by Mr P (7 August 2014). On my legal analysis in Chapter Three, such claims could have been founded on the positive language right in the *Putonghua Law*. Mr P understood, however, that at least one of these cases predated the *Putonghua Law*. This earlier case indicates that, even without the *Putonghua Law*, a normative claim to a right to Putonghua was strong. However, as these cases have not been publicly reported, I cannot confirm whether a "right" to Putonghua or other phrases and concepts from the legal discourse were used in the litigation. The participants had not heard of any cases where a legal claim was made for safely manuals, emergency call lines or other services to be in a minority language, rather than in Putonghua.

The third case was described by a Zhuangzu academic at Guangxi University (Mr C, 17 June 2014). It was said to have involved a Zhuang language advocate suing a newspaper in GZAR which ran the cartoon shown at Figure 12, which includes the following dialogue (my translation):

> Kidnapper: "Your son is in our hands, you have two days to get us 100,000RMB!"
>
> Hostage: "These two 'rabbit-toothed' bastards' accent is 'Pinched Zhuang'!"

The cartoon depicts Zhuang speech as typical of criminals and describes Zhuang speech as 夹壮 'Pinched Zhuang', which is a common and pejorative slang term. Mr C explained this is the name for the accent of Zhuang speakers speaking Putonghua, which is "贬义的" [derogatory] (field notes 17 June 2014). Linguistically, Pinched Zhuang is more than an accent: there are systematic phonological, lexical, and grammatical elements in Putonghua as spoken by first-language Zhuang speakers, but there nevertheless remains a strong stigma about this way of speaking. Even Mr J, a proud Zhuangzu whose own Zhuang-medium music was acclaimed, bewailed his children's Pinched Zhuang: "我的儿子我的女儿，还夹壮语，我觉得羞死了，羞死了" [My son, my daughter, still have Pinched Zhuang, I feel I'm dying of shame, dying of shame]. This cartoon thus reveals

Figure 12: Cartoon from the 'Guangxi News web', 2014.

a current of linguistic discrimination, referring to this variety of speech with a name reflecting the social construction of Putonghua having been corrupted by "pinches" of Zhuang. Mr C and other participants who had seen this cartoon reported feeling offended.

I eventually conducted an online interview with the advocate (Mr Q) whom Mr C reported had sued the newspaper, and soon discovered that he had not in fact sued. That is, there was actually no third legal case. Rather than suing, Mr Q said that he had had a series of contestations with police. He explained the contestations began because he was teaching Zhuang for free as an extracurricular activity at a university, which alarmed the authorities as potentially covering for organizing collective action. He alleged that he was detained without a warrant and that harassment ensued when he demanded that certain police formalities be conducted in the medium of Zhuang. If accurate – and I cannot verify whether or not it is – Mr Q's experience suggests shortfalls in the implementation of the constitutional minority language freedom, but in any case there was no litigation in response.

However, Mr Q's account to me, in his interview excerpt below, illustrates the use of the minority language freedom as a discursive resource mobilized to legitimize (to me) a claim to an entitlement to Zhuang-medium procedures.

Excerpt 4-6

Mr Q: 南宁警方非法限制壮文老师人身自由 15 小时，因壮文老师汉语水平低，要求用壮语翻译被警方拒绝……签了壮文名字，南宁警方就让他从中午 12 点等到 23: 13 分 公安说 "有一直选题给你做，签汉字名盖手印就可以回去，不签汉字名就继续留在这里' 。

[Mr Q: Nanning Police Station unlawfully limited the Zhuang teacher's [i.e. my] physical freedom for 15 hours, because the Zhuang teacher's Hanyu [Mandarin] level was low, [he] needed to use Zhuang to translate. The police declined ... [He] signed in Zhuang, the Nanning Police then made him wait from about 12:00 until 23:13. The Public Security said "There is a document for you to do, sign a name in a Hanzi character covered with a fingerprint then you can go back; if you don't sign a Hanzi character name then you will continue to stay here."]

However, this discursive resource was apparently not constructed in the policing field as having legitimacy or force – we can think of this as discourse lacking legal or other capital – so it apparently did not change the linguistic demands in the situation. Why it is that this, or any other, discourse lacks legal capital and symbolic power is a factor of predominant language ideologies, including those reproduced in the normative discourse in which legislative texts participate.

4.3 Laws and policies as discourse about linguistic justice

The law is a discourse amplified by its authority and its symbolic power, and therefore likely to have influence even if poorly understood or not well known to participants. What it means for law to be a symbolically powerful discourse is that laws can shape public conversations and inform individuals' expectations and beliefs without each law being specifically known. This wider and less direct influence is part of the naturalization of constructions of meaning that symbolically powerful discourses can achieve. The laws being analyzed in this chapter are symbolically empowered state discourses that produce both an ideology and an administrative reality of a majority-minority division. A language ideological debate between linguistic equality and national development is also deeply entrenched in the language governance framework.

The *Constitution* and other national laws reproduce the ideology of the hierarchic majority/minority division, as well as the ideology of ethnic groups as natural objects, each corresponding to a distinct language. Chapter Two has shown that these beliefs pre-date the PRC, but laws add permanence to these ideas. This is done, for example, by the current and older PRC constitutions and other national laws identifying and making distinctions between the minority minzu and the majority, between minority languages and the national language, and between the areas where minority people live and everywhere else. These texts articulate the "vision and division" (Bourdieu 1987: 852) of a citizenry divided into static ethno-linguistic polities which Chapter Two noted had been introduced into administrative practice at least by the PRC's first census. The *Constitution* therefore does not set up who the 55 minority minzu and one majority minzu are. That was done by the PRC government in its early years through a separate, official process called the Minzu Classification. The *Constitution* starts from the premise that these groups exist and is concerned to articulate how they, together, constitute a nation-state. It does this in particular in the Preamble, which reads (in its official English translation):

> The people of all nationalities in China have jointly created a splendid culture and have a glorious revolutionary tradition. [...] The People's Republic of China is **a unitary multi-national state built up jointly by the people of all its nationalities**. Socialist relations of equality, unity and mutual assistance have been established among them and will continue to be strengthened. In the struggle to safeguard the unity of the nationalities, it is necessary to combat big-nation chauvinism, mainly Han chauvinism, and also necessary to combat local-national chauvinism. The state does its utmost to promote the common prosperity of all nationalities in the country. [my emphasis]

On one interpretation, honoring this means a state commitment to "promot[ing] the use of spoken and written languages of ethnic minorities in every field", as the state itself reports to have done in (State Council Information Office of the PRC 1999: II). However, this and earlier versions of the PRC *Constitution* have created a long-lived and continuing legal discourse which subsumes minority language governance within the state's economic and cultural development and nation-building responsibilities. Like the current Preamble extracted above, the Preamble of the PRC's 1954 *Constitution* – its first official constitution – propagated a discourse of minority equality intertwined with national unity and economic development. It, too, positioned the minority polity framework as a normative challenge to Han-centric, parochial or separatist ideologies:

> All the nationalities in our country have been united in one great family of free and equal nationalities. The unity of our country's nationalities will continue to gain in strength on the basis of the further development of the fraternal bonds and mutual aid among them [...] and opposition to both big-nation chauvinism and local nationalism. In the course of economic construction and cultural development, the state will concern itself with the needs of the different nationalities[.]

The 1954 Preamble made the state's role in achieving these goals more of a normative behest, expressed as something the state "will concern itself with" (translated from 将照顾 in the authoritative Mandarin version). This is slightly different to the current, present-tense declarative description that the state *is* doing its utmost (translated from 尽一切努力 in the authoritative Putonghua version). Either way, the minzu are constructed as distinct but an integral part of the nation in a co-ordinate equality. In terms of language ideologies, this seems to reflect a principle of linguistic equality. In addition, the Preambles construct the state as having a duty to all 56 minzu, and to challenging parochial ideologies that may undermine their unity or equality. But which beliefs about language are entailed in this responsibility to the unity, equality and economic development of the minzu?

One language ideology often associated with unity is a belief that not using or not knowing the majority/national/common language is a sign of disloyalty to the nation and of separatism. Tam (2020b: 3, 2020a) explains how this view came to dominate in early PRC language politics:

> the CCP that once celebrated the authenticity of China's diverse local plebian life, that pushed back against the elitism inherent in a policy defined by standardization, that contended that linguistic homogeneity was entirely at odds with a revolution of and by the people, began to proclaim that their revolution required a strong nation, and a strong nation required a unified language. Even by the time of the Cultural Revolution [...] the party line remained, '[...] To speak the national language is to obey the party.'

That everyone should speak one language remains an important belief informing language governance currently, because national unity is a state priority (see e.g. *Communiqué on the Fifth Plenum* in Bishop 2020). Moreover, with today's emphasis on national security and coercive unity, it is a homogenizing version of this belief that dominates: i.e. that speaking the national language *and* a local language is a risk, as bilingualism is believed to work against linguistic and ideological unity. A plural version of this belief would be that everyone needs to speak the national language as a lingua franca but that bi/multilingual citizens are unproblematic or even desirable. Yet this homogenizing monolinguistic nationalism is still challenged in some public and academic discourses arguing that "the ultimate goal of *Duoyuan Yiti* ['multiple cultures, one body'] should be ethnic equality with national unity" (Wang 2016: 179) rather than the goal of assuring unity by dissolving ethnic differences. Wang, like many others, also draws on the on the discursive resources of symbolically powerful laws and policies, specifically the ideas of Duoyuan Yiti and 民族团结 mínzú tuánjié '[multi] minzu unity' expressed in the current and former *Constitutions*. This debate overlaps with the political and academic debates, introduced in Chapter Two, over the proposition that the path to equality is through ethnic dissolution (the "second generation minzu" argument). These axioms have not been formally or rhetorically discarded by the leadership but the multiplicity of cultures is now once again readily perceived as conflicting with the one whole, and it is the latter that is the leadership's priority.

Moreover, that the equality of the minzu is understood and articulated within the frame of national unity and security has recently been enhanced by a small but significant amendment to the article of the *Constitution* in which the minority language freedom is expressed. Article 4, in addition to expressing the minority language freedom, re-articulates the relationship between the state and minority peoples expressed in the Preamble. In full, it now reads (in the official English translation):

> Article 4. All nationalities in the People's Republic of China are equal. **The state protects the lawful rights and interests of the minority nationalities and upholds and develops the relationship of equality, unity, mutual assistance and harmony among all of China's nationalities.** Discrimination against and oppression of any nationality are prohibited; any acts that undermine the unity of the nationalities or instigate their secession are prohibited. The state helps the areas inhabited by minority nationalities speed up their economic and cultural development in accordance with the peculiarities and needs of the different minority nationalities. Regional autonomy is practiced in areas where people of minority nationalities live in compact communities; in these areas organs of self- government are established for the exercise of the right of autonomy. All the national autonomous areas are inalienable parts of the People's Republic of China. The people of all nationalities have the freedom to use and develop their own spoken and written languages, and to preserve or reform their own ways and customs. [my emphasis]

Shortly after my fieldwork, in 2018, Article 4 was amended to add 和谐 'harmony' in the second sentence to the list of relationships the state will uphold and develop between the minority and the Hanzu (Wei 2018). This amendment shows the ascendance of a state discourse and policy pre-occupation with stability and unity, particularly under the current leadership but also prominent during the preceding leadership, with its well-known catch-cry of 社会和谐 'social harmony'. This is linked to the underlying tension between linguistic freedom and equality, on one hand, and national unity and security, on the other, and the belief that the former are inherently antithetical to the latter.

This set of language ideologies have been present in the *Constitution* and national governance discourses since long before the current political climate but now resonate across various discourses. Benney (2013: 11), publishing just as President Xi assumed leadership of the PRC, wrote that "new developments have changed the way in which rights defence has been used and perceived. Chief amongst them are the rise of the *weiwen* [维稳] (or 'stability maintenance' discourse) from the mid-2000s onwards, and the severe crackdown on political activism which took place in early 2011". Others, too, have noted this change in tolerance. It is expressed through various state policies and practices, for example in stifling access-to-justice NGOs and lawyers especially in the South-East (e.g. Agence France-Presse 2012; Davis 2012; Franceschini 2012); in securitization-centered responses to minority group's political claims and quotidian freedoms in Xinjiang (e.g. Zenz and Leibold 2019); and in cultural disciplining at public boarding schools for minorities especially in the North-West (e.g. Leibold and Grose 2019).

Even in GZAR, this discourse of social harmony is an important, and explicit, ideological frame for language policy. The political significance of linguistic difference as an index of other differences and therefore a threat to social harmony is clear in the opening lines of the 2019 Nanning Government review of its own municipal laws on Zhuang and public bilingualism: "特别是壮汉双语和谐发展已成为我市各族人民亲如一家、民族关系十分融洽的重要体现" [In particular, the harmonious development of Zhuang-Chinese bilingualism has become an important manifestation of the closeness of the people of all ethnic groups in our city and the harmonious ethnic relations]. Note that this bilingualism is largely unidirectional, with Zhuang-speaking households and individuals adding Mandarin to their repertoires (see Chapter Two). This hints at the unequal pressure on minority peoples to be 'harmonious'. This is not a political climate in which appropriating a discursive rights framework for minority language claims will flourish.

The current and past Preambles and Article 4 also frame the equality of the minzu within economic and cultural development. This is emphasized elsewhere in the *Constitution*. For example, areas of self-government are mentioned in Article 4. There are three such areas for the Zhuangzu, one region and two at the sub-regional tier (see Chapter Two). The *Constitution* guides these areas' autonomous governments' responsibilities in Article 119, which states:

> Article 119: The organs of self-government of the national autonomous areas independently administer educational, scientific, cultural, public health and physical culture affairs in their respective areas, sort out and protect the cultural legacy of the nationalities and work for the development and prosperity of their cultures.

Within this Article 119, minority language governance is only implicitly a matter for self-government, as it potentially falls within a regional government's explicitly given roles in education, cultural administration, and the protection of cultural legacies. What does Article 119 guide an autonomous Zhuangzu government to aim for with Zhuang language? The provision envisages that the government of an autonomous area, such as the GZAR Government, will provide cultural protection for the Zhuangzu and will also work towards the "development and prosperity" of Zhuangzu culture. A cultural development frame constructs some cultural and linguistic practices and their practitioners as undeveloped, however, while others are developed.

Moreover, economic and cultural development are not necessarily compatible goals. This duality of cultural protection-oriented and economic development-oriented policy is embedded throughout China's language policy framework, and it produces an inescapable language ideological tension. It begins within the *Constitution*, both in the Article just quoted and in Article 4. The freedom to use and develop Zhuang is thus interpreted within this uneasily twinned frame of economic and cultural development. As I will explain below, of the two it is economic development which is now ascendant as the dominant policy goal.

Further, economic developmentalism can bolster the belief in the national security through monolingualism, explained above. Because lingua franca Putonghua is now realized in most of the nation, unlike in the early PRC decades, the economic argument can now be made that other languages are unnecessary for trade and labour efficiency. If multilingualism is believed to be both economically unhelpful and a threat to national security, then why implement language policies in ways that maintain many languages?

Interpreting language rights and policy through the lens of economic value did not arise only once Putonghua became a viable language of commerce across the nation. Before that, developmentalism intersected with the belief that written language practices are more valuable than oral language practices, which had become ascendant in language policy in the Republican period (Tam 2020a). It also intersected with the related belief that a standardized language was both a more developed tool than non-standardized language and a mark of cultural progression. Thus, top-down standardization and script regularization activities have long been understood as the kind of activities which the laws about "developing" minority languages are seeking. The history of PRC language policy and practice shows this pre-occupation with standardization (e.g. Bradley 2009; Kipnis 2012; Lam 2005; Premaratne 2015; Zhou and Sun 2004). This approach to development through standardizing languages and creating scripts for them works against applying language rights to support the preservation of existing or historic, organic but unstandardized language practices. With Zhuang, for instance, "the government's investment in Standard Zhuang and its consequential disuse of other Zhuang varieties has left little room for these other varieties to become useful or to gain status on any scale beyond the very local" (Grey in press).

This approach to development has also tended to Hanify the languages, which means making them become like *Hanyu* 'Mandarin'. The presiding view in China's twentieth-century language policy was that "minority languages with a healthy number of loanwords [...from Mandarin were] well-developed languages" (Zhou 2003: 364), while a 1958 article published by a government minority language agency promoting Mandarin loanwords to "enrich" minority languages was "considered as policy for minority language work" (Zhou 2003: 364). Similarly, Harrell (1995: 23–25) argues that modernization was reinterpreted as "Hanification" across twentieth-century Chinese minority language governance.

Furthermore, there is an abundance of state discourse reproducing developmentalist beliefs. Two relatively recent government *White Papers* report that the state has committed resources to "research these [minority] languages [...to] help minority people create, *improve* or reform their written languages" and that "The Zhuang, Bouyei [...] use [...] *languages which have been created or improved with the help of the government*" [my emphasis] (State Council Information Office of the PRC 1999: II; see also State Council Information of the PRC 2005b: III(3)). Legal instruments since 1982 have given priority to economic development goals by erasing other responsibilities and goals relating to language from the legal discourse. For instance, the State Council's 2005 regulations on autonomy (State Council Decree No.435) do not deal with language; rather, they "provide that People's Governments at higher levels and their functional departments should extend support to autonomous regions of ethnic minorities" in a number of stated policy areas relating to economic development, including infrastructure, developing Western China, natural resource development, environmental protection, banking, foreign trade, the production of specialized goods for ethnic minorities; and programs for economic development of border areas (Wang 2005: 78). Second, they "make provisions for promoting the development of education, scientific technological research, cultures, public health and sports, and [to improve] social security in autonomous regions of ethnic minorities". Third, these regulations direct that governments should "emphasize the consolidation of unity among all ethnic groups" and add to the legal system certain "provisions for legal responsibility for violation" of ethnic unity (Wang 2005: 78).

Recent policy texts explicitly include development goals while explicitly excluding principles about minority language stewardship or equality. They subsume language policy within development policy or present language governance as primarily about ensuring Putonghua – instrumental to the entwined national goals of developing economically and in terms of national unity – is promoted alongside minority language protections. For example, Chapter Nine of the current national *Education Policy* explicitly frames bilingual education within the national development strategy, beginning "Speeding up educational development for ethnic minorities is of far-reaching importance to promoting socioeconomic development" (Ministry of Education of the PRC 2010: 22). Foreseeing and encoding another possible tension, between minority languages bolstering minzu identity and the role of schooling in bolstering national identity, the same passage goes on to declare that "educational development" of minority schooling is of far-reaching importance "to enhancing unity between people of all ethnic backgrounds in striving for common prosperity and development" (Ministry of Education of the PRC 2010: 22). Following this, the first specific directive in Chapter Nine is that "[e]ducation in ethnic unity shall be conducted extensively in schools at all levels" (Ministry of Education of the PRC 2010: 22). This policy's combination of development and unity goals echoes the older *Basic Principles*, below. Moreover, the education laws and policies are situated within official discourses maintaining that "educational development should be future-oriented" (Yue et al. 2010), and that "[non-Han] ethnic groups [are] trailing behind in educational development" (UNESCO Institute for Lifelong Learning 2010). These co-texts frame the national *Education Policy's* support for bilingual education, discussed in Chapter Three, as support for development rather than heritage, introducing once again a familiar tension to the language governance framework.

For example, the Education Policy, the *Constitution* and other laws are officially framed within five *Basic Principles* (China Encyclopedia Compilation Group 2008: 58). The State Council Information Office describes these *Basic Principles* as underlying the "policies of the Chinese Government in handling the ethnic problems" (China Encyclopedia Compilation Group 2008: 58). They are as follows, with development emphasized at (c) and (e): (a) Equality and unity among ethnic groups; (b) Self-government of ethnic groups; (c) Developing the economy and culture of ethnic groups; (d) Training ethnic cadres; (e) Respecting and developing spoken and written languages of ethnic minorities. Specifically in relation to minority languages, principle (e) positions the "development" of minority languages as connected to respecting them.

This does not mean that any discourse of minority language equality in earlier state texts was disingenuous. Recognizing, respecting and assisting minority groups was unequivocally a genuine priority of the early PRC leadership (see e.g. Chaisingkananont 2014: 56; Whaley 2004: 142; Zhou 2004), but the ideological debates within which all language governance must be situated are dynamic. Zhou (2001: 36) has argued that the PRC's language governance has always been a "struggle between long-term and short-term development views". The vast social and ideological change since the constitutional language rights were first enshrined in the 1950s – most importantly, the ascension of market structures and ideologies – radically alter what respect and development mean and what language governance now has to achieve.

Further, leading language policy scholars also reproduce the developmentalist belief in academic discourse. Some frame linguistic development *within* linguistic equality and as consistent with appreciating an inherent value of linguistic diversity. This frame is also present in some laws, as I have pointed out. For example, one of the Chinese Academy of Social Sciences' leading minority language ethnologists, Mu Shihua, argues in an international collaboration proposing language governance reform in China (Li and Lundberg 2008: 133) that "任何一种语言，都是全人类共同的文化财富" [whichever language, each is mankind's joint cultural treasure] and "文化多样性是具有竞争优势，是文化富裕和社会稳定性的来源" [multiculturalism is a tool for competitive advantage; it is the source of cultural prosperity and social stability]. Similarly, the Chinese minority education ethnographer, Wang Ge (2016: 184–185), advocates that "all students have equal opportunities to learn multiple languages at all educational levels" and that enhancing the distinctiveness of the minority minzu is *part of* economic and other development:

> Only with a multicultural awareness and *wenhua zijue* [awareness of one's own culture; 'cultural self-consciousness'] could [Ethnic Minority Learners] build up their economic, cultural, social, and symbolic capital [...] multilingual education based on the notion of multiculturalism will not be a mission impossible but instead a key to ethnic minority development.

Wang (2016: 168) translates *wenhua zijue* as 'cultural self-consciousness', based on Fei's introduction of the term as "a kind of self-knowledge of one's culture" and situates knowledge of minority language within it. But these accounts of linguistic diversity as economically valuable are not widely found positions in official texts, hence Dr Mu and Professor Wang's gentle suggestions for reform.

By contrast, when explaining how a belief in language development this fits together with a belief in language equality, Chinese language policy expert, Zhou Minglang (2004: 84) argues that the constitutional "equality of use and development requires [...] that all minority languages have equal opportunities to undergo language development, such as graphization and standardization" . This better reflects how language policy has actually been implemented. On this belief, a minority language which has received equal opportunity for development of its script and its standard variety is then formally equal and there is no further moral or political obligation on the state. This ideology therefore guides language governance towards Zhuang being left unsupported by the government when the language no longer seems to be instrumentally useful for economic development. The linguistic landscape analyses in Part Three of this book suggests that time has arrived. Similarly, I have elsewhere argued that because the state otherwise "succeeded in teaching and using Putonghua widely, Standard Zhuang became less and less useful for communicating amongst Zhuang speakers, and is thus no longer treated even by the government as an instrument of economic development" (Grey in press).

Thus, these developmentalist discourses not only reproduce an evaluative understanding of minority languages as more or less developed but also an understanding of language as a resource which the state *should* optimize by "developing" minority languages, for the good of a minority minzu and the whole nation. These embedded, ideological frames orient language governance towards state intervention to make Zhuang a developed language and to a laissez-faire approach to language governance once the work of developing Zhuang has been done.

Within this developmentalist governance paradigm, challenging market norms in order to achieve minority language equality is an extremely hard task. Mr L articulated this: in his experience of Zhuang language advocacy, having minority language rights does not overcome the fact that decision-makers believe that socio-economic mobility comes through learning Mandarin, not Zhuang.

Excerpt 4-7

> Mr L: 现在就是在争论这个事情，他们整天拿一个例子来做一个-- 有没有用。就是以前广西民族大学的校长，他们两个儿子，在文革前一个学了汉文、一个学了壮文。最后学汉文那个他成绩很好，就出国去留学了，在中国八十年代出国的很少嘛……所以他们老拿这个例子来说，"你看，壮文没有用，学壮文的还在国内，学汉文的出去留学了"。

[Mr L: Now when it is time for disputation about it [Zhuang language policy], they always use an example to prove whether -- [pause] it [learning Zhuang] is useful or not. Previously, the Minzu University of China's president, he had two sons, before the Cultural Revolution one studied Hanyu [Mandarin], one studied Zhuang language. Afterwards, the one who studied Hanyu succeeded, went overseas for studies, very few people could leave China in the 1980s to study overseas…so they always used to say, "You see, Zhuang language is not useful, study Zhuang and remain in the country, study Hanyu and go overseas to study".]

The current economic and security-centered developmentalist ideology across governance is a guilelessly overt rather than "hidden agenda" (Shohamy 2006) of language policy. It is now open to the critique of being hegemonic. Thus, language governance faces a bigger challenge than ever if it seeks to normatively (re)value Zhuang by associating it with cultural practices which are seen as developed (i.e. investing Zhuang language with cultural capital) or seeks to organize society such that Zhuang can be considered widely useful and profitable (i.e. investing it with economic capital).

Let me now recapitulate the beliefs emerging from the participants and case law discourses, and discuss not only how they shape linguistic justice but how they may be influenced – constrained even – by the language ideologies I have highlighted are propagating in the normatively powerful discourses of law and policy.

4.4 Concluding discussion: Linguistic developmentalism further constrains minority language rights

Overall, the participants made relatively few direct comments about their understanding of China's laws about language and how, or whether, they have used these laws as advocacy or legal resources. This chapter reported that the language leaders were more likely than the student participants to have the basic knowledge that there are laws concerning Zhuang and other minority languages. Those language leaders, and some of the students who were able to comment directly on language rights in law, often felt that a lack of a legalist culture and a lack of Zhuangzu consciousness caused problems for the application of laws about Zhuang. That is, it was not the legal nature of the minority language rights, but the people's, or their leaders', or their courts' culture of not taking minority language rights into consideration that participants believed had caused such limited legal or political use to be made of existing laws.

The case law analysis demonstrated that a vastly wider pool of people have, just like this study's participants, made little use of language rights in legal proceedings. In fact, the data shows no reported cases to have invoked the constitutional minority language freedom. Participants who were aware of the language laws were also aware of this dearth of case law. I found that the freedom to participate in court proceedings in a minority language, which Chapter Three explained is enshrined in the *Constitution* and national legislation, was successfully invoked in only one recent criminal appeal and even that appeal was decided with reference only to the national legislation, not the *Constitution*. One legal scholar participant reported a few cases litigating a right to information in Putonghua, but not necessarily invoking the language right in the *Putonghua Law*. Another participant explained an experience in which he claimed a right to use Zhuang in police proceedings but was (he alleges) denied, and he did not commence legal proceedings about it.

And yet those who commented directly about language laws, as well as some other participants, had a meaningful sense of a right to Zhuang language. The epigraph states that feeling that one has rights is a starting point for the discovery of linguistic justice or injustice; this chapter concludes that it does not have to be a feeling that one has *legal* rights. An activists' pride in the long history of a minority language, or a young person's awareness that many of their community use that language, can both underpin a moral sense that one has a right to keep using the language. If that is reproduced in law, the legal right might be all the better for claiming the moral right. Or, as this chapter showed, the legal existence of the right might not offer much help in claiming an entitlement to use a language and yet still contribute to a general feeling that being able to use a language would be just.

The chapter showed that a particular belief about languages, an ideology I have called developmentalism, is widely reproduced across the official discourses of Chinese language governance. Minority languages are framed, over and again in official texts, as valuable or deficient instruments of cultural and economic development that the state should grasp. China's historic emphasis on Zhuang standardization and the creation of its Romanized script is symptomatic of this preoccupation with "developing" a language to make it more culturally and economically modern and therefore a better tool in developing the culture and economy of the Zhuang polity and the nation. There is an ideological tension between this and language equality, yet developmentalism and language equality are encoded in the foundational legal texts of the nation. As I have shown in this chapter's analysis of policy discourses surrounding the law, over time, the tension is being resolved by newer laws that explicitly prioritize economic development and remove language, linguistic diversity or linguistic equality from the state's responsibilities. Thus, developmentalism is shaping language rights and the construction of the legitimate linguistic justice that they protect.

One of the criticisms to be made of this developmentalist paradigm is that it demotes or even precludes constructions of minority languages as valuable for non-developmental reasons. As such,, it makes it hard to use – and even to think of using – the minority language freedom to seek state action to support nonstandard Zhuang language practices. It also makes it hard to defend, or to seek continued support for protecting any language that has not been very instrumental in China's economic development. That, I argue, is the particular challenge of minority language policy in China today. Grey (in press) discusses this specifically with regard to the state-led standardization and now obsolescence of Romanized Zhuang. As China marketized, Romanized Zhuang became the metaphoric Betamax to Putonghua's VHS video format, a technological almost-ran. Without economic capital or developmental cache, and given the powerful developmentalism discourses, Zhuang is now vulnerable to being constructed as outside the legitimate expectations for state policy and resourcing in regards to language.

Moreover, this developmentalist framing likely exacerbates for Zhuang a problem identified in other contexts where language rights are, like in China, part of a political discourse of "unity in diversity" (Jaffe 2004). Jaffe (2004: 276) argues that "this kind of discourse obscures the real politics of difference – the real advantages that accrue to speakers of the languages that have *de facto* dominance". In China, by analogy, we may expect that frames of national unity and formal linguistic equality obscure the fact that development-centered language governance framework works in the interests of those with better access to dominant language resources, specifically, Putonghua resources. Developmentalism is, thus, an ideology of Bourdieusian misrecognition. And, what if the following part of Jaffe's argument is likewise true for China? Jaffe's (2004: 277) argues "for majority speakers, the identity functions their language fills for them are so powerfully inscribed in the day-to-day experiences within dominant social institutions and domains of practice that they are rendered almost invisible. This invisibility makes it possible for those majority speakers […] to trivialize minority speakers' socially, politically and historically grounded experiences of identification through language".

Jaffe's critique is highlighting the naturalization of privileged access to the resources of language for identity construction by those who both speak and identify with the majority language. The addition of this naturalization and misrecognition to China's linguistic developmentalism, then, should compound the invisibility of the value of minority languages as identity resources and also the potential role of language policy as a just intervention to equalize access to identity resources for China's minority languages' speakers.

I argue that this developmentalist language ideology is therefore a major reason why there is little, and decreasing, implementation of the minority language freedom through enforceable laws and policies. Rather, these laws operate as "recursive" (Irvine and Gal 2000: 38) ideological processes, mapping certain ideological categories and values onto others. Specifically, they are vehicles for the mapping of a development hierarchy onto the ideological division between majority/minority ethnic and language divisions, thus producing an ideological association between developmental attainment and the difference between the majority and the minorities. From that perspective, minority languages correspond to pre-modernity and to peoples not yet sufficiently economically and culturally developed for their own good or the good of the nation. The law is therefore complicit in the minoritization of Zhuang language and of the peoples with whom the law associates it (the Zhuangzu), framing them as pre-modern, pre-development. If Zhuang language is interpreted this way, it is hard to see how the constitutional minority language freedom will ever be constructed as making it necessary for state officials to preserve or support Zhuang as actually practiced, so long as Zhuang speakers become proficient enough in Putonghua to integrate with, and contribute to, the national culture and economy.

And yet there remains a real, if symbolic, importance to China's the laws about minority language. The general symbolic investment of the state in language governance through law-making may become known to some even if not everyone knows the specifics of the legal rights, as some participant data here illustrated. Linguistic justice is not a natural object awaiting discovery. It, too, is constructed, and the way language rights are framed in law will impact on the broader conversations shaping expectations and beliefs about linguistic justice. Inversely, those conversations and beliefs will also shape how laws about language are interpreted. The way individuals' beliefs shape minority language rights, as well as the way cultures and courts shape language rights, was therefore the focus of the first half of this chapter. Leung makes a related point about language law and policy in many other countries which I consider important to bring into the PRC context: that symbolic jurisprudence is not meaningless or inherently unjust (Leung 2019: 249). Rather, symbolic jurisprudence is doing something valuable politically and ideationally, albeit not creating legal support. Thus, although I have concluded in the last chapter that there is little legal protection for Zhuang, and conclude here that the prevailing discourse of linguistic developmentalism further constrains the impact of minority language rights, it is still significant that there is a minority language freedom grounded in the *Constitution* and in other national laws. It has some normative significance even if it is in tension with, and cannot overcome, developmentalism. It would be politically and ideationally consequential unwelcome to remove these provisions. The question, then, is not only whether participants believe that the law protects and supports minority languages (as some do), but whether removing the minority language freedom from law now would be a move with deep political and symbolic consequences, even though it may have few legal ramifications. I believe it would: taking away something, even something largely symbolic, like the minority language freedom would create a feeling of disregard for minority rights and a sense of linguistic injustice.

Building upon this chapter, the state structures that channel and delimit the responsibility for implementing the laws and making official decisions about Zhuang are analyzed in the following chapter (Chapter Five). It will drawn out further implicit yet powerful language ideologies, especially in the legal structuring of which linguistic and minority concerns are legitimate for which organs of the state and for which peoples. Then, my ethnographically oriented linguistic landscape analyses in Part Three examine what this entwined developmentalist and symbolic jurisprudence orientation to Zhuang language policy looks like, how it is experienced, and what its limitations are, when manifest in specific, local rules and policies about public language usage. Part Three's empirical analysis will add a rich yet necessarily indirect and composite answer to this chapter's more direct evidence of what people understand the minority language freedom and the language governance framework to mean and to do.

5 The structural distribution of language governance powers

> Significant legal weight is often conferred to official language law, but the strength of the law tends to dramatically weaken during implementation. This may have to do with the fact that although elaborate institutional structures have sometimes been developed, they are non-representational and bureaucratic in character. (Leung 2019: 6)

The Guangxi Zhuangzu Autonomous Region (GZAR) has been one of the PRC's five officially autonomous regions since 1958. With the equivalent rank to a province, GZAR is the highest ranking territory officially under Zhuangzu government. It is also the most populous and largest area designated for autonomous Zhuangzu government. The other two Zhuangzu autonomous areas are geographically smaller and administratively sub-regional: Wenshan Prefecture (Wenshan) in Yunnan Province and Lianshan County in Guangdong Province, both introduced in Chapter Two. This chapter deepens the analysis of what is legally entailed or excluded by having Zhuangzu autonomous government in these areas, especially in GZAR, and argues that further weaknesses in the Zhuang language governance framework arise from the way it is structured, in addition to those identified in Chapters Three and Four. Overall, the chapter argues that the responsibility for governing Zhuang is largely channeled to the autonomous areas, especially to GZAR, but then restricted to the legally-stymied institutions of the GZAR regional government. The chapter's final section, a close-up of the structures and institutions involved in language-in-education policy in GZAR, illustrates this.

In some systems, minority language rights or other minority rights may be understood as a tool for mediating and formalizing the balance between minorities' interests and the majority's interests. That is not their role in the PRC system, because the minority language freedom is not actionable, as Chapter Three has explicated. Rather, the disempowerment of minorities is pre-empted and sought to be remedied by other formal structures in the PRC, including through rules about minority minzu participation in national and autonomous regional governments, special powers under the constitutional article on self-government (Article 119) and the *Regional Autonomy Law*, and specialized state institutions. This creates a governing structure which may at first glance appear to offer significant advantages for Zhuang language policy.

However, I have chosen as this chapter's epigraph Leung's warning about language rights being only weakly implemented by elaborate, non-representational and bureaucratic institutions, because it echoes my own contemporaneous findings in analyzing the structures of Zhuang language governance. Leung is *not* writing about the PRC's language governance; her study focuses on language governance in liberal democracies. And yet her warning rings clearly in the PRC context; I have found that the state structures offer only limited representation and responsiveness to Zhuang linguistic and other interests. Decisions are made by institutions within which no minority representation is required or institutions where minority representatives are few and whose areas of responsibility are siloed. Further, an elaborate bureaucratic "triple leadership" (Blachford 2004: 103) model of the Party, the Central government and the national minority work organizations fractures accountability. In addition, the resourcing and policy-making authority of GZAR-specific bodies such as the region's Minority Language Commission have reduced over recent decades. The problem is not that Zhuang interests are entirely marginalized from the state. They are *not* entirely marginalized, and this can lead to complacency or decoy politics. The problem is that these interests are represented and overseen by an uncoordinated and inflexible array of committees and agencies, the shortfalls of which this chapter highlights.

This chapter brings in a spatial analysis, drawing on the idea that "space is a social product" (Foucault 1984; Lefebvre 1991). In particular, it examines spaces constructed by law and the state administration system in relation to the Zhuangzu; through this, legitimate Zhuang language practices are territorialized and the responsibility and power for Zhuang language governance, as well as legitimate expectations of linguistic justice, are spatially constrained. As Sherene Razack (2002: 6), a pioneer of spatial theory in legal scholarship, argues "a spatial analysis can help us to see the operation of all the [social] systems as they mutually constitute one another." One of those systems is legal; the system which Chapter Three has critiqued. Another of those systems is the linguistic hierarchy, a system rarely acknowledged in socio-legal scholarship but centered in this book. Razack (2002: 10) makes the further point that "the production of space is also the production of included and excluded bodies" drawing on Kawash (1998) and Foucault (1984). Following this social theorization of space, this chapter will look at the production of territorial space (the geo-administrative units of the PRC) and spaces of decision-making (the PRC's state institutions) as not only producing the inclusion and exclusion of certain users of language but also of certain kinds of representative.

Chapter Two has already introduced the Zhuangzu as the minority polity officially constructed as corresponding to Zhuang language, and originally recognized by the state in the mid-twentieth century because of the practice of Zhuang dialects by the people grouped into this polity. Throughout this chapter, it becomes ever more clear that the state organizes decision-making about Zhuang language and the representation of interests in Zhuang language through the exclusive prism of the Zhuangzu polity. Language interests are legible and visible to the state as minority minzu interests, and not otherwise. For this reason, the chapter focuses on how Zhuangzu participation in government is structured through territories and institutions. This approach does not assume that all Zhuangzu people want the use of Zhuang language to be protected by the state, or that they all share any other language policy goal. Rather, this focus on Zhuangzu representation and decision-making power in government reflects the reality that the state structures representation and decision-making around recognized polities, not around languages. Thus, if Zhuangzu interests do not encompass Zhuang language interests, then those language interests will be excluded from governance.

In this way, the multi-minzu national framework sets up a fundamental exclusion of stakeholders with a stake in Zhuang language who are not members of the Zhuangzu, like the relatively small but not negligible number of first-language Zhuang speakers from other minzu noted in Chapter Two. As the following analysis of geographic boundaries in Zhuang language governance will show, the minzu framework also excludes stakeholders with a stake in Zhuang language practices who are outside recognized Zhuang areas, such as the increasing numbers of people from Zhuang-speaking backgrounds who temporarily or permanently migrate away from the "homelands". Furthermore, we will see that the Zhuang language governance structures now exclude Zhuang language interests even within the homelands in areas which no longer have a popular majority of Zhuang speakers because of language shift or in-migration of other Chinese peoples.

5.1 Geographic boundaries in Zhuang language governance

Today, the names and locations of South China's provinces largely match those mapped in the eighteenth century by d'Anville (1737, 1785), although the early PRC government shifted the Guangdong-Guangxi border somewhat, reputedly to weaken the Cantonese speaking block (Kaup 2000). The central southern territory, previously called Guangxi Province, was "discursively repurposed" (borrowing the phrase of Cartier 2015a: 3) to create the Guangxi Zhuangzu Autonomous Region in 1958. These new legal frontiers produced a Hanzu-Zhuangzu cultural difference and bound linguistic diversity firmly within this authorized, spatial organization of difference. Establishing GZAR was a major investment of symbolic power in the territorialization of Zhuang language.

Territorialization is not merely an administrative process. It is a language ideological process that has been identified in many discourses, not only law, and in countries other than China. It is a belief that language "works excellently in its own, original place, and loses functions as soon as the stable, original, 'autochthonous' [...] link between language and place is broken" and the related belief that the language people use "sets them within a particular, spatially demarcated [linguistic] ecology" (Blommaert 2004: 58–59). This belief in original language territories is central to China's language rights framework and the law adds rigidity to this territorialized belief about Zhuang. The law does this explicitly in the creation of the Zhuangzu autonomous areas under Articles 4 and 119 of the *Constitution* and the *Regional Autonomy Law*. These official territories localize where Article 4's freedom to use and develop a minority language should operate. The interaction between the territorial system and language rights is discursively emphasized in the structure of Article 4, as the language freedom comes after a number of territorial references e.g. to "areas inhabited by minority nationalities" and "Regional autonomy is practiced in areas where people of minority nationalities live in compact communities". That Zhuangzu ethnic and cultural policy are allocated to the GZAR government is also made clear in an official *White Paper* from 2005 which explains that the GZAR government's responsibilities include Zhuang language books, media and heritage (State Council Information Office of the PRC 2005b: III(7)). Li and Lundberg's (2008) edited book, a rare collaboration between Chinese and foreign scholars about Chinese language governance, highlights the ongoing importance of autonomous regions in the implementation of Chinese language policy (but leaves open for further studies, such as this one, the autonomous regions other than Tibet and Xinjiang).

The legal framework also localizes Zhuangzu affairs as a concern to be addressed by sub-regional governments in areas with high Zhuangzu populations. It does this, for instance, in the provisions of the national *Education Law* which I analyze further in Section 3 of this chapter. Those provisions permit to minority languages certain usages in schools in areas where the local population includes a numeric majority of minority minzu people. The area need not be as large as a self-governing region. Rather, the population conditions could be satisfied at the level of one county within GZAR, and then that county's government must decide upon bilingual schooling. In these ways, there is interlinked legal, geographic and ideological territorialization of Zhuang language.

Official territorialization of language is desired by some minority language speakers around the world because it offers a legal and symbolic bulwark against being wiped off the map; being officially associated with a territory means a language is at least in place somewhere. And for all that people may move or travel out of a legally or a socially constructed language homeland, "people continue to ground aspects of their identities [...] in actual places" (Johnstone 1990: 517; see also Blommaert 2004: 56). However, the delimitation of GZAR is also a limitation. There is a major weakness in the Zhuang language governance system arising from the entrenched territorialization of Zhuang language and Zhuang language governance. It is that responsibility for Zhuang language is channeled to the Zhuangzu autonomous areas' governments, especially GZAR's government, however, their self-governing powers are legally incomplete. I elaborate on this channeling, and this legal incompetence, in reverse order below.

Specifically, the *Regional Autonomy Law* gives the government of GZAR certain powers in addition to those exercised by provincial governments; however, the GZAR government's autonomous law-making powers have themselves not yet been fully enacted and so the extent to which the government of GZAR is free to manage Zhuang language is not yet formally clear. The *Legislation Law of the PRC* (National People's Congress 2000: "*Legislative Interpretation Law*") provides the technical rules for how the GZAR government is to share legal power with the Central government for making laws and regulations, including any power to regulate the use and development of Zhuang language. That law requires the Central government to endorse a plan for how decision-making power will be split between the Central and the GZAR governments, and Article 15 of the *Regional Autonomy Law* requires that regulations on the exercise of regional autonomy must then be enacted. But a plan has not been endorsed for GZAR and such regulations have not been enacted. Without satisfying these requirements in the *Legislative Interpretation Law* and the *Regional Autonomy Law*, the legal authority of the GZAR Government to practice self-government is limited.

The GZAR government has attempted to address this limitation. Between 1984 and 2000, the GZAR People's Congress approved and submitted at least fourteen drafts of regulations on the exercise of autonomy, but all were "returned to the GZAR committee for revision" (Kaup 2000: 117). Feng (2017: 65) reports that in the almost two decades since, "no regional-level autonomous regulation has been passed" across the PRC, but that GZAR has been the most active in trying. Apparently, the reasons that the GZAR government's attempts failed was "the disapproval by the central government" (Feng 2017: 67–69). Drafts were circulated to various national ministries and the National People's Congress' Ethnic Affairs Commission (shown in the organizational chart at Figure 13), but rejected after criticisms from the ministries over ceding central power and guaranteeing national funds to GZAR (Feng 2017: 68).

The consequence is that GZAR and the other four minority autonomous regions are, in practice, still lacking the autonomy that they should, in theory, have (Yu 2009: 56; see also Wang 2005: 78). This renders GZAR and other autonomous regions' governments less powerful than the governments of ordinary provinces, i.e. the territories of China which are *not* responsible for governing minority minzu concerns.

In 2005, a national law called (in English) the *Regulations of the State Council on the Enforcement of the Law on Regional Autonomy for Ethnic Minorities* (State

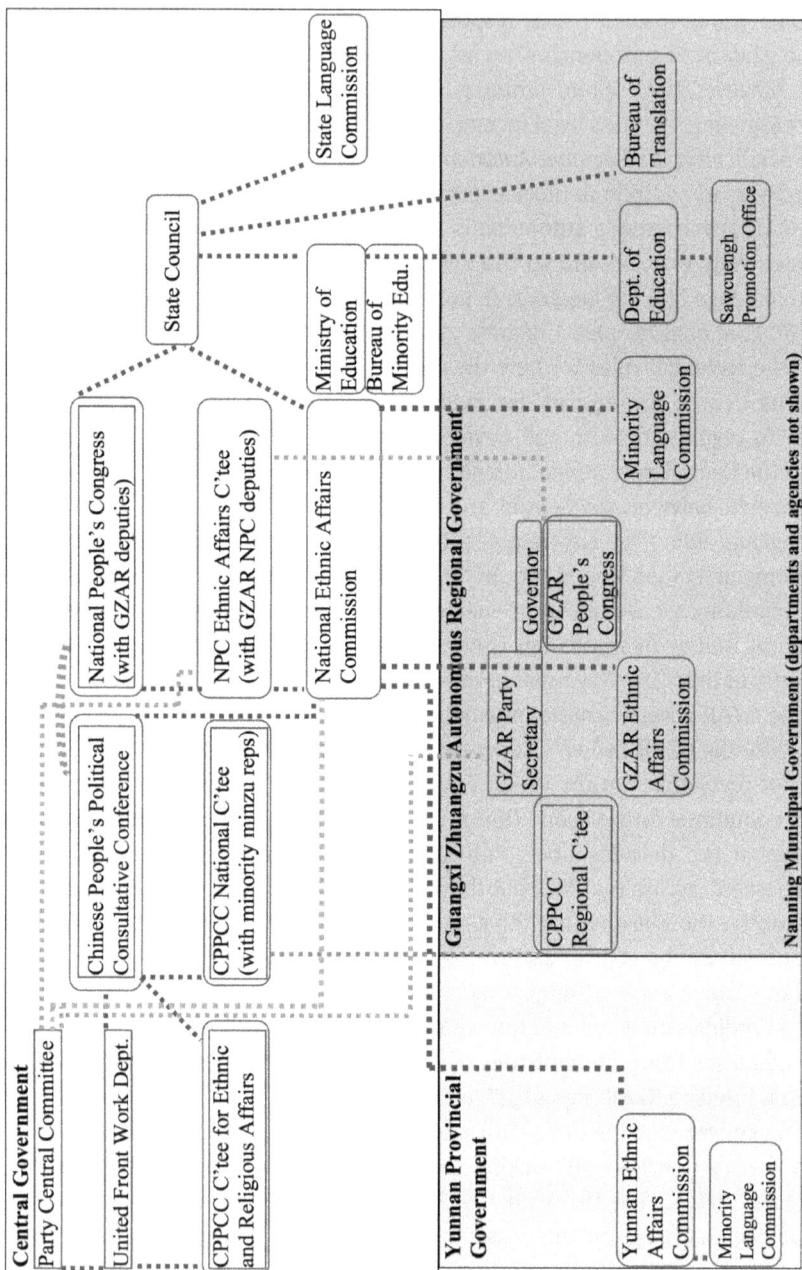

Figure 13: Zhuang language governance organization chart.

Council 2005) was passed to push national-level organs of the state to act in accordance with the *Regional Autonomy Law* after persistent failures to do so. However, this has still not resolved the impasse about GZAR's own governing power, largely because it has had little implementation: "the drafting work in the above mentioned four autonomous regions has not been re-started since the mid-1990s [when a reform of the *Regional Autonomy Law* commenced] and the central government's directives and other normative documents aiming to facilitate or promote the drafting is scarce" (Feng 2017: 67).

This incomplete process of legal devolution of power to the autonomous regional government therefore inhibits the creation or implementation of rules or plans concerning Zhuang language or linguistic diversity more generally within GZAR. Moreover, even when/if the power-sharing arrangement between GZAR and the Central Government is legally completed, GZAR law-makers will remain bound to seek approval from the National People's Congress whenever they exercise their legal power to adapt national laws to regional conditions. This may further stymie language policy.

Moreover, not only does Article 4 of the *Constitution*, in which the basic minority language freedom is granted, phrase legitimate minority freedoms as localized. It limits Zhuang language policy-making in another way. In referring to the autonomous areas, for example noting that any assistance given for realizing Article 4 will be directed to "areas inhabited by minority nationalities", Article 4 anticipates that it will be operationalized only within those areas. This means that if the GZAR, Wenshan and Lianshan governments do little to support free use and development of Zhuang in their territories, superior governments and governments in other territories are not expected to respond. However, the areas inhabited by minority nationalities have changed, both in location and in the proportions of areal populations who are from minority minzu. In 1982, when the current *Constitution* was promulgated, freedom of movement in China was limited. Nowadays, urbanization and interprovincial migration undermine the predictability of who lives where and who speaks what. In this regard, the PRC is like many other parts of the world: Blommaert and Rampton (2011: 1) have observed a breakdown of the "ethnic minority paradigm" elsewhere. However, in the PRC, the paradigm persists in these state structures. The areas that count as inhabited by minority nationalities for the purposes of the *Constitution* remain those formally recognized as such, i.e. they are the territories which were given nominal self-government because minority peoples were living there in high concentrations, often without high Hanzu population density, in the mid twentieth century.

Let us look at the example of Lianshan County. Chapter Two noted that under one fifth of the Zhuangzu living in Guangdong Province are in Lianshan.

That is, four-fifths of the Guangdong Zhuangzu live in areas that are not under autonomous Zhuangzu local government but rather under the prefectural and county branches of the Guangdong Provincial Government. For these large numbers of Zhuangzu people, their provincial and sub-provincial governments are not tasked with operationalizing the constitutional language freedom at all. Rather, all Zhuangzu people living outside the nominally autonomous Zhuangzu territories – Lianshan, Wenshan and GZAR – fall outside the scope of the language governance framework. Their interests in using or developing Zhuang language are therefore not represented in the territorialized governance system. In this sense, the system "assume[s] a spatial 'fixedness'" that Blommaert (2004: 56) has argued also pervades international law's linguistic rights framework and global scholarship. He argues that this reinforces a belief that minority languages only have local functionality and that their speakers are essentially tied to territories, such that the people and the languages are "kept in place" (pp. 57–58). I apply this criticism to the PRC: the legal structuring of minority languages as co-extensive with recognized minority polities and those polities' official territories limits the application of the constitutional language freedom and the language governance framework derived from it. Thus, not only are minority language rights in China not legal entitlements for individuals, as Chapter Three explained, but also these minority language rights have territorial limitations. This means that China's language rights suffer both the personality and territorial limitations to which Schiffman (1996: 30) drew attention in his pioneering theoriziation of language policy, following Kloss' (1965) earlier work on schemas of nationality.

The territorial and discursive delimitation of legitimate Zhuang language use and language governance are reinforced by the institutional structures for the representation of Zhuang interests.

5.2 Institutional boundaries in Zhuang language governance

The contemporary political philosophy of the PRC is self-described as socialist modernization, a people's democratic dictatorship, and democratic centralism. While none of these names mean the same thing as liberal democracy, both liberal democracies and the international organizations modelled on them share some approaches to language governance with the PRC, not least because there was a global discourse about language governance during the early and mid-twentieth century from which the PRC and its forebears were not insulated. Many models, challenges and critiques of language policy overlap across various types of political system. For example, the nature of minority language rights as freedoms, as Chapter Three has shown is the approach in the PRC, is not unusual compared to minority language rights in international law dating from a similar time. In addition, giving official recognition to languages is a common governmental response, as is the reliance on constitutions and symbolic jurisprudence rather than operative legislation in language policy (for both trends, see the many examples in Leung [2019]). The territorialization of language rights is also a common governmental response, see e.g. *the UN Declaration on the Rights of Persons Belonging to National or Ethnic, Religious and Linguistic Minorities* (UN General Assembly 1992). Nor is China alone in its language policy focus on state-led standardization, in facing either difficulties protecting individuals' as well as groups' linguistic interests, or in mitigating the tyranny of the majority over linguistic minorities. Almost all language policy the world over is vulnerable to critiques of essentialism and of certain types of practical failure because of its reliance – often naturalized to the point of invisibility – on an ideology of languages as discrete and bounded natural objects, and often also on an ideology favouring a one-to-one correspondence of language, culture and territory. This is in part because almost all linguists and policy-makers in the natiin-state era accepted these ideologies up until the late twentieth century, and also because modern democracy emerged later than language governance. Thus, when Jaffe (2004: 276) noted that essentialism often obtains when a polity is structured around "unity in diversity", may sound like she is referring to China but she is talking about the European Union, which has a similar political and legal discourse in this respect.

Where China's difference in language governance is most evident, and where this chapter's analysis therefore stands to make an important contribution, is in its structures for representing the interests of linguistic minorities. This is especially timely given language rights scholars' emerging focus on the theme of participation (e.g. Mowbray 2012; Ricento 2015; Shohamy 2006: 74; Van Parijs 2000). This Section will first look at representation in terms of minority minzu participants within organs of governance, and then look at representation in terms of the use of minority languages by organs of governance.

5.2.1 Representation through the participation of minority minzu within organs of governance

First, some basics about the organization of the government in China. The Chinese government structure has, at its core, two types of institution: first, the legislative and administrative organs of the state and second, the organs of the Communist Party of China (CPC). This is commonly called a "Party-State" model (e.g. Cartier 2015a). Much of the Party-State's structuring of power and responsibility is achieved by China's *Constitution* in its chapter on the structure of the state (Chapter III), but some power and responsibility is organized by the *Constitution of the Communist Party of China* (National Congress of the Communist Party of China, 2007: "*Constitution of the CPC*"). That *Constitution of the CPC* is not a law made by the national legislature but rather a rule adopted by the Congress of the CPC, a meeting which is held every five years. Specifically, the *Constitution of the CPC* was adopted by in 1982 by the 18th Congress of the CPC, i.e. it was adopted in the same year that China's current *Constitution* was enacted by the National People's Congress. It has been revised and re-adopted since, including just before my fieldwork in 2012, and just after my fieldwork in 2017.

The Party organs sit parallel to, and sometimes above, state organs in the institutionalized hierarchy of governing power (see e.g. Blachford 2004: 103). In addition, there is a Party Committee within every state organ. These committees check that the actions each organ will take are politically correct, and they have great influence. In this way, the Party has extensive, formal power in governance. Moreover, we should theorize that Party organs have "symbolic power" (Bourdieu 1977b, 1991) in addition to their formally allocated power. Furthermore, the integral role of the Party has recently been explicitly integrated into the state structure through a 2018 amendment to Article 36 of the *Constitution* which adds "中国共产党领导是中国特色社会主义最本质的特征" [The defining feature of socialism with Chinese characteristics is the leadership of the Communist Party of China] (Wei 2018).

Both Party and state organizations are arranged in multi-tiered structures, with a central tier at the top, provincial and autonomous regional organizations populating the first sub-national tier, and prefectural, county, town and village organizations ranking below them. Directives/orders flow downwards across the tiers. Within these Party-State structures, the governance of minority languages generally and of Zhuang specifically has an organized place rather than being totally excluded. Nevertheless, Zhuang language governance is organized across a fractured array of discrete Party and state organs. I have developed the organizational chart in Figure 13 to show this. The organizational chart illustrates not only which organs are involved in Zhuang language governance, but just how complicated the language governance framework is. Some of these organs have mandates to govern Zhuang language or to govern minority languages more generally. Other organs represent the Zhuangzu people through quotas and other forms of structured representation for minority minzu, and thus will potentially deal with Zhuang language. The most important point, from the perspective of this study, is that this fracturing creates a system in which the organs governing minority affairs and/or Zhuang language are marginalized *within* the Party-State.

In Figure 13, the organs at the central (i.e. national) tier are shown as separated from the regional/provincial organs. At this lower tier, there are organs involved in Zhuang language governance within both Yunnan Province (lower left-hand side) and GZAR (lower right-hand side). The sub-regional tiers are not shown. That is, the top half of Figure 13 charts the array of Party-State organs that govern minority languages across the PRC while the lower half charts the array of organs formally involved in governing Zhuang within specific, smaller areas. Those organs which are part of the Party structure have been shown with square corners; those which are state legislative or administrative organs have round corners (but remember even these have Party committees); and those with a formal place in both structures have both corners.

The dotted lines represent the formal advisory and supervisory connections between these governing organs; they are multiple and overlapping. Blachford (2004: 103), describes the "triple leadership" of the Party, the Central Government, and the national minority work organizations in implementing language policy. Through the lines on the chart, the complexity of this system of triple leadership is visualized. I argue that this top-down triplication obscures the lines of accountability and the interests to be represented, which can aggravate the limitations in accountability and representation of Zhuang language interests created by the fracturing of language governance across so many organs, siloed from one another, with so few Zhuangzu representatives. To elaborate this argument, I will explain each key organ and its connection to Zhuang people and language in turn, starting from the highest.

In the topmost positions on the chart are the highest ranking organs, starting with the Party Central Committee. It is "the locus of political power" (MacroPolo 2020). The Party Central Committee has a United Front Work Department which is extremely powerful in both the formal Party-State and symbolic hierarchies. It sits above the National People's Congress (NPC, the national legislature) most of the time. When the NPC is in plenary session, however, the plenary NPC then constitutes one of the two highest authorities in the Party structure (the other being the Party Central Committee itself), following Article 10(3) of the *Constitution of the CPC*. Within the state structure, the NPC sits at the apex of a pyramid of people's congresses and "all administrative, supervisory, judicial and procuratorial organs of the state are created by the people's congresses" (National People's Congress 2020). Further, the NPC has the sole authority to amend the PRC's *Constitution*. However:

> despite what the *Constitution* says, only the Party [Central Committee] can initiate the constitutional amendment process. In 2014, this long-standing practice was memorialized in a key

Party policy document, the *Decision Concerning Several Major Issues in Comprehensively Advancing Governance According to Law*. [...It] effectively forecloses any possibility that the NPC would consider any constitutional amendment proposed by a group of NPC delegates, as allowed under the *Constitution*. (NPC Observer 2017)

The NCP therefore has both high-level Party and state authority, which Figure 13 shows by giving it both square (Party) and round (state) corners, but remains less powerful than the Party Central Committee.

Further, my close reading of the *Constitution* and the *Constitution of the CPC* confirms Kaup's (2000: 114) comment that "no [...] quotas exist on the ethnic makeup of Party organizations". This means there are no formal mechanisms guaranteeing the inclusion of Zhuangzu members (or other minority peoples) in the Party Central Committee and the United Front Work Department, nor in lower ranking Party organs. Despite the lack of formally guaranteed inclusion of minorities, Blachford (2004: 103) argues that it is the national United Front Work Department of the Party Central Committee which shapes the broad outlines of minority policies. She explains that while the United Front Work Department works with the Chinese People's Political Consultative Conference (an organ I will introduce below), the United Front Work Department is "the most direct link between the CPC leadership and the national minorities". Its influence comes via this liaison function, rather than any major decision-making function.

In contrast to the lack of structured representation of the minority minzu in the Party organs, the representation of diverse interests is structured into various state organs, including the NPC. The NPC represents diverse interests by being formed of deputies elected by geographic units and from the armed forces (China Encyclopedia Compilation Group 2008: 64–68), but not through the election of representatives of each minzu. Deputies who are members of minority minzu are more likely to be elected as representatives in geographic units with high minority minzu populations and/or with minzu self-government. For instance, a Zhuangzu deputy is much more likely to be elected to represent GZAR than its north-east neighboring province, Hunan, in which few Zhuangzu live and in which there are no Zhuangzu autonomous areas. At the time of the study, the NPC included 409 minority minzu deputies, of almost 3000 deputies (National People's Congress 2013, 2016). Of GZAR's 91 deputies, 41 were Zhuangzu, and there were four other Zhuangzu deputies representing Henan (1), Guangdong (1) and Yunnan (2) Provinces. At the time of writing, the number of minority minzu deputies has increased to 439 (their names, electorates and minzu are accessible at https://zh.wikipedia.org/wiki/第十三届全国人民代表大会代表名单).

However, recent official statements promote the NPC's increasing inclusion of working migrants, young people and women, but not its inclusion of minorities (e.g. National People's Congress 2013). This suggests that minzu diversity is nowadays not especially salient to the NPC's legitimacy, while these other forms of diversity remain, or have become, salient. Likewise, the current *Constitution* removed earlier quotas for minority NPC deputies. The current *Constitution's* Article 59 merely states "[a]ll the minority nationalities are entitled to appropriate representation" whereas the 1954 *Constitution*, for example, directed that "The number of deputies to the National People's Congress, including those representing minority nationalities" was to be prescribed in electoral laws (Article 23). The current *Electoral Law of The National People's Congress and Local People's Congresses of the PRC* (National People's Congress 1979: Ch IV) mandates minority representation only for local congresses but not for regional or national people's congresses.

In addition to its plenary assembly and a Standing Committee of full-time legislators, the NCP has a number of special committees through which "guidance" is provided from higher Party organs to the NPC (Yabuki and Harner 1999: 35). Each committee is made up of NPC deputies. These special committees "examine, discuss and draw up relevant bills and draft resolutions under the direction of the National People's Congress and its Standing Committee", as per Article 70 of the *Constitution*. Article 70 mandates that one of these committees is the 全国人民代表大会民族委员会 'NPC Ethnic Affairs Committee'. This Ethnic Affairs Committee is tasked with providing the NPC guidance on minority minzu affairs. This structure allows for language issues, including Zhuang language interests, to be considered at the national level of government. A version of this committee has existed since the first PRC *Constitution* (Kaup 2000: 80), except during the Cultural Revolution; it was previously known in English as the Nationalities Committee.

However, the organization of the NPC's special committees results in minority issues being structurally separated from – and positioned as contrastive to – the focus of the other NPC committees, e.g. the Constitution and Law Committee, Financial and Economic Affairs Committee, and Education, Science, Culture and Public Health Committee. That is, minority affairs such as Zhuang language issues are considered by the NPC separately to legal, economic, cultural or public health issues. Economic issues, in particular, are a high priority and the Financial and Economic Affairs Committee therefore informally holds more than its formal share of power. Moreover, the Ethnic Affairs Committee has been criticized for its limited actual role in "minority work" (Kaup 2000: 80). This is perhaps because the members of the Ethnic Affairs Committee feel beholden to and constrained by the NPC and/or the Party (i.e. elite capture) and also because deputies are not able to be held accountable by the Zhuangzu via popular elections.

Another powerful, national organ of government is the Chinese People's Political Consultative Conference (CPPCC). The CPPCC's purpose is to advise the legislature i.e. the NPC. It has no direct equivalent in the Westminster or Washington-derived systems with which Anglophone readers may be more familiar. The CPPCC is partly but not entirely a Party organ. Its structure is not spelled out in Chapter III of the *Constitution*, which is dedicated to the structure of the state. The *Constitution's* Preamble, however, presents the CPPCC's place within the united front of efforts under the Party's leadership;

> In the long years of revolution and construction, there has been formed under the leadership of the Communist Party of China a broad patriotic united front which is composed of the democratic parties and people's organizations [...] The Chinese People's Political Consultative Conference, **a broadly based representative organization of the united front** which has played a significant historical role, will play a still more important role in the country's political and social life, in promoting friendship with other countries and in the struggle for socialist modernization and for the reunification and unity of the country.
> [My emphasis.]

The CPPCC's structures of minzu representation are different to either the United Front Work Department or the NPC. To fulfill its role as a representative organization, the CPPCC includes representatives of certain polities and interest groups, elected for 5-year terms. The General Principles of the *Charter of the CPPCC* (National Committee of the CPPCC, 1982: "*CPPCC Charter*") declare these representatives to include the CPC in a leading role and "other political parties, public figures without party affiliation, people's organizations, *ethnic minorities*, and patriots from all sectors of society [...] compatriots from the Hong Kong Special Administrative Region, compatriots from the Macao Special Administrative Region, compatriots from Taiwan, and overseas Chinese" [my emphasis]. Having read the *CPPCC Charter*, however, there do not appear to be rules to enforce this representation of ethnic minorities. Rather, the relative composition of the CPPCC chamber is a matter of convention, with the CPC and allied parties conventionally holding over two-thirds of the seats. During the study and continuing today, one of the CPPCC's Vice Chairs is Mr Ma Biao, a Zhuangzu from GZAR. Mr Ma is also a full member of the Party Central Committee, a former GZAR Governor and a former Deputy Party Secretary of the Guangxi Regional CPC Committee (MacroPolo 2020); this is rare amongst the Zhungzu.

The CPPCC has committees under it including the 民族和宗教委员会 'Committee for Ethnic and Religious Affairs', not to be confused with the NPC's Ethnic Affairs Committee. This is another organ with the potential to be formally involved in Zhuang language governance at the national level. The CPPCC also oversees a National Committee and regional CPPCC committees for GZAR and other provinces and regions. This National Committee must include minority minzu representatives (*CPPCC Charter*, Article 22). Both the national and regional CPPCC committees have Standing Committees, whose members are elected from

5.2 Institutional boundaries in Zhuang language governance — 121

the plenary of the national or regional committee and who are nominated by, amongst others, the minority minzu (*CPPCC Charter*, Articles 45 and 56). Whether the regional committees have diversity quotas, and who they include, is decided locally by each regional committee's Standing Committee in consultation with the Chairperson's Council of the outgoing committee (*CPPCC Charter*, Article 51). Thus, overall, there is more representation of the interests of the Zhuangzu ensured in the CPPCC and in its committees than in the NPC.

Another important state organ for dealing with minority interests sits within the committees of the State Council. The State Council is the last major national government organ on the chart to introduce. It ranks below the NPC. Its role is state administration, rather than making legislation. The State Council nevertheless plays a formal role in law-making, with its regulations "serv[ing] as direct legal bases for rules formulated by departments under the State Council as well as local government regulations [...providing] a connecting link between national laws on the one hand and departmental rules as well as local government regulations" (Wang 2005: 78).

The State Council oversees a number of commissions (see further Jakobson and Manuel 2016: 103; Manuel 2015). Of these, the 中华人民共和国国家民族事务委员会 'National Ethnic Affairs Commission of the PRC' (NEAC) is the national institution most relevant to Zhuang language as it deals with minority minzu cultural and linguistic research and heritage protection. This Commission is often abbreviated to NAC in the literature, reflecting its older name, the Nationalities Affairs Commission. Although the NEAC A.K.A. NAC is a commission of the State Council, a position somewhat like a Ministry, it is also formally under the leadership of the United Front Work Department, and the Party Central Committee overseas the NEAC through inspections (Baidu 2019). Moreover, both the Party's United Front Work Department and the CPPCC send guidelines to the NEAC to implement (Blachford 2004: 103). Thus, the NEAC's policy direction is largely top-down not bottom-up. This does not preclude the representation of Zhuangzu interests but necessarily transmutes them through a filter of that which the Party thinks is best for the Zhuangzu.

Moving to the lower ranks and lower part of the chart, the NEAC oversees regional Ethnic Affairs Commissions, including the GZAR Ethnic Affairs Commission (GEAC) and its counterpart in Yunnan Province, YEAC. This structure allows the state to approximate local issues, including local linguistic issues. The NEAC, GEAC and YEAC are important structures for Zhuang language governance: Kaup (2000: 80) argues, "[t]he bulk of day-to-day minority affairs is assumed by the State Council's Nationalities Affairs Commission [now NEAC] and its local branches." However, there is not structured representation of the Zhuangzu within the NEAC.

Some of the NEAC's lower tier commissions oversee or sit alongside a regional minority language agency; these agencies are the governing organs most directly connected to minority language issues. They are colloquially called 民语委 or 民语文 (both 'Minority Language Commission'). The GZAR Minority Language Commission sits at the same, regional rank as the GEAC while its equivalent in Yunnan sits below the YEAC, as Figure 13 shows. Before the 1980s, when the GZAR Minority Language Commission was established, a number of language work organs to oversee and institutionalize Zhuang language were formed and disbanded (see further Li and Huang 2004: 244). Throughout, these agencies' centered on script development, as the GZAR Minority Language Commission still does. Its forerunner (the Minority Language Work Commission) reached a highpoint of power and functional load when GZAR was named an autonomous region in 1958. The Minority Language Work Commission was then chaired by GZAR's Vice-Governor, had 151 language workers, and ran the *Zhuang News* newspaper and a school with 1500 employees. That Commission was disbanded twice in the 1960–70s, opening with a reduced staff in between. It was re-established in the 1980s with 25–35 staff, renamed the Steering Committee for the Zhuang Writing System, and later stripped of its supervisory functions in regards to promoting Zhuang writing and strengthening primary education in Zhuang communities (Li and Huang 2004: 244). The GZAR Minority Language Commission now only "coordinates the promotion of the Zhuang writing system among [the] various [GZAR government] departments" (Li and Huang 2004: 244). Moreover, while the GZAR Minority Language Commission includes government officials from various GZAR-level departments (Li and Huang 2004: 244), they are not being replaced when they retire (Kaup 2000: 143). Nevertheless, the GZAR Minority Language Commission remains a symbolically important player in Zhuang language governance, despite its waning power, and the GEAC remains both formally and symbolically important.

There is also a Municipal Minority Language Writing Committee for Nanning City, the capital of GZAR, which is an administrative department of the municipal government. It was formerly known as Nanning Municipal Zhuangwen Promotion Work Committee (南宁市推行壮文工作委员会, from 1986) then Nanning Municipal Minority Language and Writing Work Committee (南宁市壮语言文字工作委员会, from 2001–2010.) After the fieldwork in this study, its admisistrative role was subsumed into the Nanning Municipal Ethnic and Religious Affairs Commission, in January 2019. Meanwhile, the pre-2019 Minority Language and Writing Work Committee was reformed into the Nanning Minority Language Service Center (南宁市少数民族语言文字服务中心), which was classed as a public welfare agency with no administrative functions. Its organizational structure was still under review in late 2019 (Nanning Municipal Minority Language Works Commission 2019: §1.2).

This fractured array gets yet more complicated. In addition to the national and regional ethnic affairs and minority language organs, the national Ministry of Education, which sits under the State Council, has its own Bureau of Minority Education to regulate minority language schooling nationally and oversees provincial/regional education departments (Figure 13, right-hand side). Finally, separate from the NEAC and the Ministry of Education, a national agency called the State Language Commission is tasked with spreading Putonghua (Blachford 2004: 104). Amongst other things, this means that the people who govern minority affairs are not the people responsible for schooling or for promoting Putonghua. Thus, for example, the effect on Zhuang of the popularization of Putonghua in schools is not a responsibility nor necessarily even a concern of education officials.

In addition, at the regional level, the GZAR People's Congress, as well as GZAR's subordinate municipal and prefectural congresses, are authorized to regulate aspects of language use if they choose. These state organs have Zhuangzu and other minority minzu quotas. In particular, at least one of the Chairmen and Vice-Chairmen of the Standing Committee of the GZAR People's Congress must be Zhuangzu and the "head" of GZAR – i.e. the governor – must also be Zhuangzu (State Council Information Office of the PRC 2005b: II(3)). Further, the Zhuangzu and other minority minzu in GZAR must be represented in "appropriate number[s]" in the GZAR Government and its subsidiary organs (State Council Information Office of the PRC 2005b: II(3)). Whether this means representation in direct proportion to the population of GZAR, according to which roughly one third of GZAR government officials should be Zhuangzu, or some other appropriate number of representatives, is not clear.

Whatever the exact number of Zhuangzu in the GZAR Government, these quotas are a significant structure through which minority people can access some of the power to govern. Yet, even with this formalized minority representation, I found little evidence that the GZAR Congress and its subsidiary assemblies and departments actually regulate aspects of language use. Providing a rare example, Li and Huang (2004: 247) describe two official GZAR circulars from 1984 and 1991 requesting that GZAR government organizations use bilingual Putonghua-Zhuang signage. In addition, I found that in 2004, the Nanning Municipal Government issued interim provisions regulating the format of Putonghua-Zhuang signage (Nanning Municipal People's Government 2004), converting these into law in 2013. Nanning is GZAR's capital city. In 2018, the GZAR People's Congress enacted a similar law at the regional level: 广西壮族自治区少数民族语言文字工作条例 '*GZAR Minority Language Work Regulations*' (Standing Committee of the People's Congress of GZAR 2018: "*GZAR Regulations*"). In Part Three, I empirically explore the presence of the signage governed by these two circulars and GZAr and Nanning's laws.

However, after systematic searches of GZAR law databases, government websites and Chinese journal articles, I found there were no other GZAR or sub-GZAR laws concerning Zhuang language that were available to researchers. Much like the limited access to case records that I discussed in Chapter Four, not all legislation at the GZAR level is made publicly accessible. There may therefore be some other laws "on the books" that I was unable to collect, but such legislation would also be inaccessible to Zhuang speakers who wished to rely upon it as a legal or advocacy resource. This suggests that very little Zhuang language policy or regulation has arisen from the structured inclusion of Zhuangzu people in some of GZAR's governing bodies. This is likely both a result of the hard-to-coordinate structures of power, mapped above, and certain beliefs about the role of government and law in relation to Zhuang language, which I have analyzed in Chapter Four. Nevertheless, the Party-State organs analyzed here have their own language practices which are not only a form of communication but also another form of representation, separate to the structured participation of Zhuangzu people examined above, and so it is to the use of Zhuang language for governing that I now turn.

5.2.2 Representation through using minority languages within organs of governance

Political representation includes the presence of a language in the working of governance organs. In China, this is achieved by the NPC, which still provides translation and simultaneous interpreting of its proceedings in Standard Zhuang and other minority languages (reported by Mr K, Mr D, Mr E). Initially, GZAR and lower-tier Zhuangzu autonomous governments, like that of the Wenshan Prefectural Government in Yunnan Province, were also obliged to operate in the medium of Zhuang, following Article 71 of the 1954 *Constitution*. There was no equivalent constitutional rule between 1975 and 1978 (compare National People's Congress 1975 and de Heer 1978: 375), and the rule was removed again when the current *Constitution* was enacted in 1982. Now, the *Constitution* provides:

> Article 121: 民族自治地方的自治机关在执行职务的时候，依照本民族自治地方自治条例的规定，使用当地通用的一种或者几种语言文字。(中华人民共和国中央人民政府 1982)
>
> [In performing their functions, the organs of self-government of the national autonomous areas, in accordance with the autonomy regulations of the respective areas, employ the spoken and written language or languages in common use in the locality.]

This provision does not make clear whether this is a normative guideline promoting the use of local languages, or simply an acknowledgement that actual use of local languages by local government officials happens and is allowed. Moreover, this provision has to operate alongside the *Putonghua Law's* direction that Putonghua "shall be used by state organs as the official language, except where otherwise provided for in laws" (Article 9). A *White Paper* (State Council Information Office of the PRC 2005b: III(3)) sheds some light: "the organs of self-government of such areas *shall* use one or more commonly used local languages when they are performing official duties" [my emphasis], but only if this is in accordance with "the provisions of the self-government regulations for ethnic autonomous areas". There do not appear to be such regulations in GZAR, although in certain sub-regional areas the cadres are still encouraged to be trained in Zhuang under the *Opinions on Promoting Bilingual Study in Ethnic Areas-Implementation Plan* (Nanning Municipal Minority Language Works Commission 2019: §1.9). In so far as those areas may have speakers of the many minority languages known to be used in GZAR (see Figure 10), and if GZAR's regional government organs were permitted by regulations to operate bilingually, the *White Paper* explains that "the language of the ethnic group exercising regional autonomy [i.e. Zhuang] should be used primarily" (State Council Information Office of the PRC 2005b).

There is no question of Article 121 *obliging* GZAR's government organs to use Zhuang language; at best it merely permits the use of Zhuang. Participants Mr D and Mr E reported that, to their (considerable) knowledge, Zhuang is not used as a working language within the GZAR People's Congress or other GZAR government organs (Follow-up correspondence 14 November 2019). Monitoring or encouraging the use of Zhuang language in these GZAR government institutions is one role of the GZAR language governance organs introduced in the last section; that Zhuang is not a working language of the government in GZAR is an indication of the weakness of those institutions.

Nevertheless, since 1990, there has been a Zhuang branch of the Central Government's Bureau of Translation in Nanning, with about twenty staff (Li and Huang 2004: 245). Only seven of China's minority languages have these services (Li and Huang 2004: 254). This staff translates works by Karl Marx, Chairman Mao and other political philosophers into Zhuang, translates documents from the NPC and CPPCC and the Party's National Conference, and simultaneously interprets congressional sessions in the Hall of the People's Congress in Beijing. The purpose, on Li and Huang's (2004: 249) analysis, is to "reflect the equal status of Zhuang in the political life of the PRC", i.e. state-sponsored translation is seen (by those authors) as a symbolic resource in discourses of formal equality. In my view, this service enables Zhuang language to participate in a formally equal way in the outputs of governance, but without equality of input into governance over Zhuang language.

5.2.3 Perceptions of the structure of Zhuang language governance

While I find good cause to criticize the geographical and institutional structures of minority language governance, not all participants viewed these structures as deficient in their representation of Zhuangzu and/or Zhuang language interests. This is consistent with the last chapter's presentation of diverse participant views on whether the constitutional minority language freedom itself was weak, or whether Zhuang speakers had failed to mobilize to have it better implemented. Pushing for, let alone achieving, political change in the implementation of the constitutional language freedom is, in my view, made difficult by the problems I have raised with the structure of Zhuangzu representation. What participants perceived was that the same representative structures had led to differing regional applications of the national language governance texts. As I have noted above, the GZAR government is structured to include a quota of Zhuangzu people, while provincial governments are not. We might therefore predict that regional variation will show the GZAR government applying the constitutional language freedom more or better than provincial governments. This was not participants' impression; for them, regardless of the quotas in GZAR, the major problem lay in who was in the GZAR government and what that government prioritized.

Regional governance variation arose especially in discussions over a recent law concerning Zhuang and other local minority languages in Yunnan: the 云南省少数民族语言文字工作条例 '*Yunnan Province Minority Minzu Language and Script Work Ordinance*' (Standing Committee of Yunnan's People's Congress 2013: "*Yunnan Ordinance*"). I obtained a hard copy of the *Yunnan Ordinance* during fieldwork. This ordinance was enacted with a purpose:

> 一．为了加强少数民族语言文字工作，保障各少数民族使用和发展本民族语言文字的权利，保护和抢救少数民族传统文化，促进民族团结进步和少数民族文化 繁荣发展[……]。
>
> [1. To strengthen minority language and script work; safeguard each minority minzu's right to use and develop their language and script; to protect and salvage minority minzu traditional culture; to advance Minzu Solidarity and thriving minority minzu cultural development [...].]

In addition, another listed purpose of the *Yunnan Ordinance* is script development. This has long been a common emphasis in the regional implementation of the freedom to use and develop a minority language. I noted this emphasis above in the history of the GZAR Minority Language Commission, and noted the national language policy emphasis on script development in Chapter One. The *Yunnan Ordinance's* purposes illustrate the influence at the regional/provincial tier of government of the discourses in national laws and policies about the economic and cultural development of languages; they clearly shape the representation of minority language interests in the extract and in the document overall for example in its reference to "cultural development".

At the time of this research, the *Yunnan Ordinance* had not been translated into detailed regulations and impacts on public or educational language usage were not observed. However, to many of my participants, the Yunnan Government was active in minority language protection, as represented by the *Yunnan Ordinance*, and this served to highlight the relative inactivity in GZAR. Language Leader participants in both Yunnan and GZAR saw this *Yunnan Ordinance* as beneficial to Zhuang language and reported that the GZAR government had sent personnel to Yunnan to study this "很前卫" [*avant guarde*] law, as Mr A, a government minority language translator in Yunnan, described it. Participants understood that these GZAR officials had ultimately been unable to gain support within GZAR's Party-State organs for a similar law. The academic who gave me the *Yunnan Ordinance* and the participants who were aware of it attributed its successful passage into law in Yunnan to an individual politician, rather than to formal governance structures (field notes 12 June 2014). These participants usually believed that GZAR lacked an equivalent individual to turn that region's potential for language governance into action:

Excerpt 5-1

Mr N: 对，没有成功。广西的主席他不敢做这个事情，中央都把自治权给你了，广西的主席要说一句干，谁能拦得住。

[Mr N: Yes, it did not succeed. The Chairman of Guangxi does not dare do such things, the Center gives you autonomous governance rights, the Chairman of Guangxi will say some dry words, and hope that it will hold back the river.]

Similarly, Mr A expressed his surprise that the comparatively higher formal status of the GZAR Minority Language Commission compared to the Yunnan Minority Language Commission had not resulted in more actual power to support the introduction of an equivalent ordinance in GZAR. These views portray a concrete example of the structural weaknesses in representation and the organization of governing power that I identified earlier in this chapter. In the next section, a more detailed examination of language governance at the regional level is offered, focusing on GZAR's implementation of the freedom to use and develop Zhuang within the context of education.

5.3 A close up: The constrained governance of Zhuang in education in GZAR

This section offers a close-up examination of how the limitations of the *Constitution* and national structures of language governance play out in terms of education policy within GZAR. It reveals a significant discontinuity between the positive rhetoric regarding the freedom and equality of minority languages in national laws and policies, and the dearth of detailed local laws and policies to actively protect, or to normatively reproduce, this freedom and equality. Rather, we see the anticipated legal problems borne out. These laws do not entirely marginalize Zhuang, but frame it squarely within the developmentalist value system identified in national laws in Chapter Four. Reproducing the national discourses' hierarchy, Putonghua, not Zhuang, is associated with development in GZAR's education policies. Moreover, the lack of actionability of the minority language right analyzed in Chapter Three, as well as the fracturing of representation of Zhuang interests analyzed above, has made it hard for advocates of education reform to better protect Zhuang. Meanwhile, local decision-makers have been weakened by being separated from strong funding bases.

The national Ministry of Education directs – in some cases, jointly with the national NEAC – the specialized minzu universities (Blachford 2004: 103–105). By contrast, bilingual primary and secondary schooling is a localized policy decision of the GZAR Department of Education and its local subordinates (State Council Information Office of the PRC 2005b: III(7)), although they must take account of the national education policies. Chapter Four showed how those national policies frame bilingual education as an instrument of development, reproducing the general developmentalism of the language governance framework. Tsung (2014: 162), in an overview of minority education across China, found that there was great variability attributable to "the Party-state's ambivalent attitude toward bilingual education".

Following this national developmentalist orientation and ambivalence, the choices made by GZAR decision-makers are overwhelmingly for monolingual schooling in the national language. They do, however, choose bilingual schooling for a small number of communities. To support these bilingual schools, there have been prefecture- and county-level institutions training Zhuang-speaking teachers for rural primary and middle schools, and a regional institution for training Zhuang secondary school teachers, since the 1980s (Li and Huang 2004: 245). However, most often the form of bilingual schooling chosen is a form that becomes monolingual in Putonghua i.e. a transitional second language acquisition model. Putonghua – or at least an approximation of Putonghua – is introduced at most of GZAR's bilingual schools from Grade One in order to "fulfil the targets in the curriculum made by the Ministry of Education" with Zhuang retired to an auxiliary language role by Grade Four–Five (Kaup 2000: 145; Li and Huang 2004: 248; see also Wang and Phillion 2009: 1). Scholars of education in GZAR say that "subtractive bilingualism" often arises at these bilingual schools because of the "coercive power relationship" between Putonghua and Zhuang (Feng and Sunuodula 2009: 691; see also Adamson and Feng 2009: 325). Moreover, both in the very early years and later in its auxiliary role, Zhuang is typically used only in oral form; bilingual schooling is not necessarily bi-literate schooling. This surely contributes to literacy in Zhuang remaining low, as Chapter Two reported. A reliance on Putonghua in early schooling for children who have not yet sufficiently learnt the basics of first-language literacy could also be a reason for Zhuangzu people's relatively high illiteracy rates in Putonghua.

GZAR's Putonghua-Zhuang bilingual primary schools are mainly located outside of urban areas. Zhuang education specialist, Mr F, reported that 80% of rural primary schools in GZAR were using a minority language to start with. By contrast, in a relatively recent study, Zhuang student interviewees from cities and towns reported having Putonghua-medium classes from the start of their schooling (Feng and Sunuodula 2009: 691–692). The rural bilingual primary schools include Putonghua-Zhuang schools but also schools using other local minority languages such as Dong, Shui, Miao and Yao. A smaller number of bilingual primary schools in GZAR use Mandarin topolects as the second language in addition to Putonghua, and Mr F associated that type with towns.

This transitional bilingual schooling is at odds with the purpose certain participants saw for bilingual education. For example, Mr F's research expertise is GZAR's bilingual education, and he explained its purpose as passing on traditional knowledge through language:

Excerpt 5-2

Mr F: 所以就是说我们给领导人说他们要注意这一块的时候，我们也告诉他双语教育的这个根本目的之一也是保持语言文化的长远发展，我们跟他们说不是人拯救文化，是文化拯救人。

[Mr F: So we told the leaders they must pay attention to that bit of time [Zhuang lessons], we also told them bilingual education's fundamental purpose is protecting the language and culture's long-term development, we spoke with them about it not being people who save culture, but the culture saving the people.]

As Excerpt 5-2 indicates, alternative constructions of the value of Zhuang in education are not absent from policy-making discourses in GZAR, but they do not find much purchase. This is likely in part because Mr F's beliefs are not dominant amongst government officials. They may not be widespread amongst Zhuangzu communities, either, as other participants noted a lack of grassroots demand for education in Zhuang. For example, comparing GZAR to the Inner Mongolia Autonomous Region, where he now lives, university student Lloyd explained the two autonomous region's differences in applying the language freedom in official school examination policies as a bottom-up change resulting from people's language abilities and choices.

Excerpt 5-3

Lloyd: 因为法律的话，说肯定是比较照顾到各方面……说尊重少数民族肯定是为了维稳而团结吗，所以说，法律肯定是尊重少数民族的语言权利……像我们，尤其是我现在报司考……我哥们他是[说]……汉语卷还是蒙文卷，但是我估计广西就没有这个选项……我估计很少有人能出出这种有壮语，壮文这样子的卷子，所以说干脆就取消。

[Lloyd: Because, in law, there is certainly more care taken for these aspects [here] ... Take us, in particular: I am now doing exams and my buddy [said] '... take the Hanyu [Mandarin] or the Mongolian exam paper, but I'm guessing in GZAR there isn't a choice ... I'm guessing very few people could produce Zhuang language, [complete the] Zhuang writing paper, so they simply cancel it.]

The unwillingness of the government to increase Zhuang-medium schooling is also because limited budgets encourage GZAR policy-makers to prioritize the economic efficiency of largely monolingual schooling. The proviso in the *Education Law* that minority language-medium schooling be offered "where conditions exist" is indeterminate, as Chapter Three noted. Although it is unclear who holds the power to decide when linguistic conditions exist, these conditions certainly have to match up with funding conditions. The funding conditions for increasing bilingual schooling have not existed in much of GZAR. When the responsibility for funding bilingual Zhuang schools was shifted from the Central government to the typically poorer county governments within GZAR in the late 1980s, counties had to close more than half of them (Kaup 2000: 143). Mr H recalled the next major change:

Excerpt 5-4

Mr H: 到了九几年那个时候，政府感觉这个可能面太宽了一点点，所以又减掉了一部分，到了现在广西可能有三四十所……那个学校用壮文教的

[Mr H: in the 1990s, the government felt that it [Zhuang schooling] might be a little too wide, so it cut a part, so now Guangxi might have 30 or 40 schools ... Those schools use Zhuangwen [Romanized Zhuang] to teach.]

GZAR is now permitted to set a "levy of added local education fee" which will then be managed by county or township governments, under Article 57 of the *Education Law*, enabling local decision-making about the funding of bilingual

5.3 A close up: The constrained governance of Zhuang in education in GZAR 131

schooling. However, whether this levy is collected is not made public, and because Article 57 also establishes that it is to be collected at the township level, there will be little ability to raise these additional funds in poorer areas. If levies were collected across the whole region or prefectures there would be a greater range of household incomes to draw from. Moreover, Article 59 provides that the collection follows "the principle of voluntary and capacity consideration", i.e. locals cannot be compelled to fund local bilingual schools. And Kaup (2000: 137) has reported that minority schools' "teachers and students complained that the mandated government stipends were not reaching them. Villagers often rolled their eyes and said 'yeah, sure' when I mentioned special scholarships that the government supposedly supplies minority students".

However, there has been an increase in funding for some bilingual schools in GZAR. In 2002, the GZAR Department of Education increased the budget for Zhuang-medium instruction (Li and Huang 2004: 253). However, the other key aspect of this 2002 policy change was to close bilingual schools in remote areas, so the scarcity of funding is likely to have continued in the more remote parts of GZAR. The increased budget for Zhuang-medium instruction from 2002 was to facilitate the expansion of a form of bilingual schooling called "experimental schooling" in more densely-populated areas. Mr G, the magazine editor, was very enthusiastic about these experimental schools' development of young people who could speak and read Zhuang. Mr F explained this as nevertheless still being the least common type of bilingual schooling in GZAR, existing in 33 of GZAR's 123 counties. This is similar to Mr H's report, quoted above, of 30–40 Zhuang-medium schools remaining after the 1990s cut back. Mr F further explained the language of instruction at these experimental schools:

Excerpt 5-5

Mr F: [这些]有小学、有初中，它用的是壮文来教，部分那个个人他把国家的那个教材翻译成壮语……然后就对难字难句让小孩知道大致的内容，把它转过来又再讲一遍汉语。

[Mr F: [They have] preschool, primary school, junior high school, they use Zhuang to teach, they translate part of the national curriculum into Zhuang language ... With difficult sentences they [teachers] explain the difficult part word by word in Zhuang and then repeat it in Hanyu.]

That is, Hanyu [Mandarin] rather than Zhuang, is the auxiliary language for some lessons in experimental schools. Nevertheless, other parts of the curriculum, and everything after junior high (middle school), are in taught without Zhuang-medium instruction at these schools. The transition to Putonghua is completed at a higher grade at experimental schools than at the other bilingual schools. The absence of Zhuang-medium secondary schooling has been noticed by those invested in Zhuang literacy, for example the editors of the bilingual *Third of the Third* magazine:

Excerpt 5-6

Mr H: 中等专业学校那个，广西都有四所，四所都全部是教壮文的，但是现在一所都没有了，所以的话我们就少了很多那个作者，现在写的稿件多数是当时读过这个学校的学生毕业以后分到各个岗位上，像当老师啦，在政府部门里面做一点办事员啊。

[Mr H: There were four secondary vocational schools in Guangxi, all four of which were entirely taught in Zhuangwen [Romanized Zhuang], but now there is not even one, so we have a lot fewer [contributing] authors. Most of those writing the manuscripts now are those who had gone to those schools and were assigned to various positions after graduation, like being a teacher, working as a clerk in a government department.]

Mr H also remembered that there had been a drop in Zhuang-medium contributions to *Third of the Third* in the 1990s after the number of primary schools teaching Zhuang had been cut back.

Today, even with some Zhuang-medium primary schooling remaining, the various forms of Putonghua-Zhuang schools in GZAR are "太少了" [too few] in Mr F's view. According to Mr F (25 June 2014), in 2014 there were 72 bilingual primary schools and 25 bilingual middle schools in GZAR overall. That represents an increase in the number of schools, yet Mr F reported only 10,000 students overall in Zhuang bilingual schools which is less than half the 26,000 reported in 2004 by Li (2004: 248). This paucity is backed up by other sources: Zhou (2001: 56) reports that bilingual Zhuang education was not available for much of the second half of the twentieth century. As for this century, I used the most recent data available (from 2004–2005) to calculate the proportion of school-aged children from the Zhuangzu minority who were enrolled at bilingual Putonghua-Zhuang schools in GZAR in the early 2000s and found that the proportion was not quite 1% (Grey 2017: 90). And while the exact student population of bilingual Putonghua-Zhuang schools today might lie between Mr F's 10,000 and Li's 26,000, the perception that Zhuang language has too limited a place in education is not unique to Mr F.

In 2007, "a petition initiated by a group of Zhuang intellectuals and signed by more than 16,000 people called upon the Central Government to make the Zhuang language mandatory for schools in the Region" (Adamson and Feng 2009: 325). It has not resulted in significant policy change so far, consistent with a history of difficulties enacting policy in this space. Thus, as I was writing up this book, a Nanning Government review reported that:

我市壮汉双语教育存在管理体制和壮文教育体系不健全……壮语文课程建设乏力、实验模式单一、壮汉双语教师短缺，教研科研工作滞后等问题……、激励机制不完善等……目前，各相关县区财政均未设立民族教育专项资金，办学经费不足，不利于壮汉双语教育的健康发展。

[Our city's Zhuang-Chinese bilingual education has problems such as incomplete management system [...] weakness in the construction of Zhuang language courses, the single experimental model, the shortage of Zhuang-Chinese bilingual teachers, the lagging of teaching, research and scientific research [...] and an imperfect incentive mechanism.[...] At present, none of the relevant counties and districts have set up special funds for ethnic education, and the funds for running schools are insufficient, which is not conducive to the healthy development of Zhuang-Chinese bilingual education.]

(Nanning Municipal Minority Language Works Commission 2019: §2.4)

The lack of a complete bilingual education policy has arisen in GZAR, Feng and Sunuodula (2009: 691) argue, because "policy documents concerning Zhuang Language were debated, proposed and revised numerous times but were never formally promulgated and implemented". This reflects the low power of the people and institutions representing Zhuang language interests which I identified earlier in this chapter.

GZAR's change in minority education funding in 2002, the petition and the lack of promulgation of new laws about Zhuang in education in GZAR also reflect a reduction over the course of China's era of Opening and Reform, and continuing since, in the structures for supervising language governance in GZAR, especially in regards to education policy. The 2019 Nanning review just quoted goes on to report that Nanning Municipality's bilingual education remains beset by management, supervision and evaluation problems, including the fracturing of pathways to matriculation as counties are not coordinated in terms of where Zhuang-medium primary and secondary bilingual schooling is offered (Nanning Municipal Minority Language Works Commission 2019: §2.4). This has a long history. In 1992, the responsibilities of GZAR's Minority Language Commission were reduced and Central Government funding for Zhuang promotion was transferred from the Commission to the GZAR Department of Education (Kaup 2000: 143). Kaup (2000: 143) reports that just one Department of Education official was tasked with Zhuang promotion after the funding shifted. There have been further changes since. The Zhuang promotion division of the GZAR Department of Education – called the "National [i.e. minzu] Education Department Sawcuengh [i.e. Zhuang] Promotion Office" (see Figure 13) – is now only tasked to "guide and coordinate the work of minority education; formulate and implement special policies and measures for the development of minority education in our region; [... guide] minority bilingual teaching and textbook construction; [and] guid[e] students [in] the education of national unity" (Anon. 2016c). Thus, this Zhuang Promotion Office offers guideance but has little formal control over GZAR's educational regulation, financing, strategy or curricula. Those aspects are dealt with by other divisions of the GZAR Department of Education, including a Policies and Regulations Division and divisions for development planning, basic education, higher education, and occupational education (Anon. 2016c). The Policies and Regulations Division, in particular, has significant formal powers to:

> [s]tudy the strategy of education reform and development [...] Research on major policy issues, education policy information collection, analysis, and summary and reporting work; planning and drafting of local comprehensive education laws and regulations; to undertake the legal construction of the education system and the administrative law of the relevant work; [...] audit work; [... and] administrative litigation work". (Anon. 2016c)

These powers therefore potentially include suggesting language laws and regulations for law-makers to enact, which the Zhuang Promotion Office cannot do.

Moreover, Mr B, a teacher, spoke of those who had attempted to change education policy in GZAR having found that the tension between economic development and other goals of language policy was hard to reconcile in specific, operational policies:

Excerpt 5-7

> Mr B: 现在就业很困难，少数民族不太乐观……现在市场经济，他强调实用价值，经济效益。但是我们少数民族语言在这一块更多的可能是侧重这种文化价值。所以他这种好像不能产生经济效益…所以现在如果是政府不加大扶持力度，再加上我们有个培养的学生不能更好掌握一些知识，以后可能有点比较难办……
> Author: 所以每一个少数民族他们有他们的代表在中央会议嘛？……壮族的代表这些人，他们考虑语言的情况吗？还是考虑我们刚才说的就业的这些问题？他们考虑这样的问题吗？……
> Mr B: 我想他们也会考虑，但是真正要解决起来，可能就业是一个非常复杂的问题。有些专家，有些代表他们可能也会提出这方面的意见或者建议，但是具体要落实的话恐怕还是很难。

> [Mr B: Nowadays employment is very tough, the minority minzu are not very optimistic ... Now the market economy, it emphasizes practical value, economic efficiency. But our minority minzu language, in that regard, it is more likely to focus on cultural value. So they [languages] seem not to be able to produce economic benefits ... So if the government doesn't increase the level of support, and additionally if some of our [Zhuang Studies] students cannot better grasp knowledge, ultimately it's likely to be a bit difficult [to find jobs]...
> Author: So each minority minzu has a CPPCC delegate? ... The Zhuangzu delegates, do they think about language circumstances? ...
> Mr B: I think they also consider them but to really solve it, it's likely employment is a very complicated problem. Some experts, some representatives probably also give some views or suggestions, but the specific implementation is still very hard I'm afraid.]

This is consistent with my analysis in Chapter Four of the competition in laws and policies between the developmentalist language ideology and ideologies of equality/inherent value of languages. Mr B here affirms that the economic

5.3 A close up: The constrained governance of Zhuang in education in GZAR

value system is influential amongst the minzu populace and government, and propagated by the market economy. This political economy was of course absent when minority equality and economic development were first encoded alongside each other in national laws, perhaps mitigating the initial discontinuity between these ideologies. Moreover, Mr B indicates that this tension is not only a potentiality but actual at the level of the CPPCC.

This tension between developmentalism and equality manifests not only because the political economy now assists in constructing economic value as most important, but because the GZAr government, a relatively poor regional government but the nominal protector of Zhuangzu interests, must fund Zhuang language policy initiatives. Mr F had had personal experience in advising GZAR's policy-makers and reported on this economic constraint:

Excerpt 5-8

Mr F: 它这个的有原因少是什么呢……我们政府投入少……老师要多一些……少数民族所在的地方都是比较穷……因为我们是一千多万人口……这个要复杂的东西就多……甚至是几万人的那小民族还不大一样……要做双语教育它用不了几个钱……都不到我们的百分之一…所以很多人都不知道，就说你们的领导人都不同意这样做。我经常接触我们的领导人，我知道那当家的也难……广西都比广东穷。

[Mr F: Why is it [Zhuang bilingual schooling] so small? ... Our government invests a small amount ... more teachers are needed [...and] all the minority minzu areas are relatively poor ... Because our population is over 10 million ... That complicates things a lot ... even those minority minzu with tens of thousands of people are not as big ... for them to have bilingual education costs a few bucks ... they're all not even one percent of us ... So many people don't know, they say your leaders won't agree to do the same [bilingual education]. I often contact our leaders; I know it's difficult ... Guangxi is a lot poorer than Guangdong.]

Nevertheless, money *has* been forthcoming from the GZAR Government for publishing the bilingual Zhuang-Putonghua *Third of the Third* periodical about minority minzu culture. I will discuss this magazine's readership and its changing use of Zhuang language over time in Chapters Seven and Eight, but for now just provide this explanation of its funding from one of its editors. I clarified elsewhere in this interview that it is the GZAR Government, not the Central Government, who funds *Third of the Third*.

Excerpt 5-9

Mr G: 政府出钱，稿件从各地投过来，政府出钱来办，所以我们发行也是不收钱了，叫做公益性……政府办的，我们的公司印刷费都是我们国家出的，政府出的，因为我们国家对民族政策比较重视，少数民族的比较重视，有优惠政策，所以我们的民族文字呢**，这个也是国家帮我们做的，过去我们民间自己有方块字，这个是国家的，所以这个现在发行啊、出版啊、稿费啊、包括编辑人员的工资全部是国家包。

[Mr G: The [GZAR] Government pays the money, the contributions [to content] come from all over, the government pays to run it, so we do not charge for issuing it, this is called "public welfare" ... Government published: our company's printing costs are paid for by the state, government issued [funds], because our country treats minzu policies as relatively important, the minority minzu are relatively important, there are preferential policies, so our minzu script **[noise over words], that's also something the state does for us. In the past we had the Square Character Script between ourselves, this one [in the magazine] is the state one, so that's the one published now, ah; publishing, manuscript fees, and including the editor's salary that's all covered by the state.]

Moreover, in contrast to Zhuang language's limited inclusion in education in GZAR, there are detailed regional policies and proactive implementation measures for English language education in GZAR, even in "Zhuang dominated areas" (Feng and Sunuodula 2009: 691). These include English being offered at primary school, targets for tertiary institutions, special funds for training teachers, and a partnership policy to recruit English teachers from Guangzhou for GZAR's under-resourced remote schools. Feng and Sunuodula (2009: 698) emphasize that "[t]he entire system is mobilized" for English education. This is because "English is a high-stakes subject in schools in the PRC. It is a prerequisite for university study in most parts of the country and for entry into many professions" (Adamson and Feng 2009: 324). Thus, where language ideologies support the use of a language in education, the government *can* achieve it, even in GZAR.

The limited provision of Zhuang-medium education despite its legal permissibility may therefore be explained by both the developmentalist value system and local governments' lack of funding; the two are connected. Funding shortages arise because bilingual schooling is no longer a national policy priority so central funding has reduced. A de-prioritization by the Central Government reduces not only economic capital but also political capital and symbolic power. This can enforce a belief among local families and decision-makers that Zhuang schooling is not useful for individuals' or the nation's development. This study found that language-in-education policy in GZAR was not used to challenge such normative discourses.

This close up illustrates concretely and locally the chapter's identification of weakness in the representation of minority language interests and in the organization of responsibility and power in the national framework of minority language governance. It reveals language governance that is neither proactive nor even very reactive in practice, but passive in the face of changing obstacles to the freedom and equality of Zhuang in GZAR. This is not a case of the active oppression or necessarily even a deliberate marginalization of a minority language in education, but perhaps apathy in the face of the ever-building economic and mobility capital of those languages which are believed to function well beyond GZAR, namely Putonghua and, to an extent, English. Within the developmentalist system of values and beliefs which China's laws and policies invest with significant power, this focus on languages other than Zhuang in education in GZAR is naturalized as an economically rational and therefore desirable and responsible language governance choice in the best interests of the Zhuangzu and the nation.

5.4 Concluding discussion: The structures of territory, authority and representation struggle to respond to Zhuang interests

The formal organization of geography, authority and representation to govern Zhuang struggles to represent or to empower those concerned with Zhuang, as this chapter has explained. This is the case even within the seemingly advantageous but actually in-name-only system of areas of minority minzu self-government. This is not a governance system structured to adjust with agility to changing linguistic and social orders, or to hold government organs to account where language equality or minority representation are, in principle, supposed to be upheld. Rather, Zhuang speakers and even official Zhuangzu representatives are largely not empowered, through the geographically bounded and institutionally fractured mechanisms for governing the Zhuangzu, to call for different or better implementation of the constitutional minority language freedom, nor for the valuing of Zhuang language for something other than its economic potential. The relative absence of structures for representing the Zhuangzu within Party organs – or representing the interests of Zhuang speakers in other ways in Party organs – is a particular constraint. Zhuang language and Zhuang representation is kept formally and discursively in its place on the margins of governing power.

This chapter used the close-up of Zhuang language-in-education policy in GZAR to illustrate the language governance framework in practice. This gives a glimpse of concrete problems in practice that stem from the limitations of the language rights themselves, from the developmentalist ideology articulated in the law and policy texts and from the structure of language governance, problems identified by the three chapters of this Part Two. Part Three's multi-faceted linguistic landscape study will take us much further into an empirical, socially-situated analysis of language governance problems in practice. It investigates the implementation, discourse and ideologies of the language governance framework in relation to the public usage of Zhuang. This chapter's examination of the (dis)use of Zhuang language for communication in government institutions as a form of political representation dovetails with Part Three's examination of Zhuang as both a communicative and a representational resource in public built environments.

Language policy has an inherent risk of policy cleavage. Because of this, the "overt (explicit, formalized, codified) forms of policy" that have concerned us here in Part Two may be "meaningless", (Schiffman 1996: 27) has warned, if they are not paired with an analysis of the "covert (implicit, informal, unstated grassroots reality)". That reality is foregrounded in Part Three's analysis of empirical data, but it is important to note that we have already entered into an analysis of covert language policy here in Part Two. I have drawn out the implicit yet powerful language ideologies of law, both in legal texts and in the legal structuring of which linguistic and minority concerns are legitimate for which organs of the state and for which peoples.

Moreover, Part Two has revealed that cleavages arise even within the system of explicit, legally codified language policy, for example between different regions' and provinces' responses to the constitutional freedom to use and develop minority languages. Policies and rules at various jurisdictional scale-levels – and the governance organs and agents who enact and interpret them – are heterogeneous. I argue in closing Part Two, therefore, that overt language policy should be theorized as generally heterogeneous and inherently at risk of policy cleavage, not only at risk of cleavages between overt and covert, or formal and informal, or *de jure* and *de facto* policy. This is not a China-specific argument but rather the addition of a nuance to Schiffman's (and others') acknowledgement of an inherent policy-practice cleavage across language policy forms and contexts. This heterogeneity is further illustrated in the linguistic landscapes to which we now turn.

Part III: **Lived Linguistic Landscapes**

6 Visual ideologies of Zhuang in linguistic landscapes

[T]he presence (or absence) of language displays in the public space communicates a message, intentional or not [...] that affects, manipulates, or imposes de facto language policy and practice.
(Shohamy 2006: 110)

6.1 Introducing the linguistic landscape study of visual ideologies

Linguistic landscape approaches are the starting point for examining what it is that public space communicates about which languages and which speakers are "in place". What is communicated are the *de facto* language policies of which the epigraph speaks, and these *de facto* policies are a form of language ideology made visual. That is, linguistic landscapes "can be a place to see the resemiotization of policy discourses" (Hult 2018: 339) but also of powerful popular discourses. These *de facto* policies may be on their way to becoming *de jure* policies, as Chapter Nine will examine. Sometimes, *de jure* language policies are also communicated through public spaces, when governments regulate the inclusion, exclusion or formatting of languages on signage in those spaces. These *de jure* policies add to the language ideologies being communicated, and if the regulated signage is recognizably government-authored, the communication may carry additional symbolic power. Whether emergent from social practice, or imposed by law, or both, the language ideologies made visual through public displays of language have durability and a wide reach; this is their "relatively longer social life", as Lou (2016: 4) puts it. Linguistic landscape texts are thus a form of language which derives additional symbolic power from material characteristics.

The linguistic landscape analyses offered in this Part Three of the book will explore how a "linguistic landscape ceases to be a linguistic subject, but a phenomenon that highlights the dialogical relationship between language, space and place" (Lou 2016: 2), starting with this chapter's findings about the patterns of language display and their co-location with types of place: these patterns and their locations are part of the physical manifestation of language policy, both *de facto* and *de jure*. These foundations set us up to then examine the place-making work of the individual tokens of language displayed, but more especially of the patterns of language display, and the agentive role of the "linguascapers" who control and deploy visual linguistic resources to enhance particular senses of place and particular language ideologies, over Chapters Seven to Nine. Specifically, Chapter Seven draws into view more of the "semiotic aggregate" (Scollon and Scollon, 2003: 23) of the landscapes introduced here in Chapter Six. It turns to public displays of non-linguistic visual symbols which, akin to public displays of written Zhuang language, emplace references to Zhuang speakers, culture and identity. The role of viewers, examined in Chapter Eight's "lived landscape" analysis, further extends this examination of the dialogical relationship between language, space and place, revealing some of the reception and interpretation of the language ideologies communicated by these linguistic landscapes. Chapter Nine then examines how laws control who has the power to act as a linguascaper and which choices these authors of the built environment have.

This chapter analyses linguistic landscape data primarily from cities in GZAR, the autonomous region in southern China with a mandate to manage Zhuang language, but also from the three minzu-specialist universities where Zhuang Studies are taught. In particular, this chapter considers what public texts reveal about the use and status of Zhuang relative to other languages and how their "visual ideology" (following Jaworski and Thurlow 2010: 3) reproduces or resists particular linguistic and social orders. The display of language is taken to be "not only part of the visual make-up of a space but is also a form of spatial representation" of culture, power and politics (Lou 2016: 6). When we live in or experience these spatial representations, they then contribute to our socialization into structures and norms, that is, to the formation of our *habitus* (Lou 2016: 10, following Bourdieu 1977a). Thus, publicly displayed texts are treated as "maps of meaning" (Jaworski and Thurlow 2010: 6) which, in addition to publicizing specific information such as the name of a street, transform physical "spaces" into organized, socially, culturally and politically significant "places" (Lou 2016: 7–11; see also Hult 2014: 513). The representation of Zhuang in the linguistic landscapes studied here is, in part, shaped by deliberate government intervention in language display, but the patterns of the presence and absence of Zhuang also communicate that which Shohamy (2006: 110), in the passage quoted in the epigraph, calls "*de facto* language policy".

Specifically, the chapter will show that the *de facto* policy across public signage is to not include Zhuang, no matter whether the signage's author is governmental or private. This minimizes the relevance of Zhuang language in contemporary civic, commercial and educational discourses and practices. However, against the trend, there are certain patterned uses of Zhuang language on some government-authored public signage. These are made meaningful within discourses about the territory of Zhuang language and of regional cultural heritage. After the following overview of my choice of landscapes to study, the chapter provides three levels of linguistic landscape analysis: a descriptive, empirical analysis (6.3); a critical analysis of the empirical findings (6.4) and a closing discussion relating these findings to the book's broader concern with the roles Zhuang language plays within areas of autonomous

Zhuangzu government and outside these areas, as well as adding to Chapter Four's insights into the ideologies undergirding official language policy.

6.2 The choice of landscapes

I focus primarily on public linguistic landscapes within Nanning City in GZAR because Nanning Municipal Government has explicit rules about Zhuang on public signage. (These rules are extracted in Chapter Nine). Further, Nanning is GZAR's biggest city and capital and therefore imbued with a special symbolic power. The Nanning Government itself acknowledges the symbolic importance of public language usage in the city (Nanning Municipal Minority Language Works Commission 2019). Nanning's linguistic landscape norms are therefore significant in constructing the social meanings and linguistic order of GZAR. Moreover, to better understand whether the linguistic landscapes observed in Nanning were typical of GZAR overall, and in particular whether patterns in the displays of Zhuang language in Nanning were similar across GZAR's urban centers, I also studied other linguistic landscapes in the region. These were Guilin City; Wuming, a satellite town under the Nanning Municipal Government's remit; and Ping'An Zhuang Village. I observed rural areas between these centers. My fieldwork also included sites outside GZAR; I did not observe Zhuang in those linguistic landscapes other than in two university campus landscapes, in Yunnan and Beijing. Those campus landscapes are included in this chapter's analysis along with campus landscapes located within Nanning City, offering similarities and differences. The campuses are those of large regional universities within Nanning (GU) and (GUN) and of the two universities outside GZAR where Zhuang Studies is taught (YMU) in Yunnan and MUC in Beijing).

My focus on cities reflects the fact that in China (as in many countries), cities offer the greatest opportunities for mobility: they are where people come to "change their lifestyles or move up the social ladder" (Cartier 2015b: 207; see also Fan 2008: 13). Cartier (2015b: 207) argues "[p]eople in urban China [...] enjoy greater opportunities [than before. ... Their] ease of movement – mobility – [is] novel and exciting." Thus, China's cities are places where a concentration of technological and social changes, including linguistic changes, "alter the physical, cultural and linguistic landscape of a site" (Stroud and Jegels 2014: 180). Urban environments are therefore important mediums for discourses constructing the dominant identities, values and of course languages associated with mobility.

Furthermore, like cities, universities are "mobile places" (Jaworski 2014: 530) and "places of in-between-ness" as Sheller and Urry (2006: 219) theorizes in the "new mobilities paradigm". They are constructed as mobile places all the more because education is widely understood in China as a resource for better career mobility and for facilitating upward geographic and socio-economic movement. Statistics support this popular wisdom (Fan 2008: 1–13, 60). Usually, universities are located in cities and are so in this study, with universities and cities thereby co-constructing each other as centers. University campuses are therefore also symbolically powerful landscapes. Moreover, my focal campuses are part of the public urban landscape, with their exteriors forming part of surrounding urban streetscapes and their interior roads, parks and open spaces accessible to traversing members of the public. Thus, these campus landscapes offer additional sites for examining the contrasts and continuities in the role of Zhuang in public linguistic landscapes. Moreover, university environments are the part of the urban environment experienced most often by this study's cohort of student participants (in fact, daily). As such, these landscapes are integral to understanding how language in public and language in place relate to language in education and in the personal practices of individuals. The interrelations are examined across the four chapters of this Part as I build up from linguistic landscape to lived landscape approaches. Let us begin with the patterns of language on display.

6.3 An empirical analysis of patterns in language display

6.3.1 Monolingual use of Putonghua or Zhuang

Overall, monolingual Putonghua signage was the most prevalent, across all the sites, authors and genres of landscape text. I will first describe the monolingual Putonghua texts before describing the unique monolingual Zhuang text found. Government-authored signage in the urban and campus landscapes was typically monolingual in Putonghua. This observation applied across many genres of government-authored signage including parking directions at public institutions, public works notices, bus timetables and commemorative plaques. However, monolingual Putonghua signage was not necessarily limited to one script, because Putonghua officially has both logographic (simplified character) and Romanized ("*Pinyin*") scripts. Putonghua is even sometimes displayed within China in traditional characters, but in the majority of monolingual Putonghua signs only simplified characters were used. Figure 14 shows a typical example: it shows a monolingual, government-authored billboard written in simplified characters, placed on construction hoarding alongside a major, downtown road near GZAR Library in Nanning, and lauding the construction of Nanning's subway (underway in 2014–2015). This billboard exemplifies government-authored signage unrelated to an institution but

Figure 14: Billboard, curb outside GZAR Library; Nanning: Putonghua.

strategically placed alongside. Also shown immediately above the billboard is a government slogan, 求卓越 'Pursue Outstanding-ness', displayed on the side of a demountable workers' building. Monolingual Putonghua signs written in both characters and Pinyin were also fairly common in all sites surveyed, particularly for signage giving road directions. In most cases, the characters were much larger than the Pinyin: see, for example, Figure 21.

The sign in Figure 15 at the main entrance of GU, located on another main road in Nanning, is a slightly atypical example. It is similarly monolingual Putonghua and, like Figure 14, it uses only one script, but its script is traditional characters. It reads "廣西大學" [Guangxi University], and I have captured it in the process of being re-mediated through graduation day photographs. This was not the sole signage in traditional writing that I encountered, and I will describe the apparent pattern of traditional script display when I discuss Figure 35, below. For now, let us look beyond this stone sign to the small billboard and a red banner which can be observed in the background. As with the larger sign in the foreground of the picture, these background signs were also monolingual in Putonghua, as was typical for these forms of signage, and these forms were themselves typical of campus landscapes.

Furthermore, as at this entrance of GU, I found monolingual Putonghua texts surrounding all public institutions' entrances, such as signage displaying entrance rules and opening times. Figure 16 provides an example of monolingual entrance signage. Walking across the GZAR Library forecourt in Nanning, red lettering on the top of the building's façade and a scrolling electronic sign are visible; both are

Figure 15: Entrance, GU campus; Nanning: Putonghua.

Figure 16: GZAR Library; Nanning: Putonghua-only.

monolingual in Putonghua. This entrance lies on a downtown roadside beside temporary hoardings covered with monolingual government-authored texts taking advantage of the location's high visibility, including the billboard in Figure 14.

So far, the examples are all government-authored, although from differing genres. Commercial texts, whether from state-owned commercial entities or private companies, were also mainly monolingual in Putonghua. For example, Figure 17, a typical advertisement from downtown Nanning, monolingually promotes a television program for the national, state-run internet-television broadcaster. Through this advertisement's monolingual Putonghua, it anticipates that readers watch television in Putonghua and indicates that Zhuang-speakers can be marketed to jointly with everyone else via Putonghua. This expectation of a Putonghua-literate market was reaffirmed by the Putonghua-only advertisements frequently displayed below Nanning's street-name signs. For example, the advertisement in Figure 18 promotes study-coaching services, hinting at Putonghua's dominance in education. I observed the same trend in the linguistic landscapes at GU, GUN and interstate universities, as exemplified by Figure 19, an advertisement laminated onto a cafeteria tabletop at GUN. Although GUN offers Zhuang Studies and has a large

Figure 17: Billboard; Nanning: Putonghua.

Figure 18: Street-name signs with advertising panes; Nanning: Street-name: dual-script Putonghua/Zhuang, poster: Putonghua.

Zhuangzu cohort, on-campus commercial texts were mainly monolingual in Putonghua, sometimes with English borrowings, but never including Zhuang. In this way, GUN had a very similar textual landscape to GU, the regional comprehensive university in Nanning which does not offer Zhuang Studies.

I observed that monolingual Putonghua street-name signs were common in Guilin and on inter-city routes in GZAR. Monolingual but dual script Putonghua street-name signs were also common on campus at GU and GUN but only occasional on Nanning's streets (e.g. Figure 20), as most Nanning street-name signs were bilingual (as in Figure 18). Similarly, the road sign in Figure 21 uses dual-script Putonghua. Sometimes, however, road directions used English instead of Putonghua Pinyin, as I explain further below.

6.3 An empirical analysis of patterns in language display — 149

Figure 19: Cafeteria tabletop, GUN; Nanning: Putonghua.

Figure 20: Street-name sign; Nanning: Putonghua.

Figure 21: Road sign; Nanning: Putonghua.

My passage through rural GZAR confirmed my understanding of cities as places with more affordances for linguistic display. Furthermore, the signage I observed in rural areas was almost always monolingual in Putonghua, as these field notes reveal.

> Just passed through little Hezhou [GZAR] on the train from Guilin [GZAR] to Shenzhen [Guangdong Province]. Only public signage in Mando [Mandarin] characters, but really not much to be seen (a red banner at a weighing station, wall sign at a timber yard) [...] The smallest place with a station that I've yet seen. Approx. 50 mudbrick farm houses around sunny, flat fields, with a small cluster of 5 or 6-storey flats on one edge of town. A school, with clearly visible school-name in Putonghua on its roof [...] A few more village/towns, each of 50 or so usually brick, square, 3-storey buildings clustered very close, seemingly almost all residential. No visible signage. (16 June 2015)

While my observations in small places such as Hezhou were neither as systematic nor extensive as those in Nanning, Wuming and Guilin, my observations all pointed to Putonghua's preponderance in the limited textual displays of village landscapes.

Although monolingual Putonghua dominated all public linguistic landscapes, I did find certain genres of multilingual text which displayed Zhuang. Before presenting those, I will describe the one monolingual Zhuang text that I encountered. Monolingual Zhuang was exceedingly rare in linguistic landscapes, as I discovered through extensive searching, and I did not find monolingual public signage in English or any other non-Mandarin language. I found one Zhuang text inlaid in the floor of the foyer of the GZAR Library in Nanning, announcing the institution's name (Figure 22). However, the institution-name sign on the exterior was monolingual Putonghua (look back at Figure 16). While the public are free to enter this foyer, this inlaid Zhuang text was not visible from the adjacent public spaces (the street and the entrance courtyard). Like Putonghua, Zhuang can also be written in more than one script, as Chapter Two has explained. This inlaid text was in Romanized Zhuang, the script used with the standardized orthography and grammar, all of which were developed by the government in collaboration with Zhuangzu groups in the mid-twentieth century.

Figure 22: Foyer, GZAR Library; Nanning: Zhuang.

Compared to monolingual signage, bilingual signage followed slightly more Zhuang-inclusive patterns.

6.3.2 Bilingual signage

Zhuang was not only rare monolingually but even in bilingual signage the more frequent combination was Putonghua and English. Putonghua-English texts were particularly prevalent in commercially-oriented, new and temporary signage. Putonghua-Zhuang bilingual texts, by contrast, were mainly government-authored, mainly found in Nanning Municipality, and were typically street-names or public institutions' names. Bilingual signs without Putonghua were not found.

As I mentioned above, some road directions signs were bilingual in Putonghua and English, and some of exactly the same standard format were monolingual in Putonghua but dual script. My classification of the sign in Figure 23 as bilingual is not based on the named places, "HUANCHENG", "WU MING" and "HE CHI", but on "EXPWY", which abbreviates "expressway" in English. I observed many road directions across GZAR using either English or Putonghua Pinyin, but always including Putonghua characters and never including Zhuang. Throughout GZAR, English takes the second spot on road direction signage when it is not given to Putonghua Pinyin.

Figure 23: Road sign; highway between Nanning and Wuming: Putonghua/English.

A minority of other types of government-authored signs included English alongside Putonghua, for example the permanent "unrecycling" and "battery" labels on Nanning's public bins (Figure 24) and temporary texts such as Figure 25's poster promoting a design biennale. I did not observe foreign languages other than English on government-authored texts.

The biennale poster (Figure 25) is commercially-oriented although government-authored, aimed at attracting visitors and their spending. Commercially-oriented texts in Nanning were commonly bilingual (Putonghua-English), whether

Figure 24: Bins; Nanning: Putonghua/English.

Figure 25: GZAR Library entrance; Nanning: Putonghua/English.

government-authored or privately authored, although more commonly monolingual in Putonghua. Illustrating the kind of English included, my field notes record:

> Lots of English in Nanning signs, compared to Zhuang, but less than English in Hong Kong or Beijing. Shop brands / names over doors like 'Graceful' [...] Banks like CCB [China Construction Bank] have Putonghua characters and English signs, as do 'SINOPEC' servos [petrol stations] and 'CHINA MOBILE', 'Vienna International Hotel', 'Boston International Hotel', 'Walmart', 'H&M', 'Jack Jones' etc, then one-offs like 'Decedene' clothes.
>
> (10 June 2015)

As the field note records, international brands use their internationally-recognized English brand-names, and this includes Chinese multinationals like Sinopec. The list also includes hotels using the English names of foreign places and the word "international" in combination to associate themselves with marketable qualities of the lifestyle of an imagined global community. A laundromat shopfront inscribed with "UCC 国际洗衣 International Laundry", which I passed in Guilin, is another clear example of this (the characters also say 'international'). "Decedene", a unique brand-name recorded in my field note above presumably trades on customers recognizing it as an English-like foreign word or "Globalese" (Jaworski 2015).

On university campuses, English translations were sometimes included alongside Putonghua in government-authored directions, logos and building-name signage, and also sometimes in advertising texts from commercial authors. However, bilingual Putonghua-English signage was less prevalent than monolingual Putonghua direction or commercial signage at the universities, as in the cities more generally. On the sign in Figure 26, which I saw on the YMU campus and which exemplifies Putonghua-English campus texts, the Putonghua and English components are parallel in content and given close to equal space. Even the cardinal directions "<北 N" and "南 S>" are displayed bilingually. The YMU logo affixed to the left of the main sign in Figure 26 announces the university's name in Putonghua characters and slightly smaller English letters under a pictorial emblem. The logo of GUN, the minzu-specialist university in Nanning, followed the same picture-plus-bilingual-name formula.

As in Figure 26 and all the bilingual signs I have collected in this chapter, Putonghua comes before English, and its type font is never smaller than that of English. This was typical. Moreover, Putonghua was dominant in commercial signage, as the example in Figure 27 shows. This is one of Nanning's central shopping streets. In this central district, sometimes English and Putonghua together announce a brand-name, e.g. "可口可乐 Coca Cola" (in the center) and "昊天通信 Haotian Correspondence" (the name of the first shop on the left) are written in Putonghua characters and English. Less commonly, brand-names

Figure 26: On-campus street-name sign, YMU; Kunming: Putonghua/English.

and commercial slogans are in English alone, but always another part of the same sign is in Putonghua.

A more complicated combination of commercial and multi-tier government authorial interests was evidenced in promotions for the China-ASEAN Expo, a large-scale event which Nanning hosted with Central Government support in 2015. The China-ASEAN Expo was promoted on billboards, e.g. Figure 28. This example was displayed on the same thoroughfare as the GZAR Library in Nanning. In Figure 28, the Expo is explicitly linked to the Maritime Silk Road, the cornerstone international trade policy of President Xi's government (now enlarged to One Belt One Road), so it participates in a politically-oriented discourse. However, this text is more immediately commercially-oriented, seeking to attract diplomatic and business travelers.

Property development signage was another prevalent genre of bilingual Putonghua-English text on display in urban GZAR. Property development is a

Figure 27: Commercial signage; Nanning: some English, mainly Putonghua.

Figure 28: Billboard; Nanning: Putonghua/English.

significant industry in China, contributing some 15 % of China's GDP in 2015 (Barmé 2012: 114; see also Feng et al. 2013; Fung 2016). It is integral to both government and private economic growth because land is mostly leased by the state to developers (Eisberg 2015: 21). Figure 29 shows two typical property sales billboards. These advertise SINA Corporation's "O-Park" development, in

Figure 29: Billboards; Nanning: Putonghua/English.

Putonghua with some English. Under "O-Park", we see the first four characters of a property jargon term, 创智天地二维码 'knowledge and education community', often abbreviated to KIC in English jargon, and the Putonghua name of this development, 通昊 'Through Luxury'. The left-hand gives the price of 2588RMB per square meter. These all index O-Park as high-end property. Further reading on their website finds that this is a residential and commercial development in central Nanning (Sina Property 2014), featuring Nanning's first "code garden", a courtyard in which plants and three-dimensional QR codes are physically emplaced to allow for easy virtual mobility from a physical place of leisure to virtual places of leisure: mobility practices as well as leisure practices will co-construct this as a place. The developers clearly hope the Putonghua and English, and other indices of luxury and mobility, will attract tenants and visitors, proclaiming that "广大业内专业人士，媒体以及普通市民也纷纷慕名而来" ["the majority of industry professionals, media and ordinary city-folk are enticed to come here"] (Sina Property 2014).

Bilingual Putonghua-English signage typically appeared in different genres to bilingual Putonghua-Zhuang signage. The former appeared in commercial advertising genres such as the O-Park example, public order signage such as the recycling bin labels at Figure 24, and wayfaring signage such as the road directions or the YMU campus road name and history sign above. Many of these are genres in which the government is the main author, and texts that were Putonghua-Zhuang were likewise government-authored (almost to the exclusion of any other author). However, even when the texts in commercial and public order genres were government-authored, they were almost never bilingual in Putonghua and Zhuang. It was only on wayfaring signage that Zhuang was regularly included, in some sites, and even then, not on all genres of wayfaring signage. The most common bilingual Putonghua-Zhuang texts were street-name signs in Nanning City. By 2014, standard-issue Putonghua-Zhuang street-name signage had been widely installed in Nanning. (The Nanning Municipal Minority Language Works Commission (2019) reports that two of Nanning Municipality's twelve counties also erected this bilingual street-name signage: Long'An County and Wuming County, now Wuming District.) This signage has a toponym in Romanized Zhuang on the top line following Standard Zhuang grammar, above a Putonghua toponym written in simplified characters and then in Putonghua Pinyin. In a separately-colored section at the bottom of these signs, Putonghua characters provide cardinal directions alongside deictic arrows, sometimes also with adjacent streets' names in Putonghua. As Figure 30 shows, the Putonghua characters have the largest type font, while the Zhuang toponym has the smallest.

Figure 30: Street-name; Nanning: Zhuang/dual-script Putonghua.

Furthermore, the Zhuang names for the streets did not correspond intertextually to any of the large, fixed display maps, circulating paper maps or online maps that I collected and used in fieldwork, nor to the postal system. These all use Putonghua street names, sometimes with the addition of English or the option of switching to an English version. Thus, using a Zhuang street-name on a sign to locate oneself on a map, or to communicate a meeting point to a friend, would be hard. To illustrate, I have included a Mandarin-only map of a section of downtown Nanning at Figure 31. This is from the maps software of www.baidu.com, the Google of China. I relied on Baidu Maps during my fieldwork because it was available, and because many others also do: Baidu is reported to now receive "74.6 percent of the nation's online search queries" (Seth 2019). A Baidu Maps search of the Zhuang street-name in Figure 30, *VEIJVUJLU*, yields no results.

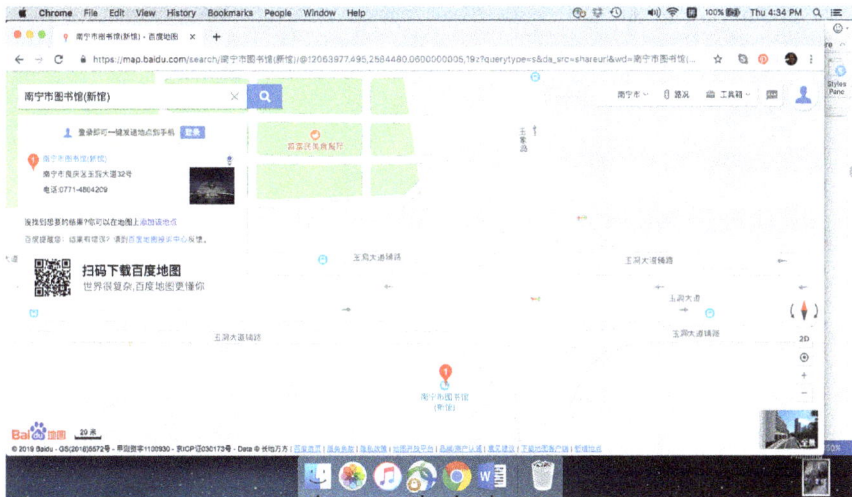

Figure 31: Screenshot of baidu.com map of GZAR Library environs: Putonghua.

Consistent with Nanning City's street-name signage, I also found bilingual Putonghua-Zhuang street-name signage in the same format in Wuming, which is a satellite town on Nanning's outskirts (e.g. Figure 32). Standard Zhuang is modelled on the variety of Zhuang spoken in Wuming. However, just as in Nanning, Wuming's commercial offerings were typically announced in Putonghua, sometimes accompanied by English but never by Zhuang, as is also apparent in Figure 32. I found no such bilingual street-name signage in Guilin City or Heping Township (urban centers in GZAR outside Nanning's remit) and photos of street-name signs Liuzhou City in GZAR suggest they too are monolingual in Putonghua ("Liuzhou Laowai" 2009).

Apart from street-name signage, no other wayfaring signage was consistently produced as a bilingual Putonghua-Zhuang text. However, some regional, public institutions were labelled in both languages, particularly in Nanning, which houses more regional institutions than other GZAR cities, being the capital. For example, I found Romanized Zhuang on exterior institution-name signs at Guangxi Nationalities' Museum and the GZAR Museum in Nanning (Figure 33) . I also found

160 — 6 Visual ideologies of Zhuang in linguistic landscapes

Figure 32: Street-name; Wuming: Zhuang/dual-script Putonghua. (Background: commercial signage; dual-script Putonghua.).

Figure 33: GZAR Museum entrance; Nanning: façade: Zhuang/Putonghua characters, banner: Putonghua, assorted signage: mainly Putonghua.

one Putonghua-Zhuang name-sign at one public school in downtown Guilin; during a 2.5-hour walk looking for Zhuang-inclusive institution-name signage I found only that sign (field notes 15 June 2015). On one bilingual entryway name-sign at each of these institutions, Zhuang was written alongside Putonghua.

Nevertheless, Zhuang institution names were not consistently part of the exterior display of public institutions in GZAR. For example, Nanning's two inter-city railway stations, Guilin's central railway station, the GZAR People's Congress in Nanning, and GU (Figure 15) did not have Zhuang on their main entrances, although GU's smaller East Gate name-sign used Putonghua and Zhuang. I found only one government department in Nanning displaying a Putonghua-Zhuang name-sign (an environment department in a peri-urban area); there may be more, but they were not obvious in downtown streetscapes. In downtown Guilin, I found bilingual departmental signage downtown at the shared entrance of the Guilin City Cultural News, Publishing and Broadcast Bureau and the Guilin City Cultural Relic Bureau (Figure 34).

Figure 34: Government agency entrance; Guilin: Putonghua/Zhuang.

Moreover, Zhuang was *not* included across the board in these institutions' exterior texts. Rather, each of the signs that included the institution's name in Zhuang was a one-off amongst surrounding texts. For example, the stone Putonghua-Zhuang entrance sign at Nanning Library (Figure 35) competed with Library's monolingual Putonghua signs shown in Figures 14 and 16, and the bilingual Putonghua-English sign shown in Figure 25. At GZAR Museum, the bilingual sign

Figure 35: Entrance stone, GZAR Library; Nanning: traditional Chinese characters/Zhuang.

which included the institution's name in Zhuang was surrounded by monolingual Putonghua and bilingual Putonghua-English signage (Figure 33). Likewise, at Guilin's cultural bureaux, the bilingual name sign hung alongside their electronic sign in monolingual Putonghua (Figure 34).

Each of these institution's Zhuang-medium labelling of itself was written in Romanized Zhuang rather than traditional, logographic Sawndip. However, in their Putonghua-medium labels, some institutions included traditional rather than simplified characters. Notably in this regard, the GZAR Museum's façade includes some traditional and simplified characters within one Putonghua name. This museum was opened in 1958 ("David" 2016), when character simplification was just beginning, which explains why the entire sign was not made exclusively in simplified characters, but which does not explain why it was never updated. However, GZAR Library's name in Putonghua is written in traditional rather than simplified characters on its much newer bilingual entrance stone (Figure 35). This recalls the traditional characters naming Guangxi University, shown in Figure 15, which are also etched into an entrance stone. There is a deictic logic to the use of traditional Chinese characters on the name signage of museums, universities and libraries; these are the institutions which house the kinds of historic texts which were written in traditional characters: literature, scholarship and records. Moreover, traditional character literacy may still be practiced (in addition to simplified character literacy) by people in these institutions working with historic texts. Moreover, other emblems are visible which co-construct these as places of tradition, such as the image of a red seal on the Library's stone sign, the graduation garb of the students at Guangxi University, the stylized, figurative art on GZAR Museum's lintel frieze, and the materiality of etched stone itself. The stone signs also reproduce the historic practice of stone boundary-marking, being placed at both the Library and the University's curb on the main road, where the institutional space meets the city. But historic Zhuang script is notably absent from the emblems of tradition that these institutions display. Rather, these signs implicate twentieth-century Romanized Zhuang in their historic symbology.

I did not find actual historic forms of logographic Zhuang writing (i.e. Sawndip) to be used in any public text, and so historic Zhuang literacy is not represented in the public linguistic landscape. However, one Zhuang logograph was – arguably – on display inside Zhuang Home-style Restaurant in Wuming. Given the consistent use of Romanized Zhuang for all institution name signs written in Zhuang, and recalling Romanized Zhuang was likewise standard on Nanning's bilingual street-name signs, I took note when I finally encountered this text. I was at 壮家人美食馆 'Zhuang Home-style Restaurant' in Wuming in 2015. Most of the restaurant's linguistic landscape, including its exterior signage and its menus, was entirely in Putonghua. Only the sign shown at Figure 36, which hung at the entrance to dining rooms upstairs, was arguably bilingual. It contained two large

Figure 36: Dining area, Zhuang Home-style Restaurant; Wuming: Putonghua/Sawndip.

characters, not in a line together, and a smaller, vertical line of characters. The topmost large character is 壯, meaning "Zhuang" in Putonghua. This is the not-yet-simplified character assigned to signify Zhuang in the early years of the PRC, during a campaign to replace the pejorative characters then used to write many minority groups' names. Prior to the campaign, 僮, a derogatory character also meaning "slave", was used for Zhuang (Chang 1968). That character can be seen in offcial usage e.g. in Guangxi Zhuang Literary History Newsroom and Guangxi Teachers College (1961) and on 1954 census records reproduced in Mullaney (2006: 142). The Putonghua character for Zhuang has since been simplified to 壮, so the sign in the restaurant is a visual anachronism.

The second large character on the dining room sign is within a cartouche and written in a calligraphic style: it is 僚; the style further conveys traditionalism. In Putonghua this translates the Zhuang word "*raeuz*" 'we/us' but it can also be read as the Sawndip character for the same word (Sinj and Loz 2008: 21), and so this sign has the potential to be read as a bilingual Putonghua-Zhuang text. Expertise is needed to read this sign in Sawndip but also in Putonghua because of the now-disused jargon character, and given the extreme brevity, this sign's semiotic function is likely to be primarily visual rather than lexical. That is, it is likely intended as a decoration. Whether read as only Putonghua or as Putonghua and Zhuang, these old-fashioned two characters index heritage, augmenting the traditionalism of eating the restaurant's eponymous "home-style" food. We will figuratively return to this restaurant in the following chapter but let us now complete the survey of collected bilingual texts.

I found one other bilingual Putonghua-Zhuang sign in public, in downtown Guilin. It did not fit the pattern, identified above, of Zhuang being included only on certain types of government-authored place-name signage. Rather, it was a government-authored billboard (Figure 37). The topmost two lines, respectively in Putonghua and Zhuang, both translate as "The Chinese minzu, one close family". The third line reads 民族团结如空气一般珍贵 'Minzu unity is as precious as air'. The first two lines physically minimize the sign's bilingualism, with the Putonghua made more eye-catching than the Zhuang through color, type-font size and by being used again for the third line, while Zhuang gets only the one line. The first, Putonghua line starts with "中华" (*zhōnghuá* in Pinyin), which is transliterated into Zhuang as "*Cunghhvaz*" in the second line. This term means Chinese in a cultural/ethnic sense, not the Chinese nation-state 中国 (*zhōngguó* in Pinyin), foregrounding the ethno-cultural rather than political element of national unity (on the inclusivity of this term, see further Lickorish 2008: 2). This sign is neither a public institution name sign nor a wayfaring sign. Rather, this sign is government messaging. It is of a piece with a multilingual poster encouraging national unity that I found displayed on the

Figure 37: Billboard; Guilin: Putonghua/Zhuang.

YMU campus (see Figure 42) and which I discuss along with other multilingual signage later in this chapter. The multiculturalism indexed by this poster's bilingualism and by this billboard's images of diversely dressed women (images which I analyze in the following chapter) is emplaced in Guilin by the recognizable representations of Guilin's iconic Elephant Tusk Park and pagoda landmarks in the background. The billboard visualizes the belief that minzu unity *should* be part of what makes Guilin the place it is, and what Guilin is known for.

We have so far canvassed relatively permanent, fixed signage, but the linguistic landscape literature has developed to also attend to circulating texts, and my study followed that lead. Bilingualism was also found amongst the circulating texts that I collected, although many circulating texts were monolingual, such as shop, taxi and accommodation receipts and the print media displayed for sale at the curbside magazine stalls which constituted another textual feature of linguistic landscapes across GZAR. Of the bilingual circulating texts, few were bilingual in Zhuang. While a government-sponsored, Putonghua-Zhuang periodical entitled 三月三 *Sam Nyied Sam* 'Third Day of the Third Month' exists, it is sold through subscription and not displayed at these magazine stalls (see further Section 7.4). A government-sponsored, monolingual Zhuang newspaper, *Gvangjsih Minzcuz Bau* 'Guangxi Minzu Newspaper', comes out irregularly. (Mr H explained that it's actually a Zhuang version of a Mandarin-medium newspaper daily, but with different content, which he and Mr G later explained as being technological, agricultural and public health information.) This newspaper was not visible in these landscapes either. *Third of the Third's* editor, Mr G, confirmed that *Gvangjsih Minzcuz Bau* is not for sale at newsstands and with his colleague, Mr H, explained that it has to be pre-ordered through the Post Office. Both also spoke of its diminished publication: Mr H: "不是很多，不是很多。现在的话就是用纸的这种都在萎缩了" [Not a lot, not a lot [of copies]. Nowadays the types who use the newspaper are shrinking], so this Zhuang text is unlikely to be seen being read in public either.

I could not find any commercially-oriented, circulating texts which included Zhuang, despite extensive searching, save one word, *CUENGH* 'Zhuang' on a gift-box of liquor on a supermarket shelf in Wuming. This barely bilingual and barely public packaging was otherwise in Putonghua (loaning the English "vol" for volume), indicating Zhuang was merely a decorative resource authenticating the box's Putonghua slogan, "壮人智慧 壮乡村户" [Zhuang People's Wisdom–Zhuang Village Household]. This was consistent with the absence of Zhuang in commercially-oriented, fixed public texts.

Finally, I will describe a different medium of circulating text in which I found Zhuang: the Putonghua-Zhuang bilingual logo/opening graphic of *Zhuang Language News*, a publicly broadcast television program. Televisions were a semi-public feature of these linguistic landscapes, playing in campus cafeterias, open-fronted shops, public buses, security gatehouses etc. In my observations, programs including spoken or written Zhuang (e.g. subtitles) were absent on these televisions. I gleaned from participants that the government-produced evening *Zhuang Language News* was the best-known, systematically-produced Zhuang-inclusive television program in GZAR, but I did not observe public/semi-public televisions tuned in to it. I nevertheless watched the show myself, as it is streamed online on the national broadcaster's (CCTV's) website after its daily broadcast on GZAR's regional public channel. It is then re-distributed for free on commercial sites like ku.com, where I accessed episodes.

I analyzed the program's language use to better understand the public, televised uses of Zhuang that people in GZAR could encounter in daily life, using a sample of streamed episodes from 2014. Episodes always include a textual display of subtitles, headlines and logos, in addition to having aural content. Each episode begins with the same Putonghua-Zhuang bilingual opening graphic, which reads "*Vahcuengh Sinhwnz* 壮语新闻" i.e. 'Zhuang Language News'; this bilingual name, in smaller font, is also overlaid on each shot (see Figure 38). Each episode delivers only a few minutes of news (contrary to reports of fifteen-minute programs e.g. Chaisingkananont 2014: 91), with some reporters speaking Zhuang and others Putonghua. People interviewed use either Zhuang or various Mandarin varieties, but Putonghua subtitles accompany all speech (e.g. Figure 38), while there are no Zhuang subtitles for Mandarin speech. Some anchors speak Zhuang and others Putonghua, either way with a banner of Putonghua character headlines scrolling underneath. Thus, while episodes typically include spoken Zhuang, the written elements are exclusively in Putonghua aside from the logos. For example, in the screen-shot in Figure 38, the reporter is named by the Putonghua characters positioned in front of her. What she is saying is transcribed in white Putonghua subtitles beside the yellow bilingual logo, which is the program name written in Romanized Zhuang and Putonghua characters. Another program logo, at the top left, is Putonghua-only. Furthermore, the program as a whole cannot be comprehended from the Zhuang content alone; the audience appears to be expected to be orally bilingual and literate in Putonghua. Because the program's news cannot be communicated fully without Putonghua and because streamed episodes must be located using a Putonghua-only webpage (CCTV n.d.), Zhuang language is positioned as less useful than Putonghua in *Zhuang Language News*.

Figure 38: Screenshot of Zhuang Language News 31 March 2014.

On *Zhuang Language News*, reportage topics include Zhuangzu cultural events like Third of the Third celebrations (the biggest of the traditional Zhuang song festivals) and prosaic stories about events in GZAR. The report in Figure 38 was about a children's choir (shown in their costumes) who performed in Zhuang for Third of the Third celebrations. Overall, Zhuang language is constructed as relevant only within GZAR by *Zhuang Language News'* localized content choices.

Thus, it appears that circulating television texts which include Zhuang (on *Zhuang Language News*, at least) are consistent with the pattern of Zhuang being included in circulating and fixed texts in public landscapes which are government-authored texts associated with GZAR. *Zhuang Language News* was also consistent with the studied landscapes in not providing parallel translations. Rather, Putonghua dominated the text of *Zhuang Language News* as it did public signage texts.

Overall, bilingual signage was more common to encounter in my linguistic landscape studies than multilingual signage; the patterns within this latter category are our next focus.

6.3.3 Multilingual signage

Signage featuring more than two languages was uncommon. When it occurred, it was typically government-authored, naming public institutions in Putonghua, Zhuang and English. In this way, it echoed the preference for either Putonghua-Zhuang or Putonghua-English bilingualism amongst authors of bilingual public texts, as identified in the last section. Combining Putonghua, English and another foreign language was extremely rare, however, some multilingual texts which I documented on the campuses outside GZAR displayed Putonghua, Zhuang and other minority languages rather than English. There are other languages with long histories of use in GZAR which are now recognized as the languages corresponding to minority minzu. The other minority minzu in GZAR all have much smaller populations than the Zhuangzu.

A typical, government-authored, public institution name sign in Putonghua, Zhuang and English is presented in Figure 39, which shows the main entrance of GUN. Displayed on a large and ornate gateway, Romanized Zhuang text names the university, sitting above a larger Putonghua name and a small English name. Another example was found on the doorway of the Literature College within this campus. The doorway displayed plaques to announce the various societies and research groups housed within the building. The writing on these plaques was engraved in a standard format, with Zhuang first, next Putonghua, then English, and with Putonghua written largest. The named societies and research groups all concerned local minzu literature but not necessarily literature in Zhuang. For example, one plaque announced the GUN Lingnan Institute of Minzu Literature in Zhuang, Putonghua and English (Lingnan is a historic term for South-Central

Figure 39: Main entrance, Guangxi University of Nationalities; Nanning: gateway sign: Zhuang/Putonghua/English. Bank sign: Putonghua/English.

China). Zhuang, being the only local language and only minority language on these plaques, and on this minzu-specialist university's main gate, therefore indexes *all* local minority traditions and supplants any alternative representation through language choice.

Moreover, these plaques were clustered together on the GUN Literature College doorway, whereas trilingual or bilingual Zhuang-inclusive texts were not generally displayed elsewhere around the GUN campus. Like the trilingual banners in the corridor of the minority language department at MUC, discussed below, these trilingual plaques are "in place" because this particular building is allocated to the study of minority languages and cultures.

Neither my participants nor I were able to find Zhuang displayed on the GUN campus other than on the trilingual gateway and the Literature College plaques. Moreover, as in the urban streetscapes presented above, even these multilingual displays were surrounded by Putonghua-dominant signage. As Figure 39 shows, next to the trilingual GUN gateway was a neighboring bank's large sign, in Putonghua and English, while Putonghua dominated the smaller information plaques at the entrance (visible at the right), and the red banners, toponym signs and maps on the roadway from this gateway into campus.

Exploring both the campuses and the urban sites, I found just two commercial texts that combined Putonghua, Zhuang and English. Both were shop-front signs at Guangxi Rural Credit Service. They announced this bank's name in a long row of Romanized Zhuang, Putonghua in simplified characters, and English, with a standardized design. This was unusual as the pattern was for Zhuang to be absent from commercial texts. I saw this trilingual sign at two branches in the Nanning area, however, confirming the dominant pattern, I found other branches of the same bank in GZAR which did not include Zhuang on their signage. Moreover, the two branches with trilingual signs also displayed monolingual Putonghua bank-name signs. In one case this included a big, neon monolingual sign on the top of the building while the trilingual sign at that branch was hung lower and was smaller. The commerciality of Zhuang is minimal for Guangxi Rural Credit Service, it would seem.

Finally, while I noted above that public institution signage which included Zhuang was rare in Guilin, I documented one trilingual Putonghua, Zhuang and English name sign atop Guilin's older, northern railway station. The Zhuang and English words were symmetrically off-set and each slightly lower than the central Putonghua words. Inside this station, however, Zhuang was not displayed. This was consistent with the linguascaping of other stations and rail infrastructure that I passed and visited in GZAR, and which I (Grey 2021a) have elsewhere argued carries cultural urbanization, including urban norms of language display, into the countryside.

So far, I have presented multilingual signage which included both Zhuang and English. Multilingual signage which included foreign languages other than English was largely absent, and I never saw Zhuang and a foreign language other than English together in one sign. I occasionally observed a non-English foreign shop-name, but only one longer text in multiple foreign languages: this Putonghua, Vietnamese and English real estate promotion at Nanning Airport (Figure 40). Consistent with the patterns already evidenced, Zhuang was absent from this commercial text. This text also builds up the pattern of Zhuang as absent from texts directed to travelers from outside GZAR, as in the China-ASEAN Expo billboards at Figure 28 or in tourism texts in GZAR's Longji Scenic Area, a ticketed tourist zone operated commercially by the government within which Ping'An Zhuang Village is located (Grey 2021a). Bucking these trends, however, there is one common, multilingual text that includes Zhuang and yet unquestionably

Figure 40: Departures entrance; Nanning Airport: Putonghua/English/Vietnamese.

participates in commercial discourses and is, moreover, directed to those from outside GZAR as much as locals: banknotes.

Banknotes are such constantly circulating texts that they should be considered enduring, albeit not fixed, parts of these (and most) linguistic landscapes. All banknotes of the PRC's *Ren Min Bi* (RMB) currency are multilingual. They display scripts representing four recognized minority minzu with large populations – the Tibetans, Uyghurs, Mongolians and Zhuangzu – in addition to displaying Putonghua. Zhuang script was added when banknotes were reissued in 1955 and in 1962, while Tibetan, Uyghur and Mongolian appeared on the banknotes even earlier. (To see, compare the images of the 2 Fen banknote (1953 issue), 5 Yuan banknote (1960 issue) and 2 Jiao banknote China (1962 issue) at https://www.leftovercurrency.com/exchange/chinese-yuan/withdrawn-chinese-yuan-renminbi-banknotes/.)

However, as with many multilingual texts, these banknotes followed and still follow the general pattern observed clearly in Nanning's street-name signs of doing informational functions in Putonghua and symbolic functions in minority languages. The front of each banknote is Putonghua-only, with 中国人民银行 'People's Bank of China' in simplified characters and the denomination in both Arabic numerals and traditional characters. The reverse side gives the denomination and year of minting in numerals, with the denomination in Putonghua Pinyin and 年 'year' as a simplified character: *yuan* 'yuan' is the denomination. Also on the reverse, under *ZHONGGUO RENMIN YINHANG*, which is Putonghua Pinyin for 'People's Bank of China', that same institutional name is transliterated in four smaller scripts, including Romanized Zhuang in the lower right position. Readers can see the front and reverse of many RMB notes at *The People's Daily Online* (Anon. 2019: http://en.people.cn/n3/2019/0429/c90000-9573899.html). The *Language Log* (Mair 2013) has analyzed these multilingual versions of People's Bank of China, identifying problems with each and of Zhuang saying: "every syllable is derived directly from Chinese, it is doubtful whether it accurately reflects the way any Zhuang people actually speak." Nevertheless, the Zhuang is there to represent those people, it is constructed through texts such as banknotes as a linguistic emblem of the Zhuangzu. In so far as four minority minzu are represented through four linguistic emblems on banknotes, this subset represents the diverse and multiple (55) official minority minzu who all, symbolically, participate in the nation's economic wealth. A similar symbolism motivates the naming of the central bank as the People's Bank. This use of minority languages to symbolize diversity within unity also appeared in the few multilingual, Zhuang-inclusive signs that I found which did not include English.

Above, I explained that the "minzu unity is as precious as air" billboard in Guilin (Figure 37) used Putonghua-Zhuang bilingualism to index the inclusion of the minority minzu (at least the Zhuangzu) in that unity. This was likewise the dominant indexicality of multilingual signage which included Zhuang and other minority languages. Official minority languages were used in visual synecdoche to represent specific minzu. I found two examples on minzu-specialist university campuses outside GZAR: Figure 41 shows trilingual Putonghua, Zhuang and Dong New Year banners in the Minority Minzu Studies Department at MUC in Beijing City; and Figure 42 shows a multilingual, government-authored poster on a noticeboard at YMU in Kunming City. The trilingual banners were hanging outside the office of some Zhuang and Dong Studies academics, offices visited by students and colleagues but not passed by the general campus population. As far as I and my participants were able to find, Zhuang was displayed at MUC only in this semi-public corridor. The banners use aphorisms written in Putonghua, Zhuang and Dong (another Southern minority language) to celebrate Chinese New Year. Zhuang and Dong are printed smaller than the Putonghua and off-set from the central line, which Putonghua occupies.

Contrasting with the *implied* message (or secondary discourse) of inclusivity of those multilingual New Year banners, Figure 42's poster at YMU *explicitly* draws attention to its own inclusion of minority languages and implicitly thus promotes the inclusion of their speakers within the frame of national cohesion, which is the theme of the poster. The poster consists of one slogan repeated in eleven different languages, including Zhuang. In Putonghua, it is: 中华人民共和国各民族团结起来 毛泽东 ['All the minzu of the People's Republic of China join together!' Mao Zedong]. The Putonghua version is highlighted in red letters

6.3 An empirical analysis of patterns in language display — 173

Figure 41: Office of Zhuang Studies academics, MUC; Beijing: Zhuang/Putonghua/Dong.

Figure 42: Campus notices, YMU; Kunming: banner and LHS poster in Putonghua, RHS poster in eleven minority languages including Zhuang, and Putonghua.

and aligned vertically in the first (right-most) line. Horizontally-aligned sentences in a smaller font then repeat the slogan in various languages and scripts. Each of these sentences ends with the name in Putonghua of the language used: thus, the Zhuang sentence ends with 壮文 'Zhuang Writing'. The Zhuang sentence also begins with *Cunghhwaz*, Standard Zhuang for 'Zhuang Speech'. These subheadings indicate that the poster intends to communicate through Putonghua to a readership who may not recognize minority languages and may therefore need to be oriented in order to consume each sentence as an "iconization" (Irvine and Gal 2000: 38) of a named language.

6.4 Analyzing the linguistic order produced by patterned multilingualism

This analysis of monolingual, bilingual and multilingual texts has revealed (at least) these patterns in the linguistic landscapes:
1. Overall, the majority of signage across genres, authors and locations is monolingual in Putonghua.
2. >Written Zhuang is publicly displayed within GZAR (i.e. within an area nominally under Zhuangzu autonomous government) more than outside GZAR, but not consistently across GZAR; it is more common in Nanning than elsewhere in GZAR.
3. Written Zhuang is always displayed along with Putonghua within the same sign, and sometimes also with English or, very occasionally, with another Chinese minority language.
4. Romanized Zhuang is written, rather than the logographic Sawndip script.
5. Written Zhuang is displayed primarily in government-authored, short, relatively old texts. Within fixed public texts, these are especially toponymic texts naming public institution buildings in GZAR and naming Nanning's streets. Within circulating public texts, only PRC banknotes habitually include written Zhuang. (Banknotes are also an exception to the pattern of commercial texts: see #8 below).
6. Written Zhuang is displayed sometimes on government-authored promotional texts (promoting unity of the minzu). Within GZAR, this use of written Zhuang is rarer than using written Zhuang for government-authored toponymic texts. Outside GZAR, using Zhuang for either government promotions or toponyms is rare.
7. Written Zhuang is included in some signage fixed to the exterior of public and semi-public buildings which are specifically and explicitly allocated to housing objects and practices of local minority cultural heritage (e.g. GZAR's public, regional museums and library, or the Literature College of the region's public, minzu-specialist university).
8. In commercial signage (whether government-authored or privately authored) and in temporary, digital, new and circulating texts, written Zhuang

is rarely used. However, a major exception exists in that all PRC banknotes still include written Zhuang and have done so for decades.
9. Homemade or handwritten Zhuang signage is not displayed in public or semi-public landscapes, whether inside or outside GZAR.
10. All the content of bilingual and multilingual signage is provided in Putonghua but it is not always fully provided in the other languages on the same signage, i.e. bilingual or multilingual signage is often "fragmentary", applying Reh's (2004) typology. Moreover, Putonghua is usually visually highlighted through its position/size/color relative to the other languages on the same signage.

So, what linguistic order and other language ideologies or *de facto* policies are these patterns of presence, absence and relative prominence communicating?

First, the empirical analysis of these largely urban linguistic landscapes shows that Putonghua is essential to public life; that Putonghua is normalized in the built environment as a written language; and that Putonghua is not out of place anywhere in these sites. It is dominant. This was ironically and thereby especially evident in the *Zhuang Language News* data; despite the name, this public television program relied on spoken and written Putonghua to convey news stories while Zhuang was not written at all, only spoken. Contrasting Zhuang with Putonghua, the linguistic orders manifest in the landscapes communicate that Zhuang is inessential in public life, especially to informing or regulating readers as Zhuang is displayed for symbolic functions more than informational functions (these functions were first proposed by Landry and Bourhis 1997: 23). For example, on Nanning's street-name signs – the only signage to categorically include written Zhuang – the cardinal directions are written only in Putonghua and the street-name itself is written in Putonghua in two different scripts, both larger than the Zhuang-medium street-name. Moreover, the Zhuang street-name is a transliteration of the Putonghua street-name rather than a name reflecting any different, local epistemology.

And indeed, there is so little written Zhuang displayed overall, for either information or symbolism, that the ideology that Zhuang *is not a written language* is communicated by linguistic landscapes, although a contrary message is communicated by the few genres and locations that *do* include written Zhuang. In Chapter Seven, I will delve into the unrecognizability of these instances of written Zhuang and how it weakens this contrary message. Here, my analysis centers on three themes: spatialized linguistic orders; commercial ideologies; and polyvocality. I will then draw these themes together to explain the relationship between this linguistic landscape analysis and the upcoming three chapters.

6.4.1 Spatialized linguistic orders

The linguistic landscapes reveal language choices to "up-scale" or "down-scale" places (Blommaert 2007; Blommaert et al. 2014), producing the spatialized linguistic orders which this section analyzes. Relatedly, they emplace the government by leveraging the localized identity of places.

I would not have expected any place in my study outside GZAR to be demarcated by displays of monolingual Zhuang. Nevertheless, it is notable that monolingual Zhuang displays were not a place-making device or public norm anywhere that I found in urban or rural GZAR, nor at the minzu-specialist universities inside or outside GZAR. Nowhere appears to be demarcated by displays of monolingual Zhuang. Rather, Zhuang is clearly included in linguistic landscape texts alongside Putonghua (and sometimes other languages) for a certain type of place-making: the identification and delimitation of space by connecting that space with the usage of Zhuang language, with Zhuang culture and heritage, and/or with inhabitation by Zhuangzu people, whether current or historic or imagined. Zhuang language is, in these materialized discourses, a feature of the landscape, part of a "geomancy" (Lickorish 2008: 203) of GZAR as the essential Zhuang homeland. The regional government's provision of *Zhuang Language News*, and the strongly local favor of that news, also participates in this co-construction of GZAR as essentially and distinctly Zhuang (but is in competition with the language ideologies propagated by the program's reliance on Putonghua). Let us call this the localizing and heritagizing display of written Zhuang. This is the pattern of meaning-making that links the inclusion of Zhuang on certain signage on Nanning's streets, on GZAR's regional museums and on minority studies department buildings on campuses. Displaying Zhuang language emplaces a "collective memory" of Zhuang heritage in Nanning and these institutions (adapting Jaworski and Thurlow 2010: 8). However, in its co-construction with local and heritage-invested places, Zhuang language is constructed as normatively out of place elsewhere.

This down-scaling usage of Zhuang language as a symbolic resource works in tandem with the display of Putonghua to scale up to the national scale, emplacing even localized linguistic landscapes and local heritage within the nation. This national place-making is enhanced by the uniformity of the Putonghua-dominant language display norm across the nation, and in GZAR it is enhanced through Zhuang language's lack of autonomy from Putonghua, which it never appears in public without. The use of Zhuang rather than any other local/minority language also makes Zhuang stand in for all other local languages, cultures, heritages and populations in GZAR in place-making, erasing them from public symbology. And even within Zhuang language there is actually a diversity of language varieties;

the actual and representational exclusion in public landscapes of all Zhuang varieties except the standard naturalizes their disuse in writing and their out-of-placeness.

Some of the studied landscapes' texts are using the choice of other languages to further up-scale the places in which they appear, in addition to or instead of down-scaling or localizing with Zhuang. This chapter's Introduction referred to linguistic landscapes as "maps of meaning" (Jaworski and Thurlow 2010: 6); the maps in this study operate on many scales. The bilingual Putonghua-English texts and the multilingual texts which include not only Zhuang but also English imply an international and/or internationally-aspiring readership, using English to further up-scale the places that these texts name or are emplaced within. Thus, signage such as the Putonghua-Zhuang-English GUN gateway (Figure 39) can simultaneously up-scale with English and localize with Zhuang, adding itself to maps of meaning on both scales. Not including Zhuang is, itself, an up-scaling or de-localizing resource. Think for example of the Putonghua-Vietnamese-English advertisement at Nanning Airport in GZAR (Figure 40), which up-scales to two different international levels, situating Nanning as a place in the PRC and in the globally-interconnected world. That most other signs which included English did *not* also include Zhuang suggests that up-scaling is more important or profitable than localizing, revealing how linguistic and social orders intersect. This becomes especially clear in the university campuses.

I described GUN above as a minzu-specialist university, and so are MUC and YMU. Recall that I found just a few trilingual signs on their campuses which included Zhuang and either English or official minority languages. Universities like GUN, MUC and YMU are more localized than other public universities by virtue of their local minority minzu orientation in enrolments, courses and research; this localization is their *raison d'être*. However, with China's tertiary education being increasingly deregulated, these minzu-specialist universities, too, need to compete for domestic and international students. Thus, up-scaling with English does important place-making work for minzu-specialist universities. As part of widening its appeal, GUN introduced Putonghua-English marketing texts including a bilingual logo which I saw displayed around the campus and online. In similar moves, at the time of my fieldwork YMU and MUC had recently erected large Putonghua-English name signs at their main entrances. This followed from updating their official English names, replacing "nationalities" with "minzu", as reported by my YMU research facilitator in June 2014 (cf. Google 2014). GUN's trilingual entrance gateway (Figure 39) seems materially older in comparison and older because it still uses the term "nationalities". Its inclusion of English nevertheless reveals an association being made between English and education and may be interpreted as attempting to portray the university as outwardly-oriented.

That orientation has had socio-political purchase since China's Opening and Reform began (1978), even before the current climate of academic capitalism. GUN's more recent campus texts respond to the increasing value of internationalism by giving a more prominent role to English, while Zhuang is absent from its newer signs.

Furthermore, the study's finding that the public display of written Zhuang in Nanning was unusual in its relative prevalence compared to the rest of GZAR indicates that the border of the autonomous region is not the only boundary delimiting where public, written Zhuang is in place or out of place. It can be out of place even within GZAR. Whether within GZAR or outside it, the campus linguistic landscapes were similar across all sites; being a place of education appeared more germane to campus linguistic landscape norms than being within GZAR, or being a university where Zhuang Studies were taught. Thus, even within campus linguistic landscapes, there were implied but tight boundaries within which signage that included Zhuang was in place. These places included public gateways interfacing between the GUN and GU campuses and Nanning City, where there is a norm of streets and public institutions being named in Zhuang, so the gateways are conforming to the surrounding linguistic landscape of which they formed part. These places also included the buildings on minzu-specialist universities' campuses inside which minority minzu languages were the object of study. The government poster insisting that "All the minzu of the PRC join together!" in Putonghua and eleven minority languages on an outdoor notice board at YMU (Figure 42) was therefore exceptional not only for that campus but for all six university linguistic landscapes that I studied, and for its uniquely extreme multilingualism.

Moreover, the exclusive use of Standard Zhuang's Romanized, government-developed script whenever Zhuang is written in public texts indexes a group for whom the government developed a script in the twentieth century *because it did not recognize previous Zhuang literacy traditions*. Thus, while symbolizing Zhuang heritage, all the Romanized Zhuang signage also has the potential to reproduce a construction of Zhuang language, culture or people as "backwards" and modernized by the state because Zhuang speakers (apparently) have had none of the traditions of literature and literary practices which attract especially high cultural capital in China, and which are associated with the majority.

There are also symbolic semantics at work that may or may not be intentional (as the epigraph foresees), but which follow a logic that considers Putonghua more important than other languages on any sign. The smaller type font of Zhuang on street-name signs and, likewise, on those few campus entrance signs that include Zhuang, as well as Zhuang's typically off-centered position in bilingual/multilingual texts, visually symbolizes that Zhuang conveys peripheral information, or is a mere decoration. Consider that, at a distance, or if walking or driving past, these little Zhuang lines will be much harder to see than the larger Putonghua: Zhuang is not positioned as important to wayfaring. This is a recurrent theme in linguistic landscape studies of minoritized languages the world over, e.g. Sebba (2010: 68, 72) found Manx was "constructed a secondary to English by being printed in a smaller typeface" on packaging and public notices on the Isle of Mann. Acknowledging these overlapping discourses can assist in resolving the ambiguities between, for example, including Zhuang on street-name signs but with a small font, or between including Zhuang on some government-authored signs but not on others. In overt discourses informing or regulating the public, Zhuang is generally not mobilized: those discourses are typically articulated through Putonghua. An overt discourse of language status mobilizes written Zhuang as a semiotic resource, but a covert discourse of language status uses semiotic resources of "visual grammar" (Kress and van Leeuwen 2006), including Putonghua's relatively prominent size and positioning, as well as Zhuang's absence on whole classes of signage and the symbolism of never having Zhuang alone without Putonghua on a sign.

Together, all these public landscape texts thus contribute organizational frames including a spatialized linguistic order to public discourses, in addition to any specific information they provide. As Sebba (2010: 59–60) notes: "public texts may have an overt purpose (for example, to inform) but may participate in other discourses as well. In the case of multilingual texts, this may be a discourse about the relative value and status of the languages used". These linguistic landscapes produce a multimodal articulation of Zhuang language's low status. In this way, the symbolic and informative functions of the language on signage interact to make meaning.

There is another, related semiotic contribution that displaying written Zhuang makes to place-making processes. It combines the symbolic use of languages for scaling just outlined with the use of written Zhuang as a metonymic symbolic resource in political discourses. The logic of this second strategy is that displaying written Zhuang indexes the Zhuangzu polity. We have seen in the data that including Zhuang in multilingual texts can symbolically reinforce an implicit and sometimes explicit government message of social inclusion of the Zhuangzu and unity between the minzu. This symbolic function of written Zhuang is especially clear in the data where written Zhuang must index the Zhuangzu to align a text's visual ideology (i.e. its visible choice of scripts, languages and imagery) with the same text's explicitly stated ideology of unity between minzu. Written Zhuang language is thus "iconized" (Irvine and Gal 2000: 38) as a symbol of the Zhuangzu polity. (This symbolism reproduces the construction of the Zhuangzu and Zhuang language speakers as coextensive groups, a language ideology which data in Chapter Two has challenged.) With this indexicality, the display of Zhuang can emplace another layer of meaning: the localization of various tiers of government. Including Zhuang language on street-name signs and public institutions' façades symbolizes a government assuming "the" Zhuangzu people's voice and/or authority to govern the Zhuangzu. In particular, the Nanning Municipal Government associates itself with Putonghua-Zhuang bilingualism through its distinctive street-name signage, positioning this government as associated with current and "ancestral" Zhuang-speaking communities. Similarly, when the regional government refers to "Guangxi Zhuangzu Autonomous Region" in Zhuang within the name signage on regional public institutions it constructs not only these specific buildings but the region – a political organization of space – as being meaningfully defined as places where Zhuang language is – or at least was – practiced. These physical emplacements of written Zhuang reveal the "semioticizing processes" called "articulation of territory" (Jaworski and Thurlow 2010: 8); but it is not only that displaying Standard Zhuang and Putonghua in the linguistic landscape articulates a claim to territory. I wish to go further than Jaworski and Thurlow here by emphasizing that the symbolic display of the linguistic icon of a minority polity builds the rooted, local identity of the government. This is part of a claim to political representativeness and thus to constructing the legitimacy of the government. This resonates with the legal and structural discourses in a governing system where minority polities officially constitute the nation (Chapters 2, 3 and 5 have explained this system) but there is no reason to think this layer of linguistic landscape meaning is unique to China.

That the inclusion of minorities through the inclusion and display of iconized minority languages is part of the legitimacy of this system can also be seen with the multilingual banknotes. Analyzing Euro banknotes from a similar perspective, Sassatelli (2017: 355) argues that "at the crossroad of money's economic and cultural significance is its reliance on trust, and therefore on the availability of a shared basis of that trust, both institutional and imagined. The images and words [...] even the very name given to the money, all must evoke trust, and together tell a story about its foundation". This holds true for the multilingual RMB ('People's Currency') banknotes, which display linguistic icons of the nation (the icon being Putonghua) and the many minorities (the icons being written Tibetan, Uyghur, Mongolian and Zhuang). The following chapter will show that the RMB's imagery also represents the Zhuangzu and other minority peoples with visual icons, augmenting the symbolic linguistic inclusivity.

Sassatelli, a sociologist, calls the linguistic and non-linguistic iconography on banknotes the "narrative of identity"; linguists might prefer to call it a multimodal discourse. This multimodal discourse represents national identity to communicate trustworthiness, which often means representing unity and/or inclusion. This sort of discourse is arguably a generic feature of banknotes and coins. While "the euro banknotes and coins' appearance has been chosen to evoke [...] the well-known rhetoric of European identity as 'unity in diversity'" (Sassatelli 2017: 356), which echoes exactly the PRC's own narrative (see, e.g. the prominence of this in constitutional texts: Chapter Four), one difference between the RMB and Euro's iconography is that in Europe "ancestral ties are [...] too controversial" (Sassatelli 2017: 263) as icons for banknotes. It shows the strength of the PRC's nation-building discourses and the strength of the concept of nation as opposed to a supra-nation that linguistic icons of four minorities appear on each RMB banknote rather than being too controversial to include. Nevertheless, whether using the Euro's anodyne but polysemic architectural iconography or the RMB's more explicit iconography of diverse languages, people and cultures, both currencies can be said to be "making a virtue out of necessity, and highlighting, celebrating the construction process [of the unification] itself" (Sassatelli 2017: 263).

6.4.2 Commercial ideologies

Patterns 5 and 8 in my list at the end of Section 6.3 emphasize that Zhuang was displayed on texts authored by the government but that Zhuang was not included in commercially-oriented government texts such as advertisements for state-owned enterprises. By contrast, I have shown that the government *did* author public texts in Zhuang in certain civic, toponymic and regulatory discourses. In fact, the absence of Zhuang from commercially-oriented public texts pertains whether the author of a public text was a private corporation/business or even an individual merchant, or a government agency/enterprise engaged in commerce. Zhuang was not found being used to communicate with, or affectively connect to, potential buyers in written advertisements or shopfront signage. It was also typically absent from circulating commercial texts such as product labels and receipts, even in shops connected to Zhuang culture like the souvenir shops at GZAR's museums (there are further examples from a department store and a tourism site in Chapter Seven). I found only one exception, the bilingual product packaging noted earlier which included the word for "Zhuang" in Zhuang. I found just two Zhuang-themed restaurants, and likewise found that the circulating commercial texts (menus, printed napkin packets etc) were *not* in Zhuang language at the one I visited. That restaurant had just one, short, possibly Zhuang-medium decorative sign inside (Figure 36). Moreover, while I did not systematically document and analyze spoken texts in the landscapes, my impression was that spoken Zhuang was not used for pre-recorded or scripted commercial texts such as the loud-speaker announcements and jingles that are often pumped out of shops to pedestrians, nor used for the rehearsed welcomes with which shop-assistants greet customers. This near-total absence of written Zhuang from commercial discourses in and outside GZAR suggests that written Zhuang has no role to play in creating associations with market actors or economic profit.

That is, the dissociation of written Zhuang from commerce is a norm of commercial discourse. Putonghua is the written lingua franca of commerce, both actually and normatively. English is included in some commercial texts in my data, to index luxury, transnational lifestyles and other positive brand associations, and potentially also as a lingua franca for texts aimed at transnational or foreign market actors, e.g. advertisements about the China-ASEAN Expo or advertising property to travelers at Nanning Airport.

This absence of Zhuang is one of the characteristics of commercial discourse across genres of public and transactional text and regardless of whether the authoring organization is a private company. I also found the absence of Zhuang to be a feature of other discourses which are built into these linguistic landscapes, e.g. informational/wayfaring discourses like road directions (I explained that even the Zhuang component of Nanning's bilingual street-name signs is not informational) and regulatory discourses like rules. We therefore have an illustration here of certain characteristics of one discourses becoming incorporated into other discourses, or more likely the back-and-forth reproduction of language norms across discourses. Of course, characteristics can cross from materialized linguistic landscape discourses to other discourses, too; this is the normative operation of linguistic landscapes. The Scollons (amongst others) call these processes "interdiscursivity" (Scollon and Scollon 2003: 193). Yet as I explained, all RMB banknotes have a little Zhuang written on them and have had for 60 years, but this practice has not moved interdiscursively beyond banknotes. Perhaps the invisibility of this multilingualism or the lack of ideological buy-in from people to the iconicity of Standard Zhuang, both revealed in the following chapter, are the reason, or the Putonghua-dominant and Zhuang-minimizing norms of linguistic landscapes have overwhelmed any influence on commercial discourses that banknotes might have had.

I have foregrounded the commerciality of discourses rather than the private nature of authors of texts in the landscape because not only private authors produce commercial texts. This is now the case both in China and around the world, meaning that the classic private/government author binary applied in Landry and Bourhis' (1997) linguistic landscape study is not helpful. This blurring is often a manifestation of a trend towards market-oriented rationales, including the corporatization of state authorities, which Coupland (2010: 93) calls "quasi public-sector" authors. In China's socialist market economy, quasi public-sector authors are likewise corporatized state authorities, e.g. state-owned enterprises. This global trend towards private-government hybridization is made additionally complex when governments regulate public texts from any author, which I analyze in Chapter Nine. In my dataset, one hybrid author explicitly named on signage is the state-owned, commercially-oriented broadcaster, China Network Television System (Figure 17). Other authors of the documented signage are corporatized state authorities, e.g. the China-ASEAN Expo Secretariat (authoring Figure 28) is backed by eleven government ministries and sixteen private or QANGO Chambers of Commerce (China-ASEAN Expo Secretariat 2016), while the entity authoring the sign about the new subway in Figure 14 is a joint entity combining a public bureau and a private organization, Nanning Rail Transport Limited.

With global corporatization trends and the symbolic power of making money to fuel interdiscursive practices (i.e. to attract imitation and convergence), I expect to see commercial discourse characteristics including the absence of Zhuang from consumer-oriented/public-oriented writing and speech propagating further through these linguistic landscapes.

6.4.3 Grassroots language practices and state ideologies of polyvocality

While public places are often regulated environments and have major state or corporate or hybrid entities authoring prominent texts within them, there are still individually authored or otherwise grass-roots texts in Chinese public linguistic landscapes. These range from the ephemeral water calligraphy that people paint on pavements in parks to graffiti, advertising stickers in transgressive places, hand-written or home-printed notices, the screens of the phones of commuters on public transport, clothing bearing writing worn by pedestrians, etc. But they are not in Zhuang.

Thus, non-government, non-commercial texts in Zhuang which played with or subverted dominant language and authorship norms were invisible, save for the Putonghua-Zhuang-Dong New Year banners displayed by Minority Studies academics in a place at MUC that was technically accessible to the public but inside and out of the way (around their office door). The academics chose to display these banners, making this the only Zhuang-inclusive "'grassroots' landscape initiative" (Coupland 2010: 99) that I found. However, the Zhuang New Year was not traditionally observed at the same time as the Han Chinese New Year. Plus, the practice of feting New Year with aphorisms on red doorway banners is a Han custom. Thus, the Zhuang and Dong couplets on these banners are re-entextualized into a mainstream textual custom without symbolically displacing the centrality of Han culture. Zhuang and Dong do not displace Putonghua from the physical center of the banners, either. As these banners cannot but be read in meaningful contrast to the typical, monolingual Putonghua New Year banners, the trilingualism is deployed for symbolic inclusivity.

The absence of grassroots public texts in Zhuang also has co-textual significance in relation to a point I made in the analysis of spatialized linguistic orders, above: that the government uses written Zhuang to publicly represent the voice of locals and thereby identify itself with/as them. A Bakhtinian (Bakhtin 1981: 263, 428) gaze upon the linguistic landscape will see that heteroglossia arises in the "social dialogue among languages" on display, but Zhuang language's part in these dialogues is government-orchestrated rather than bottom-up. Like the novelist (Bakhtin's concern), the government as author uses language choice to create an impression of heteroglossic voices, including (imagined) viewers and the body politic on whose behalf public signage is voiced. Thus, the multilingual Nanning name-signs, banknotes and billboards about government unity represent pluralism through multilingualism rather than actually voicing plural interests.

A similar point can be made by applying Goffman's production format to the linguistic landscape, following Lou (2016: 20). The *principal* speaking the words in Zhuang on the signage is not necessarily all, or any, Zhuang speakers, but rather the government, who is also the *author*. The underpinning political philosophy of the PRC is that the government speaks as the people, that author *is* principal, with government institutions mere mechanisms of animation. Yet, as Chapter Five has explained, the government is not necessarily comprised of Zhuang speakers, and indeed the locus of power to rule lies beyond the Zhuangzu and beyond the Zhuangzu's "autonomous" regional government.

Moreover, each landscape text studied here, and the texts taken together as semiotic aggregates or linguistic landscapes, predominantly use Putonghua. Thus, whatever polyvocality there may be in these linguistic landscapes, diverse authors are predominantly *not* relying on diverse languages to create the particular voice in which to express themselves.

6.5 Concluding discussion: Normatively displacing Zhuang

Overwhelmingly, these linguistic landscapes reflect Putonghua's dominance back onto places and the people within them, contributing to a continuous dynamic through which Putonghua becomes not only common but normatively hegemonic in urban and educational places and as a resource for urban, educated lives. This is an important fact against which to read reports, such as Nanning Municipal Minority Language Works Commission (2019: §1.5), that by 2019:

> 全市各级国家机关和事业单位等法定单位同时使用壮汉两种文字书写单位名称牌匾、刻制公章的比例超过 70%...市区 400 多条主要道路路名标志牌及横县、宾阳、上林、马山、隆安、武鸣主要街道路牌的用字同时使用了壮汉两种文字
>
> [more than 70% of the city's state agencies and public institutions at all levels use both Zhuang and Han characters to write [their] *danwei* name plaques and engraved official seals [...] In in Nanning Municipality, the name signs of 400 main roads in the urban area and the main street signs of Hengxian, Binyang, Shanglin, Mashan, Long'An, and Wuming [peri-urban counties/districts] used both Zhuang and Han scripts.]

Against Putonghua's dominance, even 400 bilingual street-name signs in the capital or bilingualism on most government building's name signs creates only a limited public presence for Zhuang. This Zhuang in the linguistic landscape can therefore play only a limited role in inciting change in individuals' Zhuang language practices or as a symbolic resource constructing these as places meaningfully understood as associated to Zhuang language.

Moreover, my study shows that the (central, regional and municipal) government is the main author of texts that include Zhuang and a prominent author overall in these landscapes. The government's practices of public language display reproduce and visualize beliefs in (a) Zhuang as a non-autonomous language; (b) Zhuang as a non-commercial language; (c) Zhuang as a historically unwritten language; (d) Zhuang as an immobile language; (e) Zhuang representing both the Zhuangzu all the minorities of GZAR and (f) Zhuang only being in place in GZAR, amongst others. These are complicit in territorializing and heritagizing language ideologies, and hierarchic ideologies of spatialized linguistic order, which relate not only to Zhuang but to other minority languages, Putonghua and English.

All of the linguistic landscape patterns found in this chapter are "*de facto* language policy", as Shohamy calls it in the epigraph. These *de facto* policies have the potential to enable and constrain the language practices of others, both language display practices and other language practices such as speaking, within or in association with the landscapes where such displays are seen. The linguistic landscape participates in shaping people and institutions' expectations of which languages can and should be used in which forms or mediums, in which places, in which genres/discourses and by whom. The chapter concludes that these landscapes overwhelmingly suggest that Zhuang cannot and should not be used in most forms or mediums, most places, most genres/discourses and by anyone but the government. In examining the representation of Zhuang people in these linguistic landscapes through symbols other than Zhuang language, Chapter Seven will deepen this analysis of these visual ideologies.

Moreover, some places and discourses are imbued with more symbolic power than others, as I raised in the Introduction. It follows then that features of language display associated with those places are also invested with symbolic power and thus influential. I explained why the urban places and university campuses featured in this chapter are examples of symbolically powerful places. Therefore, certain patterns of language display associated with cities or education can become not only familiar or expected but normatively valued and internalized.

Of course, these internalized norms may also be reflected upon by individuals and challenged, as an agentive theorization of habitus predicts, and which Chapter Eight illustrates empirically. All the language ideologies communicated by these linguistic landscapes and discussed in this chapter are therefore able to be reflected upon and resisted, or taken up, in the co-construction of meaning between viewers and the built environment. However, I argue that because public texts become part of the physical environment, often an enduring feature of it, and are physically and temporally removed from their producers and authors, they are easily misrecognized as non-ideological. Thus naturalized, the Zhuang-marginalizing norms of these linguistic landscapes can persist largely unchallenged in people's habitus. It is therefore a matter of critical inquiry to what extent the patterns of linguistic landscapes that this chapter has identified are not "natural" features gradually shaped by many actors without hidden agendas, but rather deliberately linguascaped by the government or other powerful actors. Chapter Nine is devoted to that inquiry.

7 New semiotic displays of old "Zhuangness"

Speaking, writing, and other semiotic codes found in space index particular localities, orient us through different levels of territorial and societal stratification including identity claims, power relations, and their contestations.   (Jaworski and Thurlow 2010: 8)

7.1 Introducing multi-modal representations of Zhuangness

Let us walk the linguistic landscapes once more, this time focusing less on language. The primary semiotic resource under analysis in the last chapter was language choice: whether Putonghua was displayed, whether Zhuang was included, whether Zhuang was displayed instead of other local languages, etc. Choice of script was one associated semiotic resource that Chapter Six analyzed – for example, non-official scripts for Zhuang were erased from view in favor of Romanized Zhuang – and the relative sizing and placement of languages were others. Chapter Six identified key patterns, or visual ideologies, in the display of linguistic resources and especially in the display of written Zhuang. These patterns of display are codes, the likes of which Jaworski and Thurlow theorize in the epigraph as actively participating in the construction of place and of socio-linguistic order. But, as the epigraph notes, "other semiotic codes" too can be emplaced, and likewise "index particular localities [and] orient us through […] identity claims, power relations, and their contestations" (Jaworski and Thurlow 2010: 8). This chapter therefore widens the linguistic lens to examine the multimodal semiotic resources that co-occur in the same landscapes and also participate in visual ideologies. *How else is reference made to Zhuangness in these landscapes, other than through the use of Zhuang language?*

There is a colloquial transparency to my term, *Zhuangness*. Zhuangness is obviously not precisely synonymous with Zhuang language or Zhuang culture or the Zhuangzu polity; rather, it labels the more emic and dynamic combinations that imbue a person or a place's "Zhuang" identity with meaning.

Given the widened focus, this chapter could have shifted to the term *semiotic landscapes*. My choice to use *linguistic landscapes* consistently throughout the book, instead, is not intended to exclude the other semiotic resources of these environments, the necessary inclusion of which Kress and van Leeuwen (2006), Shohamy and Gorter (2009), Jaworski and Thurlow (2010) and others have convincingly argued. "Linguistic landscape" is, however, a conventionalized and pleasingly alliterative shorthand (see Pütz and Mundt 2018: 1–5), and in this book it foregrounds the interrelationship between language and other semiotic resources in a way that is intentional and heuristic. Moreover, while language choice is no longer my primary concern, some of the semiotic resources that I examine in this chapter are still aspects of language use. These include displaying explicit references to "Zhuang" and "Zhuang language" in various other languages. These are analyzed in Section 7.2, which culminates in a close-up study of a complex representation in the form of a curation sign within a public museum exhibition about Zhuangzu culture. The conventionalization of representation of Zhuangness through imagery and architectural form are examined in Section 7.3. This is followed by another close-up, this time of my archival study of decades of *Third of the Third* magazines. Echoing the multimodal semiotic tropes of Zhuangness that I found in contemporary public landscapes, these magazines represent Zhuangness using both linguistic and non-linguistic resources. In fact, the similarities that I find between the representations in the magazines and in the landscapes empirically illustrate the theoretical argument made in the conclusion of the last chapter, that visual ideologies move across different spaces and discourses. While the relative aging of different signage which I analyzed in Chapter Six gave us some sense of linguistic landscapes as palimpsests or historic bodies, this media archive analysis extends our historic awareness of the conventions of representing Zhuangness which these landscapes now carry into the present.

7.2 Explicit references to "Zhuang" or "Zhuang language"

The use and display of a language by linguistic landscape authors references the use of that language by others, past and present, and Chapter Six has examined in detail how that is done for Zhuang. A language can also be explicitly named to stand in for the use and the users of the language. However, across the urban streets, cultural, commercial and commuter hubs, and university campuses that I studied, public texts did not often refer explicitly to Zhuang language, in any language. The only instances that I found were within the Guangxi Museum of Nationalities' Zhuangzu culture exhibition, in which some curation panels talked about Zhuang language in Putonghua, English and in one instance, in Zhuang (Figure 44, discussed further below); the Zhuang and Putonghua opening titles of *Vahcuengh Sinhwnz*//壮语新闻 '*Zhuang Language News*', the unevenly bilingual public television program which I analyzed in the last chapter; and the billboard at YMU promoting minzu unity by repeating a quotation from Mao Zedong in eleven languages (Figure 42). This billboard included a Zhuang translation and labelled it in Putonghua as "壮文" [Zhuang Writing].

In terms of explicit references to "Zhuangzu", the polity formed to officially recognize the speakers of Zhuang, rather than to "Zhuang language" itself, I found them often within the proper noun 广西壮族自治区 'Guangxi Zhuangzu

Autonomous Region'. This noun is displayed as part of many government institutions' names in GZAR, and such institutions sometimes named themselves on their exterior signage in Zhuang, in addition to always naming themselves in Putonghua. The last chapter provided a few examples of such institutions using both Putonghua and Zhuang for their name signs, including the GZAR Museum (Figure 33). Such naming in Zhuang aligns with the finding in the last chapter that displaying texts which include Zhuang language on campuses is normatively in place only within areas where Zhuangness is made relevant by the particular activities taking place there. Similarly, the regional museum features Zhuang culture and history. More pertinent here, naming these institutions with explicit reference to the Zhuangzu polity and its nominally autonomous region, GZAR, even in Putonghua, constructs both the polity and the region as units which derive meaning from their association with Zhuangness.

For public institutions' names, 壮族 'Zhuangzu' was the preferred referent, but I found that the adjective 壮 'Zhuang' was preferred for naming a more diverse range of products and attractions. These included references in Putonghua and English to the tourism destination "Ping'An Zhuang Village", the Putonghua-English bilingual name "黑衣壮民居//Black Clothes Zhuang House" on an attraction within the Guangxi Museum of Nationalities' "Ethnic Village" park, the bilingually-named "壮族文化展厅//Zhuangzu Culture Exhibition Hall" inside that museum, and two monolingually-named commercial restaurants in urban centers: "壮家人美食馆" [Zhuang Home-Style Restaurant] in Wuming and "壮乡美食" [Zhuang Hometown Cuisine] in Guilin. Evidently, most of these names are place-naming nouns to which the adjective "Zhuang" adds specificity; however, using Zhuang language as the medium of naming was not chosen to enhance these specific place identities. Rather, the explicit references to Zhuang in the medium of other languages within these displayed naming texts construct place by implying that Zhuangness is relevant to the place.

This is particularly clear in the example of another place which I have not yet mentioned, a souvenir stall named, in Putonghua, "壮姑" [Zhuang Auntie] (Figure 43). I found Zhuang Auntie located inside a department store of the upmarket Malaysian chain, Parkson, in downtown Nanning. Its Putonghua-dominant name-sign also featured a smaller English brand-name, "Z-girl", the Z obliquely referencing Zhuang. What makes this place Zhuang? The name constructs the souvenirs it sells as remembrances of Zhuang culture, and the souvenirs themselves materialize some of the drum and *xiuqiu* 'love ball' visual tropes of Zhuang culture which the following section will explore further. Zhuang Auntie's stock of decorative balls were embroidered with Putonghua characters, but neither the embroidered balls nor other products, signs or receipts at Zhuang Auntie contained Zhuang language to further the construction of this place or its wares or their

Figure 43: Department store stall; Nanning: Putonghua/English.

usage as associated with Zhuangness. This was consistent with the other commercially-oriented, so-called Zhuang places listed above and with the examples of commercial linguistic landscape discourse in the last chapter; practicing Zhuang language is not a common part of associating a commercial space with Zhuangness for place-making.

Before moving to non-linguistic references, I will analyze one particularly unusual and complex sign containing multiple, explicit references to Zhuang language and the Zhuangzu. I documented and photographed it during 2014's fieldwork. Within this one text, many of the discourses identified in this book meet, including discourses valorizing Zhuang language, discourses constructing Zhuang language as symbolic of the Zhuangzu and discourses constructing Zhuang language as symbolizing the "voice" of the Zhuangzu and therefore as an authentication resource, as well as developmentalist and nation-building discourses. The text is shown in Figure 44. It is a large, wall-mounted sign

Figure 44: Curation, Zhuang Culture Exhibition, Guangxi Museum of Nationalities; Nanning: Putonghua/Zhuang/English.

hanging at the entrance to the Zhuangzu Culture Exhibition Hall inside the Guangxi Museum of Nationalities.

To provide some background to the site, this is a free, public museum in Nanning which opened in 2009 as the "Guangxi Museum of Nationalities" in English. Since my fieldwork, it has been renamed "Anthropology Museum of Guangxi" in English but remains 广西民族博物馆 'lit. Guangxi Minzu Museum' in Putonghua. The museum styles itself as exhibiting and protecting the material and intangible cultural heritage of *all twelve* of GZAR's resident minority minzu (GXMN 2013; Easy Tour China 2016) and this may be why the official name does *not* explicitly refer to the Zhuangzu. The name includes simply "Guangxi" rather than the full name of the region, GZAR, thus avoiding the word "Zhuangzu". Nevertheless, the Zhuangzu have more representation and cultural and symbolic capital than the other eleven minority minzu in the sense that only Zhuangzu artifacts get their own permanent collection in this museum. This Zhuangzu collection is shown in a wing of the museum bilingually labelled the 壮族文化展厅 //Zhuangzu Culture Exhibition Hall. Upon entering this Hall, visitors face the sign at which we will now look.

The sign is entitled "僕 *raeuz[rau2]*". I debate which language(s) this character is inscribing later in this section, but *raeuz* is Romanized Zhuang. *Raeuz* is also spelled *rauz* sometimes: both spellings appear in the banner of the prominent Zhuang online community forum, *The Rauz Horizon* (www.rauz.net.cn). The bracketed part of the title, "[rau2]", indicates the pronunciation and second tone of *raeuz*. On the next two lines of the sign, subtitles in Putonghua then English provide a translation of *raeuz*: "我们咱们" 'lit. we we' in Putonghua; and "us" in English. These subtitles also announce themselves as translations, e.g. "Zhuang translation: us" (meaning 'translation from Zhuang into English: us').

Below the titles, three paragraphs in Putonghua, Zhuang and then English narrate a history of discrete, linear ethno-cultural Zhuang(zu) development and the benefits of historical inclusion in the Chinese empire. The panel is not a parallel trilingual text. All three paragraphs presents the Zhuangzu's national integration as beneficial to their development i.e. engaging the developmentalist rationale identified in Part Two. However, the Putonghua and Zhuang paragraphs also emphasize a point in time which is not emphasized in the English paragraph. This is the point when "壮族开始融入中华民族大家庭//*Bouxcuengh ongogya yungz haeuj gya hung Cunghwaz minzouz bae*" [the Zhuangzu started blending into the Great Chinese Family]. Moreover, in the quoted sentence and throughout, the Putonghua refers to the 壮族 'Zhuangzu' i.e. the officially-recognized Zhuang minzu polity, even if narrating pre-PRC times when there was no recognized Zhuangzu. The quoted Zhuang sentence uses the autonym *Bouxcuengh*, the conventional translation of Zhuangzu. The English uses "Zhuang" without the polity morpheme, -*zu*. Hidden alternatives not chosen include naming the historic group(s) as Zhuang 人 'people' or 氏族 'clans', or generic people of the Baiyue Basin, as some historians do to avoid retrospective application of the modern minzu classifications (e.g. Barlow 2011: 33–34). Historic Zhuang autonyms are also available (e.g. the autonyms listed in Li and Huang 2004: 239). Further, the Putonghua paragraph frames Zhuangzu integration as the inclusion of a minzu within the establishment of a 统一的多民族国家 'unified multi-minzu nation', which is a conventionalized reference to the PRC. Previous chapters have reiterated that this multiethnic, unified nation is an enormously influential construction of the order of society today (see further Mullaney 2011: 1). Thus, the panel legitimizes contemporary nation-building by framing it as advantageous for the Zhuangzu and, in addition in the Putonghua paragraph, as a form of state-structured ethnic harmony.

The nation-building conceptual frame and the use in the same text of "Zhuangzu" modifies the titular self-reference to we/us in Zhuang, Putonghua and English; this pronoun refers to a particular group within the state's organization of society, "we Zhuangzu". By contrast, in grassroots texts, *raeuz* 'us', whether written in a character or in Romanized Zhuang, appears to be used to index a social group transcending the official Zhuangzu grouping. For example, a CD given to me by Mr E is sub-titled "The Music of the *Rauz* People" in English but its Putonghua sub-title, also on the cover, is "壮**族**布依音乐专辑" [Zhuangzu **and Bouyeizu** Music Collection, emphasis mine]: Guangxi Nanning Dream Rauz Cultural Broadcast Company Ltd (ed) (2013). That is, in this title *Rauz* is translated as two co-referents in Putonghua, the Zhuangzu and the Bouyeizu, who are another official minority polity. Chapter Two has explained that Bouyei language is also a Zhuang variety but that Bouyei speakers are erased in the typical representation of Zhuang speakers as coextensive with the Zhuangzu. Another example of the grassroots use of the pronoun *rauz* is the *Rauz Horizon* website; it is a "prominent" (Chaisingkananont 2014: 26) transnational Tai-speakers' initiative popular with some of my participants. *Rauz* in the website name thus does not index the Zhuangzu polity but a transnational and interlingual group.

The curation sign's second paragraph is in Zhuang, although the exhibition's curation signs were not otherwise trilingual. The use of Zhuang language on this introductory sign is part of a pattern of iconic and place-making reference to (imagined) Zhuang speakers through language and script choice, a point explored at length in the last chapter. However, making this sign unusual, here the reference also is made explicit and *self-referential* through the pronominal title. The text thus represents itself as authored by Zhuang(zu) people. The Putonghua and English translations of the title represent this Zhuang voice explicably to outsiders. The self-referential title also positions the exhibition, within which the sign is emplaced and which it introduces, as being voiced and authored by Zhuang people. This is an authentication resource for the museum exhibition.

However, this indexicality, and this authentication, is complicated by the ambiguous script in the sign's title, to which I alluded above. As a reminder, the sign is entitled "偻 raeuz[rau2]". Although the subtitles in both Putonghua and English declare that the translation is 'we' or 'us', this is not completely incorrect. The usual Putonghua logograph for the Zhuang word *raeuz* is 僚 (*liáo*) rather than the 偻 (*lóu*) used here in the title. You may recall that 僚 (*liáo*) was written on a sign inside Zhuang Home-Style Restaurant which I showed in Chapter Six at Figure 36. 僚 (*liáo*) is also used to translate *raeuz* on the CD from Mr E that I mentioned above, which is trilingually entitled "*Beix Nuengx Raeuz*//贝侬僚//*Our Brothers and Sisters*" (Guangxi Nanning Dream Rauz Cultural Broadcast Company Ltd 2013). Using 僚 (*liáo*) for *raeuz* can also be found in the blog "*Bouxcuengh Raeuz*" ("浪子天涯" [Prodigal Son] 2016). Occasionally, yet another character, 滑, is used instead to translate *raeuz* (e.g. GZAR Minority Language Working Group Research Team, 1984: 631), but 僚 (*liáo*) appears to be the conventional spelling. Moreover, *Liao* was one of the pre-tenth century imperial labels for people later called Zhuang (Chaisingkananont, 2014: 33). Even the pre-PRC derogatory grapheme for writing "Zhuang" in Mandarin was not the 偻 (*lóu*) used on the curation sign but another character, as I explained in Chapter Six. Moreover, this 偻 (*lóu*) has been officially simplified to 偻, adding to the oddity of the choice on this relatively new curation sign. I therefore believe the museum's translation of *raeuz* as 偻 (*lóu*) is a mis-spelling.

Whatever the reason for it, the mis-spelling demonstrates a lack of familiarity with the Zhuang language and a failure to seek professional translation, or the translator's failure. This is remarkable for a sign purporting to speak on behalf of Zhuangzu people and with an important position relative to the exhibition's other signs. The error confounds the symbolic voice and authenticity of the signage title: which speakers are represented as saying "we *lóu* people"? Moreover, the error also potentially causes offence, because in Putonghua this 偻 (*lóu*) character actually means hunchback. Thus, this mistaken character unfortunately also works as an interdiscursive reference to the historic use of derogatory logographs to name Zhuang and other minority people. Let us move now from this unfortunate case of a linguistic reference decoupled from its referent, undermining the curation sign's symbolic use of Zhuang language, to non-linguistic visual references to Zhuang.

7.3 Non-linguistic references to Zhuangness

The symbolic role that Zhuang language plays in making "maps of meaning" (quoted in the last chapter: Jaworski and Thurlow 2010: 6) is not played exclusively by Zhuang language. Rather, linguistic and non-linguistic symbols are used co-referentially for Zhuangness. I found that there were patterns across the landscapes in the use of imagery and material form of the built environment to represent Zhuangness. This is another aspect of decoding publicly emplaced visual ideologies about what Zhuang language is, who Zhuang people are, and where both are in place. I showed a photograph of the Zhuang Auntie souvenir shop at Figure 43. Its souvenirs are good examples to begin to explain the conventionalization (and here, commodification) of non-linguistic representations of Zhuangness through the tropes of drums, love balls and costumes (particularly, costumed women in hats).

The little drums sold at Zhuang Auntie trade on the drum as a visual icon of Zhuang cultural heritage. The archetypal Zhuang drum is consistently represented as having a concave-sided shape and concentric patterns on the drumhead. Such drums were traditionally symbols of high social status and for ritual use (Chaisingkananont 2014: 6) and now serve as emblems of technological, religious and musical customs that are sometimes presented as particular to the Zhuangzu and sometimes presented as shared by historic non-Han peoples of GZAR. Such drums are central to the GZAR Museum and Guangxi Museum of Nationalities' exhibitions about Zhuangzu cultural history, and also included in the GZAR Museum of Nationalities' separate bronze drum exhibition. Both the GZAR Museum and Guangxi Museum of Nationalities sold souvenir and toy drums similar to Zhuang Auntie's drums, including inside the Museum of Nationalities' Ethnic Village's Black Clothes Zhuang exhibition house-cum-shop (field notes 16 June 2014). Images of similar drums were prevalent on circulating, Zhuang-themed texts: to name just a few, tissue packets branded by Zhuang Home-style Restaurant for its customers, the back cover of Zhang's book *General History of the Zhuang* (Zhang 1997), and the case of a CD of Zhuang-medium songs given to me by Mr E (Te Yi Lan Lu 2014). The liquor gift-box featuring the word for Zhuang in Romanized Zhuang, noted in Chapter Six, contained drum-shaped bottles. I also observed the drum image within many public texts in GZAR: the "minzu unity is as precious as air" billboard from the previous chapter serves as a good example (Figure 37). Moreover, this iconic drum is built into the urban environment: GZAR Library (Figure 16) and the Guangxi Museum of Nationalities (Figure 45) are each built in the cylindrical and geometrically-decorated form of the bronze drum, as is GZAR Museum's separate bronze drum exhibition room. However, the drum can be an indistinct symbol without linguistic co-texts. Thus, I found

Figure 45: Guangxi Museum of Nationalities; Nanning: Zhuang/Putonghua.

the representation of the drum often co-located with an explicit reference to "Zhuang(zu)", but typically not in Zhuang language. The souvenirs, museum exhibitions, tissue packets, book cover and CD mentioned above all included an explicit mention of "Zhuang" either in the place/shop name or on the object itself.

Another object constructed as having been used by traditional Zhuang people and therefore symbolic of them/their culture is the 绣球 'love ball', which is a small, silk ball made from distinctive eyelet-shaped components and decorated with embroidery and tassels. Such balls are the most numerous products displayed at Zhuang Auntie and implicated, by that shop display, in Zhuang heritage. They were also sold at the museums. Their social recognition as an emblem of Zhuangness is also apparent from their inclusion on the cover of the first edition of the *Third of the Third* magazine, from 1983 (Figure 46). Under a Putonghua and Zhuang title, the cover depicts a man and woman in traditional cloth head wraps. The woman kisses a love ball while the man watches and smiles.

This cover also hints at the cultural practice historically associated with love balls: a courtship game, rather than the contemporary cultural practices of tourism and gift-buying. However, the situated nature of this construction of the love ball as emblematic of Zhuangzu culture is apparent when we compare a similar form of embroidered ball being tossed in a eighteenth century watercolor depiction in a "Miao album" reproduced and annotated in Tapp and Cohn (2003: 23) and shown here at Figure 47. The original watercolor also included a written description confirming that this is a love ball and describing other identifying characteristics of

Figure 46: Cover of first *Third of the Third* magazine.

the people who use it. I will quote Tapp and Cohn's (2003: 23) translation of the description: "The clothing of the *Kayou Zhongjia* is dark blue. [...] In the first month of spring they perform the 'Dance to the Moon'. The women make a ball out of multi-colored cloth and throw it to the man they fancy. They often enter into illicit liaisons." Tapp and Cohn (2003: 72, 107) explain that this custom was common amongst many South East Asian groups and describe these *Kayou Zhongjia* people as "Tai speakers who referred to themselves as Pu Yi [...] and are close to the people classified today as Zhuang [...] and are called Bouyei today". My argument is not that Zhuang speakers of yore never played with love balls, but rather that it was not a cultural practice specifically associated with Zhuang language and/or the Zhuangzu until more recent discourses developed that indexicality.

This historic text also reveals that distinctive clothing has been used to index the otherness of China's minorities for centuries (as clothing has been used for belonging and othering the world over). Clothing is another Zhuangness trope that I found repeatedly in the linguistic landscapes. The Guangxi Museum of Nationalities Zhuang exhibition uses costumes to visualize and locate a variety of

198 —— 7 New semiotic displays of old "Zhuangness"

Figure 47: A section of Plate 13 from Tapp and Cohn (2003).

Zhuangzu sub-groups on a map of GZAR (Figure 48). Multiple costumes are represented as emblems in this map and in other examples, but all are unlike the modern, western clothes that most people across the PRC now wear daily. They are also unlike imperial Chinese clothes, in having features such as short, pleated skirts, geometrically embroidered cloth and elaborate, folded headwear. Banknotes offer another example of the costume trope. In Chapter Six, I analyzed the Romanized Zhuang text which is found on all RMB banknotes. Now, let us focus on the pictorial representations on the five-*jiao* (50 cent) note: readers can see it on *Language Log* (Mair 2013) https://languagelog.ldc.upenn.edu/nll/?p=7013. The reverse side depicts two traditionally-clad people who are identified elsewhere as being people from the Miaozu and Zhuangzu (Wang 2013: 145).

The conventional interpretation is that the Zhuangzu representative is the person on the right-hand side. The costume worn by this figure resembles that in

Figure 48: Map of GZAR with Putonghua toponyms and images of Zhuang costumes, Guangxi Museum of Nationalities; Nanning.

an old photograph of Zhuang farmers which I observed in Ping'An Zhuang Village's cultural exhibition hall (fieldwork 15 June 2015). It is, however, unlike most of the representations of Zhuang costumes that I collected in that it is undyed and unadorned. By contrast, there were silver filigree headdress and bright clothes presented as the Zhuang costume for tourists to hire within the Guangxi Museum of Nationalities Ethnic Village's "Black Clothes Zhuang House". The "minzu unity is as precious as air" billboard at Figure 37 depicts a similarly colorful, high-sheen dress and folded headdress, and both resemble the colorfully clad women painted into a mural in Nanning's downtown, riverside park. I also saw variations of this colorful, high-sheen costume repeatedly displayed within Nanning and Guilin on advertising posters and in a video promoting GZAR for tourism which I analyze in (Grey 2021a). Mr T, a participant who works as a Zhuang folk singer, posted pictures on social media dressed in such a costume for a television appearance in 2015. Likewise, this "look" is often represented on the cover of *Third of the Third* magazine (e.g. issues 2014–5, –6). Somewhere between these rustic and gaudy representations is the dark outfit worn by a figure labeled 壮 'Zhuang' in Putonghua in a set of 萌羊娃 'Adorable Sheepie' postcards which I purchased in the GZAR Museum shop (Figure 49). Each postcard names one minority minzu and depicts a cartoon sheep in a different traditional costume, constructing the costumes as emblematic.

Across these various media, the people represented in these costumes are almost always women. This imbalance is illustrated clearly in Figure 50, which

200 — 7 New semiotic displays of old "Zhuangness"

Figure 49: Postcard purchased at GZAR Museum gift shop; Nanning.

shows another display in the Guangxi Museum of Nationalities Zhuangzu Cultural Exhibition Hall near the costume map of GZAR which I showed in Figure 48. In this collage of some 60 photographs of people in bright versions of traditional costumes, the overwhelming majority are women. This pattern echoes Turner's (2010: 155) finding that GZAR's tourism discourses rely on representations of women, and Schein's (2000) exposition of the gendered nature of "internal orientalism" in other parts of China.

All these representations which make costume salient serve the interests of spectacularization of diversity, creating visual resources to distinguish products or places. It goes almost without saying that these costumes are essentialist, and performative. I did not see people in everyday life wearing these costumes, even in rural areas. I did observe people – mainly women – employed in cultural tourism wearing more simple and uniform versions of such costumes in one tourism site, Ping'An Zhuang Village, but I did not see staff wearing these costumes in cities, even within Nanning's museums, the Ethnic Village park or Wuming's Zhuang restaurant. The Zhuang speakers whom I interviewed do not generally wear these

Figure 50: Images in the Zhuangzu Cultural Exhibition Hall, Guangxi Museum of Nationalities, 2014.

costumes, they report. However, some of the female students wished they could afford one of these bright and elaborate costumes to wear for festivals, reminding us that these visual discourses have a real-world impact in reshaping what is understood as authentic and attractive Zhuang culture and in doing so can price people out of their own cultural inheritance. Arguably, the governments' insistent use of written Standard Zhuang while most Zhuang speakers are just that, speakers, also prices people out of their culture, because attaining Standard Zhuang literacy comes at the cost of learning materials, private tutors and time.

Further, it is notable that the multiplicity of costume emblems contrasts with the singular script emblem, Romanized Zhuang, the only script used for writing Zhuang in public texts. The multiplicity also contrasts with the sole language variety, Standard Zhuang, which those written displays encode. These costumes may be reductive and performative; nevertheless, it appears that the diversity of Zhuang practices has not undergone as much erasure in the representation of clothing as it has in the representation of language. Why is it that actual or even historic linguistic diversity is never represented, but clothing diversity is? I suggest that linguistic diversity undermines the construction of a socially or politically meaningful Zhuang(zu) group in a way that clothing diversity does not. The government has standardized language but not clothing; now, the representation of Zhuang linguistic diversity may threaten the construction of the one-minzu, one-language paradigm of socio-linguistic order, or challenge standardization-centered language policy.

Another answer relates to the specificity of the constructed group. The variety of emblematic costumes makes costumes indistinct in their indexicality, blurring their minority minzu referents. Costume is a trope that is meaningful in indexing a non-Han quality, foregrounding both visual "otherness" and traditionalism (Gladney 2004: 58). It adds what is called in Putonghua "民族味道" [ethnic flavor] without specifically indexing one culture or group. Sometimes in my data, an accompanying word made explicit the particular referent of a costume, e.g. the title on the costume map in Figure 48 says "壮族" [Zhuangzu]. But by contrast, in the "minzu unity is as precious as air" billboard, explicit reference to the Zhuang(zu) is not made, so the costumed women depict the more general referent, "minority minzu", or "minority minzu of Guilin" if the billboard's representations of Guilin's landmarks are also read for meaning.

This use of distinctive costumes to index minorities *generally* is a discourse that goes beyond the construction of the Zhuangzu and other minorities in GZAR. There is a national visual ideology of showing groups of people each in differently exotic costumes which is used often by the government to represent the unity and/or inclusion of the minzu. Examples encountered on fieldwork included a picture of a parade celebrating the establishment of GZAR as an autonomous region in 1958 on display inside the Guangxi Museum of Nationalities (shown in Grey in press) and a billboard in the forecourt of that museum (Figure 51). But before encountering these examples, I had seen this imagery elsewhere. Figure 52 shows a similar billboard which I photographed on a street in Urumqi, the capital

Figure 51: Minority peoples on billboard, Guangxi Museum of Nationalities' forecourt, 2014.

Figure 52: Billboard on a road in Urumqi, 2013.

of the Xinjiang Uyghur Autonomous Region in 2013. That one additionally includes text explicitly articulating the theme of "民族团结" [minzu unity] and people in military uniforms, while its background, a skyline of skyscrapers, is a relatively unusual update of the trope to situate diversity within a modern city. While these billboards clearly mobilize visual diversity of dress to metonymically represent diversity of ethno-cultural groups, they do not rely on each costume specifically indexing a particular minzu. Rather, the multiplicity represents these groups' most significant shared trait: that they are non-Han.

Combining these visual tropes with an explicit reference to "Zhuang" or to "Zhuang language", in any language, is a tactic for clarifying that the referent is the Zhuangzu rather than the more general minority minzu. A similar clarification can be achieved by representing the location, such as Guilin in the "minzu unity is a precious as air" billboard or Urumqi in Figure 52, or by combining visual tropes with writing in the medium of a minority language, like Uyghur in the official Arabic script in Figure 52. This clarification can be conveyed with co-text in written Zhuang language, too, provided a viewer can recognize the written language as Zhuang. However, as Chapter Eight explores, the recognizability of written Zhuang should not be assumed. If written Zhuang is not recognized, the

Romanized Zhuang script may be another indistinct visual trope, representing "non-Han language" with unspecific indexicality.

Many of these visual tropes have a history of usage – often usage without the co-textual written Zhuang – in the *Third of the Third* magazine.

7.4 Referencing Zhuangness in the "Zhuang" magazine, *Third of the Third*

The bronze drum, love ball, costumes, and even written Zhuang visual tropes recur now as emblems of Zhuangness in the landscapes that I studied, but these conventions of representation started earlier and in other media. They have been re-entextualized as emplaced public texts. I will explore these older representations through a dive into the archives of *Third of the Third* magazine, which has been printed in GZAR since 1983. During my fieldwork in 2014–2015, I discussed, collected editions of, and interviewed the editors of this magazine, and it was generally held up as the preeminent Zhuang-language publication. At that time, *Third of the Third* was a bilingual Zhuang-Putonghua publication, but both before and since that time it has been a monolingual Putonghua-medium magazine. With the generous purchasing of an extensive collection of *Third of the Third* by the National Library of Australia, I have analyzed editions from throughout *Third of the Third's* publication history. It is an excellent illustration of how something comes to be meaningfully "Zhuang", including through its use of the visual emblems of Zhuangness that I also found in the linguistic landscapes. The magazine archive also reveals how Zhuang language can vary between being used as a visual resource for stylization and as a linguistic resource for conveying information. As elucidated over the next few paragraphs, the magazine has changed its types of content, its format, its publication schedule, its publisher and its use of various languages over the last four decades. There is no clear correspondence between the changes; a new publisher, for instance, has not always heralded a change in language choice. I will integrate, below, what one of the magazine's editors, Mr G, explained to me about the reasons for *Third of the Third's* transformations.

Third of the Third began as an A4-size short story magazine with the bilingual Putonghua-Zhuang title "三月三 *Sam Nyied Sam*" ('Third Day of the Third Month'), shown above in Figure 46. Early on, it sometimes used the subtitles "小说专号" [Short Story Special Issue] or "中篇小说专号" [Novella Special Issue], and was mainly a magazine of fiction writing. The *danwei* (i.e. work group, an organ of the state's administrative apparatus) responsible for its publication was listed in the 1980s as 广西民族出版社 'Guangxi Minzu Press'. *Third of the Third* came out monthly and bimonthly at various times. Mr G recounted that the magazine

7.4 Referencing Zhuangness in the "Zhuang" magazine, *Third of the Third*

began its focus on Zhuang language and culture in September 1986 with top-down direction:

Excerpt 7-1

Mr G: 那么为什么我们当时推行壮文呢，1986 年推行壮文搞得比较热，这个形势很好，当然图书也出来了，出版社出版的壮文图书有了，报纸也有了，但是唯一还没有壮文的刊物，这样我们自治区民语委根据这个形势去党委宣传部打报告，要办一个民族文化期刊，《三月三》，86 年的 9月，到现在已经 30 年了。

[Mr G: So why did we promote the Zhuang language at that time? In 1986, Zhuang language implementation was relatively "hot". This situation was very good. Of course, books had also come out. There were Zhuang language books published by publishers, there were also newspapers, but there still wasn't a Zhuang language periodical. Our autonomous region's Minority Language Commission reported the situation to the Propaganda Department of the Party Committee; it is necessary to run a minzu cultural journal, *Third of the Third*, in September of 1986. It has been 30 years now.]

According to my review, during the late 1980s, the magazine included occasional articles in Putonghua about Zhuang culture. For example, I found one about Zhuang tones in music in edition 1987(4) (pp. 62–63) and one about Zhuang language in edition 1987(10) (pp. 51–53), but both were written in the medium of Putonghua. I found the first instances of written Zhuang inside the magazine in this same era. The 1987 article about Zhuang music included a few Romanized Zhuang words as examples, and the 1987(8) edition shows Romanized Zhuang clearly on a bilingual banner within a photograph that is printed in the inner back cover. The page's heading is "壮族作家创作促进会成立大会剪影" [Photos of the conference for the promotion of the creations of Zhuang writers] and the banner reads: "COZGYAH BOUXCUENGH CANGOZ GU[ ]//壮族作家[ ]作促进会成立大会" ['Conference for the promotion of the creations of Zhuang writers' with some words/characters obscured].

This was part of a growing focus in the magazine on minority culture but not always specifically on Zhuang culture. The magazine began including unlabeled cover pictures of women in traditional costumes of minority minzu styles (e.g. Figure 53 from 1990) amongst cover imagery which otherwise romanticized modern, urban lifestyles (as in Figure 54 from 1987). In 1989, the December cover pictured a maiden in a traditional costume dancing between bamboo poles held by four men in cloth hats. A group version of the same dance is photographed for the "三月三记" [Remembering the Third of the Third] article on page 16 of the 2018(2) edition. I also saw it advertised as an upcoming cultural activity at the Guangxi Museum of Nationalities. This is a traditional game-dance which the GZAR government claims as a local custom on http://en.gxzf.gov.cn and which the *Shanghai Daily* (Zhang 2014) describes as a tradition

Figure 53: 1990 *Third of the Third* cover.

practiced by the Li people of Hainan Island, whom it describes as descendants of "the ancient Baiyue tribe who lived in today's Guangxi Zhuang Autonomous Region". That is, this game-dance is a tradition shared by many people of South China who are now officially classified into different minzu.

In the 1989 editions of the *Third of the Third*, I started to find explicit references to various official minority minzu in the captions of photographs: "壮乡情" [Zhuang Nostalgia]; "苗族姑娘" [Miaozu Girl]; "苗妹织苗锦" [Miao Sister Does Miao Embroidery]; and "瑶家的欢笑" [Yao Family's Mirth], respectively from editions 1989(-4, -7, -8, and -9). However, during this same period commercial advertising was added to the magazine, at first with back cover advertisements for mod-cons such as microwaves and showers. The advertising was monolingual in Putonghua.

By the early 1990s, the magazine was starting to experiment with a bilingual cover, including adding the Zhuang-medium title "*Sam Nyied Sam*" and sometimes also the Putonghua Pinyin transliteration of the title "*San Yue San*" (e.g.

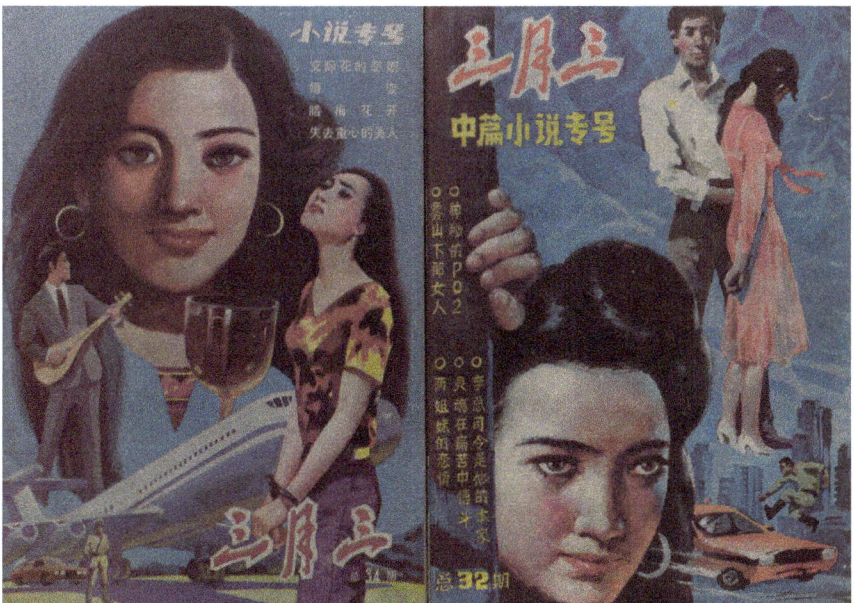

Figure 54: 1987 magazine covers.

Figure 53). At this time the magazine's publisher changed to 三月三杂志社 'Third of the Third Magazine Publisher', an entity which the magazine declared was under the responsibility of two danwei: 广西壮族自治区民族事务委员会 'GZAR Minzu Affairs Committee' and 广西壮族自治区少数民族语言文字工作委员会 'GZAR Minority Minzu Language and Script Work Committee'. It now very occasionally included Romanized Zhuang, e.g. again on a banner in a photograph on the inside cover under the heading "第二届壮族文学奖颁将大会剪影" [Photos of prize night for the 2nd Zhuang Language Studies Prize] in 1993(2). Nevertheless, the content was still monolingual in Putonghua. By 1998, *Third of the Third* had been restyled to resemble a women's fashion magazine, with a monolingual Putonghua cover but still with the occasional cover photo of women in traditional costume (e.g. lefthand cover in Figure 55).

It was only during the 2000s that the magazine transformed into a somewhat bilingual magazine about GZAR and Zhuang culture and language. For example, a language leader participant gave me the 2010(4) edition of *Third of the Third*, and its uneven bilingualism, albeit with a high proportion of Zhuang-medium content, was characteristic of other samples from the 2010s period which I collected or examined in the library (including the one in Figure 56). The 2010(4) edition contains a bilingual contents page that translates Zhuang titles into Putonghua but

Figure 55: 1998 *Third of the Third* covers.

not Putonghua titles into Zhuang. All Zhuang is printed in Romanized Zhuang. It also separately provides an English-medium contents page, although none of the content is in English. Throughout, the section headings are bilingual in Zhuang and Putonghua, e.g. "*SAWCUENGH BOUXCUENGH* 壮人小说" [Zhuang People's Fiction], so the magazine is navigable to anyone reading either language, but certain information like the publication and editorial contact details are only in Putonghua (p. 1).

Moreover, the content itself is not bilingual, with one exception: a story published in both Zhuang and Putonghua within the "Garden of Translation" column. The Zhuang-medium content is creative and subjective, whereas the Putonghua-medium content is in genres that are characterized by factual, objective styles. The Zhuang-medium content includes seven stories, one folk song and personal reflection essays written only in Zhuang. The Putonghua-medium content includes two event reports with photograph spreads on the inside covers and three academic articles, all about Zhuang linguistics. This edition also includes contemporary lyrics from the Sam Nyied Sam folk song festival and it is only in this content that we see a slight blur in the otherwise firm division between the genres for which each language is made appropriate. The "Selected folk songs of publizing [sic] the spirits of the Third Plenary Session of 18th CPC [Chinese Communist Party] Central Committee" are printed in Putonghua, while the songs on "The profound significance of the Third Plenary Session of 18th CPC Central Committee" are printed in Zhuang. These are not parallel bilingual song texts but are equivalent in theme. In both languages, new creative works (songs) have been written.

7.4 Referencing Zhuangness in the "Zhuang" magazine, *Third of the Third* — **209**

Figure 56: 2014–2 *Third of the Third* front and back covers.

Because the topic of the songs is a then-current political event, Zhuang language is brought slightly closer to the reportage genre.

The early 2010s was the highpoint for Zhuang content, as it turned out, because Putonghua has carried an increasingly heavy load in the magazine since my fieldwork ended in 2015. The publishers had already started publishing a separate, monolingual Putonghua, A5 spin-off in addition to the bilingual A4 magazine in the 2000s, editions of which I collected during fieldwork and which I discussed with the *Third of the Third* editors in 2014: they and their 13 staff were then producing both magazines. The smaller format magazine was still bilingually called "三月三 *Sam Nyied Sam*", but it described itself inside as the "《三月三》汉文版" [《*Third of the Third*》Han Writing Edition] and the content was all in Putonghua. The editors explained the place of this second magazine:

Excerpt 7-2

Mr G: 我们还有一本这个杂志是汉文的。
Mr H: 这个是汉文。
Mr G: 汉文就编故事，《三月三》的故事，全部是故事，这里面的故事都是用汉文来写的。刚才那个是文学的，那本…这里的故事，编那种故事的，这个卖给那种打工仔，来打工啊，他闷了他可以去书摊，这个在书摊上面可以找到，就广东那边啊或者哪里打工的，他闷了可以去书摊里面可以买到，但这个呢像书摊没有办法，这个要提前订，订了有多少它才印。

[Mr G: We also have a version of this magazine that is Han Wen [written Putonghua].
Mr H: This is Han Wen [giving me a copy].
Mr G: The Han Wen [version] is fiction stories; *Third of the Third's* stories, they're all fiction, the stories inside this are all written in Han Wen. That one just now [the recent edition just given to me] was literature ... The stories inside, that sort of fiction story, that's sold to wage earners, those who go to work, and if they're bored they can go to the bookstall, at the bookstall they can find it [this magazine], so if they're working some place in Guangxi or anywhere they can go to into a bookstall and buy it, whereas this one [A4 bilingual version] it's like a bookstall won't have a way [to sell it], this one has to be ordered in advance, you order however many and then they're printed.]

By 2017, only this monolingual Putonghua, small version appears to have been printed; even on-demand bilingual printing seems to have ceased because the National Library of Australia did not receive bilingual editions, only Putonghua, in its orders from this period. However, now the contributing authors' minzu were listed on the contents page, to exhibit their minority minzu connection. In these 2017 mini-editions, Putonghua Pinyin is used in addition to Putonghua characters for headings, e.g. "少数民族作者作品选 SHAOSHUMINZU ZUOZHE ZUOPINXUAN" [Selection of Minority Minzu Authors' Works] and "SANJIE GETAI 三姐歌台" [Third Sister Songs]; "third sister" referring to the folktale heroine and Zhuangzu icon, Third Sister Liu (see e.g. the celebrated film retelling from 1960). As is obvious from these headings, the content continued to feature minority culture. At this point, one of the responsible danwei had also changed: the GZAR Minzu Affairs Committee had been replaced by the 广西壮族自治区民族宗教事务委员会 'GZAR Religious Affairs Committee'.

We might assume this 2017 change to the *Third of the Third* format was an effort to increase the subscriber base and circulation, because even during the early 2010s' Zhuang content highpoint, circulation was dropping. Mr G reported that circulation in 2014 was around 2000, down from a high of 5500 copies per edition. However, this assumption cannot fully explain the change, as by the 2010s the magazine was in fact no longer funded by paid subscriptions:

Excerpt 7-3

Mr G: 钱呢都是由政府出的，这个杂志是政府出的。所以我们现在基本上是送的，不收钱，以前就有人订。

[Mr G: The money is all issued by the government, this magazine is issued by the government. So we basically send it out now. No money is charged. People used to subscribe.]

As noted in a comment on the policy of funding *Third of the Third* in Chapter Five, it is the GZAR Government, not the Central Government, who funds the magazine. Perhaps, instead, it was the departure of the GZAR Minzu Affairs Committee as the responsible government body that heralded the return to a Putonghua-only *Third of the Third*, or perhaps this Committee's departure had been precipitated by a push from elsewhere to change the magazine's language choice.

In 2018, the magazine transformed again into a quarterly, A4 magazine, for reasons that I have not been able to confirm. Since that change, *Third of the Third* still only has monolingual Putonghua content, as Figure 57 illustrates, but once again has its Zhuang-Putonghua bilingual title. It continues the new practice of publishing each authors' minzu on the contents page. The contents page contains the only Zhuang language that I could find, in the bilingual phrase "*Banj Sawgun* 汉文版" [Han Writing Edition]. A Zhuang-Putonghua bilingual edition of the magazine appears no longer to be published. Other changes have been made, also. The current format uses higher-quality paper stock and has a much greater emphasis on professional, high-resolution photography, featuring local scenes that I would describe as cultural spectacles and rustic charm. The example in Figure 57 provides the captions "蓝衣壮妇女在刺绣" [Women of the Blue-Clothes Zhuang doing embroidery] and "糍粑画展示" [A show of glutinous rice cake art]: the women's embroidery is geometric in keeping with local traditions but their rice-cake painting includes Chinese zodiac and PRC flag motifs. The women's uniform blue costumes, and their embroidered wares, are reminiscent of those I saw as souvenirs on sale in the Guangxi Museum of Nationalities' Ethnic Village's Black-Clothes Zhuang House in 2014 (Figure 58), illustrating convergence of visual tropes across modes.

Figure 57: Pages from 2018(3) edition of *Third of the Third*.

Figure 58: Embroidered shoes and dolls on sale at the Guangxi Museum of Nationalities Ethnic Park's Black-Clothes Zhuang House, 2014.

However, *Third of the Third* occasionally also does something the other discourses do not do: representing people as both associated with Zhuang culture and Zhuang language and yet participating in cosmopolitan, modern, mainstream life. Even in the small selection shown in this chapter, we have seen real people wearing western suits and modern jackets while talking at conferences about Zhuang issues, under a heading in Zhuang (Figure 56). The magazine can be said to be representing Zhuangzu people *to Zhuangzu people* not to tourists or consumers. By contrast, I found that other representations in the landscapes depicted minority/Zhuangzu people almost exclusively in "traditional" costumes in natural landscapes, as in Figures 37, 50 and 51, and doing traditional cultural activities such as picking tea and dancing or simply standing, decoratively, near the subject of an advertisement (see further examples in Grey 2021a). Indeed, in museum, tourism and advertising texts, showing people who looked "normal" would not be eye-catching or distinctive and would not convey the idea of "minority" or "Zhuang" without extra textual explanation and the challenging of dominant norms of representation.

Nevertheless, we can see from the archival comparisons that over time the normative representations of practicing Zhuang culture and being Zhuangzu have largely been replicated. Wearing bright and traditional clothing, wearing and doing embroidery, and being female are the most frequent characteristics represented. The love ball is represented and invested with the symbolic clout of being on the very first cover, as I noted above. The drum trope, however, is rarely shown. Moreover, being in GZAR is represented over and again in the magazine's content, reproducing the territorialization of Zhuangness. However, reading and writing Romanized Zhuang has not been continually demanded of readers, and nor has any other Zhuang literacy, although Romanized Zhuang is now, and has often been, represented through the magazine's bilingual title. Putonghua began and has now again won out as the means to reach a readership for *Third of the Third*. Nevertheless, Zhuang language has been represented from time to time as a Zhuang cultural practice in other ways, including as an object of study in articles about Zhuang music and linguistics, in making creative writing in the medium of Zhuang a visible practice by publishing it (at least for a few years), and in printing photographs of cultural events explicitly named as Zhuang writing events. Moreover, through the photographs and reports of those events, Zhuang language has been represented as a cultural practice which has been officially celebrated beyond the pages of the magazine, at the 1987 Zhuang Language Studies Prize Night and the 1993 Conference for the Promotion of the Creations of Zhuang Writers.

That is, for a time the magazine represented back to its readership a community who wrote stories, read and made music in Zhuang. However, Zhuang cultural practices such as telling stories or singing folk songs are also, and often, represented in the magazine as being done in the medium of Putonghua. For example, the Third Sister Songs in a number of editions are only given in Putonghua.

Tracing these visual but not always linguistic tropes for constructing Zhuangness over mediums and landscapes and over the last four decades through the *Third of the Third* archive, I have concluded that Zhuang language as a living, spoken language is not a common or conventionalized semiotic resource for representing or emplacing Zhuangness. Rather, as the concluding section discusses, Zhuangness is largely an *unspoken* feature of the landscape. Indeed, as the conclusion then argues, this feature is perhaps best understood as minority-ness, not specifically Zhuangness.

7.5 Concluding discussion: Temporal and cultural otherness is made visible in the landscape

The analysis of linguistic landscapes in the preceding chapter found, ultimately, that in GZAR and especially in Nanning City, Zhuang language plays a limited role as a symbolic resource co-constructing these as places as meaningfully understood as associated to Zhuang culture and as places where the government identifies itself with ancestral Zhuang speakers. This chapter adds three points to the analysis: first, across textual and other mediums in the built environment, Zhuangness is made meaningful to GZAR primarily through the authorship of the GZAR government. Second, the Zhuang language with which the government associates itself, and its territory, and with which the government associates the Zhuangzu polity, is not represented as a living or varied language. Third, displays of Romanized, Standard Zhuang language are part of a suite of visual symbols which ambivalently index not only the Zhuangzu but local minority peoples generally.

Chapter Six commenced the first of those arguments, showing that the use of written Zhuang in public texts was almost exclusively done by government authors. This chapter developed the point, showing that the government also authors many of the public discourses that explicitly refer to the Zhuangzu polity or Zhuang language, or which use the non-linguistic tropes of Zhuangness that I have identified. Museum graphics and texts, souvenirs sold at shops inside public museums, the architectural form of public cultural institutions, public murals and the *Third of the Third* magazine – all of which this chapter collected data from – are government-authored and make Zhuangness meaningful to GZAR.

However, unlike written Zhuang in public landscapes being written almost exclusively by government authors, I found that private authors in addition to the government used the shared non-linguistic visual tropes of Zhuangness. This included the marketing products of the Zhuang cuisine restaurants or the Zhuang Auntie Z-girl souvenir shop. Between the government and the non-government authors, these visual tropes were also being used across a range of genres, whereas Chapter Six showed that public, written Zhuang was limited to just a few genres of place-naming public signage.

Looking at the kind of Zhuang language or culture or person represented in the data, I found these visual tropes to reference a nebulous Zhuangness and to only rarely represent Zhuang language being spoken, written or read as part of Zhuangness. Neither writing nor speaking Zhuang, as personal or group activities, have become tropes in the public representation of Zhuangness: there is little visualization of people "doing Zhuang language". Explicit reference to Zhuang language in the linguistic landscapes was, likewise, rare, even in texts that were otherwise emplacing or commodifying Zhuang culture. The only representations of people practicing Zhuang language are found within on again-off again content in the *Third of the Third* subscriber-only magazine. Moreover, the representation of the actually-existing and diverse Zhuang varieties is entirely absent: even *Third of the Third* represents culture and creativity as practiced through Standard Zhuang. Zhuang language practices are, I conclude, under-represented in urban and cultural linguistic landscapes. This interacts with the norm of excluding Zhuang and other minority languages from most genres of public texts, especially from newer signage, higher-tech signage, temporary signage about current events, and commercial texts, which Chapter Six has identified, and which implied Zhuang language's absence from current, communicative language practices.

Further, this absence of representations of contemporary, lived Zhuang language practices shines another light on the last chapter's finding that public usage of written Zhuang language was almost exclusive to government-authored, non-commercial texts, most of which were in Nanning. Not only does this limited generic and geographic distribution make for limited representation of Zhuang language practices, but it *only represents the government using Zhuang language*. While such signage may imply that other people have a practice of reading (or even writing) Zhuang, this pattern coupled with the non-linguistic visual tropes identified in this chapter together enforce in public an ideology that people – even Zhuangzu people – do not interact in Zhuang language, speak Zhuang, use diverse Zhuang varieties or write Zhuang themselves.

The absence of "doing language" from representations of Zhuang culture or people constructs Zhuang language as a less important part of *current* Zhuang culture and personal Zhuang identities, as well as a less important part of GZAR's identity. This is consistent with contemporary Zhuang culture being made almost meaningless by the narrative of Zhuang assimilation which I introduced in Chapter Two, and in the legal construction of the only valuable minority language being a developed language, as analyzed in Chapter Three. Furthermore, the static form and memorializing functions of many of the objects, buildings and texts that use the drum, love ball and costumes heighten the heritage symbolism of emblems of Zhuangness rather than indicating that these cultural objects or the practices associated with them are part of contemporary practice. In Grey (2021a), I found a corresponding absence of Zhuang language in performance and in representation within GZAR's tourism advertising discourses and tourism landscapes, even in destinations explicitly described as "Zhuang".

However, in this chapter I found that *Third of the Third* did, atypically, occasionally represent people as *both* Zhuang(zu) *and* modern *and* urban. In the recent past, it represented Zhuang language users in mainstream clothing in urban environments from time to time, particularly in photographs. Nevertheless, the magazine's recent shift back to Putonghua-only content and new style of photography, featuring high-resolution images of scenic cultural events and landscape vistas, follows the trend of excluding Zhuang language practices from the representation of being a Zhuangzu today.

Thus, I have shown that both the language and the imagery of these varied static and circulating texts, all accessible to the public if not on public streetfronts, are highly naturalizing, visual ideological processes which construct Zhuangness and Zhuang language as inherently tied to GZAR and yet which construct Zhuang language as a visual feature of the landscape, without human agents and without living speakers. This is heightened within the heritage discursive frame, identified in Chapter Six. Visual symbols of Zhuangness work together with the government's displays of Standard Zhuang to emplace a "collective memory" (Jaworski and Thurlow 2010: 8) of the region's heritage which has become a visualized relic.

This representation of Zhuang as a disembodied feature of GZAR landscapes is further heightened, I argue, because popular non-linguistic visual tropes of Zhuangness are designed to facilitate the visual consumption of Zhuangness. These are displayed alongside or even instead of the visual symbol of written Romanized Zhuang language. This chapter identified a number of visual tropes referencing Zhuangness which are currently used by a variety of authors, but with the GZAR government still prime among them. The chapter also showed these have previously been conventionalized over time and over various media. They include drums; love balls; and distinctive costumes, or more precisely, women in distinctive costumes. The reliance on these visual and often non-linguistic representations can enforce a habituated expectation of encountering Zhuang culture as a visual motif or spectacle.

Government representations of marginal cultures, such as those studied here, can be something marginalized people's seek. However, in my view, these conventionalized usages and displays of linguistic and non-linguistic visual symbols of Zhuangness orient us to a stratification of languages and people associated with the modern/urban/current over those associated with the pre-modern/rustic/past. This is an ideational legacy already mapped onto a majority vs minority group division.

Moreover, this conventionalized imagery is not necessarily made explicitly "Zhuang", but could be read as symbolizing all local minorities. With tropes such as the love ball, for instance, the discourses are now relatively consistent in representing this as part of Zhuangness, but with its history of a less fixed symbolism and outside the context of a shop display with a sign saying "Zhuang", it is unclear whether the love ball would be taken to symbolize the Zhuangzu or the indistinct minority minzu. This sort of ambiguity may be intended by some authors, for example to make a normative association between GZAR and ethno-cultural diversity rather than to make a normative association specifically with the Zhuangzu. I observed in the analysis above that the ambiguity of referent was not always clarified when the intended symbolic message was the coming together of many minority peoples whose similarity to one another in having non-Han culture was being made their most salient feature. At other times, I found that the ambiguity was clarified by a co-textual use of written Zhuang language or an explicit reference to "Zhuangzu" or "Zhuang".

An identity dilemma is not necessarily being produced by these ambiguous linguistic and non-linguistic visual tropes in public discourses. This is because a Zhuang-specific construction of GZAR and the pan-minority identity of GZAR both tap into similar hierarchic ideologies noted just above and explicated in Chapter Four vis-à-vis development, civility and Mandarin. The general minority identity does not necessarily negate or undermine the Zhuang identity, but simply expands it, reproducing a localized and metonymic relationship between the Zhuangzu and the many other minority minzu who associate themselves, or who are associated, with the region.

Being alert to this ambivalent identity of the one place also entails an acceptance that even written Zhuang language in linguistic landscapes need not be intended, or interpreted, as a symbol only of Zhuangzu people. Written Zhuang, too, can function as a visual representation of non-Han local languages *plural* and of their speakers. Romanized written displays of this non-Han language, like a bright costume, are not necessarily displayed to index one specific group but as a spectacularly non-Han language. However, the next chapter explains that the distinctiveness of written Zhuang as something different to Mandarin is not as obvious to the public as policy-makers and government authors may assume.

In the next chapter I will also extend my linguistic landscape analysis to inquire what Zhuangzu people or Zhuang speakers make of the patterned semiotic resources in urban public spaces, and how (or whether) they take up these semiotic resources to construct their Zhuangness. The chapter also explores the extent to which the authenticity of these visual representations of Zhuangness are validated by viewers. Do they feel these texts, which are stylized through language choice and imagery to be in "their" voice, actually voice their perspectives?

8 The multiple meanings of Zhuang displays in lived landscapes

Identity is never a one-way street. (Anderson 2011: xx)

8.1 Introducing the lived landscape approach

From Chapter Six and Seven, we now have a thorough understanding of key semiotic environments in which my participants, and many others, can learn or remake their own identities as well as the identities of their minzu and of the places they inhabit. This chapter continues the investigation of the role of Zhuang in these public landscapes, adding insight into Zhuang speakers' interactions with the language displays and language norms of the built environment that were set out in the preceding two chapters. In Chapter Six, I referred to a news article about the policy of including Zhuang on certain signage in Nanning (Sina News 2009). That article also reports an investigation by Guangxi News into complaints over new signage at a major intersection; residents had complained that the place-name on the sign was misspelled in Putonghua Pinyin, but the journalists reveal that the place-name was actually written in Romanized Zhuang. That people had assumed the name must be in Putonghua, and did not recognize it as Zhuang, illustrates the perceived abnormality of public Zhuang writing. What would encourage such a perception? Recall, from Chapter Six, how few public texts are written in Zhuang; the linguistic landscape encourages this perception. The example demonstrates that the meanings of Zhuang-medium public texts are co-constructed by viewers, that a linguistic landscape is a lived experience through which a habitus is formed and in which reading habits are inculcated or, perhaps, challenged.

Nevertheless, linguistic landscape studies have tended to overlook viewers and indeed other relevant social actors whose experiences direct and interpret the usage of language in linguistic landscapes. Blommaert (2013, reiterated by Hult 2018: 346) therefore prevails on researchers to "look behind the signs" into lived experiences of linguistic landscapes. Noticing the same shortfall, Jaworski (2014: 525) observes that linguistic landscape studies which include "the role of social actors in producing space through their embodied actions [...] and interactions with the environment" are relatively rare. These rare examples include Scollon and Scollon's (2003) identification of place as a meaning-making resource beyond the linguistic aspects of landscapes in their pioneering "geosemiotic" work on "discourses in place", and the study of "image participants" within that work. In that vein, Sloboda et al. (2010) and Zabrodskaja (2014) have interviewed viewers about their attitudes to linguistic landscapes in contexts where language policy has intervened in those landscapes. In a different vein of research into social actors' interactions with linguistic landscapes, Malinowski (2009), Papen (2015) and Eclipse and Tenedero (2018) focus on the perceptions of authors of signage. Social actors can be types of interactant other than authors and viewers of landscape texts and images, depending on the media of the landscape under investigation: see e.g. Pennycook and Otsuji (2011) on the spatialized semiotics of "smellscapes" and Hu (2018) on listeners in public soundscapes. Many other approaches to investigating people's interactions with and judgments of linguistic landscapes are emerging in the literature, too, including multimodal studies incorporating interviews (Sharma 2019); public signage rewriting simulations (Shohamy et al. 2019); studying "the body as a corporeal landscape" (Peck and Stroud 2015: 133) and the "dialectics between t-shirt producers and consumers" (Caldwell 2017); collecting tourists' online re-mediations of linguistic landscapes (Thurlow and Jaworski 2014); surveying potential signage viewers (Draper 2016); and Hult's (2014) "drive-thru" documentation of texts. Lou (2016) has foregrounded the Bourdieusian aspect of such studies, explaining that displaying language is "a form of spatial representation" of culture, power and politics and that living amongst or experiencing these spatial representations therefore contributes to the formation of people's habitus (Lou 2016: 10, following Bourdieu 1977a). The seeds of these newer ethnographically-oriented studies of participants' interactions with linguistic and semiotic landscapes go right back to Lefebvre's (1991) 'lived space' and the (non-ethnographic) survey of participants in Landry and Bourhis' (1997) first linguistic landscape study. The inaugural edition of *Linguistic Landscape* calls this a "critical turn" and Shohamy calls it a "phase" in which "the people who create, contest and interact in the linguistic landscape are at the center of attention" (reported by Pütz and Mundt 2018: 4, 13, respectively).

However, these people-centered approaches are not so far recognized as a set of brushes in the paint box of researchers wishing to produce accounts of linguistic landscapes. What is emerging is a suite of lived landscape methods all aiming to foreground the agency and the subjectivities of people co-producing space, identity and meaning through their actions and interactions with linguistic landscapes. These 'lived landscape' methods to bring greater ethnographic thickness into the literature which is particularly important in Chinese linguistic landscape research, as its ethnographic turn is less developed and the connection between linguistic landscapes and language policies less firmly established. The thicker ethnographic analysis of people's socially-situated interactions with linguistic landscapes, to which these works pave the way, is what I have started calling a "lived landscape" approach (see also Grey 2021b). For me, it involved inquiring into participants' subjective making of meanings from the identity affordances and other semiotic resources of linguistic landscapes, as well as their landscape reading practices (this chapter) and inquiring into the laws that shape agency to participate in linguistic landscape authorship (Chapter Nine).

Of particular influence in ethnographically-oriented methods of linguistic landscape study – the methods I suggest we draw together as a "lived landscape approach" – has been Stroud and Jegels (2014: 180) response to Jaworski's observation on the overall paucity of such research. In their response, Stroud and Jegels draw subjectivity into the foreground, exploring the interplay between displayed language and individuals in the "affectual" navigation of public space through "narrated walks", a method now increasingly used by scholars e.g. Banda and Jimaima (2015) and of course this study. Szabó and Troyer (2017) have recently reviewed walking and other multimodal, mobile methods in the linguistic landscape literature. Stroud and Jegels' (2014) narrated walks bolstered my own contemporaneous choice of commented walks, a very similar method with a slightly different name that I adopted from a human geographer human geographers studying Cantonese language politics: Qian (2014). My commented walks, like Stroud and Jegels', investigated individual subjectivities, in this case, Zhuang-speaking participants' interactions with Zhuang-Putonghua bilingual toponym signage of the kind displayed and regulated in Nanning and presented in Chapter Six.

Chapter Six presented instances of Zhuang language on urban signage. While I found these to be marginal in Putonghua-dominant, text-dense urban landscapes, my study also revealed certain norms about Zhuang display: Zhuang is rare in commercial and privately-authored public texts but it is included in certain toponymic genres of government-authored signage, especially street-name signage in Nanning (see Figure 30 for an example) and some public institutions' façade or gateway name signage. Chapter Six also explained that many of these Zhuang-inclusive displays are regulated by explicit policy, namely a Nanning municipal law about the format of bilingual public signage.

Now, this chapter deepens that analysis, following the rationale that "merely representing what there *is* [in a linguistic landscape] does not capture what is imagined to be, nor how what there *is* is transformed and transmuted and 'read' in alternative ways in situated interactions" (Stroud and Jegels 2014: 183). In order to explore how such Zhuang-inclusive signage is "transformed and transmuted and 'read'", this chapter explores alternative language-ideological visions of the urban landscapes. After all, government organizations, whom Chapter Six showed to be almost the sole agents displaying written Zhuang in these landscapes, "are not the only agents in the process, and their framings are not necessarily definitive" (Coupland 2012: 23); the other important agents are viewers. The semiotic resources offered by public texts are necessarily open to viewers' multiple uptakes, as this chapter vividly reveals. Neither the place identities of the streets displaying Zhuang-inclusive signage, nor the identities of those who author this signage, nor the personal identities of those walking or driving along these streets, are determined by the Nanning language policy's intervention in streetscape signage. "Identity", as Anderson (2011: xx) explained in a fortuitously apt simile, "is never a one-way street".

I investigated the multiple meanings made of public texts in Zhuang through my commented walks and other interviews with my cohorts of university student and language leader participants. Most participants were Zhuang speakers. In their roles as residents, visitors, pedestrians and road-users in Nanning or at minzu-specialist universities where we had also found some Zhuang-inclusive language displays, these participants had personally experienced the linguistic landscapes in this study. This chapter is about their perceptions of Zhuang-inclusive signage. These perceptions were articulated in my walks with participants past instances of Zhuang-inclusive signage and in interviews in which we discussed participants' own experiences of the Zhuang-inclusive signage of the kind that I had documented in my fieldwork.

Analyzing this data about the participants' personal and everyday ways of seeing their linguistic landscapes, Sections 8.2–8.5 examine how public displays of written Zhuang are misrecognized, not read despite being recognized, evaluated as tokenistic, or evaluated as contributions to heritage maintenance. (Here, tokenism is an emergent idea contrasting with substantive state support, and thus not necessarily invoking Arnstein's (1969) well-known theory of tokenism as a low-order form of citizen participation.) These perceptions are often interrelated or overlapping, especially in so far as Zhuang-inclusive signage was read symbolically and criticized in reference to language-in-education policies which have failed to support Zhuang literacy. Section 8.6 then foregrounds the common thread – perceptions of widespread illiteracy in Zhuang – and examines the participants' belief that Zhuang literacy is attained only through specialist training. Section 8.7 discusses the various themes of participants' perceptions of publicly displayed Zhuang writing through the prism of "activating" semiotic resources in identity construction, following Jaworski and Thurlow (2010: 5). The analysis reveals how participants view linguistic landscapes through a habitus that reflects language norms and this, I argue in the concluding discussion, undermines assumptions about the increased visibility and symbolic valorization achieved by publicly displaying marginalized languages.

8.2 Misrecognition of Zhuang displays

A key theme emerging in discussions with participants about Zhuang on display in linguistic landscapes was the language's misrecognition: certain participants did not actually realize that the Zhuang toponyms written on signage were in Zhuang. Specifically, Romanized Zhuang had been misrecognized by participants themselves and people they knew as Putonghua Pinyin (as in the news report mentioned earlier) but also as English. For example, two Zhuang-speaking GUN students – in fact, they were majoring in Zhuang Studies – reported the misrecognition of Zhuang as Putonghua Pinyin and English in Excerpt 8-1.

> *Excerpt 8-1*
>
> Laurel：因为它这个是拼音文字，没什么人看，看不懂。略过去也觉得它是英文或者是拼音这种，但是又不是拼音，所以他不会觉得这个是壮文。
> Author：对啊。
> Zeina：看起来像英文一样，我觉得。
>
> [Laurel: Because it [signage] is Pinyin script, no one pays it any regard, they can't read it. In the recent past, people even thought it was English or [Putonghua] Pinyin, something of that nature, but it is not [Putonghua] Pinyin, so they could not conceive of it being Zhuang script.
> Author: Right.
> Zeina: To look at, it looks the same as English, I think.]

Zeina's comment highlights the significance of the alphabetic form of Romanized Zhuang in the language's misrecognition; while the orthography is different from English, the script is the same because Zhuang shares the 26 letters of the English alphabet. These 26 include the 25 letters used to write Putonghua Pinyin (A-Z without V), so the alphabetic form is also vulnerable to misrecognition as Putonghua Pinyin.

Laurel's comment suggests the additional significance of habitus: to conceive of a text being written in Zhuang, a viewer must have a mental representation of Zhuang as a written language, and then recognize it. However, being a Zhuang speaker does not automatically mean having a mental representation of written Zhuang, or even having an idea that Zhuang can be written. Laurel's comment reveals metalinguistic awareness about this, and the excerpts across this chapter build up the picture of Zhuang speakers who do not (or did not) know Zhuang could be written, let alone know what its standardized writing conventions look like.

Laurel here suggests people previously thought Zhuang was Putonghua Pinyin, implying people now know better. Other data, however, suggest some

Zhuang speakers (and others) still cannot recognize written Zhuang, including Laurel's own surprise, later in our interview, to be shown the line of Zhuang written on every banknote (see Excerpt 8-3). Other students discussed the idea of coming into knowledge, explaining the role of formal education in their transition from someone who misrecognized written Zhuang as English or Putonghua Pinyin to someone who recognized it. For example, Sunny described acquiring the knowledge to recognize and read Romanized Zhuang.

Excerpt 8-2

Sunny：所以说没有去了解这个壮文啊，它壮文也有壮文的拼音— 你如果没有了解它那个壮文，像之前我刚来的时候看到广西大学旁边写的 "GVANGJSIH DAYOZ"，这个是用壮文写的，然后我那时候就用英文去拼，可是拼着它拼不出来是那个啊。如果是英文的话是 "Guangxi University"，但是如果是要大写的首写字母也拼不出这个，所以呢我就-- 然后我加入到这个协会学了一节那个拼音，壮文的拼音，然后就去看了一下，"哦，原来是这样子念"。

[Sunny: So to speak if you don't come to understand that Zhuang script, that this Zhuang script also has Pinyin [Romanized orthography]-- If you don't understand that Zhuang script, like before when I had just come [to university] I saw written on the side of Guangxi University [East Gate] "GVANGJSIH DAYOZ", that's written in Zhuang script, so at that time I used English to sound it out, but it can't be sounded out like that. If it were English it would be "Guangxi University", but if it were written in big alphabetic letters it wouldn't come out like that, so I was -- Then I entered that [Zhuang students'] association and studied that Pinyin a bit, Romanized Zhuang, then I went to take a look: "oh, all along it was read out like this".]

Excerpt 8-2 reveals the role of university in gaining the knowledge to recognize Zhuang writing, but Sunny's accounting degree courses were not instrumental. Rather, she learnt Romanized Zhuang through classes offered by an extracurricular student association at GU.

The role of knowledge in recognizing Zhuang is explained further in Excerpt 8-3, in which GUN Zhuang Studies students affirm the need, in their view, for specific knowledge about written Zhuang rather than simply knowledge of how to speak Zhuang in order to recognize it.

Excerpt 8-3

Luke：每个人都有人民币，RMB，但是其实没有多少人懂得这个是壮文。
Author：对--
Laurel: -- 有壮文呢？！
Author：我最近-- 写什么啊？
Laurel: 写的吗?
Author：对啊。

Luke：中国人民银行，十元。[都在笑着]
Laurel：我爸妈都不一定懂哦。写什么啊？对啊。
Luke：中国人民银行，十元。
Zeina：我爸妈都不一定懂哦。

[Luke: Everyone has *Renminbi*, RMB, but in fact not many people know this [pointing on the note] is Zhuang script.
Author: Yes --
Laurel: -- It has Zhuang script?!
Author: I recently -- [To Luke] What's written?
Laurel: Written?
Author: [To Laurel] Right.
Luke: [reading from note] The People's Bank of China, 10 yuan. [General laughter]
Zeina: My dad and mum wouldn't necessarily understand.]

Zeina positioned her parents, whom she reported were speakers of Zhuang, as unable to recognize Zhuang on banknotes because of their lack of formal education in Zhuang. The excerpt demonstrates that oral proficiency in Zhuang is frequently divorced from the ability to read Zhuang, hence speakers may not recognize Zhuang when it appears in the linguistic landscape.

The extracts above show Romanized Zhuang is misrecognized as Putonghua or English, but I found it is also sometimes misrecognized as an unspecified foreign language, as Excerpt 8-4 illustrates. Referring again to the GU campus East Gate, which gives the university's name in Zhuang and Putonghua, Mark, a science undergraduate, said:

Excerpt 8-4

Mark：因为很多人却是看不懂的，像我们只会说语所以我也是上了大学才知道有壮文这个东西……我看到［东门］，我以为是其他国家的文字，也没看得懂。

[Mark: Because many people actually can't read it, like we can only speak the language, also I only knew there was that Zhuang script as a thing once I started university ... I saw [the East Gate], I thought it was another country's writing, I didn't understand it.]

Mark had not encountered Romanized Zhuang in his childhood in GZAR, or had not been made aware if he did encounter it. He rationalizes his misrecognition by arguing that Zhuang is a spoken language and that therefore recognition of written Zhuang ought not to be expected.

The contention that the oral nature of Zhuang was the cause of misrecognition also emerged in a group interview with GUN students who, with the exception of one student, Luke, had only become familiar with Romanized Zhuang at university.

8.2 Misrecognition of Zhuang displays — 225

Excerpt 8-5

Yana：我以为只是说，但是没有那个字，我不知道它有没有字。然后上大学之后就知道他们在学壮文嘛，然后就说怎么会有壮文，就觉得很神奇，我不知道，以前不知道。
Author：所以以前没看到牌子这样的还是没看到比如, 我拿出来, --
Luke: -- 三月三 --
Author：-- 这个杂志？这样的东西？是用壮语写的。
Yana：看到我也不懂啊，我看不懂。
Luke: 没什么人懂。

[Yana: I thought it was only spoken, but didn't have these written graphemes, I didn't know whether or not it had a script. Then after I started university I understood they [co-interviewees studying Zhuang Studies] were studying Zhuang script, then I thought "how can there be Zhuang script?" I thought that was really miraculous, I didn't know, before, didn't know.
Author: So beforehand you had not seen signage and things like that, or had not seen, for example, I'll get it out … this magazine? --
Luke: *Third of the Third* [title of bilingual magazine] --
Author: -- Those things? Written in Zhuang language.
Yana: Seeing them I still didn't understand; I could not read.
Luke: Nobody understands it.]

It was ironic that Luke proclaimed nobody (else) understood written Zhuang, as he was literate in Zhuang so he knew literacy was possible. Luke's response highlights how unusual his Zhuang literacy is. GUN has taught its Zhuang Studies students that a script for Zhuang exists and that knowledge – although not necessarily the knowledge to read it – has been transmitted by the Zhuang Studies students to students in other majors, including Yana.

Contrasting with those emphasizing the need for specialist education to recognize written Zhuang, other participants wondered how they, being Zhuang speakers, could have failed to recognize written Zhuang automatically without training. To them, the typical orality of Zhuang language practices did *not* naturalize the misrecognition of written Zhuang (unlike the students quoted above). For example, Huw, at GU, previously thought Romanized Zhuang was Putonghua Pinyin, like those in the Guangxi News report. Huw recounted that he came to know how to read Zhuang script after moving to university and that he had initially misread GU East Gate's bilingual sign as a dual-script, monolingual Putonghua sign. Now that he had learnt to recognize written Zhuang through the extracurricular student association's classes, it made sense to him that Zhuang speakers be expected to recognize it, and he turned this expectation on himself:

Excerpt 8-6

Huw: 看到这个我的感觉就是，基本上就是广西南宁啦，政府那牌子写的名字上旁边才用壮文。然后我说怎么看不懂？又不是英文，又不是拼音。

[Huw: Seeing these signs my feeling is, basically it's Guangxi Nanning, so the government, next to the names it writes on signs it then writes Zhuang script. So I say "how was I unable to read it?" It's not English, nor is it [Putonghua] Pinyin.]

Excerpt 8-6 also reveals that it made particular sense to Huw that Zhuang writing be displayed in Nanning; the language is "in place" in GZAR's capital.

The implication of perceiving displays of Romanized Zhuang as another language is that Zhuang's symbolic capital is vitiated, and no association can be made by such viewers between Zhuang language and traditional or contemporary literacy practices. This reduces both the perceived utility and the symbolic power of the displays. However, when a viewer is highly literate in Zhuang – as Mr B, who has a PhD in Zhuang and teaches Zhuang Studies is – the bilingual signage can be recognized and become symbolically powerful:

Excerpt 8-7

Author：你在路上看到用壮语写的牌子会有什么感觉？
Mr B：觉得挺亲切的，还觉得是自己的东西。
Author：这个可以理解，特别是历史上汉语和少数民族语言不能公开的写在一起。
Mr B：被歧视，地位不高。

[Author: In the street, when you see signage written in Zhuang, how might you feel?
Mr B: It feels very familiar, I also feel it's my own thing.
Author: That is understandable, especially as historically Hanyu [Mandarin] and minority languages would not be publicly written together.
Mr B: There was prejudice against it, the status wasn't high.]

Mr B is referring to experiences seeing Zhuang-inclusive signage in GZAR, where he is from, not in Yunnan, where he now lives.

Finally, the dissociation between Zhuang writing and Zhuang language may persist even when a viewer is aware of Romanized Zhuang, because their knowledge about Romanized Zhuang is incomplete. The following quotations from Jane and Tansy's interviews illustrate this. Jane, a Zhuang Studies undergraduate at YMU, declared "我们语言也是这个汉语拼音写的" [our language is also written in this Hanyu Pinyin]. "Hanyu Pinyin" is Putonghua Pinyin. Here, the majority language is perceived by Jane as useful even for transcribing Zhuang, in a misperception nurturing Putonghua's hegemonic status. This is a slightly different misrecognition to seeing Zhuang as Putonghua or English because Jane knows the language being written is Zhuang. She misrecognizes the tool used to write it; Jane associates literacy practices with Putonghua rather than Zhuang, not recognizing that Zhuang has its own orthography.

Yet another version of misrecognition emerged in an interview with Tansy. In Excerpt 8-8, Tansy associates the practice of writing Zhuang with a dialectal group other than her own, misrecognizing the writing as "Yulan Zhuang" and therefore as a specific symbol which offers her no generic Zhuang communicative or identity affordances.

Excerpt 8-8

Tansy: 壮文看不懂。像我们那边的壮语就只是口口相传的，没有书面，书面类型。像那个，中国的那个人民币上，不是有那个壮文吗？但是那个壮文应该是，就是玉兰他们那边的，因为就是玉兰他们那边应该是有文字保留下来的。他们那边是正统的壮语。

[Tansy: I can't read Zhuang script. Like, our Zhuang language from there [hometown in GZAR] is only word of mouth, it's not in books, in book form. It's like that, on the Chinese RMB, isn't there Zhuang script? But that Zhuang script must be that of Yulan, theirs, because those from Yulan should have kept Zhuang script going. There they have orthodox Zhuang language.]

This normative role proposed for "Yulan Zhuang" appears to be idiosyncratic; official, standard Zhuang is based on the Wuming dialect (Li and Huang 2004: 241). Tansy's view reveals a hierarchy of orthodox and heterodox Zhuang dialects on a localized scale familiar to her. To Tansy, the written form of Zhuang represents the strictly preserved minority language practices of a specific place. As that kind of orthodox language is not associated with her hometown, she places no expectation on herself to be able to read or write Zhuang. This is potentially also because, while a Zhuang speaker, Tansy is not classified as Zhuangzu. Similar to participants in Excerpts 8-4 to 8-5, Tansy considers that an ability to recognize written Zhuang should not be expected of Zhuang speakers raised within an oral language tradition.

The above excerpts illustrate participants explaining the misrecognition of Zhuang – as alphabetically-written Putonghua, English or another foreign language – either as a mistake of their former selves or of less educated others, not a mistake they now make. Tansy is the exception, presenting herself as still not literate in Zhuang because her kind of Zhuang is not the literary kind.

Taking Zhuang Studies or extracurricular Zhuang classes may appear to be the sort of education which enables a viewer to correctly recognize written Zhuang. However, the surprised reaction of Laurel upon learning banknotes display Zhuang writing (Excerpt 8-3) reveals that a viewer can be familiar with Zhuang writing – as Laurel is from her Zhuang Studies major – and yet not "see" it. Section 8.3 delves into this other form of subjective invisibility, the habitual overlooking of public, written Zhuang.

8.3 Overlooking Zhuang displays

Even where displays of Romanized Zhuang are recognized *as Zhuang*, the recognition may engender only a fleeting interaction between the text and a Zhuang-speaking viewer if the viewer's reading habitus tends towards attending to, and reading, another language on the same multilingual sign. This section explores such experiences of overlooking Zhuang writing. I found some viewers noticed Zhuang displayed on signage in the sense of recognizing that the signage included Zhuang, but reported themselves habituated to ignoring it while reading the signage's other language(s), especially Putonghua.

Ignoring Zhuang was particularly evident with reference to Nanning's bilingual street-name signs. For example, in a group interview at GU, I discussed Nanning's street-name signs with Liz and Hope. These students considered Zhuang their first language, and grew up in Zhuang-speaking areas of GZAR, but neither had learnt to read Zhuang. Their major was English Language and they likened reading Zhuang on signage to their experiences learning to read English.

Excerpt 8-9

> Author：然后我有一个问题，你在路上看到，每一条路的名字有壮文，然后有普通话的汉字，然后有普通话的拼音，汉语拼音，这三个语言。你们看到这样的有什么样的感觉？
> Hope：一般的话直接看普通话。
> Liz：对……
> Hope：就像看美剧，有时候双语的话我们也会直接看普通话。要练习英语的话，有的时候就听听，就做一些听力了也。

> [Author: Now then, I have a question, have you seen on the street; each street's name sign has Zhuang script, then Putonghua characters, then Putonghua Pinyin – Hanyu Pinyin – those three languages. When you see them how do you feel?
> Hope: Generally, I really only look at the Putonghua.
> Liz: Yes …
> Hope: So it's like watching American television [with subtitles], sometimes where there are two languages we will really only look at the Putonghua. If we are practicing English, sometimes we listen and do some "Listening Strengthening" also.]

Hope's television analogy reminds us that permanent, fixed, street-name signage can be experienced as temporary text, akin to subtitles which change during a show. Evidently, these students consider reading Putonghua takes them less effort than Zhuang and is therefore preferable when one has only a moment to read. Hope thinks the common reading habit is to look to the language you already know. This need not be true for everyone; this is Hope's own reading habit and her classmate, Liz, affirms it in the same excerpt. They have developed a language learning practice of breaking the habit of reading Putonghua, with effort, when intentionally reading English to better learn it.

Others professed never paying attention to Zhuang displays. I specifically discussed Nanning's street-name signs in my RUC group interview, given the interviewees' GZAR origins. In Excerpt 8-10, from that interview, Freddy and Zac acknowledge Zhuang-medium (bilingual) signage exists but Zac dismisses any expectation that he would read it.

> *Excerpt 8-10*
>
> Author：我在南宁看到每一条路牌名字用普通话写，然后壮语写，然后拼音写。看到这样的公开的壮文，你们有什么样的感觉？
> Freddy: 嗯。好。
> Zac: 哈哈我们没有注意到这个东西，对完全没有注意到这个东西。
>
> [Author: In Nanning, I saw that each street-name sign is written in Putonghua, then it is written in Zhuang, then in Pinyin. Seeing that kind of public Zhuang script, how do you feel?
> Freddy: Hmm. Yeah.
> Zac: Haha! We haven't paid attention to that, yes, paid completely no attention to that.]

Zac expresses his response as "we", not just "I"; thus including his peers or possibly even the wider group of all Zhuang speakers as oblivious to Nanning's Zhuang-inclusive street-name signs.

Excerpts 8-9 and 8-10 reveal how Nanning's Zhuang-inclusive signage may be ignored by Zhuang speakers. Moreover, the data revealed the overlooking of Zhuang on more widely encountered Zhuang-inclusive texts, such as banknotes. In Excerpt 8-3, I quoted Luke bringing into our conversation the example of banknotes as public texts partially written in Zhuang. His fellow interviewee, Goldie, then commented that banknotes were multilingual texts in which Zhuang writing was typically not noticed unless a viewer had developed Zhuang literacy through education "这种没有专门学过壮文的人是不会去注意这个事的" [With these things, if somebody hasn't specifically studied Zhuang script, they would not pay any attention to this thing.] Luke provided our group interview with another example of a similarly common but overlooked multilingual text, official identity cards:

> *Excerpt 8-11*
>
> Luke：而且在身份证上有，我们广西的身份证上都有。然后但是他们没有人去注意，或者说可能觉得是英文。
>
> [Luke: And moreover our identity cards have it, our Guangxi identity cards all have it. But then, they don't have anybody paying attention, or we could say they probably think it's English.]

Here, Luke combines lack of attention with misrecognition. These two processes form a continuum that serves to render Zhuang invisible to viewers even if it exists in the public linguistic landscape.

Finally, the oversight was sometimes a matter of scale. This involved noticing certain Zhuang texts but not noting them as part of a wider practice of displaying Zhuang, thereby overlooking some of the significance of public Zhuang texts. For example, Huw, in Excerpt 8-12, had known of banknotes' Zhuang script since high school but did not perceive banknote multilingualism to be part of a policy of writing in Zhuang in public until he moved to Nanning, because he had not encountered any other public Zhuang-medium texts in his hometown, Guigang, which is another urban center in GZAR.

Excerpt 8-12

Huw: 我在高中的时候就去知道，基本每一张那个钱是有壮文的……但是说有些比较有名的地方方面都标有壮文，我是后面才知道的，因为我那边好像很少有。

[Huw: While at high school I came to know, basically every banknote had Zhuang script. … But that some relatively well-known places are marked in Zhuang script, I only knew that afterwards, because there [home town] seems like it has very few [such signs].]

Huw perceived bilingual Zhuang signage to be a particular feature of Nanning landscapes, in contrast to Guigang landscapes. As he expresses in Excerpt 8-6, above, this is rationalized as being in line with Nanning's distinction amongst GZAR's cities (it is the capital).

So far, the chapter has described the misrecognition of Zhuang as other languages, and the overlooking of Zhuang on multilingual signs by viewers habituated to focusing on the Putonghua version of the text. These are variations in the ways people read (or do not read) public Zhuang-medium texts for lexical meaning. In addition, even when written Zhuang on signage is recognized as an icon of Zhuangness and thus read symbolically, it is likewise subject to multiple readings. In particular, the inclusion of written Zhuang signage may be perceived as tokenistic.

8.4 Zhuang displays as tokenistic

Mr C, a scholar of Zhuang, emphasized that the addition of Zhuang to Nanning's public signage was a "符号的" [symbolic] change, and that its purpose was *not* to be understood for linguistic meaning (field notes 17 June 2014). Investigating this symbolism apparently prioritized by the government in displaying bilingual signage, this section presents perceptions of written Zhuang displays as problematic and potentially even a slight to the Zhuangzu group, within a frame of identity politics. Displays of written Zhuang were perceived by some participants as an inauthentic symbol of language practices. I found Zhuang signage was perceived as inauthentic for two reasons: first, Zhuang was widely perceived as a spoken rather than written language, as I demonstrated in Section 8.2. Participants with this view included some who thought viewers were unable to read or correct Zhuang signage because Zhuang literacy had been insufficiently supported in the public school system, rather than accepting the orality of Zhuang as some participants above did. Second, some considered Romanized Standard Zhuang, specifically, as inauthentic because it encoded and represented what they considered to be a Hanified variety of Zhuang. Either way, the inauthenticity of the symbolic public display of written Zhuang by the government read to them as a superficial practice without the substance of Zhuang language and disconnected from support for Zhuang language i.e. tokenism.

To illustrate the view that writing rather than speaking Zhuang is tokenistic, I will present extracts of my interviews with Mr N, a language leader, and Barbara, a student. Mr N is a Zhuangzu historian. Barbara was then a Chinese Language major at GU who voluntarily co-taught extracurricular classes in Zhuang writing at GU which certain other participants had attended (e.g. Sunny: Excerpt 8-2). Each perceived Nanning's Zhuang-inclusive signage cynically, explaining that they associated the signage with the absence of schooling enabling people to learn to read it. Excerpt 8-12 comes from my discussion with Mr N about his understanding that GZAR offered a limited number of bilingual schools, the quality of which were questionable, resulting in few opportunities to learn Zhuang literacy.

Excerpt 8-13

Author: 壮文学校都不教授壮文了？
Mr N: 是的，它不教了，成了普通高中了，只挂了一个壮文学校的牌子，其实已经不教了。

[Author: None of the schools [nominally] for Zhuang writing are teaching Zhuang writing?
Mr N: That's right, it's not taught, they've become mainstream secondary schools, they just hang up a Zhuang script school sign, but they're not teaching it.]

Further, these comments reveal how public Zhuang displays can be perceived as indexing the minority language policy framework of which they are part, foregrounding a governance discourse in tension with the discourse of language valorization in which the same Zhuang displays symbolically participate. This point is illustrated further by Excerpt 8-14.

Excerpt 8-14

Author: 但听说是经常写错。
Mr N: 是的，经常写错。毕竟国家给她这个地位了，人民币上也印上了壮文，所以广西政府不得不这样做，但这种东西哪怕写错了也没有人能看得出来，因为广西人没有任何机会能接受到壮文的教育，谁能看懂？广西有那么几所小学，装模作样的教授壮文，教了两三年又不教了，广西的小学有那么一万到两万人能享受到双语教育。但对于一个人数由两千万的民族，只有两万人会壮文，这跟没有是一样的。等于官方只做了一些门面上的工作，社会上有没有人看得懂壮文，他的错误就更没有人指出来了。

[Author: But I've heard it's often written wrongly.
Mr N: That's right, it's often written wrongly. After all, the nation gives it [Zhuang language] that status, the *Renminbi* [banknote] has Zhuang script printed upon it, so the Guangxi government has no choice but to do likewise, but no matter how erroneously those sorts of things are written there is no-one who can pick that out, because Guangxi people have no opportunity to receive a Zhuang script education; who can read and understand? Guangxi has however many primary schools, making a pretense of teaching Zhuang script, teaching it for two or three years or not teaching it, Guangxi's primary schools have ten to twenty thousand people who are able to receive bilingual education. But with a minzu population of twenty million, only having twenty thousand people who can use Zhuang script, it's like nothing else. It equals the government showing a bit of superficial work, in society there isn't anybody who can read Zhuang script, so there is nobody to point out their errors.]

Here, Mr N refers to "门面上的工作" [*lit.* door-front work], a figurative reference emphasizing the image-projection role of multilingual public texts, including the work of erecting the largely government-authored texts collected in Chapter Six.

To Mr N, the use of Zhuang name signage by these schools and institutions is a mere token, given that substantive government efforts to develop people's literacy in Zhuang are lacking. Barbara, although many decades younger than Mr N, shared a similar perception:

Excerpt 8-15

Barbara: 我觉得啊壮文以前国家是从于挺广的，就是在每个县会看壮语吧……后面的话是心痛顺社会，所谓的民族班就发钱，但是不教壮语，只是跟普通的班系一洋就的教汉语的东西，所以使用人群少，而且在家也没有任何的经济佳绩，没有提供很多的工作岗位，所以你必要壮文的话其实心痛去升，只是说国家意识形态比加好看一点 "如果我们再提高壮文我们再使用壮文"，这样的。

[Barbara: I think ah Zhuang script was previously widespread across the country, in each county you could see Zhuang language ... After, it sadly went the way of society: so-called "minzu classes" cost money, but they don't teach Zhuang language, they're just the same as the common class stream so they teach Hanyu things, so people who use it [Zhuang writing] reduce in number, moreover in the home it doesn't have any economic value, not offering many company jobs, so times when you have to use Zhuang writing are actually sadly falling, it's only to make the national ideology a little better looking: "if we again offer Zhuang writing we will use Zhuang writing again", like that.]

Barbara's term "minzu classes" is a common expression referring to public schooling provided at least partly in the medium of a minority language (GZAR's manifestations of minority education were canvassed in Chapter Five). Excerpt 8-15 illustrates how displaying Zhuang on signage can be perceived as tokenistic because the teaching of Zhuang in the education system is also seen as tokenistic. Because of the current problems with Zhuang-medium education, Barbara is concerned that Zhuang speakers will not be more inclined to value Zhuang language, nor use it more, just because the government now displays some written Zhuang in GZAR. Mr C, a linguist and the convener of the extra-curricular Zhuang class which Barbara co-teaches, expressed a similar view that "public signage won't change youth opinion, low prestige" (field notes 17 June 2014).

Moreover, Mr N expressed his perception that the use of Zhuang signage represents a false pretense of government commitment to maintaining Zhuang language. The following excerpt also illustrates how the treatment of Zhuang language may be taken as representing an overall tokenism in the government's treatment of the Zhuangzu.

Excerpt 8-16

Author: 当你看到这样的牌子你会怎么想?
Mr N: 这简直就跟开玩笑一样，用中国话说就是"挂羊头卖狗肉"，就是装门面，他们内心对壮文没有任何尊重，为了装门面，广西壮族自治区，才挂上去。不信的话问那些官员尊不尊重壮文，他们绝对没有这种意识。本民族的官员都觉得自己的民族是一个很可笑的民族。

[Author: So when you see those signs [on government institutions in GZAR], what do you think?
Mr N: It's simply a joke, to use Chinese national language it's "to hang up a sheep's head and sell dog meat" [Idiom: false pretenses], so it's on the façade, but in their hearts there is no respect; for the façade, "Guangxi Zhuangzu Autonomous Region" gets hung up. Don't believe the talk, those officials don't respect Zhuang script, they have absolutely no such consciousness. Our minzu officials think their own minzu is a foolish minzu.]

A similar view was expressed by a manger who offered to show me around the Guangxi Museum of Nationalities' Ethnic Village on my first visit. He explained his view that often government talk about the minorities is more for a show of care than anything else, and that government measures for the minorities often "有限" [are limited] (field notes 16 June 2014).

The irony of the GZAR government being a nominally "Zhuangzu" government exacerbated the perception of tokenism in that manager's views and in Excerpt 8-16; to Mr N, Zhuang language protection is normatively in place in GZAR but has not sufficiently materialized. This supports my finding in Chapters Four and Five that the language governance framework constructs Zhuang language practices as taking place only amongst Zhuangzu people within the Zhuangzu autonomous territories, and Zhuang protection as the responsibility of those territories' governments.

Other participants perceived displays of Romanized Standard Zhuang, specifically, as tokenistic, because the development of this script and orthography was seen as part and parcel of the Hanification of Zhuang through the government's standardization of the language. For example, Excerpt 8-17 comes from my interview with Hoz, a political science student at YMU. Hoz led me to the only piece of Zhuang-inclusive signage which he knew of on his campus, the multilingual national unity poster shown at Figure 42. Hoz pointed out a grammatical mistake in the Zhuang on that poster, and explained:

Excerpt 8-17

Hoz: 这个壮文，实际上，这个语法在我看来是一个很错误的用法……是完全汉化了的壮语。

[Hoz: This Zhuang writing, frankly, this grammar is in my view a really erroneous usage ... it's completely Hanified Zhuang language.]

This echoes Excerpt 8-14, where Mr N noted that Zhuang displays often contain errors but few people can tell. While the YMU poster's display of minority languages may have been intended as inclusive symbolism, displaying mistakes causes Hoz to interpret the text as offensive. Hoz's offense is further explained by his belief that the Zhuang writing used on the poster was not legitimate:

Excerpt 8-18

Hoz: 我们壮文主要的目的反对那种、不认可那个广西方面的那种所谓的标壮，一个原因是它掺用了太多的汉语，包括语法方面他们没有坚守我们母语的语法，所以我们就比较反感。

[Hoz: Our Zhuang script must have as its goal opposing that, Guangxi's so-called Standard Zhuang which is not endorsed [by Zhuang speakers]; one reason is that it mixes in too much Han Language, including from the grammar aspect it doesn't stick to the grammar of our mother tongue, so we feel relatively disgusted.]

That is, the Romanized Standard Zhuang is perceived as a symbol of government regulation and reformation of Zhuang. A more authentic way of writing, on this view, might use the older, unstandardized Sawndip script, in which Hoz claims some literacy, or a new, grassroots orthography which he explained he hopes to develop after graduating.

As the chapter's introduction posited, there are multiple readings of public Zhuang texts. For example, another symbolic reading was likewise critical of the quality of the Zhuang in public displays, but did not perceive such displays as tokenistic government efforts. This view was expressed particularly by Mr S. He, too, regretted the loss of meaning and knowledge that is conveyed by displays of Zhuang of declining linguistic quality, as he saw it, but Mr S explained this as a problem with Zhuangzu people, not a policy problem. He considered that Zhuangzu people shared an expectation of limited governmental use of Zhuang language.

Implicit in these participants' commentaries on Zhuang displays as tokenistic is the acknowledgement that when the government publicly displays Zhuang-inclusive signage, it does so to contribute a symbolic resource for Zhuang heritage and/or language maintenance, albeit a choice of symbol which the participants in this section saw as wrong-headed. The next section further explores evaluations of Zhuang writing displays as – positive or negative – symbolic resources in heritage and language maintenance.

8.5 Zhuang displays as contributions to heritage and language maintenance

A fourth perspective on Zhuang signage revealed in the interviews evaluated the contribution of displaying written Zhuang to maintaining Zhuang heritage. Both positive and negative evaluations are evident in my data. To see public texts partially written in Zhuang as a tool of heritage preservation, viewers must see such texts as symbolizing Zhuang heritage, but this was not an automatic way of seeing, as the sections above have demonstrated. Furthermore, I found those who saw written Zhuang displays as symbolic of Zhuang heritage struggled to dissociate this symbolism from the functional problem of the public being unable to read Zhuang signage. Some also perceived written Zhuang displays as ineffectual contributions to heritage maintenance due to negative associations with Zhuang culture, the exclusive association of Zhuang displays with government language practices, or the dissociation of the standardized language variety on display from authentic Zhuang heritage.

First, some people saw Zhuang-inclusive signage as positively contributing to Zhuang heritage maintenance. For example, I asked Dora how it made her feel to see Zhuang writing in public and she replied:

Excerpt 8-19

Dora: 我觉得有的话还是挺好，但是我觉得没有用，没有多少人看得懂的。她们甚至不知道有壮文这么东西存在。

[Dora: I think sometimes it's really good, but I think it has no use, there are not that many people who can read it. They don't even know Zhuang script exists as a thing.]

Inquiring further into this tension between a viewer perceiving Zhuang signage as both positive and useless, I asked how Dora would feel if she knew a sign was in Zhuang although she could not completely read its meaning. She reaffirmed her positive evaluation, giving a specific example: "我觉得挺好，就像我们学校的东门" [I think that's really good, like on our campus' East Gate.] That is, despite recognizing the limitations of displays few people can read or recognize, Dora evaluated the public display of Zhuang positively.

Others were less equivocal about the positive contribution of Zhuang writing in the linguistic landscape. For example, at the time of our interview, Mr S's book on the history of GZAR was being translated from Putonghua into Zhuang, printed in the Romanized script, to become a circulating Zhuang text in the public realm. Although he expected that the translated edition would be rarely read because of low Zhuang literacy, and explained it was expensive to translate, Mr S nevertheless believed publishing in Zhuang served a symbolic purpose. My field notes record his explanation: "It [a Zhuang edition] seems proper to do given it is about the locality and local language, so it 'should be in the local vernacular'". That is, he sees producing a Standard Zhuang-medium book as an act of valuing Zhuang heritage. Similarly, the manager I spoke with at Guangxi Museum for Nationalities explained that he thought of the museum as being able to raise the status of minority languages although archiving written Zhuang was not going to create more every day communications in Zhuang (field note 16 June 2014).

For others, a positive reaction to public Zhuang displays was diminished by their awareness that few people can read such displays. For example, in Excerpt 8-20, Liz doubts her own positive evaluation of Zhuang signage's contribution to maintaining heritage.

Excerpt 8-20

Liz: 我觉得还是很有价值的吧，就是保护我们的壮族文化。但是可能因为我们毕,我们有些都不太理解不太懂，所以可能我们就觉得好像也无所谓这样的。

8.5 Zhuang displays as contributions to heritage and language maintenance — 237

[Liz: I think it [Zhuang on signs] still has value, it's to protect our Zhuangzu culture. But maybe because we are relatively --, we all don't understand that well, don't read, so maybe we think it's a good symbol yet also "whatever", like that.]

Mr E expressed a similar view during a commented walk in GZAR Museum. While Mr E was pleased that Romanized Standard Zhuang appeared on curation signage in the standing exhibition on Zhuang heritage because he perceived this, and the whole exhibition, as valorization, he expressed dismay that most people had no training to read the Zhuang on the signage.

While Dora, Liz and Mr E saw public Zhuang texts as contributing to Zhuang cultural heritage preservation, albeit also as reminders of Zhuang's low readability, others who perceived Zhuang language displays as a symbolic way of maintaining heritage evaluated them negatively because of their low readability. One even discounted that Zhuang signage could be for heritage protection if it could not also be communicative (Excerpt 8-22 below). Like the participants in the last two excerpts, the participants in the following two excerpts questioned the heritage value of erecting signage that most Zhuang speakers cannot read. In contrast to the participants above, however, these participants did not then conclude that such signage nevertheless made a contribution. The first example is from my group interview at RUC. Freddy's comments in Excerpt 8-21 generalize his and his co-interviewees professed habit of not reading of Zhuang on public signage (stated in Excerpt 8-9) to their wider community, questioning whether it matters that there is a heritage policy about Zhuang displays if the resulting signage is habitually not seen despite being in public places.

Excerpt 8-21

Author : 啊。哪，所以你来北京你们没有发现没有壮文呢? 没注意到北京有, 广西有--
Freddy: 我觉得区政府这么做，南宁市政府那么做，他只是为了凸显一个我们是壮族人，所以我们的路牌一定要有壮文而已，但是说实话用壮文写的路牌有多少人会去看，我觉得比较少。

[Author: Ah. So, then, when you came to Beijing you didn't realize there was no Zhuang script? Didn't pay attention to Beijing having, Guangxi having --
Freddy: I think the areal government did that, Nanning Municipal Government did that, it is only for highlighting a bit that we are Zhuang people, so our street signage must just have Zhuang script, but frankly speaking, street signage using Zhuang for the writing will have how many people seeing it? I think relatively few.]

Freddy does not personally affirm that the symbolism of displaying written Zhuang has value to him, but rather presents what he thinks is the value it has to the government. Excerpt 8-21 reveals how viewers make meaning from both the symbolic *and* informational functions of signage together; meaning is not derived through just one channel. Freddy thinks Zhuang signage must maintain some utility as an informational resource in order to be a positive symbolic resource. This is exemplified also in Excerpt 8-22, from the same group interview, which further illustrates the perception that public Zhuang texts do not contribute to Zhuang heritage maintenance because of the Zhuangzu's habituation to reading Putonghua. Thus, Zhuang is no longer considered necessary for public communications.

Excerpt 8-22

> Leroy: 我觉得就是可能能吸引来游客，但是对于保护语言文字的话我觉得作用确实比较小，因为这个东西本身大的趋势上来说本身确实是要被普通话所取代的，我觉得，因为确实用不到这个东西了，它没有，可以说已经没有存在的必要了，因为确实现在普通话普及了之后，生活环境里头确实这个已经没有使用的必要了，等就是-- 你想在我们下一代再下一代的时候，估计上基本上就是听不到这样的语言在存在了，因为现在接受的都是普通话的教育，所以大家都习惯于用普通话来交流。那既然习惯于用普通话来交流的话，别的语言就容易慢慢的退化了，就被取代了。所以它的那个刻字的行为，我觉得保护的作用不大，基本上就这样。

> [Leroy: I think that [Zhuang on public signage] may be able to attract tourists, but for the protection of language and script then I think the effect is relatively small, because speaking of the big trend, it is actually to replace these things with Putonghua, I think, because indeed these things are unusable, they do not have-- We can say there is no longer a need for them to exist, because in fact now that Putonghua has been popularized, there is already no need to use it within the environment in which we live, so-- I think, in the next generation and the one after that, I estimate, basically, you'll not hear that kind of language in use, because now all education is received in Putonghua, so everybody is accustomed to communicating in Putonghua. So given we are accustomed to communicating in Putonghua, it's easy for other languages to fade away, to be replaced. So it's – that lettering behavior, I think its function as protection is not big, basically that's it.]

That is, to Leroy, Zhuang signage today represents language practices that are already fading from existence and it is too late to protect them through public use. He sees signage as primarily about communication rather than visualizing heritage. Supporting Leroy's observation about the low communicative value of Zhuang were comments from a Zhuang language professional, Mr K, who previously worked for a GZAR government translation bureau translating and interpreting government announcements, rules and broadcasts from Putonghua into Zhuang for public dissemination. Mr K reported that the need for government information to be translated into Zhuang in order for the public to understand it has died away, whereas previously there were many readers illiterate in Putonghua who were expected by the government to read Standard Zhuang instead. (It is not clear that they actually did.)

8.5 Zhuang displays as contributions to heritage and language maintenance

A different, negative evaluation of the efficacy of Zhuang signage's contribution to heritage maintenance arose from the perception that it targeted tourists rather than regular users of Zhuang language, thus producing very little uptake of Zhuang language in new domains. This is similar to perceiving Zhuang-inclusive displays as inauthentic and tokenistic, as explored in 8.4, except that these viewers were not offended and did not perceive written Zhuang as a false show of respect by the government. Rather, these viewers considered Zhuang was simply displayed for a purpose other than heritage protection: the purpose of attracting tourists. For example, Freddy, continuing after Leroy in Excerpt 8-22, said:

Excerpt 8-23

Freddy: 我基本上也是同意他们两个的意见，然后我觉得说你用这个方式来保护民族的文化的话我觉得其实用处也是真的不太大，因为说你本民族的文化、本民族的语言还是要你本民族的人来说，然后你用这个去吸引游人、吸引一个外来人，他可能看的时候觉得挺有兴趣的、挺新奇的，但他走了回到自己家了之后他也不会记得什么东西，所以我觉得说，我们要想说保护我们本民族的语言和文化的话，应该还是说在本民族，在教育啊那些方面多下点功夫，而不是靠这些旅游的东西。

[Freddy: I basically agree with the views of the two of them [Leroy and Zac], so I think, say you use that method to protect minzu culture, actually I think the usefulness is not that great, because speaking of our minzu culture, our minzu language or our minzu people, and then you use this to attract tourists, attracting people from outside, when they see it they might think it's pretty interesting, very novel, but when they go back home they won't remember anything, so I think, if we want to talk about protecting our minzu language and culture, for this minzu it should be in education and those sorts of things, put in a bit more effort, rather than relying on these tourist things.]

To the participants in Excerpts 8-21 to 8-23, Zhuang on signage was perceived as useless for lexical communication and a means of attracting tourism and could not simultaneously be seen by Zhuang speakers as a symbol of their own cultural heritage. For these participants, practical contributions to protecting Zhuang heritage are more valuable than symbolic contributions. Moreover, while tourism may be a reason for the government displaying written Zhuang, it is not clear that such symbolic displays are recognizable as Zhuang by tourists either, given that even Zhuang speakers cannot recognize written Zhuang and given the local ethnicities and languages of GZAR are rarely explicitly constructed as distinct from one another or named in tourism discourses (Chapter Seven; Grey 2021a).

Freddy, in Excerpt 8-21, articulates a common perception amongst participants that Zhuang-inclusive signage is *only* a government language practice.

Mr N also made this clear as we discussed the characteristics of areas of Zhuangzu autonomous governance:

Excerpt 8-24

Author: 在公开的地方会有壮语吗？
Mr N: 在政府公开的牌匾上有壮文。

[Author: In public places will there be Zhuang language?
Mr N: On the government's public signs there is Zhuang script.]

This view accords with my linguistic landscape findings in Chapter Six: the public usage of written Zhuang is almost exclusively government-authored. One consequence for heritage maintenance of this view is that the government's Zhuang-inclusive signage does not readily encourage others to use written Zhuang because writing Zhuang in public is not perceived as a normal personal activity, nor as a personal heritage maintenance responsibility. This echoes the finding in the preceding chapter that 'doing' Zhuang language was not represented publicly as a personal or current activity.

Another evaluation of Zhuang displays as contributing very little to Zhuang heritage maintenance arose for those who associated Zhuang language with a culture they did not value; if Zhuang is perceived as having limited cultural capital, displaying it may not have much symbolic power. An example is given in Excerpt 8-25, from an interview with a Zhuangzu student at RUC. This student, Una, did not see Zhuang language in any mode as having cultural capital, and therefore its written display was perceived as futile heritage maintenance. Her comments reveal the interaction between the displacement of Zhuang language practices from urban and educational settings – norms that the landscape findings in Chapters Six and Seven have explored – and broader language ideologies. To this student, using Zhuang language – even the government using it for public texts – could not be disassociated from low-status rustic customs.

Excerpt 8-25

Author: 对，我发现是这样的，所以很多人觉得壮语没用。哪我在广西的时候看到有的公开的地方比如博物馆还是民俗他们都用壮文写，这样的东西我觉得可能有这个象征性--
Una: 什么性？
Author: Symbolic性。就是，不是很有用的，但是让人，怎么说，高兴，这样的，让人骄傲，还是让人高兴看到自己的语言，你觉得有这样的吗？
Una: 没有，因为我觉得在我眼中，因为壮族就是现在就是还这么保存着这种风俗其实是很山里面的，所以对我们来说，已经完全同化了，就没有什么概念了。而且，因为在我们那边，他们壮族如果是很纯的话，他们穿的衣服说话跟我们都不一样，所以就会觉得很奇怪。有一点，我没有那种认同感。因为我小时候看到那种她们不穿胸衣的，然后就

8.5 Zhuang displays as contributions to heritage and language maintenance — 241

会觉得他们穿自己的衣服，自己做的那种壮锦，然后就出来觉得很奇怪，也不梳头发，就用那个筷子。
Author：不洗头发？
Una: 不梳头发，就是不像我们这样放下来，她们就是用筷子或者是梳子挽起来，特别大的一把，你见过吗？
Author：见过啊
Una：特别纯那种，她们本也不说话，她可能从山里出来……就带着她们的孩子，都很脏的，我觉得，不太讲卫生。就觉得是那样的。

[Author: Yes, I realized it was like that, so many people think Zhuang language has no utility. So when I was in Guangxi I saw some public places – for example the museum – all using written Zhuang script. That kind of thing I think may have this symbolic nature--
Una: What nature?
Author: Symbolic nature. That is, it's not very useful but it makes people, how to say it, happy, like that, it makes people proud, and makes people happy to see their own language, do you think there is that [symbolic nature]?
Una: No, because I think in my eyes, because Zhuangzu is now-- Howsoever it's still maintaining that kind of custom, in fact that [language] is really inside the mountains [i.e. remote villages], so in regards to us, already completely assimilated, there is not any concept of it. Moreover, because in our area [home in GZAR], these Zhuangzu if they're really pure, the clothes they wear, their speech, are not at all the same as our ways, so we will think it's really strange. It's a bit, I don't have that kind of feeling of identification. Because when I was small and saw them not wearing bras, then I would think they wear their own style of clothing, that kind of Zhuang brocade they make themselves, so then the thought emerged that it's really strange, also they don't comb their hair, they use those chopsticks [hairpins].
Author: They don't wash their hair?
Una: They don't comb it, so it's not like our hair let down like this, so they use chopsticks or combs to pin it up, a really big bun, have you seen that?
Author: I've seen it.
Una: Especially pure that type, they fundamentally don't speak, they probably come out of the mountains ... carrying their children, all filthy, I think, not very hygienic. So I think it's like that.]

Una's comments reveal a strong ideological emplacement of Zhuang language in rural areas, while Zhuangzu practices are completely out-of-place in the city even for heritage maintenance. In Excerpt 8-25 she reports having "not any concept" of written Zhuang although we had previously discussed her knowledge that Romanized Zhuang exists and she had demonstrated some ability to recognize it. She almost overlooks my report of Zhuang writing in city museums, despite knowing Zhuang writing exists, because it cannot fit within her understanding of all Zhuang cultural practices as rural and pre-modern. For Una, Zhuang language has no place in the city, even in GZAR.

Yet another reason for negatively evaluating the efficacy of Zhuang displays as heritage maintenance tools was the perception that the Zhuang writing displayed was inauthentic, i.e. a misleading symbol. This extends from the critique of inauthentic signage as government tokenism analyzed in the preceding section. For example, extending our discussion of the multilingual poster at YMU in Excerpt 8-17 to written Zhuang displays in general, Hoz noted that Zhuang signage often transliterates Putonghua proper nouns, such as place names, into Zhuang, rather than inscribing Zhuang proper nouns. Further, he noted that the Zhuang word for street would not be at the end of a toponym in grammatical Zhuang although he had seen it placed terminally in street-names following the rules of Putonghua. We have seen this too, in photos of Nanning's street-names signs in Chapter Six, e.g. Figure 30. Hoz then summarized his evaluation:

Excerpt 8-26

Hoz: 我觉得像这种的壮语，我感觉的话给人一种造成不利的影响。因为感觉这种好像是四不像，既不是汉语，又不是壮文，到底是什么文字？……但是这种很官方化的语言一般我们都不太认同、不太喜欢。

[Hoz: I think this Zhuang language; I feel it gives people a kind of adverse effect. Because I feel this kind is neither fish nor fowl, i.e. it's not Hanyu [Mandarin], nor is it Zhuang writing, in the end what kind of writing is it? …But this kind of very official-speak language, usually we all don't really identify with it, don't really like it.]

That is, the display of Hanified Zhuang language was perceived as detracting from Zhuang heritage maintenance.

Finally, some participants valued Zhuang-medium texts positively as contributions to heritage maintenance but prioritized other kinds of text much more than public signage in Zhuang. Moreover, they felt Romanized Zhuang was perfectly adequate for conveying their heritage. The magazine editor and former Zhuang teacher, Mr G, remarked:

Excerpt 8-27

Mr G: 你用壮文来写的文章很生动，但是你用汉语来它有时表达不出它那种……还有我们壮语山歌的*押韵，那种东西用汉歌来表达很难表……所以这个杂志它对弘扬民族文化、保护民族文化它有重要的作用

[Mr G: The articles you write in Zhuang are very vivid, but you sometimes can't express them in Hanyu … and the *[noise over word] rhyme of our Zhuang mountain songs [a folk song genre], that sort of thing which is really difficult to express in Hanyu. … So this magazine plays an important role in promoting and protecting national culture.]

Meanwhile, Mr F, like many other participants, believed that few people could read Zhuang, however, he explained that his goals were to preserve a written archive in Zhuang and "instill a passion" for written Zhuang in his Zhuang

Studies students; it is Romanized Zhuang that he and his students use for such writing. Making a comparison between the heritage maintenance value of genres of written Zhuang, Mr H, another editor of *Third of the Third*, emphasized the heritage value of *personal* Zhuang texts and explained why this – in addition to its being literary – gave the magazine an advantage over the waning Zhuang-medium newspaper. His reasoning implies that public signage is likewise less useful for maintaining heritage than personal copies of creative and expressive works. Mr H's comparison, in Excerpt 8-28 below, used an example of a folk song printed in the magazine that we were looking at.

Excerpt 8-28

Author: 所以你觉得，怎么说，这个有用的价值以外，这样的报纸、这样的杂志也有象征性的价值吗？
Mr H: 有，肯定有收藏的价值……像这个情歌，这个歌啊，一般你把它收集起来，过了几年以后你再拿来翻一翻，这都是很宝贵的东西，过了就没有了。

[Author: So do you think, how to say, besides this useful value, do such newspapers and magazines also have symbolic value?
Mr H: Yes, there's certainly value as a keepsake ... like this love song, this song, you usually collect it, and after a few years you take it out again and flick through. These are all very precious things, and as time passes they'll be gone.]

It must of course be noted that those who were positive about the heritage maintaince value of these other texts in Romanized Zhuang were all people who were literate in Romanized Zhuang: Mr F, G and H have long taught and written in Romanized Zhuang and still use it for work. Yet they all perceived that Zhuang literacy was low amongst generations younger than themselves and amongst city folk, in this way aligning with the many other participants who noticed the same illiteracy and were oftentimes themselves part of that trend. We have seen that perceived problems with Zhuang literacy became central to many evaluations of public, written Zhuang displays as symbolic resources for heritage maintenance, just as Zhuang literacy had been central to perceptions of public written Zhuang as tokenistic, as other languages or as not worth bothering to read, in Sections 8.2–8.4. Let us now look further into the construction of the problem of literacy and its place in Zhuang identity construction.

8.6 Perceptions of learning to read Zhuang displays

So far, this chapter reveals the participants' great variety of perceptions and discursive constructions of written Zhuang displays. Across these personal narratives, and integral to them, is a consistent theme of not knowing the Romanized Zhuang writing system and/or believing that others do not know it. The realization that Zhuang could be written was a life moment that a number of participants remembered vividly and which had prompted a new desire in some to formally study Zhuang, as excerpts above have shown. In addition, the interviews revealed a common perception that Zhuang literacy is difficult and so a Zhuang speaker must be formally trained to become literate in Zhuang (see e.g. Excerpts 8-2, 8-3, 8-13, 8-14). This diverges from the belief of language-policy makers who Romanized Zhuang so that written Zhuang would be transparent to Zhuang speakers and thus "easy to learn" (Li and Huang 2004: 244) with basic instruction; enabling rapid mass literacy was the policy goal behind all the minority languages' Romanization (Premaratne 2015; Rohsenow 2004; Zhou 2001, 2003). This section foregrounds the belief that Zhuang literacy must be taught rather than being an ability naturally inhering in Zhuang speakers.

This belief stands out against the universal perception amongst my participants that few speakers of Zhuang are actually literate in the language. That belief arises in their lived experience of widespread *illiteracy* in Zhuang. While Barbara in Excerpt 8-15 contrasts the present with a past in which Zhuang literacy was more widely taught, Zhuang writing was *never very* widely taught (Zhou 2001: 56; Feng and Sunuodula 2009: 690–693). Moreover, in Chapter Two I have analyzed data indicating that the limited specialist education which does exist today is not sufficient to create and maintain Zhuang-literate communities, although Mr G, the *Third of the Third* editor, did report in our 2014 interview that a recent, bilingual Putonghua-Zhuang book by the Editor-in-Chief of the *Guangxi Minzu Newspaper* had sold out 10,000 copies. In Chapter Six I have shown that written Zhuang is marginal in public displays, and was even more so before Nanning's street-name signs went up in the last decade or so.

Illustrating the perception that Zhuang literacy is associated with being especially educated, Mr M, an academic specializing in Southern Chinese minorities, maintained that there were some people literate in Zhuang but described the specialization of such readers. My field notes record:

Excerpt 8-29

He thinks those magazines [*Third of the Third*] and the minzu newspaper are still popular, for example his office mate [sharing his profession] reads them. The kind of people who read them are his university classmates. (field notes 27 November 2014)

Mr G, an editor of *Third of the Third* magazine, one of the few producers of public Zhuang-medium texts whom I could access, similarly expressed a view that those literate in Zhuang have had specialist, formal training:

Excerpt 8-30

Mr G: 社会青年也有，读者就很多了，读者有专家的，在北京，你见过 [-]，这些都是读者；也有大学生的，现在我们广西民大就有本科生；也有那个研究生；原来以前教的大专生、中专生都有，现在有实验小学啊，我们德保、东兰、黄江很多县都有这个壮文实验学校，有的初中有，有的是小学有，大部分在小学，那我们现在***主要发行到小学。

[Mr G: We also have as readers the young of society, readers are numerous, readers include professionals, in Beijing, you met [names of participants teaching Zhuang Studies], they are both readers; there are also university students, now we have some Bachelors students from GUN; also those research students; there are college and middle school students whom I originally taught, now there are experimental primary schools, our Debao, Donglan, Yellow River [counties], many places all have this Zhuang script experimental schooling, some are middle schools, some are primary schools, the majority are primary. Now we [the magazine] are ***[noise over words] mainly distributed to primary schools.]

We have heard the view of Mr G's colleague, Mr H, in Excerpt 5–6 that a decrease in literate Zhuang contributors to the magazine has resulted of the closure of GZAR's four technical secondary schools, which used to teach in Zhuang and which trained many of the region's civil servants.

However, it is worth noting that Mr G (in Excerpt 8-31 below) and Mr H each made it clear that *Third of the Third* has many rural readers and writers; so many, in fact, that they do not bother trying to sell through urban newsstands but rather distribute the magazine only through mail order. This rural readership challenges any assumption that education in Zhuang literacy is a feature of urban lifestyles, whereas there is a general association between education and urban lifestyles in China.

Excerpt 8-31

Mr G:我们这个杂志的很多读者都在农村的。
Author: 真的吗？
Mr G: 嗯，农村的。
Author: 所以在农村的小杂志摊--
Mr G: 有过去学过的，有的农民来给我们投稿，也有农民的。有大学生、有中学生、有时候有农民、也有专家……
Author: 所以他们写的壮文一样吗？还是他们用，怎么说，各种不一样的文字来写？
Mr G: 他们学壮文呢！他们学壮文，但是有的是学，有的原来在学校学的，有的在农村扫盲的时候学的，很多人自学，在电脑上面也可以自学，我们民语委开了一个网站，上面可以自学，学壮文。

[Mr G: Many readers of this here magazine are in rural villages.
Author: Really?
Mr G: Mm, rural villages.
Author: So at a small, rural magazine stand –
Mr G: They've studied. Some farmers come and contribute [magazine content] to us, there's also farmers [emphatic repetition]. There's university students, there's secondary school students, sometimes there are farmers and there are also experts …
Author: So is the Zhuangwen [Romanized Zhuang] that they write all the same? Or do they use all sorts of different scripts to write?
Mr G: They study Zhuangwen [Romanized Zhuang]! They study Zhuangwen, but some of them are learners, [while] some studied it back at school. Some of them learnt it during the Eliminate Rural Illiteracy campaign [i.e. early 1950s], many people study it themselves. You can also study it yourself online; our Minority Languages Commission started a website [and] on it you can study by yourself, study Zhuangwen.]

Thus, I found widespread beliefs that those who have attained Zhuang literacy have done so through specialist education, albeit with the report of informally self-taught Zhuang writers too, from Mr G.

I also heard from many of the participants had encountered the Zhuang illiteracy of others. We have heard, for instance, from Zeina that her Zhuang-speaking parents do not read Zhuang (Excerpt 8-3), and from Mark, Yana and Tansy that in their Zhuang-speaking childhood communities they had not encountered Zhuang literacy practices (Excerpts 8-4, 8-5, 8-8). Moreover, the participants at GUN joked that their Zhuang-literate classmate, Luke, was the "我们班的宝贝" [teacher's pet] in their Zhuang Studies cohort because his Zhuang literacy far exceeded that of the other students, many of whom started reading and writing Zhuang only when they commenced this degree.

The participants and I were together occasionally able to encounter members of the public struggling to decode Zhuang on signage, although literacies which viewers did *not* have were obviously rarely on show. A particularly clear instance arose during my commented walk through GZAR Museum with Mr E. While he was explaining the Zhuang orthography to me in reference to the museum's trilingual curation signs, a local woman working as a museum attendant came to join the "lesson", explaining that she had never known how to read Zhuang (Figure 59). A number of Chinese museum-goers joined in the impromptu tutorial which then ensued. Encounters such as these serve to contextualize the belief of my participants that illiteracy in Zhuang is commonplace.

The belief that Zhuang literacy is a specialist skill that can only be accessed through specialist training then creates identity affordances, as reading Zhuang can be taken as a marker of social distinction. In concluding the chapter, I will discuss this affordance.

Figure 59: Mr E gives an impromptu lesson in reading Zhuang to staff-member at GZAR Museum.

8.7 Concluding discussion: Mobilizing signage as an identity resource

This chapter took the linguistic landscapes described and analyzed in the preceding two chapters and investigated them as lived landscapes. I did this primarily through interview data, although other ethnographic data also informed the chapter, and more ethnographic data would make for an even richer lived landscape study. Zhuang language displayed as public text in the participants' physical environments was experienced by them and mobilized within multiple semiotic systems. Jaworski and Thurlow (2010: 5) have argued that the physical environment offers "a symbolic system of signifiers with wide-ranging affordances activated by social actors to position themselves and others in that context" (see also Thurlow and Jaworski: 307; Coupland 2014: 33; Kramsch and Whiteside 2008: 688). My lived landscape approach allows some of these activations to be seen and analyzed. In revealing the participants varied ways of "reading" Zhuang-inclusive street-name signage and other public texts, the chapter shows that "identity is never a one-way street", as my epigraph playfully quotes from Anderson's (2011) foreword to Mullaney's (2011) history of China's minorities' construction in nation-building. The chapter also allows us to start seeing how interacting with signage is mobilized variously as an identity-making resource.

Moreover, I analyze how the beliefs about, and experiences of, illiteracy in Zhuang provide the context in which reading public Zhuang-medium signage offers affordances for identity construction. Given the perception that public Zhuang texts are largely unable to be read, because readers with the necessary specialist training are believed to be few, being able to read Zhuang-medium signage allows for a performance of Zhuang literacy to construct and embody special and authoritative Zhuang identities. I interpret Barbara and Hoz's critical evaluations of Zhuang signage (Excerpts 8-15, 8-17, 8-18) and their problematization of *others* not being able to read it as discursively positioning themselves with authoritative Zhuang identities. It is no coincidence that, of the students, these two were among the most passionate about doing Zhuang language work after graduating, and among the few literate in Zhuang. This self-construction is particularly intertwined with perceptions of public displays of written Zhuang as tokenistic – which both Barbara and Hoz expressed – because to evaluate the accuracy, historicity and frequency of displays of written Zhuang, and to be seen to do so legitimately, relies on Zhuang literacy. Similarly, Mr E enthusiastically embodied an authoritative Zhuang identity through emplaced interactions with the trilingual museum signage in the impromptu literacy lesson captured in Figure 59.

Hoz, in Excerpt 8-26, goes further, explicitly identifying himself in opposition to the Zhuang identity that he perceives the displays of Romanized Zhuang to represent. This exemplifies what Lickorish (2008: 27), studying subaltern minzu identities elsewhere in China, has called an "oppositional ethnic consciousness". During my study, Mr E and Mr D were learning to read and write Sawndip using resources shared on social media amongst a small network of Zhuang cultural revivalists. This, too, is an embodiment of an oppositional ethnic consciousness, as they see Sawndip writing as a more authentic alternative to the Romanized script and one with which they identify. Through dint of their own learning and usage, Sawndip literacy practices are becoming a resource for them to use to strengthen their own and the group's Zhuang identity. Since my fieldwork, Mr D has reported to me that the group is now also involved in the recreation of traditional Zhuang costumes (follow up talk on 8 October 2019), a rejection of the now-conventionalized representations of Zhuang costumes identified in Chapter Seven which runs in parallel to the rejection of Romanized Zhuang as an icon of Zhuang identity.

It is worth clarifying that this re-signification of the linguistic and other visual symbols of Zhuangness does not necessarily mean rejecting a Chinese identity or accepting that Han language varieties (i.e. the Mandarin dialects, including Putonghua) are essentially affiliated with a Hanzu, not Zhuangzu, identity. Nor does it mean accepting that Putonghua is inherently affiliated with literacy in a way that Zhuang is not. The symbolism and embodiment of Han literacy practices, and other Han language practices, are also semiotic resources with multiple affordances. For example, Mr D is also passionate about teaching Putonghua, which is his current job, and has proudly shared with me examples of his children's acquisition of simplified characters. He constructs his own Zhuang and Chinese identities as concurrent and concordant. His opposition is not to China or Han language, but to the top-down construction of Zhuang identity, including opposing the dominant belief that Zhuang-Putonghua bilingualism is problematic or impossible to achieve. Indeed, his view is that speaking and writing in Zhuang, Putonghua and English is achievable and desirable.

Beyond affording viewers an opportunity to claim linguistic and cultural capital by performing Zhuang literacy, the Zhuang-inclusive texts in these linguistic landscapes afforded many other symbolic identity resources. A subject may mobilize – or "activate" in Jaworski and Thurlow's terms – the face-value and policy-intended affordance of these Zhuang displays. For example, a subject may read Zhuang-inclusive signage as a valorization of the Zhuang language and, metonymically, of Zhuang speakers and/or the Zhuangzu people, and therefore feel their Zhuang pride is bolstered by such public displays. Mr B exemplified this in Excerpt 8-7, reproducing an indexical link between Romanized Zhuang, his own identity and a Zhuangzu group identity. However, this "Zhuang pride" activation was relatively uncommon amongst my participants (compare Sections 8.4–8.5).

Of particular importance given that this finding is not prominent in other studies, this chapter showed how affordances may *not* be activated. For instance, government officials who are intentionally increasing the amount of Zhuang in a linguistic landscape – for example through making Nanning's street-name signage bilingual – may expect that a subject who identifies with Zhuang language will read this signage as a localizing symbol and thus feel in place where such signage exists. Notably, however, this "at place" activation is absent from my participants' reports of their perceptions of actual Zhuang-medium signage. Mr B's comments that such signage feels pleasantly familiar is the closest we get.

Rather, the participants show us a number of reasons why these linguistic landscapes' affordances for self-affirmation and belonging were *not* activated. These include the misrecognition of written Zhuang as Putonghua Pinyin or English rather than as Zhuang, for reasons of not knowing Zhuang could be written or having become habituated to reading the "easier" non-Zhuang language in a bilingual display. I referred to this as the subjective invisibility of publicly displayed Zhuang, emphasizing that this is a product of viewers' habitus, not only literacy skills. Other reasons shown in the data for not activating a self- or group-valorizing affordance of public texts written in Zhuang include perceiving Romanized Zhuang as an inauthentic symbol of the Zhuangzu or as a symbol of neglectful literacy policies, and perceiving Romanized Zhuang displays as intended for tourists rather than locals.

All of these reasons, but particularly the misrecognition of written Zhuang as a majority language, foreclose the government's intended iconic affordances of displaying Zhuang language. The misrecognition and overlooking of written Zhuang in public found by this study thus extends Jaworski's (2014: 528) argument that reception of linguistic displays begins with noticing, and that noticing in itself is situated: "the noticing (or not) and reading of the poster (its uptake) is thus dependent on the knowledge, experiences, skills, capacities, and goals that social actors bring into their encounter with this particular instance of discourse in place, their historical bodies".

Thus, foregrounding lived landscape data in linguistic landscape research allows us to see in more detail how noticing is socially-situated and what the implications of landscapes' texts, imagery and patterns are for various users of these spaces. This Zhuang case study has revealed how and why certain semiotic resources in the linguistic landscape – particularly, texts written in a minority language – may not be noticed at all, or noticed as symbols of something other than what the authors intended. This has immense implications for language policy makers, and is therefore a theme of my reflection on implications language policy research and policy-making in Chapter Eleven. To lead up to that reflection, Chapter Nine revisits official language policy, theorizing the government's language policy interventions in GZAR's linguistic landscapes not only as authorship but as "linguascaping".

9 Linguascaping through language policy

To the casual beholder a landscape simply is[...]. Yet it is in fact a product of social action and of a social history[...]. And this applies also to the 'semiotic landscape'.
(Kress and van Leeuwen 2006: 35)

9.1 Introduction

A linguistic landscape is oftentimes not an accidental product of social history, but deliberately shaped by law-makers through legal interventions controlling who can participate in making a linguistic landscape, and what they can do. Thus, the role of laws in linguascaping is the concern of this fourth and final perspective on Nanning's linguistics landscapes. It is prompted by the argument of Kress and van Leeuwen, in the passage quoted in the epigraph, in support of the problematization of linguistic/semiotic landscapes. Examining the role of laws is central to inquiring into the social actors and histories which produced this study's linguistic landscapes. This book has argued throughout that policy is dynamic and multi-agentive discourse and practice, and here that argument is brought to bear in analyzing who does the linguascaping, and whom laws empower to do so. Specifically, this chapter looks to the empowerment, through law, of *linguascapers*.

Coupland (2010: 78) asks whose designs and priorities the characteristics of a linguistic landscape respond to. I have long thought this a great question, and the elephant in the room during many a descriptive presentation of a linguistic landscape. It is asking not only who a landscape benefits, or responds to, now and going forward, but whose designs and priorities influenced its making. Whom a text in a linguistic landscape is intended to benefit or what that text is intended to achieve and whose priorities that text actually reflects can diverge, especially when law-makers and policy-makers intentionally intervene in linguistic landscapes. The priorities of law-makers may not fully anticipate, or reflect, the needs of those whom they intend to use or to benefit from the places that they are creating. Moreover, regulation means that bottom-up public texts may actually express the designs and priorities of the "top" i.e. of those who made laws constraining the agency of authors, complicating the characterization of texts by private authors as bottom-up (e.g. Backhaus 2007). Thus, texts by commercial or grassroots authors may respond to the priorities of the state. This not only complicates their assignation as "bottom-up" texts but the interpretation of such texts as "revolt", "resistance" or "subversion" against official policy script (see e.g. Hult 2018: 336; Lanza and Woldemariam

2009: 190); public texts may resist or subvert in some respects, e.g. their lexical content or their authorship, while reproducing the ideas and enforcing the rules of official language policy in other ways, e.g. in using a rule-compliant script. Is a non-compliant shopfront sign resistance to the rules by its author or resistance by the local authority that has failed to have corrected, or neither? This question indicates that the characterization of texts by government authors as top-down (e.g. Gorter 2006) is also complicated; higher level governments can regulate lower level government authors with divergent language ideologies and agendas, yet, as this chapter will show, the hierarchy of authority does not always determine which actors within the government get the final say in shaping the linguistic landscape.

This divergence in the priorities, purposes and participating authors and regulators behind linguistic landscapes is a concern particularly in this study because, as I have argued in Chapter Five, there are significant disconnections in the mechanisms for accountability and representation of minority language speakers and minority peoples in China's language governance framework.

I therefore propose "linguascaping" as a frame for organizing an answer to Coupland's question. Specifically, this chapter advocates linguascaping as a conceptual tool of critical language policy analysis. I (Grey 2021a) recently introduced linguascaping as an analytic tool which "further foregrounds *agency and power* in semiotic landscape studies", noting that "[c]hoices about language use and display (i.e. linguascaping) are strategic, processual 'deployment[s]' of linguistic resources which do semiotic place-making work and language ideological work" (citing Jaworski and Piller 2008: 304).

This focus on linguascaping is another step in my development of the ethnographically-oriented, lived landscape approach to researching linguistic landscapes and, more broadly, to researching language policy, following the literature canvassed in Chapter Eight. Chapter Eight examined lived linguistic landscapes using data on the agency and subjectivity of viewers, while this chapter's theoretical linguascaping perspective and use of legal data foregrounds control over the agency and subjectivity of authors and creators of linguistic landscapes. Laws and policies can support the agency of some authors or creators more than others, but they cannot completely control all agency and all subjectivity in linguascaping. This chapter therefore takes the examination further by investigating how both laws about language and the language ideologies they encode organize and entrench agency for linguistic landscapers. In this way, the chapter is also extending Spolsky's (2004: 5) and Hult's (2018: 347) approach to studying language policy as a dynamic interaction between official "management", language ideologies and the habituated language norms of the society.

The concept of linguascaping arose outside language policy research but close to home, in sociolinguistics (Jaworski and Piller 2008; Thurlow and Jaworski 2010; Chen 2016). The verb "linguascaping" is a coinage derived from "landscaping" – i.e. the physical shaping of terrain – in order to emphasize the active creation of the linguistic elements of a landscape. It is a heuristic for critical sociolinguists: the term's originators, Jaworski and Piller (2008: 303–304) explain that, "[b]y referring to linguascapes and linguascaping [...] we mean also to reveal the very particular deployment and devaluing of local languages [... by] powerful ideological mediators". In Jaworski and Piller's (2008) initial study, the powerful ideological mediators to which they refer are television travel shows, or more specifically, the people who make these shows (the agents) as well as the shows themselves (the representations made by the agents). It may be familiar to think of a television show as a creation, but linguistic landscapes are also creations – *built* environments – and important ones at that in constituting social realities. Because linguistic landscapes are often enduring and encompassing, with people living inside these representations, linguistic landscapes have a more powerful capacity than television shows or many other representations to elide their creators and creation. But, because of these same features, linguistic landscapes also have many more agents creating and recreating them than a television show does. This is where policy can have a crucial intervening role: policy, I argue, is a significant mechanism for empowering some agents and some types of creation, while marginalizing others. Through the Chinese language policy framework, even the linguistic landscapes of a big city can end up with just a few dominant creators and standardized representations of languages, cultures, people and power.

The first purpose of this chapter is to reveal that this study's linguistic landscapes are linguascaped by government agents through law, in Section 9.2. The second purpose is to explore how linguascaping laws are not inescapable or immutable constraints, in Section 9.3. Rather, laws may empower a range of heterogeneous linguascaping agents, including various state organizations with their own varied interests and policies about adhering to the laws, and laws often operate in contexts where norms precede laws. Thus, linguascaping laws may be reinterpreted or resisted, just as the meanings of the symbols and patterns in the linguistic landscape were shown to be in Chapter Eight. This can cause the underapplication but also the over-application of linguascaping laws, as I will illustrate with examples from Nanning.

At the national level, the main regulation covering the linguistic landscapes which I studied is the *Putonghua Law*. In operation since 2000, the *Putonghua Law* can be seen as a translation into specific rules of the general constitutional mandate that "the state is to promote Putonghua in the whole country". National rules about place names also come into play. At the subnational level, the main regulations covering these linguistic landscapes at the time of this study were the 南宁市壮文社会使用管理办法 '*Management Measures for Social Usage of Zhuangwen in Nanning*' (Nanning Municipal People's Government 2013: "*Nanning Measures*"). These *Nanning Measures* had then just replaced their prototype, the 南宁市社会用字管理暂行规定 '*Nanning Municipality Interim Provisions on the Management of the Usage in Society of [Written] Characters*' (Nanning Municipal People's Government 2004: "*Interim Provisions*"). Both the *Nanning Measures* and the *Interim Provisions* are rules about bilingual public and official texts.

In 2018, GZAR People's Congress enacted a related, regional law which fits above the *Nanning Measures* and below the *Constitution* and national laws about language in the legal hierarchy. This regional law is the 广西壮族自治区少数民族语言文字工作条例 '*GZAR Minority Language Work Regulations*' (Standing Committee of the People's Congress of GZAR 2018: "*GZAR Regulations*"). This is another linguistic landscape intervention: it adds a regulatory framework within which the public usage of written Zhuang is both encouraged and regulated across GZAR, while public, written Zhuang continues also to be more specifically regulated within Nanning Municipality by the *Nanning Measures*. These new *GZAR Regulations* also support certain roles for Zhuang in education, research and employment, including establishing tests and quotas for language workers in the GZAR civil service; those developments are not closely related to linguistic landscapes and so I do not delve into those aspects of the regulations in this chapter.

Both the linguistic landscape rules and the other aspects of these new *GZAR Regulations* were surprising to me, given the contraction in Zhuang-medium education, the indicia of language shift amongst the Zhuangzu, and the musty aroma of tradition and thinning threads that I felt permeating government efforts in regards to Zhuang. Moreover, a number of my language leader participants had told me that Zhuang language was not taken seriously enough by the GZAR government, and GZAR government officials had failed to get a similar law enacted earlier in the decade, despite being spurred by the neighboring province, Yunnan, passing a pro-minority language ordinance in 2013. The politics behind the 2018 *GZAR Regulations*' enactment will hopefully one day be available to researchers, but for now we can content ourselves with an examination of what these new rules add. A forecast of these new rules' prospects frames the chapter's concluding discussion. Let us start by examining what the laws allowed or mandated in the linguistic landscapes that I studied, and the extent to which those landscapes conformed to the rules in 2014–2015.

9.2 Laws intervening directly to regulate linguascapes

First and most obviously, the linguistic landscapes that I studied show that the national *Putonghua Law* is adhered to. The *Putonghua Law*, which I introduced in Chapter One, orders that Putonghua "shall be used by state organs as the official language, except where otherwise provided for in laws" (Article 9). It regulates this official usage in detail, including rules about where, for which public-facing functions, and in what script Putonghua must be used. It is therefore not surprising that some aspects of GZAR's public linguistic landscapes conform to specific provisions of the *Putonghua Law*. However, it is also clear from this quotation of Article 9 that the rules about public Putonghua can be modified by other laws. This is what we see in the *Nanning Measures* and now the *GZAR Regulations*; these laws are otherwise providing for the use of Zhuang as an official language alongside Putonghua. It is through Article 9's permission for law-makers to allow a second official language in certain places or texts that law-making bodies other than the national legislature can also claim significant agency in linguascaping, as the Nanning Municipal Government did through its *Interim Provisions* and then *Nanning Measures*. 2018's *GZAR Regulations* also do this to an extent, making the GZAR People's Congress another linguascaper. Those regulations (Reg 13(4)), in turn, leave a legal space within which the Nanning-level government can continue to linguascape its own municipality through its own laws, which it was already doing before 2018.

My empirical examination found that linguistic landscapes reflected, but did not entirely comply with, the two-tiered (and now three-tiered) regulation of public text under these laws. Let us walk through the legal stipulations and the evidence of their application in public linguascaping.

The default position since 2000, when the *Putonghua Law* was enacted, has been that Putonghua must be included in many modes of civic and commercial discourse found in linguistic landscapes: simplified Chinese characters are mandatory as "the basic characters" in services, and workers in service trades are "encouraged" to use Putonghua (Article 13) while Putonghua "shall be used as the basic spoken and written language in [...] facilities in public places; [...] signboards and advertisements; [...] names of enterprises and other institutions; and [...] packaging" (Article 14). Furthermore, publishing, broadcasting, television, and information processing must be in Putonghua (Articles 11–12 and 15), and this also affects the circulating texts in linguistic landscapes, such as the newspapers for sale or television broadcasts visible on public and semi-public screens. Moreover, television presenters and others working in broadcasting must meet a standard of Putonghua ability, or must be trained up to meet it (Article 19). In this way, the National People's Congress, the legal authority behind the

Putonghua Law, is linguascaping public places across the country. My landscape analysis showed empirically that these rules are consistently followed in practice. For instance, the types of commercial discourse listed in Article 14 and which I documented and analyzed in Chapter Six (signboards, advertisements, packaging) not only included Putonghua but were usually monolingual in Putonghua. Likewise, Putonghua-medium newspapers and magazines dominated displays at curbside stalls reflecting the *Putonghua Law's* rules about the language of publishing. The shows on the public and semi-public television screens which I have noted were widespread in the landscapes that I studied also complied with the *Putonghua Law's* rules about television.

The constitutional freedom to use and develop Zhuang language does not override these articles of the *Putonghua Law*. This means that Zhuang-medium signage is never permitted to be monolingual, but rather must always include Putonghua, and that there must be a law allowing it before Zhuang can be added to public signage at all. That is what the Nanning Municipal People's Government has sought to provide, thus creating agency for Zhuang speakers or, more accurately, for Zhuang-writing government officials.

Nanning Municipal People's Government first used the *Interim Provisions*, from 2004, to regularize bilingual public texts (or to regularize "social word usage", to literally translate the *Provisions*). It then upgraded to the *Nanning Measures* in 2013. The *Interim Provisions* stated purpose was to "为加强社会用字管理，促进社会用字规范化、标准化，更好地为经济发展和社会交流服务" [strengthen the management of the public usage of script, promote the regularization and standardization of the public use of words, and better serve economic development and social exchanges]. The *Nanning Measures'* purpose was more simple: "为推动壮文在社会使用中的规范化、标准化" [to promote the regularization and standardization of Zhuang script in public use]. That is, any economic purpose was left only implicit/discarded in the 2013 law, echoing the national language policy trend identified in Chapter Four of no longer framing minority language as instrumental for economic development.

Specifically, both the *Interim Provisions* and the *Nanning Measures* are concerned with standardizing the scripts and formats of multilingual signage and other public-directed texts which include Zhuang and/or foreign languages. In sum, Article 6 of the *Interim Provisions* ruled that written Zhuang could not be displayed by itself on public texts, but when it was included it should be in the first-line position (on top in a horizontal text, or on the right in a vertical text). Subsections (iv) and (v) also mandated the visual separation of Zhuang and English (or other foreign languages) in public texts: Zhuang was to go above Putonghua, and English below. In the *Nanning Measures*, a similar separation was mandated, with additional rules for circular texts (Zhuang on the left or the outer ring) and multi-panel signage (Zhuang panel above). This consistent formatting – linguascaped by governments – provides a systematic way that Zhuang and English could be recognizable as different languages, despite their shared alphabetic script. However, recall from Chapter Eight that people confuse the two: this systematic distinction did not seem to be known amongst my participants.

While the stipulated formatting may not have been noticed, it was adhered to in most public texts in Nanning. In my data, there were no multilingual circular texts, but otherwise multilingual public texts mostly followed the governments' preferences, as expressed in these legal rules. For example, Nanning's street-name signage, which was mainly erected during the time of the *Interim Provisions* circa 2009–2010 (see e.g. Chou 2010), has Zhuang taking the top line, above the Putonghua toponym. This indicates that the *Interim Provisions* were treated as authoritative rules and followed by the Nanning Government itself, the author and producer of that signage. The Guangxi Museum of Nationalities opened in 2009, while the *Interim Provisions* were in force. It, too, adhered to the rules: e.g. above its main doorway, the Zhuang version of the institution's name was placed above the Putonghua name. There were even compliant signs that pre-dated the *Interim Provisions*, e.g. the façade of the GZAR Museum places that institution's Zhuang name atop its Putonghua name: I will return to this idea of norms preceding laws, below.

Despite the general compliance of these linguistic landscapes, there were nevertheless some instances of non-compliance in terms of formatting inside both museums on their bi/trilingual curation signs. Specifically, the line and panel order in both museums incorrectly placed Zhuang below Putonghua. These had not been corrected at the time of my fieldwork, even though Article 10 of the *Nanning Measures* required older, non-compliant signage to be brought up to standard by July 2014, and Article 8 required the local minority language work agency to help with corrections at no cost. However, the general tendency to comply appears to have continued since the *Nanning Measures* replaced the *Interim Provisions*: e.g. signage for the new Nanning subway, which was being built during my fieldwork, is now on display and complies.

At least, Nanning's subway signage complies with the linguascaping rules as much as Nanning's street-name signage does, in format but not necessarily in content. There are parts of these signs that are *not* transliterated/translated into Zhuang. On street-name signage, this is the names of adjacent streets and cardinal directions, which are only in Putonghua, while the street name itself is bilingual and formatted compliantly. On photos of the new subway signage that I have inspected, the far left and right of station-name signage is bilingual in only Putonghua and English, e.g. 1 号线//Line 1, while the station name itself is trilingual and formatted compliantly, e.g. *Camh Gvangjsih Dayoz*//广西大学站//Guangxi University Station.

This uneven or "fragmentary" (Reh 2004) multilingualism within one sign is not ad hoc but consistent across types of signage; so are the linguascaping rules about bilingualism being misapplied? Previously, no, but since 2013, arguably yes. This is because the *Nanning Measures* introduced, from mid-2013, an obligation that certain public signage include Zhuang. Technically, the preceding *Interim Provisions* allowed signs to include Zhuang and required certain formatting *if* a sign *did* include Zhuang, but did not demand the inclusion of Zhuang on any public signs. So, prior to 2013, the street-name signage could be fully or partially translated from Putonghua into Zhuang, or even remain monolingual in Putonghua. Such signage would then have needed to be renovated to meet the standards of the *Nanning Measures* in 2013–2014. However, while the 2013 *Nanning Measures* are clear that certain types of signage must include Zhuang, they are less clear about whether the entire content of these signs must be bilingual. In my view, they have introduced a legal obligation for complete or "duplicating" (Reh 2004) bilingualism. This is because Article 4 requires that "为表达同一个内容而同时使用壮文、汉文两种文字的，壮文的含义应当与汉文的含义一致" [Where Zhuang and Chinese are used simultaneously to express the same content, the meaning of Zhuang shall be consistent with that of Chinese] and no explicit allowance is made in the *Nanning Measures* for partial translation.

Nevertheless, the empirical reality is one of partial bilingualism on Zhuang-inclusive, government-authored public signage in Nanning. As such, some discretion has been taken by the municipal government, as author and as regulator, in applying the *Nanning Measures*. The government has decided that these rules require Zhuang to be included on certain types of signage but then to duplicate only some of the content. These decisions are a kind of language policy that is not necessarily in legal form yet which does further linguascaping work.

Here the crucial agency allowed to the municipal government in the law is that of both author and of regulator of the linguistic landscape. Specifically, Article 3 provides that Nanning's public security, civil affairs and transportation departments will inspect and supervise the public usage of written Zhuang and Article 9 directs minority language work institutions to provide them technical help for inspections and supervision. Ultimately, the public security, civil affairs and transportation departments thus decide whether the legal standards about displaying Zhuang are being sufficiently met and whether to respond by changing the landscape if they are not. In this way the law provides these departments with far more agency for linguascaping than that given to any other institution (including the state's minority language work institutions), community group or language user. We will return to this point, but first let us complete the assessment of the linguistic landscapes against the legal standards.

To which types of signage do the 2013 rules apply? The *Nanning Measures'* Article 5 lists five types of public text that must be bilingual in Zhuang and Putonghua: (1) nameplates of administrative divisions; (2) plaques and official seals of the names of state organs and institutions; (3) names of the government affairs websites and local government newspapers; (4) signboards and signs for the names of public places such as airports, railway stations, bus stations, ports, museums, exhibition halls and libraries; (5) signs and banners used for large-scale conferences and major events in cities and counties. These are all government-authored texts, with the possible exception of some major event signage.

In this regard, the *Nanning Measures* are more precise about public linguascaping but also more onerous than the *Interim Provisions*. The *Interim Provisions'* Article 3 listed nine types of public text which had to be formatted as per the rules *if* they included Zhuang, but those *Provisions* did not require that such texts had to include Zhuang at all. The nine types included the government-authored texts for which bilingualism is now mandatory under the *Nanning Measures*, but also some that could be authored by others, such as advertisements, slogans and product packaging, for which bilingualism is still not mandatory. In terms of those other authors, now "enterprises, social organizations and individuals are encouraged to use both Zhuang and [Putonghua]" but not obliged (Article 5, *Nanning Measures*). (Likewise, the *GZAR Regulations*, which are now in force in addition to the *Nanning Measures*, do not oblige non-state signage authors to include Zhuang, nor require government authors to include Zhuang on new types of signage. Rather, the *GZAR Regulations* make some of the types of texts which were already required to be bilingual within Nanning under the *Nanning Measures* now also bilingual across the region: seals and name plaques of state institutions, government website names etc.: Reg 13). In this way, the law allows for the agency of non-government linguascapers in their language choices although expressing a preference, and directs how their texts should look if non-government authors do choose to be bilingual.

Furthermore, although the *Nanning Measures* increase the obligation on the government to add Zhuang to the listed types of public texts, I found it was not always being adhered to in practice, at least in 2014–2015. For example, the then-new *Nanning Measures* required signage for major conferences and events to be bilingual in Zhuang and Putonghua. In my data, I documented the signage in Nanning for two such events in 2015, the China-ASEAN Expo and the Design Biennale. The signage was not compliant; it excluded Zhuang. China-ASEAN Expo events were held at multiple locations, e.g. Guilin, so perhaps a government decision was taken that the Expo signage shown in Nanning need not comply with rules specific to Nanning but rather needed to be consistent across GZAR. However, a different decision could have been taken to include Zhuang on all the Expo signage to keep it consistent across GZAR while also complying with the *Nanning Measures*. Both the China-ASEAN Expo and the Design Biennale signage was in Putonghua and English. As with the pattern of "fragmentary" bilingualism noted above, this choice of languages reveals a *de facto* language policy which is modifying the application of the laws; the government, as signage author and the signage regulator under those laws, has the agency to do this.

Finally, in terms of the standards, let us assess how Putonghua and Zhuang share the space on public signage. When the *Nanning Measures* replaced the *Interim Provisions*, they added a rule about relative font size: "the font width of the Zhuang script should be more than one third of the width of the Chinese font" (Article 7(4)). Many of the public texts in my study pre-dated the *Nanning Measures*, which commenced in July 2013. Nevertheless, they met this standard. On the two museums' bilingual entrance signs, for example, the Zhuang is as wide as the Putonghua script. Typically, the Putonghua street-names in Nanning were written in three large characters and the Zhuang name above them took at least the width of one character, i.e. a third. (These wide Zhuang street-names were, however, in a much shorter font than the Putonghua characters or the Putonghua Pinyin on the street-name signs, thus rendering them relatively small and subtle, as Chapter Six has noted.)

Why is there some evidence of compliant signage even before there were legal obligations to comply with, and evidence of both compliance and non-compliance even by government authors once the rules were in force? It is because laws about linguistic landscapes participate in broader and dynamic discourses, as the next section will examine. That examination will help me predict in the final section how the *GZAR Regulations* will or will not intervene in linguistic landscapes across GZAR in the next few years.

9.3 Laws about linguistic landscapes as dynamic discourses

We can empirically see in this study that language laws are not implemented to-the-letter in linguistic landscapes. Rather, a language law's intervention to preserve or change linguistic landscapes is but one of several forces shaping the norms of public language use and display. This limited implementation and enforcement may not be a surprise, whether a reader is simply cynical about law or has read linguistic landscape studies such as Eclipse and Tenedero

(2018), which found very low compliance in the Manila Central Post Office with a nationwide legal directive that Filipino be included on public signage of the kind on display in that Post Office. This section develops the thinking about the empirical phenomena of non-compliance, arguing that legal rules about linguistic landscapes can be minimized or challenged by language ideologies and by other laws, and that this can undermine the linguascaping agency of certain law or policy-makers. I will explain this argument with reference to the continued display of English place names in GZAR's urban linguistic landscapes and certain institutional language policies that the data reveal. These are illustrations of language norms over-powering language laws, and laws being *under-applied* as a result. Moreover, laws about language also participate discursively themselves, propagating and amplifying norms which can then shape linguistic landscapes even when the laws do not legally impose those norms on those landscapes. I will explain this discursive influence through examples of the *over-application* of language laws in the landscapes.

9.3.1 Under-application of language laws

China has a national law restricting foreign languages in public linguistic landscapes, the 1996 地名管理条例实施细则 '*Detailed Implementation Rules for the Management of Place-Names Ordinance*'. It forbids foreign place-names (Anon. 2016b) and the Vice Minister of Civil Affairs renewed policy efforts in 2015 to enforce this ban, specifically against English names, as a response to English's perceived invasion (Anon. 2016b). Yet this ban is clearly not fully applied in the landscapes I studied, in which English location, street, property and shop names were displayed. Despite the national place-name rules and official policy supporting them presenting a powerful discourse which constructs English as out of place and to be weeded out, English dominates over other foreign languages in road directions and in commercial signage in my data. This was clear in the advertisements for "O-Park", a high-end property development in Nanning, which I analyzed in Chapter Six: indexicalities of mobility, futurism, commerciality and being accessible to an urban community are integral to O-Park's sense of place, as its advertising explicitly tells us. Zhuang was not deployed to index these qualities in O-Park's advertisements, whereas English was, in addition to Putonghua. Global discourses construct English as the main language associated with international places and the mobility of international people between them (see Piller and Grey 2019); the display of English names for places like O-Park in GZAR thus up-scales the named places from local to international. This belief that English is a valuable index of an international identity is also reproduced by the commercial texts of various government authors, not only in private businesses' signs. For example, the government includes English but not Zhuang in the Biennale signage at GZAR Library and GZAR Museum (Figure 25), the China-ASEAN Expo advertisements (Figure 28), and in university logos and texts. However, the government was less likely than private authors to include English in place names. Thus, the local government partially follows the national place-name rules itself but does not strictly enforce the rules against others in Nanning. This is an example of "covert" or informal language policies overriding rather than extending "overt" and legally-codified policy. (This covert/overt distinction follows Schiffman 1996; Shohamy 2006). Specifically, the norms around using English are shaping local, non-legal policies in Nanning.

Returning to the introductory question, to whose designs and priorities does the linguistic landscape respond, we can get a more nuanced answer here by looking at who exercises legal and practical agency in linguascaping. English place names in Nanning respond to the designs and priorities of businesses and of the Nanning government agencies who are responsible for regulating the linguistic landscape, rather than only responding to the priorities of the national law-makers who passed the place-name rules or the National Ministry of Civil Affairs who is pursuing the ban.

Another illustration of the dynamic role of laws in linguascaping is provided when laws interact with institutional policies. My signage data reveal how language laws may be reconstructed within specific institutional language policies. Institutional policies can simply be a norm embedded in an institution's culture or shared by its staff, but they can also be formal policies: explicit, recorded and made by a decision-maker as part of their official work. Institutional policies may even have the strength of a rule rather than a mere guideline within that institution, but they do not have the legal nature or general application of a law. Nevertheless, in practice, it may be that institutions' rules transform the application of laws about linguistic landscapes, rather than the other way around.

Let us consider this using examples of signage at Nanning's public institutions. At each museum and regional/municipal bureau, decisions about many signs have to have been made, and there were clear patterns in terms of when public institutions chose to include Zhuang in their public texts. The data showed that Zhuang-inclusive exterior signage was limited to signage that was not time-sensitive. By contrast, Zhuang was excluded from newer or time-sensitive signage at these places, such as the updatable, scrolling digital signs at the library and museums in Nanning (Figures 16 and 46). The relatively portable signage at public institutions was likewise never in Zhuang: for example, the red banners at the entrance to universities, car park rules on sandwich boards at museums, etc. This indicates that there are institutional language policies about not producing temporary, new or expensive-to-fabricate Zhuang texts. It may have been that the GZAR government had not structurally facilitated cheap access to Zhuang language work for public institutions, given the lack of renovation of Zhuang-inclusive signage. That the incorrect sign in the Guangxi Museum of Nationalities' Zhuang Culture Exhibition Hall (see Figure 44) remained on display is perhaps further evidence that minority language work is seen as not worth the cost by public institutions' decision-makers, however, the *Nanning Measures* have required the local Minority Language Commission to translate signage for free since 2013. It is therefore likely that poor/absent translation also reflects the shortage of Zhuang translators which a Nanning Government report noted, in 2019, had still not improved (Nanning Municipal Minority Language Works Commission 2019: §2.2). Institutional language policies have been guided, therefore, by more than simply the expense of language work. They reflect a belief reproduced at levels higher than the institution, and by the market, that having just some bilingual signage is sufficient, especially publicly-visible institution-naming signage, and that operating bilingually is not expected or required. This may change, at least within Nanning, because the city's 2019 civil service reform saw the creation of the Nanning Minority Language Services Centre (see Chapter Five: 5.2.1) to increase access to Zhuang translation services. But will this greater access – if realized – change the evident *de facto* policy across many public institutions of identifying themselves in written Zhuang and then "set and forget"? There is no need, from that perspective, to take up translation services even if they are available. Nevertheless, as the following section examines, in other respects there was more Zhuang displayed than the law required. So, institutional culture may also change to enthusiastic uptake of translation and increased/corrected displays of Zhuang.

9.3.2 Over-application of language laws

Covert and *de facto* policies about public language not only limit the application of language laws; sometimes they expand it. Moreover, and more specifically the point I wish to highlight here, the law itself can make a pre-existing idea about language display more powerful. These norms, existing before a specific law does, and enhanced by being encoded into legislation, can cause an over-application i.e. a normative rather than a strict application of law.

The existence of norms before laws may explain why the *Interim Provisions* appear to have been over-applied in Nanning earlier this century. Recall that these *Provisions* did not mandate that any signage had to include Zhuang, but rather regulated the format *if* a sign were to be bilingual. Nevertheless, in commentary upon these *Provisions*, Sina News (2009) expressly described the *Provisions* as the reason why an increased number of public texts in Nanning were becoming Zhuang-inclusive, including street-name signage. Moreover, it listed a number of texts that the *Provisions* allegedly regulated: "全市党政机关、社会团体、企事业单位名称牌、公章都使用壮汉两种文字，公共场所设置的挂牌、路牌、标志牌也同时标注有壮文拼音文字" [All of the City's Party and state organs, social organizations, enterprise and work unit-name signage, and official seals must use both the Zhuang and Han types of script, and all listed public places' installed road signage, street signage, direction signage must also display Zhuangwen Pinyin text [i.e. Romanized Zhuang]]. This report goes further than the *Provisions* actually did. And so, of course, did actual linguascaping practices: the municipal government converted its street-name signage from monolingual Putonghua to bilingual Putonghua and Zhuang. Both Sina News and the Nanning authorities were reproducing norms rather than reproducing the law. These norms, it seems to me, were built up by an accretion of formal policies (but not laws) and more limited Zhuang-inclusive signage practices in GZAR over decades.

We can excavate traces of this history of institutional naming policy in the documentary records, not only in the built environment. In 1984 and 1991, GZAR regional circulars were published which requested that GZAR's state organizations use Putonghua and Zhuang for their own institutional signage (Li and Huang 2004: 247). These were internal institutional rules but not general laws. There may have been other written directives like these that are not recoverable. These circulars are probably why some of Nanning's public institution name-signage appears to predate the twenty-first century laws about including Zhuang. This is likely also why I found some bilingual government bureaux signage matching Nanning's *Interim Provisions* and/or the *Nanning Measures*' stipulated format outside the Nanning Municipal Government's remit in Guilin, another city in GZAR. This previous, internal regional policy of including Zhuang on government-authored, public institution name signage is consistent with the landscape evidence. It is evident in the data that some of the Zhuang-inclusive name signage around Nanning pre-dates the *Interim Provisions*. Think, for example, of the bilingual signage on the front of the old regional museum in downtown Nanning or the trilingual gateway at the entrance of GUN (Figures 33 and 39). These institutions pre-date even the GZAR circulars. Perhaps their façade signage was designed to include Zhuang as part of the recovery of minority languages and cultures after the Cultural Revolution. Further, we can see, because we have the full text of the 2004 *Interim Provisions* and the 2013 *Nanning Measures*, that the latter re-entextualized many of the standards articulated in the former. There is every reason to think that this incremental and derivative process of regulating the linguascape commenced well before the *Interim Provisions*. I therefore suggest that Nanning's *Interim Provisions* and then the *Nanning Measures* and *GZAR Regulations* about landscape texts were based on pre-established norms of bilingual government signage formatting which had arisen under or been amplified by the older regional policies.

Moreover, in becoming law, these pre-existing norms gained symbolic power. In recognizing that Zhuang-inclusive bilingual signage *could* exist, the *Interim Provisions* suggested that it *should* exist. That normative resource was then available to be taken up by linguascapers. Thus, the Nanning municipal road authorities undertook the wide-spread replacement of Putonghua-only street-name signs with Zhuang-Putonghua signs in the years following the *Interim Provisions*' introduction, and reputedly did so *because of* the *Provisions*, without that having been the legal direction given to them by the municipal law makers.

A different type of over-application of language laws is evident in the use of English on road direction signage around Nanning, which I also documented in Chapter Six. There is international language policy in the form of law which regulates the languages to be used on road directions signage: the *Vienna Convention on Road Signs and Signals* (1968). Article 14(2) of this *Vienna Convention* stipulates: "The inscription of words on informative [road] signs […] in countries not using the Latin alphabet shall be both in the national language and in the form of a transliteration into the Latin alphabet reproducing as closely as possible the pronunciation in the national language." The PRC is not a signatory to the *Vienna Convention* so the *Convention* does not apply as law in Nanning. Nevertheless, signage which conformed to this international rule was oftentimes observed in GZAR. That is, many road directions were displayed in both Putonghua characters and Putonghua Pinyin (being the alphabetic transliteration which most closely reproduces the pronunciation of the national language). At other times, as I have noted in Chapter Six, road directions were displayed in Putonghua characters and English (e.g. Figure 23). This vacillation between Putonghua Pinyin and English on road directions is not unique to GZAR in China. Displaying Putonghua characters and English is *also* consistent with the *Convention*, as Article 14(4) permits two languages, but no more, on road direction signage.

The government has thus aligned Nanning's signage with global norms of road direction signage, which are highly influenced by the *Vienna Convention*, without actually applying the *Vienna Convention* as law. The agency in this aspect of linguascaping is, therefore, maintained by relevant Chinese law-makers rather than the international law-makers, although the Chinese agents converge towards one norm of the international genre of road directions signage, the inclusion of the Roman alphabet. This Romanized look is a way to linguascape China's streetscapes to look – and indeed to be – modern, international and accessible. This is similar to the Beijing Government mandating the addition of English to Putonghua street-name signage for the 2008 Olympics, a linguascaping law which Zhang (2011: 88–95) has analyzed. Moreover, China's transport ministry's (or ministries') ruling to provide Romanized content in addition to Putonghua in simplified characters on road directions manifests in practice as both Putonghua Pinyin (e.g. HE CHI SHI, *shi* meaning city) and as English (e.g. HUANCHENG EXPWY). Writers in China do not always differentiate these as distinct languages, as I have learnt from my observations of other signage and from discussion on the subject with my participants, Liz, Mae and Hope, while I participated in a survey assignment that they were doing about the translation of texts for tourists. Thus, there is both an appropriation of the normative value of English in modern road design from overseas legal discourses and linguistic landscapes, and a modification through its interaction with the agents' belief about whether a script, by itself, defines a language. This road directions example highlights the distinct, normative power of laws as discourses, rather than their legal power as laws, in that the international *Vienna Convention* law is appropriated at a national scale, but it also illustrates the dynamic interaction of norms with rules.

9.4 Concluding discussion: What this linguascaping analysis implies for the new *GZAR Regulations*

Nanning's Zhuang-inclusive street-name signs, its Zhuang-inclusive institution-name signs, and its abundance of monolingual Putonghua signage are all closely shaped by laws about the linguistic landscapes, as I have demonstrated in Section 9.2. The analysis has revealed how the government exercises a domineering agency in linguascaping as the law-maker, using laws to prioritize its views on how linguistic landscapes should look and read, but I also highlighted how "the government" is actually various law-making bodies with differing legal ranks and diverse designs and priorities for the linguistic landscape. Moreover, despite the power law-makers wield, legal interventions in the linguistic landscapes here primarily constrained other government agents, not enterprises and individuals. Rather, Nanning's laws (and now GZAR's new law) explicitly preserve some of the agency over language choice of commercial enterprises and individuals, encouraging them to include written Zhuang but not obliging it. The public texts that *must* include Zhuang are overwhelmingly those that will be authored by government bodies. Putonghua, by contrast, is obligatory for all under national law. All public texts must respond to the priorities of the national government in this regard and everyone's agency over public language choice is thus constrained.

Further, through the lens of linguascaping, I have drawn forth the way that government bodies exercise linguascaping agency by being legally empowered as regulators, in addition to being empowered as law-makers. As regulators, government organizations enforce or choose not to enforce the legal standards against others. Further, under the *Nanning Measures*, the local government is an agent of linguascaping in yet another way. This is as a co-author, with the state's minority language work agency (i.e. a part of the local government) being legally obliged to help both governmental and private authors of public texts to add or correct Zhuang.

Let us consider these laws about who can or must participate in linguascaping, and how they must participate, as "moves" in what Coupland (2012: 4) has called the "evolving discourses of cultural definition". These moves, while symbolically empowered by their legal form, are not all-powerful. Rather, as I argued in Section 9.3, using law to challenge or reshape existing norms about linguistic landscapes is vulnerable to being undermined or filtered by preexisting norms, although I showed that those pre-existing norms can sometimes also expand the application of the law.

Until recent decades, Zhuang was constructed as inappropriate for most public texts (and many other formal functions), whereas Putonghua was quickly becoming appropriate, even in GZAR, building on a history of earlier national Mandarin varieties being used and considered appropriate. Similarly, in Coupland's (2012: 7–8) study of changes in language policy in Wales, he found that the "organizational premise" for language display was that Welsh was "inappropriate for use as a public code" whereas English was appropriate; the concept of an "organizational premise" here is applied from Goffman (1974). Against this history, pro-Welsh language policy sought to "assert or propose" a new "'shape' of bilingual culture" (Coupland 2012: 4), and that is what Nanning's *Interim Provisions*, then the *Nanning Measures*, and now the *GZAR Regulations*, seek to do for Zhuang. But, akin to the Welsh case, this new shape is not immediately a dominant cultural-linguistic norm in China, even within GZAR. My study shows clearly the ongoing dominance of Putonghua in public in GZAR. Looking beyond GZAR, Zhou (2004: 87) reports that in most minority autonomous areas of China most government services and signs are not in the local minority language. And while the local decision to include Zhuang on Nanning's street-name signage challenges the ideological subordination of Zhuang, these signs also conform to local and national rules about always including Putonghua.

Laws that direct how linguascaping is to be done often remove agency. However, as the chapter illustrated, in the wider operation of laws as discourses the agents of linguascaping may retain their legal agency but appropriate and re-interpret normative discourses, deliberately or unconsciously. This can allow for certain agents, especially local decision-makers, to modify or thwart the agency of other linguascapers, especially further-away law-makers, but it can conversely also allow symbolically powerful law-makers elsewhere to exert influence beyond their legal limits. Thus, in the dynamic discourses in which language laws participate, linguascaping agency can be regulated by laws but not entirely constrained or directed. Rather, norms (i.e. covert language policies) and formal but non-legal policies can cause various agents to under-apply, over-apply or otherwise modify the application of laws. Thus, while it might be thought that the relatively tightly regulated linguistic landscapes in this study are ulikely to "suggest a *de facto* language policy [...] that could be formally codified in de jure policy in order to align policy with sociolinguistic experiences in daily life" as Hult (2018: 344) has suggested following Schiffman (1996: 49), in fact even these linguistic landscapes continue to be able to propose *de facto* policies which differ from the official position. The disjunction between the regulation of the format of Zhuang-inclusive texts and the interpretation of such regulations as requiring Zhuang-inclusive texts reveals more of these ideological "struggles" over Zhuang's "authoritative entextualization" (Blommaert 1999: 9). So too do the disjunctions between the inclusion of Zhuang on some public, government-authored texts while it is excluded from others in the same city, or between the even, duplicate bilingual format described in the rules and the uneven, fragmentary bilingual format that is produced. We therefore need to accept that any desire on the part of law-makers to challenge or reshape existing norms about linguistic landscapes is vulnerable to being undermined by the enduring strength of pre-existing norms. Of course, that goes for language laws about other aspects of usage too: law by itself does not shape or reshape beliefs and practices, and the law-makers are rarely the only agents.

Because decision-makers' language ideological struggles and institutional policies have colored the interpretation of the *Nanning Measures,* and of the older rules, they are likely coloring the interpretation of the new *GZAR Regulations* nowadays too. However, the *GZAR Regulations* only became effective from 1 August 2018, so it is yet too early to comprehensively document or evaluate their impact. Nevertheless, we can already see that these regulations have been drafted to directly address certain previous hurdles and ambiguities. For instance, they add enforcement mechanisms, which Chapter Three noted are absent from minority language laws at the national level. Enforcement penalties do not feature in the *Interim Provisions* or *Nanning Measures,* although those regulations provide that the responsible entity can be assisted to correct non-compliant texts and should do so. By contrast, the *GZAR Regulations* enforcement mechanisms are relatively tough: the GZAR Minority Language Commission and its subordinate branches can order that people correct signage (Reg 30), and infractions can result in not only an order to correct but in fines, administrative penalties and even criminal penalties (Regs 28–31). The *GZAR Regulations* are thus a new move in evolving cultural discourses, not a repeat of old moves. Might they therefore succeed in reshaping language ideologies, as well as linguistic landscapes?

I argued in Chapter Three that it is a problem that the national laws do not empower individuals concerned about Zhuang to initiate legal proceedings to protect their own language usage, or others'. Under the new *GZAR Regulations*, this problem persists but it is ameliorated by giving the local Minority Language Work Commission officers the power to order corrections, which could be used in response to citizens' complaints. However, the administrative penalties require there to have been adverse consequences caused by state officials/departments. It will be interesting to see over time whether, and how, this threshold is met. When public signage in Zhuang is wrong and is not corrected, it offends certain Zhuang speakers, including some from whom we heard in Chapter Eight. But what adverse consequences could be demonstrated in such an instance in order to trigger this new legal liability? In addition, the new *GZAR Regulations* (Reg 14) give the Zhuangzu and other minority minzu a "right" to sue in court in their own language. This is a local re-codification of a right which Chapter Three pointed out exists already in the *Constitution* and a national law about legal proceedings. There is nothing wrong with rearticulating it clearly and in a more localized context, especially if it is matched with local government funding to provide more interpreters in courts. However, as with the national laws, there are no rights in the *GZAR Regulations* about language use or protection upon with people can sue. This right is to enable Zhuang speakers to litigate everyday contract, criminal or property cases in their best language, not to empower them to challenge the authorities and businesses linguascaping their environments.

Moreover, despite these more robust penalties in the *GZAR Regulations*, these regulations will likely face constraints. In particular, and following the arguments made in Section 9.3, this new law may be narrowed in its application by agents' adherence to pre-existing norms of language display. Neither the repeated practices of governments in regulating bilingual signage in Nanning prior to 2018, nor their practices of actually putting Zhuang into the linguistic landscape, appear to have engendered a general norm favoring Zhuang-inclusive public text. To the contrary, I have shown that many public institutions which were once provided with government-authored Zhuang-inclusive building name signage have since excluded Zhuang from all their newer public signage. In addition, other genres of public text like shop names, advertisements, public announcements, plaques and directions signage, have not adopted Zhuang-inclusive bilingualism, despite legal encouragement. I therefore cannot see the *GZAR Regulations* as being over-widely applied to other signage types or by other authors; that is, I do not foresee those who are not strictly bound by the new rules nevertheless following them as norms.

Furthermore, although the *Interim Provisions* and then the *Nanning Measures* sought to create textual parity and equivalence between Putonghua and Zhuang, I discussed in this chapter my finding that equal, duplicate bilingual texts are oftentimes not produced in Nanning, even on signage which has otherwise been created in conformity with the rules. I therefore expect this convention of partial inclusion of Zhuang to carry over into the application of the *GZAR Regulations*. Similarly, I do not expect the norm of displaying only Zhuang amongst the local minority language to change, even though GZAR Regulation 13 provides that other minority languages can also be used for official functions such as public signage.

My biggest concern with the *GZAR Regulations* is that their obligations to use or provide Zhuang are constantly qualified by phrases like "in accordance with actual needs" and "where minority peoples live in concentrated communities". In this way, the *GZAR Regulations* are not likely to increase Zhuang in public texts or services in GZAR's cities, which are already drawing Zhuangzu people away from concentrated communities to new, multi-minzu urban communities, and still growing. This is not a regulation to expand the public presence of Zhuang language, for either functional or symbolic purposes. Nor is it a regulation to assist multilingual Zhuang speakers who live outside concentrated Zhuangzu communities, even if they would feel more comfortable using Zhuang for services or official purposes. As such, it will not encourage people to remain multilingual within cities or to raise Zhuang-speaking, multilingual children there. These blind spots perhaps hint at why this law was enacted, which I queried in this chapter's Introduction; a law that is not expected to cause big changes is easier to pass, and to pass off as a caring or appeasing political move. But this is a language policy that seems to dodge many of the key challenges facing Zhuang and other minority languages today, the circumstances of a *changing* China.

I therefore conclude that the current Zhuang linguascaping laws, being the *Nanning Measures* and the *GZAR Regulations*, are not creating the physical or ideological impetus for a change to Zhuang language being included more in publicly-displayed discourses. In particular, we should consider the legislative "encouragement" on non-state actors to use Zhuang found now in both the *Nanning Measures* and the *GZAR Regulations*. An encouragement provision is a purely normative use of law. This singular style of legislating is not uncommon in Chinese laws. However, there is not much to "fill up" the "ideological or implementational space" (Hornberger 2005: 605) created by this suggestion for commercial enterprises and individuals to use Zhuang on public signage. This space runs the risk of simply being filled up with existing beliefs in and habits of the public desuetude of Zhuang.

Rather, it is arguably in the face of the increased complexity of scales, authors and discourses in today's changing China that adherence to high-scale normative language practices – like the association of Putonghua with education, national identity and government functions, or English with global commerce and mobility – plays an ever greater role in producing a linguistic order within GZAR. This is what fills up the ideological and implementational spaces in contemporary language governance. That is, although the state technically leaves open the linguistic landscape choices of many agents, this does not mean that their choices will be free from the influence of state-amplified norms and discourses about what should be included in or excluded from public text, for what purposes and in which places. This should inform our reading of GZAR's new, and on their face relatively robust, regulations about public-facing uses of minority languages.

Finally, I see the *GZAR Regulations* as confirmation of a trend in the type of problem that concerns language policy-makers in China at the moment. In Grey (2017: 305), I argued that Nanning's *Interim Provisions* exemplified language governance directed at "allocat[ing] functions and/or uses for particular languages [... i.e.] status planning" (quoting Johnson and Ricento 2013: 7). In this way, I argued, Nanning was a bellwether harkening a shift away from "preparing a normative orthography, grammar, and dictionary for [...] a non-homogeneous speech community" (Johnson and Ricento 2013: 7) and the *Interim Provisions* represented a move beyond twentieth century Zhuang language governance's focus on "corpus planning". The earlier focus on corpus planning was not limited to Zhuang language policy but was characteristic of minority language policy across the board in China in the twentieth century (see further Chapter Four). That the *Nanning Measures* then strengthened the *Interim Provisions* with additional specificity and legal force showed that the shift from corpus to status planning was consolidating during my study. Now, 2018's *GZAR Regulations* have taken this shift in language policy up a government scale-level to the regional scale, and strengthening the language policy focus on status planning for minority languages, adding greater legal authority and enforcement mechanisms to bolster the long-favored mechanism of public displaying written minority languages. I do not expect this shift to be unique to Zhuang language policy. My proposed reasons for the shift include the appropriation of a Zhuang linguistic identity by the government for political and place-product profits during a time of political nationalism and commodification of place in response to the increasing mobility of tourists and re-settlers within China. Further, I argue that as Zhuang language usage comes under pressure, particularly in the context of intergenerational illiteracy in Zhuang and the double domination of Putonghua and English, the needs of Zhuang speakers and the expected performances of this minority language are shifting from individuals to institutionalized representatives, including representative places. I suggest this same shift is affecting many, if not all, other Chinese minority languages. As people increasingly cannot, do not want, or do not need to use Zhuang themselves, they / their governments want their linguistic identity to be "voiced" publicly, ventriloquized, through the places they live and the symbolic practices of their officials. In this climate, regulatory linguascaping arises but does not seek to force largescale changes in the practice of a language. I will take this argument further in the book's next and final chapter, critiquing the assumption that linguascaping through law to increase the public presence of a minority language encourages change in language practices (let alone forcing change) or raises a minoritized language's status.

Part IV: **Conclusions**

10 Summary and conclusions regarding language rights in a changing China

> *How to learn about law and legal institutions as they developed through the millennia of one of the world's oldest legal systems [...] require[s] knowledge of history, philosophy, society, economics, politics and culture as well as analysis of usual and unusual legal materials.*
> (Cohen 2015: 6)

China's legal system stretches beyond language governance, but in making this interdisciplinary study of it through the prism of languages and the people associated with them, I have revealed significant elements of the history, philosophy, society, economics, politics and culture shaping the making and use of laws in China today. Language is central to the state's structuring of territory, polities and governing power. Reducing use of minority languages in favor of Mandarin (i.e. increasing language shift) and changing beliefs about minority languages and multilingualism are key to current political debates about reforming the structures that shape the nation and re-setting its priorities. The increasing marginalization of minority language rights and language governance organizations shown in this study exemplifies a broader trend in law-making and the form of legal rights in China today. This is a trend from the purpose of laws being to make declarative, normative statements to the purpose being actionable, specific legal rights, which the minority language freedom has not been reformed to become. But this study of language rights in a changing China also speaks to general issues in language rights scholarship and practice around the world. In concluding, I therefore devote Chapter Ten to reflecting on the state of language rights in China and the directions in which Chinese language policy is heading, and Chapter Eleven to generalizations and implications that reach well beyond either the Zhuang language or China to global questions.

10.1 Conclusions regarding language rights in a changing China

This study combined sociolinguistic, ethnographic and legal approaches in research over the period 2013–2020. It investigated how China's laws and policies about minority languages, which were a priority for the early PRC government, are implemented and understood in a much-changed China, a nation rapidly urbanizing, globalizing, marketizing, mobilizing, securitizing and reforming its conception of itself as a proud global leader in the twenty-first century. Specifically, this project investigated the operation and impact of China's constitutional freedom to use and develop minority languages, the legislative right to learn and use the national language, Putonghua, and some derivative legal rights e.g. to have court proceedings translated, through a case study of China's most-spoken official minority language, Zhuang. After an examination of the framework of laws and organizational structures in the governance of minority peoples and languages in China, the book used an empirical linguistic landscape study to examine national, regional and local laws relating to Zhuang language. This provided "usual and unusual legal materials", to borrow from Cohen's quotation in the epigraph; indeed, this approach is unusually comprehensive and interdisciplinary for linguistic scholarship, not only for legal scholarship. The approach was made in response to the general theorization of public space as a key instrument of *de facto* and *de jure* language policy (Shohamy 2006: 57) and because language policy about or materialized through public space had not been examined in depth in the language rights and policy literature.

This was an interdisciplinary study of minority language governance in China which combined legal analysis with Bourdieusian critical sociolinguistics. Thus, in addition to examining the legal nature and limitations of the constitutional freedom to use and develop minority languages, the study examined the understandings and uses made of language rights and the associated framework of laws and policies, as well as the laws and policies' interaction with beliefs about languages' value, appropriateness and association with certain social categories. It did this using multi-sited and multi-modal ethnographic data collection anchored in specifically selected urban and university sites in GZAR and in three other provinces across China, and the purposive selection of participants for both interviews and ethnographic interaction (see Figure 5 and the tables in the Appendix). The participants comprised 43 university students who were either Zhuang speakers or Zhuangzu members, and 20 Zhuang language leaders. Of my 43 student participants, 18 were Zhuang Studies undergraduates and postgraduates at three of the anchoring minzu-specialist universities while 23 were students at the three anchoring comprehensive universities. The 20 language leaders were people doing Zhuang/minority language work in cultural heritage, Zhuang policy, education, popular culture and media, language professions, and law.

Following, I will summarize the study overall and then recapitulate the key findings and arguments of Parts One (Foundations), Two (Laws and Governance Structures) and Three (Lived Linguistic Landscapes). **Part Four** provides a recapitulation (this **Chapter Ten**) and a reflection on the wider implications of this study (**Chapter Eleven**). All three parts used the Zhuang case study to develop the analysis of the minority language governance framework as it pertains to all minzu in China. This chapter ends with a section looking ahead to policy predictions and policy recommendations for Zhuang and China's other minoritized languages.

10.1.1 The findings, overall

In 2019, the Nanning Municipal Minority Language Works Commission, under the auspices of the Nanning Municipal Ethnic and Religious Affairs Committee, reviewed and evaluated the *Nanning Measures*. The *Measures* are a piece of local rule-making passed in 2013 in support of Zhuang language which this study examined both through the linguistic landscape analysis in **Chapters Six to Eight** and the theorization of linguascaping laws as discourse in **Chapter Nine**. The 2019 review reonnates with my own initial assessment (Grey 2017) and this book's fuller assessment of minority language governance; the following encapsulation of the problems at the Nanning level echoes my overall findings at the regional and national scales:

> 当前，壮文在我市壮族聚居区学校使用壮汉双语教学、机关壮文使用、在壮语文的翻译、古籍整理、广播电视，以及利用壮语山歌等形式向少数民族群众宣传党和国家的方针政策等方面都取得了阶段性成效。但是……也存在着一些亟待解决的困难和问题，这些问题的产生，既有个人的语言态度原因，也有国家强力推行国家通用语言文字政策、学习使用壮语文制度保障缺失、评价机制未建立、财政扶持有限等客观原因。

> [At present, Zhuangwen [i.e. written Zhuang] is used in Zhuang-Chinese bilingual teaching in schools in the Zhuang ethnic communities of our city; the use of Zhuang language by government agencies; translation into Zhuang language; the collation of ancient books; radio and television; and the use of Zhuang language folk songs to promote the Party and the state to minority people. [Nanning's] Guidelines and policies have achieved initial results. However [...] there are also some difficulties and problems that need to be solved urgently. These problems arise due to personal language attitudes, as well as objective reasons such as the country's strong implementation of the national common language policy, and the lack of systemic guarantees for learning and using of Zhuang language, the failure to establish an evaluation mechanism and limited financial support].
>
> (Nanning Municipal Minority Language Works Commission 2019: §2)

One further overarching problem that this study has found is reflected in but not acknowledged by the review: that Zhuang language policy is preoccupied with the Romanized, written form of Standard Zhuang, Zhuangwen.

Overall, my study finds that China's circumstances are causing the existing minority language rights to become obsolete rather than engendering new practices and norms. In particular, the norms of culture invested with symbolic power by their association with urban places and lives, including the convergence towards dominant cultural practices and the normative exclusion of Zhuang language in the material discourses of urban landscapes, heighten the minoritization of Zhuang language. This *cultural urbanization* can affect language norms and the socio-linguistic order well beyond cities (as Grey 2021a argues) but in this book I have focused on the roots of cultural urbanization by examining cities themselves. Laws about language do very little to challenge this cultural urbanization. I have explained how the *Nanning Measures* and *GZAR Regulations* do intervene to "linguascape" some public landscapes such that they include some written Zhuang, but that these laws do not oblige widespread change in Zhuang usage, nor empower agents of change. The national language rights are not empowering, either. Rather, promotion efforts such as these local laws run up against the strong developmentalist ideologies in legal discourses, which devalue Zhuang in the development of the nation. The language governance framework's developmentalist bent is amplified, nowadays, by synergies with the marketized ideologies of the globalized new economy, despite initially arising from Communist ideologies about remedying imperial socio-economic oppression and developing an inclusive nation-state. This development is indexed by the urban places, practices and discourses from which Zhuang is largely absent. Thus, the linguistic toleration of China's overarching language rights is becoming complicit in the marginalization of minority languages. Moreover, the idea of linguistic justice as equal support for use and development of languages is being reformed through law, policy and government practices into equal support for the curation of linguistic heritage. In addition, there is a growing trend elsewhere in China towards security-focused language governance. Freeland and Patrick (2004: 5) have argued that "[n]ation-state ideology creates one of the central paradoxes of claiming minority rights in a discourse based on equality, individual liberties, and national unity". This study shows such a tension is unavoidably embedded in the foundations of China's language governance framework, in the constitution of this multi-minzu nation-state. It is therefore unlikely that Zhuang language will be isolated from the trend towards securitized language policy that mistakes homogeneity for unity.

There is little in this context to push policy-makers and law-makers to consider that Zhuang is anything other than already sufficiently equal, after previous language policy interventions, or to prompt them to make Zhuang language more instrumental or more widely used. Some participants in the study, but not all, shared this ideology, and did not expect Zhuang language policy to create such value, or to fix current challenges that the language and its speakers face.

10.1.2 Recapitulating Part One

To reach these conclusions, **Part One** (**Chapters One and Two**) first denaturalized the officially recognized Zhuangzu minority and Zhuang language, putting these "natural objects" back into the social and political history from which they arose. This offered an especially clear illustration of how "it is the nation-state that creates linguistic minorities" (Freeland and Patrick 2004: 5).

But we must understand that China is not alone in creating linguistic minorities: countries such as Vietnam, Canada and Spain recognize official linguistic minorities within their diverse legal systems, as does the *European Charter for Regional or Minority Languages*. It was significant in this case that I showed the Zhuangzu ethno-linguistic minority group to have been created by the state in the twentieth century *without* disputing that a Zhuang identity now has meaning for both people and the state. This extends Kaup's (2000) claim that the government "created" the Zhuangzu, and sets us up to see such social construction not as a horrifying surprise (as Kaup implies) but as an expected, ongoing process to the benefit and detriment of various interests. To this end, I also explained that the various dialects grouped as Zhuang are not only spoken by the official Zhuangzu polity, that members of the Zhuangzu polity are no longer necessarily Zhuang speakers, and that Zhuang speakers, whether Zhuangzu or not, likely do not speak or write the government-created Standard Zhuang. This changes the nature of whom Zhuang language policy should target or exclude.

Moreover, Zhuang speakers are nowadays typically multilingual and Zhuangzu people are no longer necessarily located in rural, concentrated Zhuang-speaking communities because many Zhuangzu people are mobile and have moved to cities. Zhuang language is not moving to cities with them, or at least not remaining there. This was anticipated by the earlier literature and is shown vividly through my data; I propose that this as part of cultural urbanization (see also Grey 2021a, on cultural urbanization beyond the city limits). Nevertheless, most Zhuang speakers do still live in GZAR, an autonomous region on the southern border of China. GZAR is a poor province in comparison to its Eastern neighbors, and is just recently experiencing the investment and growth that many parts of China have already experienced. As a result, Zhuang language policy has not necessarily been well resourced and Zhuang language practices are especially vulnerable to being understood as indexing poorer, less modernized places and communities. However, GZAR also has self-governing autonomy, seemingly increasing the power of Zhuang speakers over language policy. The remainder of the book interrogated that apparent power.

10.1.3 Recapitulating Part Two

GZAR is autonomous in name. The legal analysis in **Part Two** (**Chapters Three to Five**) has shown the tight limits of this, and that this is a legal devolution problem for all five of China's nominally autonomous regions. **Part Two** also made it clear that, despite GZAR's lack of legal autonomy, Zhuang language governance is channeled through the autonomous regional structure; governing Zhuang language is a responsibility of the state inside delimited Zhuangzu areas. However, the authority of governments within these Zhuangzu areas to provide regulatory or material support for Zhuang language is marred by the incomplete, formal processes of power-sharing between the central and regional governments, as is common across China's five autonomous regions.

There are certain strengths to the system. Most decisions about Zhuang language are made by regional and sub-regional decision-makers closer to the issues than the Central Government; and many tiers of government have a structured inclusion of Zhuangzu officials, notionally representing the interests of Zhuang speakers, as well as having minority language organs for the purposes of informing and executing language policies. However, my analysis concluded that the structures to represent the Zhuangzu in decision-making are removed from input of or accountability to Zhuang speakers, that the organs of the Party-State in which those representatives are included are too limited, and that there is a high level of structural un-coordination between relevant decision-makers, advisors and influences. The freedom to use and develop minority languages in the *Constitution* and the laws that derive from it do not remedy these problems by empowering people or organizations to participate in, or challenge, decisions.

Rather, my analysis found that the constitutional minority language right is not a legal entitlement to claim anything of the state in regards to Zhuang language. Moreover, there are no processes through which an individual or even the Zhuangzu group can use this freedom to use and develop Zhuang to make a legal claim against the state or other entity to do something, or stop doing something, in order to protect the freedom: "法律有一个保证 ...... 你用不上就像那个水在那里你喝不了" [*The law has a guarantee, but ... it's like there is water there but you cannot drink it*], as Mr F put it (my translation).

Moreover, Zhuang language is not all that is at stake when people are inadequately represented amongst powerful decision-makers. In **Part One**, I introduced a foundational idea, that language policy is a structure which organizes (sometimes by proxy) socio-economic power and marginalization (following Costa 2013 and Lafont 1997). Thus, participating in, being represented in, or controlling decision-making that affects Zhuang language (or any other language) is a form of access to power. However, my study has explained that Chinese language rights are not designed to re-balance or to create access to this power in language governance.

Yet we can imagine that removing the current freedom to use and develop minority languages from Article 4 of the *Constitution* would be deeply offensive and unwelcome. The symbolic import of having this constitutional language right is to validate minority people's languages as languages, and by extension their legally-created minzu idenities and Chinese national identities as meaningful. A right to be free to use and develop minority languages has been included in successive constitutions as part of resisting long-held and negative, even demonizing, beliefs about China's non-Han peoples. This remains important even though Article 4 does not offer anything much in a strictly legal sense and even if speaker numbers decrease.

Furthermore, **Part Two** explained that the Zhuang language governance framework entrenches the normative position of various language ideologies. Prime among them is territorialization, not unlike in other language governance frameworks known to the literature, and developmentalism, which I identified in **Chapter Four** as an ideology predominant in the Chinese context but which researchers may find a helpful concept in explaining language ideologies elsewhere. Within a territorialized paradigm, a language "loses functions as soon as the stable, original, 'autochthonous' [...] link between language and place is broken" (Blommaert 2004: 58), especially functions of communication in daily life, work, education and civic participation, but also cultural and affiliative functions. **Part Two** concluded that China's language governance framework reproduces the construction of territories as essentially corresponding to minority languages and minority minzu, building on **Part One's** exposure of an ideology in both state and academic discourses of Zhuang language and the Zhuang minzu being natural objects with an essential correspondence. From **Part Two** onwards, this book has argued that the corollary of the territorialization of Zhuang as essentially and only linked to Zhuangzu autonomous areas (mainly GZAR, the biggest such area) is the production of a normative invalidity of Zhuang use and development outside these areas.

Moreover, within the developmentalism paradigm, languages are understood as developed or undeveloped (or moving between), and this is ideologically mapped onto what it means for minority languages – and the speakers and peoples categorized as corresponding to them – to be valued as modernized, civilized and worth governing. I have made the point that this developmentalist language ideology includes a normative component: that the state *should* develop languages. This has a social permanence in part because it comes from China's *Constitution* itself. National law and policy discourses frame development of languages in terms of economic and cultural development and, relatedly, the development of standardized writing technologies. Through this study, we saw Zhuang often being constructed as under-developed, or developed to its limits but with no more potential, or of low value and not instrumental to any further advances in China's (economic) development. Zhuang is obviously not the only minority language in China to suffer this construction, given the entrenchment of this ideology in many national laws and policies and given the ascendance of developmentalism over an ideology of equality between languages which I have pointed out is evident in China's more recent laws and policies. These ideologies close the "implementational and ideological spaces" (Hornberger 2005) within which language policies or language and identity practices could change as China changes.

Finally, **Part Two** also analyzed the *majority* language governance framework. I concluded that language right to learn and use Putonghua, found in national legislation rather than the *Constitution*, was more legally forceful than the constitutional minority language right. Moreover, by making Putonghua the official national language in both the *Constitution* and national legislation, the state has mobilized its legal authority to monopolize extensive domains of language use exclusively for Putonghua and to mandate the inclusion of Putonghua in others. The freedom to use and develop Zhuang cannot impinge on legally sanctioned and mandated uses of Putonghua. The empirical examination of linguistic landscapes in **Part Three** bore this out.

10.1.4 Recapitulating Part Three

Through the application of pre-existing and new approaches to studying linguistic landscapes in **Part Three (Chapters Six to Nine)**, I examined how legal mechanisms supported or inhibited Zhuang language and constructed Zhuang people in public in urban and mobile places. This allowed me to examine the built environment instantiating both *de jure* and *de facto* language policies (including language ideologies) as well as how various social actors control linguistic landscaping and respond to the language policies made visible, impersonal and powerful through their physical landscape presence. **Part Three's** four chapters analyzed public Zhuang from four angles. This included linguistic and semiotic landscape analyses of the government's choices as a public author and an analysis of how public displays of Zhuang language are *linguascaped* through regulation. It also included a unique examination of people's responses to Zhuang's presence and absence in linguistic landscapes. I called this a *lived landscape* approach in **Chapter Eight**.

Together, the chapters of **Part Three** showed that patterns of public language display differ depending on the formal level of authority and autonomy of the Zhuangzu polity over that place. However, Zhuangzu autonomous areas do not legally or normatively mandate the inclusion of Zhuang on all public signage, nor challenge the Putonghua dominance of public linguistic landscapes. The government usage of Zhuang in public is not even consistent across areas of Zhuangzu autonomous government; public Zhuang more common in GZAR's capital city, Nanning, than elsewhere in GZAR, though not prominent overall even within Nanning's semiotic aggregates. Zhuang is generally not displayed even by the government unless the government has at least a normative prompt from law-makers, if not a legal obligation.

In terms of specific findings, **Chapter Six** found that there were some patterned inclusions of Zhuang language in public landscapes. Ten patterns are listed at the start of Section 6.4. These include the finding that Romanized, Standard Zhuang is always used instead of other varieties or scripts, and it is used mainly for bilingual signage naming GZAR's public institutions and the streets of its capital, Nanning. My analysis in Chapter Six concluded that public linguistic landscapes constructed and emplaced linguistic and social norms which largely marginalized and even excluded Zhuang, even in GZAR. In addition, some of the most consistent and widespread patterns were: the use of written Putonghua in all public texts, most of which were monolingual; the absence of any minority language other than Zhuang in government-authored public texts in GZAR; the absence of Zhuang and other minority languages from commercial public discourses (whether authored by the government or private entities); the smaller type font and off-centered placement of Zhuang relative to Putonghua on most bilingual signage; Zhuang usage being limited to relatively short, fixed, non-digital texts; fragmentary multilingualism (i.e. all content in Putonghua, only some also in Zhuang); the inclusion of English on some public texts, especially newer ones; and that homemade or handwritten Zhuang signage is not displayed. These patterned divisions between the public signage that includes Zhuang and that which excludes Zhuang reinforce a belief that writing Zhuang is not a normal personal activity, nor a personal heritage maintenance responsibility, and that Zhuang is of low value in commercial activities. Moreover, through these patterned linguistic landscapes, Zhuang is normalized as out of place in cities, and in the pursuits and technologies that typify city life.

Chapter Seven re-analyzed the same landscapes through a different lens in order to examine patterns in the non-linguistic, public representation of "Zhuangness". Specifically, it found multimodal "Zhuang" tropes across public imagery and architectural forms representing "love balls" (a toy for traditional courtship games in South China), geometrically patterned bronze drums, and women in colorful, traditionally-inspired costumes and hats. However, **Chapter Seven** also identified that there were minimal explicit references to "Zhuang" or "Zhuang language" in any language in these linguistic landscapes. I argued therefore that the linguistic and non-linguistic "Zhuang" symbols on public display were not necessarily clear references to Zhuang language, culture or people as opposed to a general minority reference. And on the other hand, I acknowledged that these emblems' emplacement within the region in which the Zhuangzu are titular may suggest that the Zhuangzu are the *only* local minority. Either way, the linguistic landscapes are erasing local diversity.

Further, the government's dominance of authorship over the signage types and specific signs that include Zhuang language and other emblems reveals the interests of the government in forming a local identity for itself. The government's usage of written Zhuang on certain types of public text in parts of GZAR – one of the last, active areas of Zhuang language governance intervention – maintains an ideological space that the state itself can continue to fill with representations of Zhuangness, including written Standard Zhuang and people it categorizes as Zhuangzu. However, even with this interest, local government interventions are not so widespread as to make Zhuang central to GZAR city landscapes.

This study has shown Zhuang language and Zhuang imagery to be emplaced largely in places that are not "on the move" but rather on the immovable edifices of the kinds of large public institutions that claim posterity not mobility, and the inside of museums. Even at mobile places like major train stations and universities, Zhuang is used (if used at all) only on the most static of texts – older and permanent façade names, signs and plaques – and Zhuang is typically absent from physically mobile (i.e. circulating) public texts, temporary texts such as banners, and newer technologies, such as digital signage. Thus, Zhuang language is not a symbol used to make the sites of its emplacement seem more mobile, but precisely the opposite. Zhuang language is a symbol of rootedness and historic association. **Chapter Nine** explains the legal interventions which led to the newer, bilingual street-name signs in Nanning which expand public Zhuang usage beyond such static places, but even these bilingual street-names trade in Zhuang's rooted symbolism, place-branding Nanning with resources symbolizing its Zhuang history (albeit with a twentieth-century Romanized script as the symbol). Because Zhuang is constructed in law and policy discourses as a highly localized and immobile language, as discussed in **Part Two**, it is a semiotic resource available to linguascapers to "make" the staticity of places. I have therefore argued that the government's Zhuang identity construction performatively emplaces heritage rather than reflecting or promoting Zhuang as a contemporary, living language.

Despite the patterns found in **Chapters Six and Seven** causing public landscapes to look fairly predictable, the meanings of public landscapes as discourses are not always predictable, as **Chapter Eight** investigated. Chapter Eight's lived landscape analysis revealed the participants making various socially-situated meanings of the linguistic and semiotic resources offered by these landscapes: they variously took up, ignored or even rejected the linguistic landscapes' affordances for Zhuang identity construction, misrecognizing Zhuang on signage as either Putonghua or English and habitually overlooking Zhuang signage. However, learning to read Zhuang and/or critically engaging with Zhuang language and identity politics was shown, in some participants' experiences, to overcome these dispositions. Participants also criticized the symbolism of Zhuang-inclusive signage. The widespread beliefs that few people can read Zhuang and that acquiring Zhuang literacy requires specialist formal training underpinned many of their views. These findings are consistent with the theoretical argument made by Wee (2011) and set into this study's foundations in **Chapter One** that there is a reflexive dynamism in an individual's habitus. My lived landscape approach offers one way of researching this dynamism, and I hope to see many more.

Closing out my multi-angled analysis of linguistic landscapes, **Chapter Nine** turned back to the role of law, examining how current laws from the Nanning and GZAR law-makers about public texts create and constrain the agency of linguascapers. This chapter argued for linguascaping as a conceptual tool of critical language policy analysis to foreground the ways that agency over landscape authorship is organized, complementary with the lived landscape approach. My linguascaping analysis drew out the normative rather than strictly legal effect of laws on these landscapes, illustrated by under-applications but also over-applications of linguascaping laws in Nanning. Language ideologies, including those identified in **Part Two** as being propagated with symbolic power through national laws, inform how laws are implemented in concrete, local terms in linguistic landscapes. The chapter therefore concluded that the linguistic landscapes in this study reflected but were not completely shaped by the key legal instruments. (These instruments are the 2018 *GZAR Regulations*, the 2013 *Nanning Measures* and Nanning's 2004 *Interim Provisions*, as well as the national *Putonghua Law* from 2000.) Moreover, those laws were shown not only to provide a dominant linguascaping role to the government as *both author and regulator*, but also to constrain the agency of other linguascapers without completely removing it. Rather, laws may be reinterpreted or resisted by various authors with some agency, just as the meanings of the languages, symbols and patterns in the linguistic landscape were shown to be reinterpreted or resisted by various viewers in **Chapter Eight**.

Finally, in my concluding discussion of linguascaping in **Chapter Nine**, I examined what the operation of the *Interim Provisions* and *Nanning Measures* suggests for the operation of the new *GZAR Regulations*. They are likely to be under-applied. And while they expand the geography of where certain kinds of public signage needs to include Zhuang from Nanning City to the whole region, they do not expand the types of signage or the types of authors who are obliged. In particular, commercial public texts and non-government authors *can* legally continue to exclude Zhuang and I predicted that they *will*, given the current normative exclusion and devaluing of Zhuang resonating between legal and material (landscape) discourses. Moreover, I placed the *GZAR Regulations* within a trend in minority language policy towards status planning and away from corpus planning, relying on the long-favored status-raising mechanism of public displaying written minority languages (which I will critique in Section 10.2). My proposed reasons for the shift – relevant to all minority languages in China – include the appropriation of a minority linguistic identity by the government for political and place-product profit during a time of increasing political nationalism and commodification of place. Further, as minority languages comes under pressure from intergenerational illiteracy and the double domination of Putonghua and English, I argue that the expected performers of minority languages are shifting from individuals to institutionalized representatives, including representative places. In this context, linguascaping public bilingualism through law *may* represent the interests of the notional inheritors and remaining speakers of a minority language, but it is not necessarily representative.

10.2 Looking ahead for Zhuang and other Chinese minority languages

This study serendipitously captured a period of change in Zhuang language governance. My theory on the changes so far in the twenty-first century is that, in the late twentieth century, laws and policies about Zhuang were not updated, and the implementation of older laws petered out. When this became apparent, there was something of a reactionary, urgent attempt to breathe life into now-minoritized Zhuang and/or to placate its speakers and preserve their cultural heritage, crystalizing in the recent Yubao Language Protection project introduced in Chapter One. This may also have been a reaction to the scale of social change, which was becoming incontrovertible in the 2000s. Similarly, the massive social changes in wake of the Cultural Revolution and the very beginning of Opening and Reform had seen a phase of activity and change in Zhuang language governance. So, will the 2020s mark a retreat from policy support for Zhuang and another period of petering out? I postulate that we are about to enter another phase like the late twentieth century, with the *Nanning Measures* and *GZAR Regulations* now on the books but a complacency and gradual diminishment of resourcing, political capital and new ideas on how to implement them to follow. If so, regaining momentum in Zhuang language governance will be hard. The systemic problems – problems that this book has argued have made the current language governance framework insufficiently agile in a changing China – still remain. There are relatively high numbers of people who still speak Zhuang, mainly multilingual people, but Zhuang is indubitably *minoritized* in the sense of "remaining restricted in its use in higher-status functions" (Deumert and Mabandla 2018: 201) despite its speaker numbers. Further, there are signs in this study that intergenerational language transmission is breaking down on a large scale and that this is associated with urbanization. Signs of an approaching wave of non-transmission of Zhuang amongst urban households were noted by Kaup (2000). Unless language rights and policies respond to the biggest changes in contemporary China – marketization, urbanization and the spread and symbolic power of Putonghua – language governance will be complicit in rendering Zhuang dispensable this century.

In the next section, I set out what would I like to see from twenty-first language policy. This complements the recommendations made to the Nanning Government in late 2019 by the Nanning Ethnic and Religious Affairs Committee (2019: §4), which I summarize as:

1. Upgrade the *Nanning Measures* to local regulations made by the municipal congress.
2. Intensify publicity for the resources that the legal system provides regarding minority languages and strengthen minority language training for cadres and workers in minority minzu areas.
3. Innovate through policy mechanisms to strengthen the training of talented, Zhuang-Mandarin bilingual personnel.
4. Promote the establishment of special funds for Zhuang language work in counties and districts to provide financial security for the promotion of Zhuang language.
5. Continue to steadily promote the implementation of Zhuang language across multiple domains and mediums, and do more detailed research on the actualities of Zhuang language use and diverse needs, as a basis for policy-making.

10.2.1 A letter to twenty-first century Zhuang policy-makers

"I want to go back to China and work to protect minority languages," a Linguistics student told me at the University of Sydney in 2018. I had just given his class an overview of this study and he was sharing an ambition that had been brewing throughout his degree. "What do you think policy-makers should do for Zhuang?" he then asked.

What a tough question. So practical, so hopeful. Could I say, "It's what they un-do that will make the difference"? Would it ever be helpful for me to say, "It may be too late"? The following is what I would most like to see policy-makers do, and not only for Zhuang but for other minority laguages in China, although I have centered my answer on Zhuang.

Change 1. Securitization and ideologies of monolingual nationalism are of immediate concern and therefore something for language policy to challenge (rather than amplify) across the country. The most concerning ideologies right now for Zhuang are territorialization and developmentalism, with its construction of minority languages as having low educational, economic and national value. These two ideologies also present challenges for all minority languages and their speakers and affiliates in China. Social changes and associated changing beliefs – especially marketization, urbanization and globalization – aggravate the pre-existing friction of territorialism and developmentalism against linguistic equality that is embedded within China's laws. Yet these are changes to which minority language laws and policies have so far barely responded in the now multiple decades in which these transformations have flourished in China. Nor have the makers and implementers of language laws and policies been called upon to respond to these challenges, because of the fractured and disempowering structures of minority language governance. Unfortunately, violence to languages and their speakers can happen through the banality of language policy that is not responsive to changing conditions, not only in highly conflictual or oppressive contexts. The shortfall of language rights in China today is that they do not sufficiently prompt, or empower, government or social actors to respond to changes in the sociolinguistic economy of Zhuang and other minoritized languages. The first change, then, would be to make the existing minority language rights actionable against the government (or at very least against non-government people and entities) and an obligatory consideration in national law-making. That is, language rights need legal force. A related change would be to put resources behind the realization of the rights that are already on the books to interpretation and translation in courts, rather than repealing these limp laws. This should be an explicit goal in the next national five year plan for court reform, going beyond the Supreme People's Court and NEAC's *Opinions on Further Strengthening and Improving the Training and Training of Bilingual Judges in Ethnic Areas* and the related trying out of bilingual judges in some local courts in GZAR. To support the legal force of any of China's minority language rights, they will also need the interdiscursive force that comes from aligning formal policies, governing structures, institutional practices, and public landscapes, which is what the remainder of the reply focuses on.

Change 2. Bourdieu (1977a) says that "the social value of linguistic products is only placed on them in their relationship to the market". This is especially true in China because of the entrenched developmentalist paradigm in language governance discourses and practices. To protect Zhuang, twenty-first century policy therefore has to create markets for it. Ideally, markets that ascribe Zhuang monetary value: profits that can be made by employing people who do various sorts of Zhuang language work, and income for those workers. In my view, this is now crucial, as China continues to marketize on so many fronts. But there is little of that sort of policy currently, and decreasing numbers of those sorts of jobs. The *GZAR Regulations* of 2018 are a valuable step in attempting to create some Zhuang language-based employment, as is the current funding for Zhuang Studies research positions, but meanwhile the dissociation of Zhuang from commercial discourse is not dealt with by the *GZAR Regulations*, although it could have been.

Change 3. As part of policy attempts to increase the economic value of Zhuang, the government must also make education reforms. People have to be given reasons to believe that Zhuang will be useful and appropriate at school and beyond school when they go to exchange their education capital on the job market. Currently, Zhuang language practices, especially Zhuang literacy practices, are excluded from almost all schooling even in the Zhuangzu autonomous region. The twenty-first century emergence of the Putonghua language right, and other legal supports for Putonghua, have aggravated this. Now, education policy and practice reflects and amplifies a belief that Zhuang is inappropriate for education. Learning Zhuang is widely believed to be detrimental to children's attainment in their educational and employable languages, Putonghua and English. In Grey (2017), I identify this as a "zero-sum language ideology". To rectify this situation, multilingualism must become part of the state's portrayal of a good student, and both the time and rewards for minority language multilingualism must be increased within the public education system. Further, the current push for universities to teach the languages of ASEAN to contribute to China's foreign policy's goals should leverage any advantages that minority language speakers may have over first-language Mandarin peers in learning related ASEAN languages, such as Zhuang speakers learning Thai. Likewise for any languages of China's western, northern and eastern neighbors that are the same or closely related to official minority languages within China. This would require more coordination between minority language education and foreign language education policy-makers but could also up-scale minority language practices to national human resources, similar to how China's marginal areas have been up-scaled to strategic transborder trade zones, investing these languages with increased educational, mobility and economic capital.

Change 4. Moreover, policy to create markets for Zhuang has to extend to "markets" in which value is not quantified in money, such as cultural markets. There have to be fields in which using Zhuang language creates cultural prestige, especially as this study has found that in some circles being a Zhuang person who does *not* speak Zhuang is becoming socially acceptable. Perversely, language policies which have minimized opportunities for gaining literacy in

Zhuang have turned personal literacy practices in Zhuang into resources of cultural distinction. This uncommon cultural resource can be embodied and made seminal in the construction of authoritative Zhuang identities. Nevertheless, the twentieth century government's attention to standardizing Zhuang and the recent government efforts to recognize and represent Zhuang language and culture as part of GZAR's local heritage have alleviated many people's shame in being Zhuangzu, which is an important start, even if the same language policies have not given Zhuang speakers much access to or control over their own cultural resources. It may seem that recent language policy is creating more cultural prestige for Zhuang, for instance by valorizing Zhuang language through including written, Standard Zhuang on public texts. But does this create cultural prestige for a *speaker* of *actual* Zhuang, whether in the eyes of other Zhuang speakers or more broadly? One of the most important findings of this study is that the cultural impact of the state's display of written Zhuang in Nanning is indirect and its symbolism is ambivalent, not least because the texts are not necessarily recognizable as Zhuang by Zhuang speakers themselves, nor by other locals or tourists.

In support of Changes 2 – 4, the government's linguistic landscape interventions can be made more widespread, consistent or representative. Likewise, *Third of the Third* can return to the simplified character and Romanized Zhuang publication that it was in the early 2010s rather than remain the monolingual Putonghua publication is has become.

Change 5. Moreover, while there are existing cultural fields in which Zhuang speakers and writers are valued, these fields do not necessarily exist because of policy support. The state recognition's of Zhuang language achievements through writing competitions and song festivals and the recent 100 Films in Zhuang project (Nanning Municipal Minority Language Works Commission 2019) have helped to some extent. However, we saw in this study that other Zhuang language practices which are currently not supported by the state, such as learning Sawndip, are nonetheless valued cultural practices within some communities. Furthermore, some language policy support has recently fallen away: my examination of the transformations to *Third of the Third* magazine revealed that this key, government-financed publication through which Zhuang cultural traditions and creativity could be both practiced and accessed is no longer published in Zhuang. Vastly increasing literacy in Zhuang would help. Future policy must at least support more access to training in Standard Zhuang in order to make creative endeavors in that medium more widely meaningful. But preferably, policy will also support a range of other Zhuang language practices, including new and non-standard Zhuang language practices which communities themselves value as part of their culture and for communications.

Change 6. The language ideology that only Mandarin is essential to national Chinese culture is strong, and the ideology that promoting other languages is anti-national is re-emerging. The common result of these two language ideologies – securitized language policy – was not yet a key part of governance in GZAR during my fieldwork in 2014–2015, but it was already in practice elsewhere in the country and these language ideologies have only become more powerful since. Future Zhuang language policy-makers and heritage officials therefore need to be aware of this securitization trend, to take leadership in critiquing it, and work to counteract its spread. It is clear throughout this study that people identify as Chinese *and* Zhuang, not one or the other, even people who are passionate about their own and others' Zhuang language practices. The dominant, oppositional view of identity as either Chinese or Zhuang should not be forced upon them through the ideologies or structures of policy and Zhuang language governance needs to continue to refrain from treating minority language practices threatening or criminal. Indeed, Zhuang language policy should actively promote conceptions of dual identity and multilingualism.

Change 7. Most of all, it is crucial that any language policy aiming to protect Zhuang language grapples with urbanization and the mobility and dispersal of minority groups. The economic, educational and cultural value of Zhuang has to be expanded beyond remote and concentrated Zhuangzu communities into multilingual, multi-ethnic communities in urban places and into the modern lifestyles associated with them. In effect, Mandarin-minority language bilingualism or Mandarin-English-Minority Language trilingualism has to become an urban cultural norm. If it is believed that languages survive better when speakers use them in distinct but equally symbolically powerful domains (Fishman 1968[1972]: 135–161) then policy has to create ideological and practical structures within which people can be *both* traditional and modern Zhuang speakers, alongside being speakers of lingua francas. That may require more social heterogeneity and individual agency: Chapters Three, Four, Five and Nine have highlighted the current constraints on the agency of individuals but also of groups and organizations in Zhuang language governance.

Other options. It may be that policy-makers prefer to save people rather than languages. Mufwene (2002: 377) raises this as a choice facing many minoritized language communities and their leaders, so Zhuang language policy is not necessarily going to aim for language protection in the future. However, this may be a false dichotomy, at least in terms of saving *a people* as a group. Maintaining a people requires maintaining a common identity in their own eyes and the eyes of others and is therefore hard to achieve without saving their language, especially if the language is central to that group's shared identity, as it is with Zhuang. Some participants have told me that saving Zhuang language is integral to saving people, e.g. "So we told the leaders [... that Zhuang] bilingual education's fundamental purpose is protecting language and culture's long-term development, *we spoke with them about it not being people who save culture, but the culture saving the people*" (Mr F, my translation, my emphasis, see original in Excerpt 5-2). Increasing the economic wellbeing of Zhuangzu people at the expense of maintaining Zhuang language would not be ideal, but rather a salvage operation within a hegemonic, minoritizing socio-linguistic order. Proactive language policy can avoid this sorry choice but it may be too late, and Putonghua too dominant, to (re)create the value of Zhuang language and its contemporary speakers.

Perhaps the state wishes to re-create the Zhuangzu such that language is not central to their group identity; this will entail putting the state's discourses and other resources behind people becoming non-Zhuang-speaking Zhuangzu people. This is arguably what the current Yubao 'Language Protection' archival project is doing under the guise of heritage preservation.

An even more extreme version would be to re-create the Zhuangzu as Chinese with no formal or substantive sub-national group identity. Some second generation minzu policy advocacy seeks this, while some seeks to retain the 56 formal minzu classification but evacuate the legal content of the classifications. I made the point in Chapter Two that constructing the Zhuangzu as different and traditional is part of maintaining a necessary "Other" to replicate self-interested boundaries of a majority Hanzu identity (there citing Gladney 2004 and others). Having now seen throughout the study how strongly this ideological "vision and division" (Bourdieu 1987: 852) has been made across forms of discourse, one can predict that this fundamental boundary would be replicated, re-mapped onto other perceived markers of difference, even under the second generation paradigm in which formal distinctions between ethno-linguistic groups are removed from the laws.

Thus, economic salvation and increased access to symbolic power will not necessarily arise from language shift from Zhuang to Mandarin/Putonghua, and so language policy should not apathetically permit that shift. Rather, linguistic ghosts – language ideologies of the current, minoritizing, developmentalist language rights and policy framework – will keep shaping what value and authenticity look like. No longer being classed as Zhuangzu but living in a society where people who speak like you are discriminated against, for example, will not be progress. Nor will being unmoored from any heritage by losing the label Zhuangzu, not being taught Zhuang language, yet being denied legitimate mainstream identity. This is what systemic, intergenerational oppression often looks like, and it can result from overly-instrumental, callously rational, pro-majority-language policy.

In my view, therefore, households and communities should not be left to give up their own and future generations' Zhuang language practices, as now, and only supported to do so if they have been provided with information, other options and agency in their decision-making, including through reformed government representation. Moreover, any policy that focuses on saving the Zhuangzu rather than Zhuang language must include active, society-wide policies to ensure that people are not relegated into a minority which is socially meaningful but invisible to the government because it ceases to be explicitly named in legal discourses.

Thus, on any of these options (and any more that readers or policy-makers may have in mind), future Zhuang language policy-makers should be prepared to confront and change beliefs about and markets for language. According to a leading theorist of language policy, Bernard Spolsky (2004: 222), "[u]nless the management [of language] is consistent with the language practices and beliefs, and with the other contextual forces that are at play, the explicit policy written in the constitution and laws is likely to have no [...] effect". This study has shown that beliefs about majority and minority languages are propagated and amplified by laws as well as by significant contextual factors such as the lack of policy support for Zhuang literacy, government and non-government social actors' practices of excluding Zhuang from most commercial, informational and circulating public texts and the regimentation of how language can appear in the landscape under linguascaping laws. These factors shape the practices and beliefs with which new language laws must be consistent in order to have effect, or those new laws have to very effectively reshape those practices and beliefs as their own foundation for operating.

If it is to protect Zhuang language, twenty-first century Zhuang language policy should aspire to change the behavior of more people in more places than previous policies, including people and places not traditionally associated with Zhuang, rather than apathetically avoiding engagement with changes in the significant contextual factors surrounding language governance. Zhuang (or any other official minority language) will be more likely to be sustained as a language in use and with social significance if reform is not limited only to language policy but rather comprehensive and inter-connected policy reform and investment.

I do not expect such reform to be a government priority in China any time soon, or indeed in any nation; this is a demanding vision for language policy. But I hope students like my interlocutor are thoughtful and active and take the institutions of language governance, their local laws and the nationwide freedom to use and development Zhuang and other minority languages as far as they can to order to keep minority languages in use, especially in cities.

11 General implications for language rights and policy research and practice

> *[I]f we do not understand how linguistic diversity intersects with social justice and if we are unable to even recognize disadvantage and discrimination on the basis of language, we will not be able to work towards positive change.* (Piller 2017)

Legal discourses typically have high symbolic power relative to other discourses shaping ideas of what it means to have (linguistic) justice. The legal discourses surrounding China's constitutional minority language right envisage and legitimize only certain claims to linguistic justice. This linguistic justice does not include the free use of forms other than Standard Zhuang. Writing Standard Zhuang – *Zhuangwen* – has long been constructed by policy as the culturally developed form of usage but not actually widely taught, so language policy does not seem to legitimize any substantive claim to the equally free use of Standard Zhuang by all. Moreover, state protections or support for people to use Zhuang are not framed as legitimate if the people are outside concentrated communities of Zhuang speakers, even within GZAR and even under the newest laws, the *GZAR Regulations*. This is significant because it means policy interventions in cities, where Zhuang speakers are less concentrated, are beyond the normative scope of the constitutional freedom to use and develop Zhuang.

The book has emphasized that the constitutional minority language right, rather than being operative or a discursive resource for Zhuang's speakers and protectors, is a discursive resource of those governing. Now, it legitimizes as linguistic justice the documentation and archiving of the linguistic and cultural patrimony of Zhuang speakers in ways that further marginalize Zhuang language in the socio-linguistic order by further decoupling it from contemporary life. This raises themes of relevance to all contexts of language policy: what linguistic justice is and whether heritage-focused language policy is just. The following two sections take up these themes, first responding to Leung's (2019) important, recent theorization of linguistic justice, and then critiquing the nationalization of heritage. In both sections readers will find echoes of critiques of colonization and coloniality. Coloniality is not a mainstream frame for talking about and analyzing the PRC and the extent to which it would be useful is a project beyond the scope of this book, but that is a project I am not alone in being curious to pursue (e.g. Roche and Leibold 2020; Roche, Leibold and Hillman 2020). In the book's final section, I reflect on a third theme of wide relevance: the methodological, theoretical and policy-making implications of this study's lived landscape approach and its findings.

11.1 Linguistic justice

This study illustrates a strong language policy orientation towards the symbolic valorization of minority languages. As part of this, China has a language rights regime which relies on law as a norm-forming discourse, not so much for the legal pathways it creates. To my mind, this is a significant characteristic of the Chinese language governance framework, without which it cannot be properly understood. I believe there will be other cases around the world where foregrounding this orientation is also analytically useful. In a well-timed publication about other nations' language policy regimes, Leung (2019) offers a label which I will apply to this orientation: *symbolic jurisprudence*, which is neither inherently good/just/moral nor bad/unjust/immoral. Leung's work traces the causes of the now global phenomenon of official state multilingualism, and some of its consequences, particularly in liberal states and particularly for access to legal processes and the interpretation of laws made in multiple, theoretically equally-authoritative languages. The following discussion is a complement to Leung's work, a conversation grounded in this empirical study of official *minority* languages and multilingualism in China, which are topics her book carves out. Leung (2019: 44, 71) surveys only China's official bilingualism in the Special Administrative Regions of Hong Kong (Chinese and English) and Macau (Chinese and Portuguese), and acknowledges multilingualism on the Mainland only in terms of the diversity of Mandarin dialects. She avoids China's minority language regime because her project is not concerned with sub-national official multilingualism. However, China's minority languages *are* officially recognized even at the national level. But they are officially *minority* languages. Most of the other nations with official multilingualism that Leung considers do not have an official language hierarchy, but multiple, formally equal official languages. An official language hierarchy like China's disrupts the theorization of equality in multilingual legal orders, and indeed the following reflection is just the first step in the extension of Leung and others' theories of linguistic justice which could springboard from this and other studies of China.

As with the many nations Leung surveys, China uses its *Constitution* as the primary means of endowing a language with status: it does so for both Putonghua and official minority languages. The Chinese case therefore supports Leung's (2019: 258) observation that "language still lies at the heart of national narratives". This book has delved into long-standing tensions in those narratives, and their interplay with China's current changes. China's deepest national narrative tensions are between unity and diversity, and (linguistic) equality and development. It is in this respect, however, that China departs from the taxonomy of equality that Leung (2019: 254–259) applies and from which application she concludes that multilingual legal orders offer "shallow equality", being neither difference-blind nor difference-aware. Difference-aware, or substantive, equality seeks to equalize people or groups who begin from different levels or types of disadvantage, and thus may precipitate preferential policies. This describes the Chinese approach to the minority minzu vis-à-vis each other and vis-à-vis the Hanzu majority, although the book has noted current, second generation minzu policy debates in China which seek to depart from the difference-aware pursuit of equality. In acknowledging that China has preferential language and other policies, I am not arguing that all inequalities in access to the national language (Putonghua) are equalized, or that such equalization is even attempted by policy. The ongoing prejudice against "Pinched Zhuang" (the way first-language Zhuang speakers typically speak Mandarin), for example, is a difference in access to the linguistic *and social and symbolic* resources of Putonghua of which policy seems unaware. The right to learn Putonghua, and Putonghua promotion policies overall, are already largely difference-blind. Moreover, the difference-aware educational pathways to Putonghua which responded to differing needs are being dismantled across China, for example in Inner Mongolia (Baioud 2020). Rather, like many other national standard languages before it, Putonghua is now considered by policy-makers a "purely referential medium of communication available to all for the conduct of common affairs and the government of the nation, thus, in principle, affording to all who can acquire such a medium the (at least theoretical) possibility to take part without the burdensome interference of social or geographic provenance" (Costa et al. 2018: 5). But Hu (2012, with Alsagoff 2010) has shown inequality in access to Putonghua education, particularly for the minority minzu. Moreover, social or geographic provenance and other categories of distinction remain socially significant – some, like class, are *increasing* in significance in China, as Tomba 2014 argues – keeping variations in Putonghua as far from neutral, pure referentiality as language has always been. We can look to the extensive literature on World Englishes to see an analogy of vast linguistic inequality amongst people who all speak "the same" language (e.g. Kachru 1985; Piller and Grey 2019: 6–9). Formally equal access to Putonghua is a shallow justice.

Leung contrasts difference-aware regimes of multilingualism with those that legally recognize languages as "a mechanism of establishing and maintaining distinctiveness, based on a politics of recognition". But China's language regime aims at both. With the two fundamental tensions described above, language rights and policies since the inception of the PRC have been unsteadily strained between both difference-aware equality for languages and their speakers (albeit limited to languages of the official 56 minzu) *and* actively partaking in a politics of recognition which moves against the previous non-recognition and oppression of certain peoples. This politics of recognition is itself difference-aware, an explicit attempt to rectify the historic difference in different groups' cultural and political capital through the investment of the symbolic resources of the state. I do not believe this parallel pursuit of difference-aware equality and political recognition of marginalized ethno-linguistic identities is unique to China or to political systems like China. What is particular about China and systems like it is the inability to reconcile these competing aims through popular and participatory processes.

Yet despite China not fitting neatly into Leung's theorization, Leung's study and mine align closely in concluding that "the dependence on legal intervention for the vitality of minority languages is a worrying trend [...] considering the misalignment between the motivations of law-making and the needs of language communities" (Leung 2019: 251). The key misalignment Leung addresses is legal frameworks "handling group-based demands as a matter of individual rights", the perennial bug-bear of liberal accounts of minority rights. That is not China's problem. Rather, it is the absence actionable or enforceable language rights for either individuals or groups because the constitutional minority language right is a normative declaration as opposed to a right that citizens can enforce against the state. Moreover, China *does* handle language demands as group-based in the way it organizes political participation and representation through the 56 recognized ethno-linguistic groups. In China's case, the misalignment arises from the lack of coordination, power, representation and accountability in the language governance structure. This is why I conclude that legal intervention is not reliable for maintaining minority language vitality in China today. Thus, I come from a different direction but to the same point as Leung (2019: 251): "existing institutions dispossess minority speakers of [agency] in favor of a bureaucrat acting as their spokesperson". Not only do bureaucrats acting as spokespeople dispossess diverse peoples in China of agency in defining, representing and controlling their language and culture, these bureaucrats then have very little power themselves in the Chinese language governance structure, as Chapter Five shows.

The problems that led me to the conclusion that minority speakers in China are disposed of agency may also be problems in liberal systems, in addition to the individualized group rights problem. Moreover, this study has revealed that legal intervention is unreliable because law is just one discourse interacting with multiple agents, discourses and ideologies. On a Bourdieusian view of law as discourse and/or on the basis of evidence in this study, law should be considered an *inherently* unpredictable tool of language policy in any legal system.

China is not a nation in which formal linguistic equality masks a "refus[al] to commit to any substantive redistribution of resources for marginalized communities", a problem which Leung (2019: 257) and others identify elsewhere and against which their prescribed safeguards are "the enhanced autonomy of minority groups and their political representation". But China does lack such safeguards and so there will be little recourse when Chinese minority language policy stops redistributing resources and abandons any further pursuit of multilingual equality. Does this mean China must have such safeguards in order to achieve linguistic justice? Such safeguards are unrealistic. Could there be other, socially-situated safeguards instead? This is a question for further theorization; is linguistic justice impossible within "democratic socialism" i.e. the Chinese political framework? If linguistic justice is possible only within liberal frameworks, then it must be vulnerable to the same claims of ahistoric fallacy as liberalism. What is the suitability to places like China of alternative theories of linguistic justice, such as Todd's (2013, 2015) proposition of linguistic reparative justice to provide both acknowledgement of harm and a form of resource redistribution when languages can no longer be viably recovered, and is the suitability different in liberal democracies?

Is a social justice frame more helpful than a linguistic justice frame? A key work on this, Ingrid Piller's (2016) *Linguistic Diversity and Social Justice*, which the epigraph describes, "draws on the work of the philosopher Nancy Fraser and conceives of social justice as constituted along three dimensions, namely, economic redistribution, cultural recognition and political representation" but explains how linguistic diversity is integral in all three dimensions (Piller 2017). Readers will be able to look back over this book, or even just to my "letter to twenty-first century language policy-makers" in Chapter Ten and see my own focus on linguistic diversity in those three dimensions in a Chinese context. The findings and analysis relating to economic redistribution and cultural recognition are likely to echo across political economies. This book's analysis of political representation may seem less relevant to liberal democratic contexts because this is the dimension in which the China context diverges most. However, I urge readers to think carefully about this Chinese counterpoint and the generalizable problems with representation that this study identifies: fractured responsibility across institutions; lack of participation by minority language speakers in both legislative and administrative law-making, and lack of accountability to them; incomplete devolution of legal power; and the locus of power being somewhere other than where the law says it is. Recall that my critique of the representation of Zhuang interests in Chapter Five began with a quotation from Leung's (2019) critique of the bureaucratization of language governance in liberal democracies that was deeply resonant with the Chinese case.

Leung (2019: 252) concludes that standardization of a language can "threaten the perception of authenticity" (akin to Costa et al. 2018: 2). This study likewise shows that it can, but that it does not always; we have heard perspectives accepting as well as disputing the authenticity of cultural practices and representations in Romanized Standard Zhuang in Chapter Eight. Standard Zhuang has certainly attracted some "variety shifting [i.e.] the association of a group's acts of identity with the supradialectal norm" (Costa et al. 2018: 3) amongst Zhuang speakers and particularly writers, but the study has also shown the lightening-rod affordance of Romanized Standard Zhuang in the construction of anti-establishment Zhuang identities.

However, there is nothing in this study to support Leung's conclusion that "official use of a language necessitates its standardization". Costa et al. (2018) problematize the origins of that assumption, while Deumert and Mabandla (2018: 218) remind us that standardization is tool of (colonial) domination over alleged "epistemological disobedience" (quoting Walter Mignolo). It is through a legal construction of officialization as standardization that law often incites this misrecognition, by which I mean legitimating the creation or sustenance of a power relationship such that it is seen to be the objective nature or order of things even by those it disempowers (following Bourdieu 1987; see Chapter One-1.3). Moreover, as I have argued previously, standardization has not future-proofed Zhuang language (Grey in press). I therefore caution against the reproduction of standard language ideology in academic discourses. The more important question, to my mind, is whether "access to the public sphere" (Costa et al. 2018: 16) necessitates standardization; or better still, asking how that access can be facilitated *without* the double-edged sword of language standardization.

Overall, Leung's (2019) work exposes the "shallow" reality of liberal, equality-centered philosophies of linguistic justice. On one view, this study contributes an illustration of the shallow reality of an illiberal but also equality-centered philosophy of linguistic justice. But on another view, it has exposed how ideas of justice are shaped in dynamic and interdiscursive processes in which the state's institutions, laws, public landscapes and individuals participate unequally without seeking to test whether or not any abstract philosophy of linguistic justice is made real in China. That, I believe, is this book's most important contribution to scholarship on linguistic justice, but pointing out that illiberal systems can also have foundational language rights which are in some important ways similar to international and liberal nations' language rights, and similarly vulnerable or weak, is also a useful contribution. This work follows Piller's (2016: 5, 2017) "pragmatic approach that is not concerned with 'perfect justice'", but it nevertheless seeks to prompt further critical theorization on what justice may be in relation to languages and their speakers.

11.2 The nationalization of heritage

In addition to the orientation towards symbolic jurisprudence which I have noted in Chinese language governance, Shen and Gao (2019) make a convincing argument that the new, national Yubao Language Protection project, introduced in Chapter One, has a "resource orientation" (using the three orientations of Ruiz 1984; see also Li 2015). It turns languages into both commercial and heritage resources (sometimes both). However, as they warn, rather than being a fundamental shift in revaluing linguistic diversity, this could be a "makeshift delay tactic in response to linguistic diversity that is essentially seen as a problem" (p. 4). Moreover, I argue that within the ideological frame of developmentalism, this resource orientation manifests differently to the way other studies present it. Not all languages are constructed as equally resourceful under Yubao. Rather, only certain languages are resources for development (because they assist international trade, mainly) and therefore worthy of significant investment; these are generally not the official minority languages. Moreover, developmentalism reshapes the field of culture, introducing an ideological structure of developed and less developed cultural practices. This has particularly affected minority languages. Thus, even as cultural resources, the value of minority languages under the Yubao policy lies in their conversion into stable, displayable written artefacts and performances. Moreover, a developmentalist resource orientation rewards and invests in the standardization of culture as a recognizable product. This developmentalist ideology is likely not unique to the PRC; I believe this reflection on its implication for resource oriented language policy can helpfully expand our general theories of language policy.

This brings me to the subject of the nationalization of cultural capital through policies of heritage preservation, which is a subject of wide relevance as language policies around the world often engage in heritage preservation. It is, arguably, the newest of the challenges facing China's minority languages. Within this Zhuang case study, I have shown the trend emerging in regional and municipal laws and practices, particularly as regards the government's selective use of written Zhuang in public linguistic landscapes and the interdiscursive, public representations of "Zhuangness" absent of people "doing" language (see Chapter Seven). Looking back over the many data relevant to this point throughout the book, I now wish to emphasize the laws, policies and state practices which reform cultural practices into archives, museum artifacts and place-branding resources are nationalizing cultural capital. This heritage-focused turn in language policy may be intended by governing authorities to benefit individuals and the Zhuangzu group by taking over the responsibility for maintaining Zhuang language and making Zhuang culture (both the language and the knowledge it encodes) accessible to future generations at a time when more and more people face pressures that make it difficult and costly to pass Zhuang on themselves. In that sense, Yubao is a policy that is very responsive to the changes China is undergoing.

But if barely anyone has access to learning Zhuang literacy now, how accessible Zhuang heritage be? The government's reliance on Romanized Standard Zhuang as the key technology of cultural preservation *without* policies to create widespread access to that technology, in addition to the preservation of linguistic and non-linguistic emblems of Zhuangness that seem to have been constructed predominately by the state top-down, call into question what culture is being aided to survive. This approach marginalizes current and potential future users of Zhuang language both from the practices of Zhuang language and culture and from the meaning making associated with those practices. Further, Costa et al. (2018: 6) have shown that written media coming "to be part of the definition of legitimate knowledge" is inherent in standardization rooted in European traditions, and I have argued in Chapter One that these traditions, along with China's own tradition of written language standardization, merged in China's language policy. Against this ideological backdrop, preserving Zhuang heritage almost exclusively in written Standard Zhuang amplifies the disempowerment of the notional inheritors of Zhuang and the empowerment of the government in both defining and accessing that heritage.

Moreover, the distinction and profit from the practice or performance of Zhuang heritage come to be accrued by the government. Examples include the economic profit of deploying Zhuang heritage resources in government-operated tourism sites and museums, the political profit from localizing the government's identity through government-authored Zhuang signage in Nanning, and the place-making distinction gained through displaying Zhuang. This is a tricky issue, however. Heritage preservation is symbolically important as a mark of current government respect against a history of more obvious symbolic violence, and heritage preservation is also too expensive to achieve without government support. Moreover, for all my concerns about the government defining Zhuang language and culture and which practices are valuable, and then monopolizing those practices itself instead of facilitating individuals to use them, some people *do* identify with Standard Zhuang and other Zhuang icons used by the government, and see the government's efforts as useful in preserving their culture, especially when they will not be shut out because they are already literature in Standard Zhuang.

Moreover, this is tricky because government investment in Zhuang heritage – like funding museums and displaying bilingual street-name signage in Nanning – makes Zhuang linguistic heritage visible and accessible for people to use as a resource in constructing their own identities, even if they do not, or do not often or fluently, speak Zhuang themselves. This is particularly useful because the study found that an "imaginable" or "plausible" community of Zhuang speakers (to adopt Mullaney's 2011: 69–91 terms) was significant for many participants to the Zhuangzu remaining a meaningful social grouping even as they and people they knew stopped speaking Zhuang it. However, the study also found that the state's mobilization of Zhuang language as an emblem of the Zhuangzu is very limited and that is it subjectively invisible; some people do not notice when the government uses Zhuang in public. Further, the law does not dispute the classification of non-Zhuang speakers as Zhuangzu, concerning itself instead with parentage requirements. As such, the government's heritage maintenance efforts may be insufficient to keep an imagined Zhuang speaking community plausible over the lifetime of my university student participants.

And of course, this official canonization of Zhuang history reproduces the association between Standard Zhuang and Zhuang-speaking people, and the disassociation between the Zhuangzu and the Bouyeizu, despite Zhuang and Bouyei being arguably the same language as Chapter Two explained. However, the government's efforts to document and display aspects of Zhuang heritage continue to counter a previously widespread belief that people who did not speak Mandarin, including Zhuang speakers, were barbaric, uncultured and not part of the nation. The Zhuangzu social group will therefore likely keep drawing on this canonized heritage, but as living Zhuang language practices continue to shift, will the Zhuangzu people feel that this Zhuang heritage is theirs to embody?

11.3 Implications for policies of minority language display

The final implication affects both the study of linguistic landscapes and the advocacy or making of language policy. Through my lived landscape study, we started to see that public texts in Zhuang are not necessarily recognized – *or even recognizable* – as Zhuang. Public Zhuang was also sometimes interpreted as Putonghua or English, symbolizing quite different people and cultures. We started to see how this subjective invisibility of public Zhuang can arise from a habitus informed by multiple discourses and practices which marginalize Zhuang. Not least of those discourses are the public linguistic landscapes themselves, which remain largely Putonghua dominant even though a few types of signage now include Zhuang, as Chapter Six established. A linguistic habitus is formed in part through the environmental influence of living amongst these landscapes: their patterns "become an inescapable part of everyday life and, even if only tacitly, shape one's social and ethnolinguistic identity" (Hult 2014: 510; see also Dong and Blommaert 2009). The education system also contributes to the predisposition to not see Zhuang even when it is displayed. The study also reveals how government authorship of minority language signage can function to draw attention to political ironies, with that signage symbolizing the government rather than the Zhuangzu. Bilingual government signage in this study thus emplaced and foregrounded contested discourses evaluating official minority language and education policies. As government-authored, publicly displayed Zhuang is not seen as Zhuang, or is recognized and "read" as a symbol of the government's policy failings, I cannot agree with Li and Huang's (2004: 247) evaluation of the laws' encouragement of Zhuang on public signage as "symbolizing Zhuang's successful role in local politics".

These findings are in contrast to the presumption often made, in literature and actual language policies, that official displays of a minority language offer resources for constructing more positive and valorized minority identities and normatively challenge the marginality of that minority language *because they make that language publicly visible*. Official displays do not necessarily increase visibility. Thus, while government signage is theorized as having symbolic capital (Bourdieu 1991), my study concludes that we should not assume that increased respect or changed language behaviors will ensue from a government displaying a minority language in public.

In this respect, the book raises a question of relevance beyond the Zhuang case study: what is the point of language policies which focus on publicly displaying a written minority language, if such measures are likely to go unrecognized or to be perceived as invalid in that language ecology? By no means am I arguing against displaying minority languages. Rather, I am arguing that in most cases, other policy-led action is needed in addition to these displays in order to direct their symbolic meaning (see further Grey 2021b). I recommend that advocates and policy-makers answer the following questions for themselves, preferably on the basis of ethnographic research, before implementing policies: what else needs to be done in addition to publicly displaying this language to achieve the recognizability and readability of this language? Where will this language be displayed; on which texts, by and for whom, and what varied symbolic messages might these choices send?

Further, the theoretic implication of this subjectivity in viewing is a reminder that the separation of landscape signage into mobile or fixed, Language A or Language B etc is merely a heuristic to be avoided or, as in my study, supplemented, because in its lived experience signage slips outside these categories. In addition to including various actual subjective readings of the landscapes – and wishing I could have gone far further with that data collection – I have tried to analyze linguistic landscapes as semiotic aggregates and as having interdiscursive connections between sites in order to get closer to the way linguistic landscapes are experienced holistically.

These implications of the study are key reasons why it is important to include people's experiences of linguistic landscapes in language policy analyses: discourses in place afford situated meanings that may not be transparent to the researcher without ethnographic inquiry. By extension, investigating situated and dynamic meaning-making and use of policy is important to all language policy studies, not only to studies of linguistic landscapes. This reiterates the argument that Costa et al. (2018: 1) made recently about studying language standardization policy; their edited book also models how social-actor-centered language policy research can be done. My This study's ethnographic data, its triangulation of theory, and its lived linguistic landscape approach have enriched the analysis of China's language rights framework with social information. My lived landscape analysis, and the precursors outlined in Chapter Eight, echo the trend towards ethnographically-oriented language policy studies which I canvassed in Chapter One. However, the ethnographic turn within linguistic landscape studies and the very similar turn in language policy studies have not fully cinched together, and ethnographically-oriented studies specifically on language rights are lagging behind. Linguistic landscape studies have started to be integrated into studies about language policy in education and Coupland (2010) has modelled the integration of a linguistic landscape study into an ethnographically-oriented language policy analysis in his research on policy "from above" and "from below". Occasionally, the insights of linguistic landscape research into participants' perspectives have also been made directly relevant to language policy-makers. For example, Draper (2016) used questionnaires to investigate the public's desire for and expectations of new Isan language-inclusive public signage in one province of Thailand on behalf of local policy-makers.

This book closes with the argument that *lived* linguistic landscape studies not only *can* be integrated into language rights and polices studies, but that *it is important to integrate them*, especially in regards to public landscapes. This book seeks to provide critical, socially-situated linguistic research to inform language policy, and to encourage others to do the same.

Appendix

Table 2: Student participants' profiles.

S#	Pseudonym & minzu if not Zhuangzu	F/M	University the student attends (and was interviewed at, unless otherwise indicated)	Major, stage in summer 2014	Home (Province, area)	Speaks Zhuang (Y/N)	Interview details
1.	Monica	F	Yunnan Minzu University (YMU)	Zhuang Studies, undergraduate	Yunnan, Wenshan	Y	11.6.2014 Group Interview A
2.	Jane	F	YMU	Zhuang Studies, undergraduate	Yunnan, Wenshan	Y	11.6.2014 Group Interview B
3.	Louise	F	YMU	Zhuang Studies, undergraduate	Yunnan, Wenshan	Y	11.6.2014 Group Interview A
4.	Nola	F	YMU	Zhuang Studies, undergraduate	Yunnan, Wenshan	Y	11.6.2014 Group Interview B
5.	Tara	F	YMU	Zhuang Studies, undergraduate	Yunnan, Wenshan	Y	11.6.2014 Group Interview A
6.	Blaine	M	YMU	Zhuang Studies, undergraduate	Yunnan, Wenshan	Y	11.6.2014 Group Interview B
7.	Hoz	M	YMU	Political Science, Masters	Yunnan, Wenshan	Y	11.6.2014 Individual Interview C
8.	Damien	M	YMU	Zhuang Studies, undergraduate	Yunnan, Wenshan	Y	11.6.2014 Individual Interview D
9.	Jack	M	Yunnan University – interview at YMU	Materials Science, undergraduate	Yunnan, Wenshan	Y	15.6.2014 Group Interview E

Table 2 (continued)

S#	Pseudonym & minzu if not Zhuangzu	F/M	University the student attends (and was interviewed at, unless otherwise indicated)	Major, stage in summer 2014	Home (Province, area)	Speaks Zhuang (Y/N)	Interview details
10.	Fay	F	Guangxi University of Nationalities (GUN)	Zhuang Studies, undergraduate	GZAR, Laibin	Y	27.6.2014 Group Interview H
11.	Gina	F	GUN	Zhuang Studies, undergraduate	GZAR, Liuzhou	PARTIAL	27.6.2014 Group Interview H
12.	Luke	M	GUN	Zhuang Studies, undergraduate	GZAR, Guigang	Y	27.6.2014 Group Interview I
13.	Laurel	F	GUN	Zhuang Studies, undergraduate	GZAR, Nanning	Y	27.6.2014 Group Interview I
14.	Danielle	F	GUN	Zhuang Studies, undergraduate	GZAR, Hechi	Y	27.6.2014 Group Interview H
15.	Zeina	F	GUN	Zhuang Studies, Masters	GZAR, Wuming	Y	27.6.2014 Group Interview I
16.	Yana	F	GUN	Chinese, undergraduate	GZAR, Tiandeng	Y	27.6.2014 Group Interview G
17.	Goldie	F	GUN	Zhuang Studies, PhD	GZAR	Y	27.6.2014 Group Interview I
18.	Liz	F	Guangxi University (GU)	English, undergraduate	GZAR, Nanning	Y	27.6.2014 Group Interview J
19.	Mae – Yaozu	F	GU	English, undergraduate	GZAR, Laibin and Nanning	N	27.6.2014 Group Interview J

Table 2 (continued)

S#	Pseudonym & minzu if not Zhuangzu	F/M	University the student attends (and was interviewed at, unless otherwise indicated)	Major, stage in summer 2014	Home (Province, area)	Speaks Zhuang (Y/N)	Interview details
20.	Hope – Dongzu	F	GU`	English, undergraduate	GZAR, Liuzhou	Y	27.6.2014 Group Interview J
21.	Barbara	F	GU	Chinese, undergraduate	GZAR, Hechi	Y	17.6.2014 Group Interview F
22.	Mark	M	GU	Mathematics and Information Science, undergraduate	GZAR, Guilin	Y	17.6.2014 Group Interview G
23.	Dora	F	GU	Chinese, undergraduate	GZAR, Baise	Y	17.6.2014 Group Interview F
24.	Huw	M	GU	Mechanical engineering, undergraduate	GZAR, Guigang	Y	17.6.2014 Group Interview G
25.	Quentin	M	GU	Mechanical engineering, undergraduate	GZAR, Laibin	Y	17.6.2014 Group Interview F
26.	Sunny	F	GU	Accounting, undergraduate	GZAR, Hechi	Y	17.6.2014 Group Interview G
27.	Ivy	F	GU	Labour management, undergraduate	GZAR, Liuzhou	Y	17.6.2014 Group Interview G
28.	Norm	M	Peking University – interview at MUC	Thai, PhD	Yunnan, Wenshan	Y	30.6.2014 Group Interview K
29.	Yvonne	F	MUC	Zhuang Studies, Masters	Yunnan, Wenshan	Y	30.6.2014 Group Interview K

Table 2 (continued)

S#	Pseudonym & minzu if not Zhuangzu	F/M	University the student attends (and was interviewed at, unless otherwise indicated)	Major, stage in summer 2014	Home (Province, area)	Speaks Zhuang (Y/N)	Interview details
30.	Yazmin – Hanzu	F	MUC	Zhuang Studies, undergraduate	Yunnan, Wenshan	Y	30.6.2014 Group Interview L
31.	Lucy	F	MUC	Zhuang Studies, undergraduate	GZAR, Baise	Y	30.6.2014 Group Interview L
32.	Willow	F	MUC	Zhuang Studies, undergraduate	GZAR, Hechi	Y	30.6.2014 Group Interview L
33.	Farah	F	Inner Mongolia university of Science & Tech. (IMUST)	Law, undergraduate	GZAR, Nanning	N	2.7.2014 Group Interview M
34.	Penny	F	IMUST	English, undergraduate	GZAR, Nanning	Y	2.7.2014 Group Interview M
35.	Tansy – Hanzu	F	IMUST	Chinese, undergraduate	GZAR, Congzuo	Y	2.7.2014 Group Interview M
36.	Tom	M	IMUST	Finance, undergraduate	GZAR, Hechi	PARTIAL	2.7.2014 Group Interview N
37.	Morris	M	IMUST	Finance, undergraduate	GZAR, Hechi	Y	2.7.2014 Group Interview N
38.	Quinn	F	IMUST	Construction, undergraduate	GZAR, Laibin	Y	2.7.2014 Group Interview N

Table 2 (continued)

S#	Pseudonym & minzu if not Zhuangzu	F/M	University the student attends (and was interviewed at, unless otherwise indicated)	Major, stage in summer 2014	Home (Province, area)	Speaks Zhuang (Y/N)	Interview details
39.	Lloyd	M	IMUST	Law, undergraduate	GZAR, Wuming then Nanning	Y	2.7.2014 Group Interview N
40.	Una	F	The People's University of China (PUC)	Law, undergraduate	GZAR, Liuzhou	N	9.7.2014 Individual Interview O
41.	Zac	M	PUC	Digital and information systems, undergraduate	GZAR, Liuzhou	N	9.7.2014 Group Interview P
42.	Leroy	M	PUC	International economics and trade, undergraduate	GZAR, Guigang	Y	9.7.2014 Group Interview P
43.	Freddy	M	PUC	Accounting, undergraduate	GZAR, Nanning and Wuming	Y	9.7.2014 Group Interview P

Table 3: Language leader participants' profiles.

LL#	Minzu	Pseudonym	Interview Place and date	Profession/Role	Home province	Speaks Zhuang (Y/N)
1.	Naxizu	Mr A	Kunming (13.6.2014)	Translator/ trainer	Yunnan	N
2.	Zhuangzu	Mr B	Kunming (14.6.2014)	Zhuang Studies academic	GZAR	Y
3.	Zhuangzu	Mr C	Nanning (17.6.2014)	Linguistics academic / Zhuang language tutor	GZAR	Y
4.	Zhuangzu	Mr D	Nanning (17.6.2014) and Sydney (7.5.2015)	English & Putonghua teacher / Education Studies academic / Zhuang language singer-songwriter	GZAR	Y
5.	Hanzu	Mr E	Nanning (25.6.2014)	Zhuang language songwriter/researcher / Zhuang language tutor	GZAR	Y
6.	Zhuangzu	Mr F	Nanning (25.6.2014)	Education Studies / Zhuang Studies academic	GZAR	Y
7.	Zhuangzu	Mr G	Nanning (26.6.2014)	Zhuang language magazine editor	GZAR	Y
8.	Zhuangzu	Mr H	Nanning (joint interview with Mr G)	Zhuang language magazine co-editor	GZAR	Y
9.	Hanzu	Mr I	Nanning (27.6.2014)	Zhuang language singer-songwriter / GZAR State TV music role	Northern China	Partial
10.	Zhuangzu	Mr J	Nanning (joint interview with Mr I)	Policeman/ Zhuang language singer-songwriter	GZAR	Y
11.	Zhuangzu	Mr K	Nanning (28.6.2014)	Putonghua-Zhuang Translator	GZAR	Y
12.	Zhuangzu	Mr L	Beijing (30.6.2014)	Zhuang Studies academic	GZAR	Y

Table 3 (continued)

LL#	Minzu	Pseudonym	Interview Place and date	Profession/Role	Home province	Speaks Zhuang (Y/N)
13.	Zhuangzu	Mr M	Beijing (27.11.2014)	CASS Institute of Ethnology academic	Yunnan	Y
14.	Zhuangzu	Mr N	Beijing (30.7.2014)	Zhuangzu historian / documentary maker / teacher	GZAR	Y
15.	N/A	Mr O	Beijing (1.8.2014)	China Director of an international legal rights NGO	USA	N
16.	Hanzu	Mr P	Beijing (7.8.2014)	Chinese law academic	Heilongjiang	N
17.	Zhuangzu	Mr Q	Online, Nanning-Sydney (19–20.8.2014)	Activist/ Zhuang language tutor	GZAR	Y
18.	Unknown	Mr R	Online, Beijing-Sydney (29.1.2015)	Chinese political science researcher	China	N
19.	Zhuangzu	Mr S	Nanning (15.6.2015)	GZAR Local History Compilation Committee member	GZAR	Y
20.	Zhuangzu	Mr T	Nanning (16.6.2015)	Zhuang language folk singer/ GZAR State TV music role	GZAR	Y

Table 4: Student participants' places of origin and of university.

Place of origin (Province/Region/City-State)	Total number of students from each place of origin	University the students now attend (number of students at each university from each place of origin)
Yunnan Province	12	**Yunna Minzu University (YMU)**, Yunnan Province (8)
		Yunnan University (YU), Yunnan Province (1)
		Minzu University of China (MUC), Beijing (2)
		Peking University (PKU), Beijing (1)
Guangxi Zhuangzu Autonomous Region	31	**Guangxi University for Nationalities (GUN)**, GZAR (8)
		Guangxi University (GU), GZAR (10)
		Inner Mongolia University of Science and Technology (IMUST), Inner Mongolia Autonomous Region (7)
		MUC, Beijing (2)
		Renmin University of China (RUC), Beijing (4)

Acknowledgements

Many thanks to the many participants and contacts who loaned or gifted me otherwise hard to access bibliographic materials, including Messrs C, D, E, G and S; Pan Chaoyang, editor-in-chief of the *Guangxi Minzu Newspaper*; Dean Huang Binlan of Guangxi University; and Cathryn Yang of SIL International. Thanks also to Dean Yang Hongyan at Yunnan Minzu University, Guo Jian at Inner Mongolia University of Science and Technology, Professor Luo Yongxian at Melbourne University and Dean Wang Ge at Zhongnan University for Economics and Law for assisting me with initial fieldwork connections.

This project was funded by generous Research Extension Funding from the Macquarie University Department of Linguistics, National Library of Australia grants from the Australian National University's Centre on China in the World and the University of Sydney's China Studies Centre, and publishing support grants from the same China Studies Centre.

Drafts of this book were thoughtfully reviewed, discussed and proofread by many friends and family. Particular thanks to Dr Rosemary Grey; Dr David Houseman; Ian Grey; Dr Sofie Hongye Bai (Gegentuul Baioud); Dr Janette Wujian Han; Dr Li Jia; Dr Gerald Roche; Professor Marian Baird; Professor Ed Rubin; Professor David Atwill; Professor Elana Shohamy; Professor Lionel Wee; Professor Amita Batra; Professors Ofelia García and Francis Hult and the 2018 Joshua A. Fishman Award judging panel; this book's anonymous reviewer; Distinguished Professor Ingrid Piller and the Macquarie University Language on the Move Reading Group; the Sydney Law School Feedback Club; and the attendees of my Birkbeck Department of Applied Linguistics and Communication seminar and University of Sydney seminars in the Law School and Department of Linguistics.

Dr Alexandra Grey, April 2021
University of Technology Sydney, Faculty of Law,
Ultimo NSW 2007, Australia.

References

Reference list of legal sources

People's Republic of China

"Common Program"
    中国人民政治协商会议共同纲领 [Common Program of the Chinese People's Political Consultative Conference], 1949 (Chinese People's Political Consultative Conference).

"Constitution"
    中华人民共和国宪法 [Constitution of the People's Republic of China], 1982 (National People's Congress).People's Republic of China Constitution (Authorized English Translation)

"1978 Constitution"
    中华人民共和国宪法 [Constitution of the People's Republic of China], 1978 (National People's Congress).

"1975 Constitution"
    中华人民共和国宪法 [Constitution of the People's Republic of China], 1975 (National People's Congress).

"1954 Constitution"
    中华人民共和国宪法 [Constitution of the People's Republic of China], 1954 (National People's Congress).

"Constitution of the CPC"
    中国共产党章程 [Constitution of the Communist Party of China], 2007 (National Congress of the Communist Party of China).

"Criminal Law"
    中华人民共和国刑法 [Criminal Law of the People's Republic of China], 1979 (National People's Congress).

"Criminal Procedure Law"
    中华人民共和国刑事诉讼法 [Criminal Procedure Law of the People's Republic of China], 1979 (National People's Congress).

"CPPCC Charter"
    中国人民政治协商会议章程 [Charter of the Chinese People's Political Consultative Conference], 1982 (Chinese People's Political Consultative Conference).

"Education Law"
    中华人民共和国教育法 [Education Law of the People's Republic of China], 1995 (National People's Congress).

"Electoral Law"
    中华人民共和国全国人民代表大会和地方各级人民代表大会选举法 Electoral Law of the National People's Congress and Local People's Congresses of the People's Republic Of China, 1979 (National People's Congress).

"GZAR Regulations"
    广西壮族自治区少数民族语言文字工作条例 [GZAR Minority Language Work Regulations], 2018 (GZAR People's Congress).

"Interim Provisions"
: 南宁市社会用字管理暂行规定 [Nanning Municipality Social Word Use Management Interim Provisions], 2004 (Nanning Municipal People's Government).

"Legislative Interpretation Law"
: 中华人民共和国立法法 [Legislation Law of the People's Republic of China], 2000 (National People's Congress).

"Nanning Measures"
: 南宁市壮文社会使用管理办法 [Management measures for Social Use of Zhuangwen in Nanning], 2013 (Nanning Municipal People's Government).

"Putonghua Law"
: 中华人民共和国国家通用语言文字法 [Law of the People's Republic of China on the Standard Spoken and Written Chinese Language], 2000 (Standing Committee of the National People's Congress).

"Regional Autonomy Law"
: 中华人民共和国民族区域自治法 Law of the People's Republic of China on Regional National Autonomy, 1984 (Standing Committee of the National People's Congress).

"Yunnan Ordinance"
: 云南省少数民族语言文字工作条例 [Yunnan Province Minority Minzu Language and Script Work Ordinance], 2013 (Yunnan People's Congress).

International

Declaration on the rights of persons belonging to national or ethnic, religious and linguistic minorities,1992. adopted by the UN General Assembly on 18 December, 1992, without a vote[1], by resolution No. 47/135.

Vienna Convention on Road Signs and Signals, opened for signature 8 November 1968, 1091 UNTS 3 (enetered into force 6 June 1978).

International Covenant on Civil and Political Rights, opened for signature 16 December 1966, 999 UNTS 171 (enetered into force 23 March 1976).

Cases

阿苏尔且、吉达达果与阿说尔几、阿说日木盗窃罪二审刑事裁定书, 辽宁省大连市中级人民法院 刑事裁定书 （2017）辽02刑终86号 [Second Instance Criminal Verdict of Azurchi, Jeddah Dago, Ashuorji and Ashuori for Theft, Intermediate People's Court of Dalian City, Liaoning Province Criminal ruling (2017) Liao 02 Xing Zhong No. 86] (published 27 September 2017) *China Judgements Online* http://wenshu.court.gov.cn/website/wenshu/181107ANFZ0BXSK4/index.html?docId=9ff8c9d854574bd2b147a7fa016a918c

Reference list of secondary sources

Adamson, Bob & Feng Anwei. 2009. A comparison of trilingual education policies for ethnic minorities in China. *Compare: A Journal of Comparative and International Education* 39 (3). 321–333.

Agence France-Presse. 2012. Crackdown on China workers' rights groups. *New Straits Times*. http://www.nst.com.my/latest/crackdown-on-China-workers-rights-groups-1.141732. Archived at https://www.worldlabour.org/engs/node/531/. (2 September 2020).

Ager, Simon. 2016. Zhuang language and alphabet. *Omniglot: the online encyclopedia of writing systems and languages*. https://omniglot.com/writing/zhuang.htm (2 September 2020).

Ager, Simon. 2018. Bouyei (Haasqyaix). *Omniglot*. https://omniglot.com/writing/bouyei.htm (2 September 2020).

Anderson, Benedict. 1991. *Imagined communities: Reflections on the origin and spread of nationalism*. London & New York, NY: Verso.

Anderson, Benedict. 2006. *Imagined Communities: Reflections on the Origin and Spread of Nationalism*. 2nd ed. London and New York: Verso.

Anderson, Benedict. 2011. Foreword. In Thomas Mullaney (ed.), *Coming to terms with the nation: Ethnic classification in modern China* (Asia: Local Studies / Global Themes 18), xv–xx. Berkeley & Los Angeles, CA: University of California Press.

Anon. 2016a. Rich province, poor province. *The Economist*, 421 (1 October 2016). 41–42.

Anon. 2016b. 民政部: 将重点清理"洋地名"等乱象 [Ministry of Civil Affairs: We Will Focus on Cleaning Up the Mess of 'Foreign Place Names' Etc]. *新京报* [The Beijing News]. Beijing: Beijing News Agency.

Anon. 2016c. Guangxi Department of Education. *Shared Encyclopedia* http://www.et97.com/view/5912381.htm (4 October 2016).

Anon. 2019. China to issue new RMB bills in August. *The People's Daily Online* http://en.people.cn/n3/2019/0429/c90000-9573899.html (24 October 2020).

Appadurai, Arjun. 2006. *Fear of Small Numbers: An Essay on the Geography of Anger*. Durham and London: Duke University Press.

Arnstein, Sherry R. 1969. A ladder of citizen participation. *Journal of the American Institute of Planners* 35 (4). 216–224.

Asher, R. E. & Christopher Moseley (eds.). 2007. *Atlas of the world's languages*, 2nd edn. London & New York, NY: Routledge.

Backhaus, Peter. 2007. *Linguistic landscapes: A comparative study of urban multilingualism in Tokyo*. Clevedon: Multilingual Matters.

Baioud, Gegentuul (Bai Hongye). 2018. *Performing linguistic and cultural authenticity: Contemporary Mongolian wedding ceremonies in Inner Mongolia*. Sydney: Macquarie University PhD thesis.

Baioud, Gegentuul (Bai Hongye). 2020. Will education reform wipe out Mongolian language and culture? *Language on the Move*. https://www.languageonthemove.com/will-education-reform-wipe-out-mongolian-language-and-culture/#comments (30 August 2020).

Baidu. 2019. 中华人民共和国国家民族事务委员会 [National Ethnic Affairs Commission of the PRC]. https://baike.baidu.com/item/%E4%B8%AD%E5%8D%8E%E4%BA%BA%E6%B0%91%E5%85%B1%E5%92%8C%E5%9B%BD%E5%9B%BD%E5%AE%B6%E6%B0%91%E6%97%8F%E4%BA%8B%E5%8A%A1%E5%A7%94%E5%91%98%E4%BC%9A/3700504?from

title=%E5%9B%BD%E5%AE%B6%E6%B0%91%E6%97%8F%E4%BA%8B%E5%8A%A1%
E5%A7%94%E5%91%98%E4%BC%9A&fromid=2278337 (Renders as https://baike.baidu.
com/item/中国人民共和国国家民族事务委员会/3700504?fromtitle=国家人民事务委员会&
fromid=2278337.) (2 September 2020).
Baines, Donna & Ian Cunningham. 2013. Using comparative perspective rapid ethnography in international case studies: Strengths and challenges. *Qualitative Social Work* 12 (1), 73–88.
Bakhtin, M. M. 1981. Discourse in the novel. In Michael Holquist (ed.), *The dialogic imagination: Four essays*, 259–422. Austin, TX: University of Texas.
Banda, Felix & Hambaba Jimaima. 2015. The semiotic ecology of linguistic landscapes in rural Zambia. *Journal of Sociolinguistics* 19 (5). 643–670.
Barlow, Jeffrey. 1989. The Zhuang minority in the ming era. *Ming Studies* 1989 (1). 15–45.
Barlow, Jeffrey. 2011. 壮族：他们的历史文化与民族性 [The Zhuangzu: their history, culture and minzu form]. Nanning: Guangxi Minzu Press.
Barmé, Geremie (ed.). 2012. *China story yearbook 2012: Red rising red eclipse*. Canberra: Australian Centre on China in the World, The Australian National University.
Beckett, Gulbahar H. & Gerard A. Postiglione (eds.). 2012. *China's assimilationist language policy*. London & New York, NY: Routledge.
Beckett, Gulbahar H., & Gerard A. Postiglione. 2012. China's language policy for indigenous and minority education. In Gulbahar H. Beckett & Gerard A. Postiglione (eds.), *China's assimilationist language policy*, 3–17. London & New York, NY: Routledge.
Ben-Rafael, Eliezer, Elana Shohamy, Muhammad Hasan Amara & Nira Trumper-Hecht. 2006. Linguistic landscape as symbolic construction of the public space: The case of Israel. *International Journal of Multilingualism* 3 (1). 7–30.
Benhabib, Seyla. 2002. *The claims of culture: Equality and diversity in the global era*. Princeton, NJ: Princeton University Press.
Benney, Jonathan. 2013. *Defending rights in contemporary China: Reserving the right* (Routledge/Asian Studies Association of Australia East Asian 12). London & New York, NY: Routledge.
Bian, Aidi. 2019. New Gaokao in Zhejiang China: Carrying on with Challenges. *International Education News* https://internationalednews.com/2019/03/06/new-gaokao-in-zhejiang-china-carrying-on-with-challenges/ (12 October 2020).
Bishop, Bill. 2020. The Fifth Plenum. *Sinocism* https://sinocism.com/p/the-fifth-plenum?token=eyJ1c2VyX2lkIjoyMDIzNywicG9zdF9pZCI6MTU4ODU3MDAsIl8iOiJPa1BJYiIsImlhdCI6MTYwNDAyMzg4NSwiZXhwIjoxNjA0MDI3NDg1LCJpc3MiOiJwdWItMiIsInN1YiI6InBvc3QtcmVhY3Rpb24ifQ.YP_JrFd7sE4qbEwzNWWy6-C0dvpp42TXI6odClBAmwo (30 October 2020).
Blachford, Dongyan Ru. 2004. Language spread versus language maintenance: Policy making and implementation process. In Zhou Minglang & Sun Hongkai (eds.), *Language policy in the People's Republic of China: Theory and practice since 1949* (Language Policy 4), 99–122. Boston, MA: Kluwer Academic Publishers.
Blommaert, Jan. 2004. Rights in places. In Jane Freeland & Donna Patrick (eds.), *Language rights and language survival*, 55–65. Manchester: St Jerome Publishing.
Blommaert, Jan. 2007. Sociolinguistic scales. *Intercultural Prgamatics* 4 (1). 1–19.
Blommaert, Jan. 2016. Superdiversity and the neoliberal conspiracy. *Ctrl+Alt+Dem* https://alternative-democracy-research.org/2016/03/03/superdiversity-and-the-neoliberal-conspiracy/ (31 August 2020).

Blommaert, Jan. 2013. *Ethnography, superdiversity and linguistic landscapes: Chronicles of complexity*. Bristol: Multilingual Matters.
Blommaert, Jan (ed.). 1999. *Language ideological debates*. Berlin & New York, NY: Mouton de Gruyter.
Blommaert, Jan & Ad Backus. 2013. Superdiverse repertoires and the individual. In Ingrid de Saint-Georges & Jean-Jacques Weber (eds.), *Multilingualism and multimodality: Current challenges for educational studies*, 11–32. Rotterdam: Sense Publishers.
Blommaert, Jan & Dong Jie. 2010. *Ethnographic fieldwork: A beginner's guide*. Bristol: Multilingual Matters.
Blommaert, Jan & Ben Rampton. 2011. Language and superdiversity. *Diversities* 13 (2). 1–22.
Blommaert, Jan, Elina Westinen & Sirpa Leppänen. 2014. Further notes on sociolinguistic scales. *Tilburg Papers in Culture Studies* (Volume 89) https://www.tilburguniversity.edu/sites/default/files/download/TPCS_89_Blommaert-Westinen-Leppanen_2.pdf (1 September 2020).
Bodomo, Adams. 2010. Documentation and revitalization of the Zhuang language and culture of southwestern China through linguistic fieldwork. *Diaspora, Indigenous, and Minority Education: Studies of Migration, Integration, Equity, and Cultural Survival* 4 (3). 179–191.
Bodomo, Adams & Pan Yanqin. 2007. *A proficiency course in Zhuang: Fieldwork documentation and revitalization of a language and culture of southwestern China*. Hong Kong: Linguistic Society of Hong Kong.
Bourdieu, Pierre. 1977a. The economics of linguistic exchanges. *Social Science Information* 16 (1), 645–688.
Bourdieu, Pierre. 1977b. Sur le pouvoir symbolique. *Annales. Histoire, Sciences Sociales* 32 (3). 405–441.
Bourdieu, Pierre. 1984[1979]. *Distinction: A social critique of the judgement of taste* (Richard Nice, Trans.). Cambridge, MA: Harvard University Press.
Bourdieu, Pierre. 1987. The force of law: Toward a sociology of the juridical field. *The Hastings Law Journal* 38 (July). 814–853.
Bourdieu, Pierre. 1991. *Language and symbolic power*. Cambridge: Polity Press.
Bradley, David 2009. Language policy for China's minorities: Orthography development for the Yi. *Written Language & Literacy* 12 (2). 170–187.
Caldwell, David. 2017. Printed t-shirts in the linguistic landscape. *Linguistic Landscape* 3 (2). 122–148.
Cartier, Carolyn. 2015a. Territorial urbanization and the party-state in China. *Territory, Politics, Governance* 3 (3). 294–320.
Cartier, Carolyn. 2015b. Urban, mobile and global. In Geremie Barmé, Linda Jarvin & Jane Goldkorn (eds.), *China year book 2014: Shared destiny*, 206–225. Canberra: ANU Press.
CCTV. n.d. 壮语新闻[Zhuang language news]. *China Central Television*. http://tv.cntv.cn/videoset/C14051 (29 September 2016).
Chaisingkananont, Somrak. 2014. *The quest for Zhuang identity: Cultural politics of promoting the Buluotou cultural festival in Guangxi, China*. Singapore: National University of Singapore PhD thesis.
Chan, Kam Wing. 2013. China, internal migration. In Immanuel B. Ness (ed.), *The Encyclopedia of global human migration*. Oxford: Wiley-Blackwell.
Chang, Chi-Yun (ed). 1968. *Encyclopedic dictionary of the Chinese language* (Volume 39 Index 1). Taiwan: Institute for Advanced Chinese Studies.

Chen, Hailun. 2005. 广西语言文字使用情况调查报告 [Report on the investigation into the circumstances of language and script usage in Guangxi]. In Chen Hailun & Li Lianjin (eds.), 广西语言文字使用问题调查与研究 [Investigation and research on the subject of the usage of Guangxi languages and scripts], 16–23. Nanning: Guangxi Education Press.

Chen, Hailun & Li Lianjin (eds.). 2005. 广西语言文字使用问题调查与研究 [Investigation and research on the subject of the usage of Guangxi languages and scripts]. Nanning: Guangxi Education Press.

Chen, Hailun & Wang Liping. 2005. 广西少数民族母语使用现状及趋势分析 [Status quo and development trend of the use of ethnic mother tongue in Guangxi]. In Chen Hailun & Li Lianjin (eds.), 广西语言文字使用问题调查与研究 [Investigation and research on the subject of the usage of Guangxi languages and scripts, 49–55. Nanning: Guangxi Education Press.

Chen, Xiaoxiao. 2016. Linguascaping the other: Travelogues' representations of Chinese languages. *Multilingua* 35 (5).

China-ASEAN Expo Secretariat. 2016. *The China-ASEAN Expo Bulletin*. http://eng.caexpo.org/html/news/Notice/ (2 September 2020).

China Encyclopedia Compilation Group. 2008. Ethic minorities. In State Council Information Office of the PRC (ed.), *China Encyclopedia (English Version)* (Vol. 5. 38–63). Beijing: China Intercontinental Press.

Chinafolio (Cartographer). 2016. *Guangxi province*. http://www.Chinafolio.com/provinces/guangxi-province/ (2 September 2020).

Chou, Bruce. 2010. Nanning Street Sign. *Nanning Here blog* http://www.nanninghere.com/nanning-street-sign (6 October 2015).

Chung, Kimmy. 2018. Top beijing official Li Fei to lead newly renamed Constitution and Law Committee. *South China Morning Post*. https://www.scmp.com/news/hong-kong/politics/article/2136898/top-beijing-official-li-fei-lead-newly-renamed-law-and (2 September 2020).

Clyne, Michael. 2005. *Australia's language potential*. Sydney: UNSW Press.

Cohen, Jerome A. 2015. Establish Yourself at Thirty: My Decision to Study China's Legal System. *Chinese (Taiwan) Yearbook of International Law and Affairs* 33. 1–10.

Cole, Matthew A., Robert J. R. Elliott, & Zhang Jing. 2009. Corruption, governance and FDI location in China: A province-level analysis. *Journal of Development Studies* 45 (9). 1494–1512.

Costa, James. 2013. Language endangerment and revitalisation as elements of regimes of truth: Shifting terminology to suit perspective. *Journal of Multilingual and Multicultural Development* 34 (4). 317–331.

Costa, James, Haley De Korne and Pia Lane. 2018. Standardising Minority Languages: Reinventing Peripheral Languages in the 21st Century. In Pia Lane, James Costa and Haley De Korne (eds.) *Standardizing Minority Languages Competing Ideologies of Authority and Authenticity in the Global Periphery*. New York, NY: Routledge. 1–23.

Coupland, Nikolas. 2001. Introduction: Sociolinguistic theory and social theory. In Nikolas Coupland, Srikant Sarangi & Christopher Candlin (eds.), *Sociolinguistics and social theory*, 1–26. Harlow & New York, NY: Longman.

Coupland, Nikolas. 2010. Welsh linguistic landscapes 'from above' and 'from below'. In Adam Jaworski & Crispin Thurlow (eds.), *Semiotic landscapes: Language, image, space*, 77–101. London: Continuum.

Coupland, Nikolas. 2012. Bilingualism on display: The framing of Welsh and English in Welsh public spaces. *Language in Society* 41 (1). 1–27.
Coupland, Nikolas. 2014. Language, society and authenticity: Themes and perspectives. In Véronique Lacoste, Jakob Leingruber & Thiemo Breyer (eds.), *Indexing authenticity: Sociolinguistic perspectives*. Berlin: De Gruyter.
Cox, Wendell. 2011. China: Urbanizing and moving east: 2010 Census. *New Geography* https://www.newgeography.com/content/002218-china-urbanizing-and-moving-east-2010-census (2 September 2020).
Dal Negro, Sylvia. 2009. Local policy and modeling the linguistic landscape. In Elana Shohamy & Dirk Gorter (eds.), *Linguistic landscape: Expanding the scenery*, 206–218. New York, NY: Routledge.
d'Anville, Jean Baptiste Bourguignon. 1737. *Carte la plus generale et qui comprend la Chine, la Tartarie Chinoise, et le Thibet*. La Haye: Chez Henri Scheurleer.
d'Anville, Jean Baptiste Bourguignon. 1785. *Nouvel atlas de la Chine, de la Tartarie Chinoise, et du Tibet*. Amsterdam: Chez Barthelemy Vlam.
"David". 2016. Guangxi Museum. *Nanning Attractions* http://www.chinatravel.com/nanning-attraction/guangxi-museum/ (17 September 2016).
De Heer, P. 1978. The 1978 Constitution of the People's Republic of China. *Review of Socialist Law* 4 (1) 309–322.
De Saint-Georges, Ingrid. 2013. Multilingualism, multimodality and the future of education research. In Ingrid de Saint-Georges & Jean-Jacques Weber (eds.), *Multilingualism and multimodality: Current challenges for educational studies*, 1–8. Rotterdam: Sense Publishers.
De Swaan, Abram. 2001. *Words of the world: The global language system*. Cambridge: Polity Press.
De Varennes, Fernand. 1996. *Language, minorities and human rights*. The Hague & Boston, MA: Kluwer Law International.
Davis, Bob. 2012. Labor NGOs in Guangdong claim repression. *The Wall Street Journal*. https://www.wsj.com/articles/BL-CJB-16196 (2 September 2020).
Deng, Jinting. 2016. A functional analysis of China's guiding cases. *China: An International Journal* 14 (2). 44–70.
Deumert, Ana & Nkulueko Mabandla. 2018. Beyond colonial linguistics: The dialectic of control and resistance in the standardization of isiXhosa. In Pia Lane, James Costa and Haley De Korne (eds.) *Standardizing Minority Languages Competing Ideologies of Authority and Authenticity in the Global Periphery*. New York, NY: Routledge. 200–221.
Diller, Anthony V. N., Jerold A. Edmondson & Luo Yongxian (eds.). 2008. *The Tai-Kadai languages*. London: Routledge.
Dong, Jing & Jan Blommaert. 2009. Space, scale and accents: Constructing migrant identity in Beijing. *Multilingua* 28 (1). 1–23.
Draper, John. 2016. The Isan culture maintenance and revitalisation programme's multilingual signage attitude survey: Phase II. *Journal of Multilingual and Multicultural Development* 37 (8). 832–848.
Easy Tour China. 2016. Guangxi Museum of Nationalities. *Easy Tour China*. http://www.easytourChina.com/scene-v830-guangxi-museum-of-nationalities (1 September 2020).
Eclipse, Abegail N. and Pia Patricia P. Tenedero. 2018. The linguistic landscape of Manila Central Post Office: A macro-linguistic analysis. *Asian Journal of English Language Studies* 6. 157–176.

Edmondson, Jerold A. & Li Jinfang. 1996. The language corridor. *Pan-Asiatic Linguistics* 3. 981–989.

Education Department of Inner Mongolia Autonomous Region. 2020. 秋季学期起我区民族语言授课学校小学一年级和初中一年级使用国家统编语文教材 [From the autumn semester, the national language teaching schools in our district will use the nationally compiled Chinese textbooks for the first grade of primary and junior high school] (press release 26 August 2020) https://www.google.com/search?q=translate&oq=translate&aqs=chrome.0.69i59j0l2j69i59j0j69i61j69i60j69i61.1861j0j4&sourceid=chrome¡UTF-8 (12 October 2020).

Eisberg, Neil. 2015. Boom and bust? *Chemistry & Industry* 79 (8). 21.

Fan, Cindy. 2008. *China on the move: Migration, the state, and the household* (Routledge studies in human geography 21). London & New York, NY: Taylor & Francis.

Feng, Anwei & Mamtimyn Sunuodula. 2009. Analysing language education policy for China's minority groups in its entirety. *International Journal of Bilingual Education and Bilingualism* 12 (6). 685–704.

Feng, Xingyuan, Christer Ljungwall & Xia Yeliang. 2013. Protection of property rights as a key to economic success in China. *Center for International provate Enterprise Blog* http://www.cipe.org/blog/2013/09/26/protection-of-property-rights-as-a-key-to-economic-success-in-China/#.V9eAkJN96T8 (2 September 2020)

Feng, Yang. 2017. The legislation in autonomous areas of China: Progress, limitations and recommendations. *Asian-Pacific Law & Policy Journal* 18 (2). 46–82.

Finder, Susan. 2013. Supreme People's Court's 4th Five Year Reform Plan sees the light of day. *Supreme People's Court Monitor*. https://supremepeoplescourtmonitor.com/2015/02/26/supreme-peoples-courts-4th-five-year-reform-plan-sees-the-light-of-day/ (12 October 2020).

Finder, Susan. 2020. Supreme People's Court's New Vision for the Chinese courts. *Supreme People's Court Monitor*. https://supremepeoplescourtmonitor.com/2020/05/04/supreme-peoples-courts-new-vision-for-the-chinese-courts/ (12 October 2020).

Fishman, Joshua A. 1968[1972]. *Language in Sociocultural Change*. Stanford, CA: Stanford University Press.

Fishman, Joshua A. 1999. *Handbook of language and ethnic identity*. Oxford: Oxford University Press.

Foucault, Michel. 1984. 'Space, power, knowledge' interview with Paul Rainbow. In Paul Rainbow (ed.), *The Foucault Reader*. New York, NY: Pantheon.

Franceschini, Ivan. 2012. Another Guangdong model: Labour NGOs and new state corporatism. *The China Story blog* http://www.thechinastory.org/2012/08/post-labour-ngos/ (4 August 2012).

Freeland, Jane, & Donna Patrick. 2004. Language rights and language survival: Sociolinguistic and sociocultural perspectives. In Jane Freeland & Donna Patrick (eds.), *Language rights and language survival*, 1–33. Manchester: St Jerome Publishing.

Fung, Esther. 2016. China housing revival buffers economy. *Wall Street Journal*. http://www.wsj.com/articles/China-housing-revival-buffers-economy-1463288631

Gao, Shuang. 2015. Multilingualism and good citizenship: The making of language celebrities in Chinese media. In *Working papers in urban language and literacies* (Paper 166). London: King's College.

Gal, Susan. 2018. Visions and revisions of minority languages: standardization and its dilemmas. In Pia Lane, James Costa and Haley De Korne (eds.) *Standardizing Minority*

Languages Competing Ideologies of Authority and Authenticity in the Global Periphery. New York, NY: Routledge. 222–242.

Gladney, Dru. 2004. *Dislocating China: Reflections on Muslims, minorities, and other subaltern subjects*. London: University of Chicago Press.

Goebel, Zane. 2015. Infrastructures for ethnicity. *Working papers in urban language & literacies* (Paper 175). London: King's College.

Goffman, Erving. 1974. *Frame analysis: An essay on the organization of experience*. Cambridge, MA: Harvard University Press.

Google. 2014. *Minzu University of China*. https://www.google.co.uk/search?q=central+minzu+university+beijing;utf-8œutf-8&gws_rd=cr&ei=taNiV628C5CvgAarhrLABQ (2 September 2020).

Gorter, Dirk. 2006. Introduction: The study of the linguistic landscape as a new approach to multilingualism. *International Journal of Multilingualism* 3 (1). 1–6.

Grey, Alexandra. 2015a. Guangxi bombings: Corruption and power-abuse take their toll. *Lowy Interpreter blog* https://www.lowyinstitute.org/the-interpreter/guangxi-bombings-corruption-and-power-abuse-take-their-toll (31 Octover 2020).

Grey, Alexandra. 2015b. Guangxi bombings: Does speculation of ethnic minority activism hold up? *Lowy Interpreter blog* https://www.lowyinstitute.org/the-interpreter/guangxi-bombings-does-speculation-ethnic-minority-activism-hold (31 October 2020).

Grey, Alexandra. 2017. *How do language rights affect minority languages in China? An ethnographic investigation of the Zhuang minority language under conditions of rapid social change*. Sydney: Macquarie University PhD thesis.

Grey, Alexandra. 2019. A polity study of minority language management in China focusing on Zhuang. *Current Issues in Language Planning* 20 (4). 443–503.

Grey, Alexandra. 2021a. Tourist tongues: High-speed rail carries linguistic and cultural urbanisation beyond the city limits in Guangxi, China. *Applied Linguistics Review*. 12 (1) Ahead of Print. 11–37.

Grey, Alexandra. 2021b. Perceptions of the invisible Zhuang minority language in LLs of the PRC and implications for language policy. *Linguistic Landscape*. 0 (0) Ahead of Print.

Grey, Alexandra. (in press). How standard Zhuang has met with market forces. In Nicola McLelland & Hui Annette Zhao (eds.), *Language standards, norms, and variation in Asia*. (unpaginated). Clevedon: Multilingual Matters.

Grey, Alexandra & Gegentuul Baioud. (in press). English as Eastern: Zhuang, Mongolian, Mandarin and English in the linguistic orders of globalized China. *International Journal of the Sociology of Language*.

Guangxi Language Reform Commission, Language Research Centre. 1989. 武鸣壮语语法 [A grammar of the Zhuang dialect of Wuming]. Nanning: Guangxi Minzu Press.

Guangxi Nanning Dream Rauz Cultural Broadcast Company Ltd (ed.). 2013. Beix Nuengx Raeuz 贝侬僚 *Our Brothers and Sisters; Deb Rom Fwen Hauq Raeuz* 壮族布依音乐专辑 *The Music of Raeuz People*. Nanning: Guangxi Quanhaiwan Audiovisual Production Company.

Guangxi Zhuang Literary History Newsroom & Guangxi Teachers College, Department of Chinese. 1961. *Guangxi Zhuang nationality literature*. Nanning: Guangxi Zhuangzu Autonomous Region People's Press.

Guo, Long-Sheng. 2004. The relationship between Putonghua and Chinese dialects. In Zhou Minglang & Sun Hongkai (eds.), *Language policy in the People's Republic of China: Theory and practice since 1949* (Language Policy 4), 45–54. Boston, MA: Kluwer Academic Publishers.

Guo, Rongxin. 2013. *China's ethnic minorities: Social and economic indicators*. Abingdon & New York, NY: Routledge.
Guo, Rongxin et al. (eds.). 2015. *Multicultural China: A statistical yearbook (2014)*. Verlag, Berlin & Heidelberg: Springer.
GXMN. 2013. Introduction to GXMN. *About GXMN*. http://www.gxmn.org/eng/news-detail.php?ID=2998 (30 September 2016).
Gyausou, Yauzcuz & Saugangh Loz (eds.). 2010. *Sam Nyied Sam* [Third of the Third] 2010 (4). Nanning: Guangxi Guangxiang Colour Printing Corporation.
GZAR Bureau of Statistics & Office for the Sixth Population Census of GZAR. 2010. 广西壮族自治区 2010 年人口普查资料1 [Tabulation on the 2010 population census of GZAR (book 1 of 4)]. Beijing: China Statistical Press.
GZAR Minority Language Working Group Research Team. 1984. *Sawloih cuengh gun* 壮汉词汇 [Zhuang Han dictionary]. Nanning: Guangxi Minzu Press.
Han, Huamei. 2013. Individual grassroots multilingualism in Africa Town in Guangzhou: The role of states in globalization. *International Multilingual Research Journal* 7 (1). 83–97.
Harrell, Stevan. 1993. Linguistics and hegemony in China. *International Journal of the Sociology of Language* 1993 (103). 97–114.
Harrell, Stevan. 1995. Introduction – civilizing projects and the reactions to them. In Stevan Harrell (ed.), *Cultural encounters on China's ethnic frontiers*, 3–36. Seattle WA: University of Washington Press.
Harrell, Stevan. 1996. The nationalities question and the Prmi problem. In Melissa Brown (ed.), *Negotiating ethnicities in China and Taiwan*, 274–296. Berkeley: Berkeley Institute of East Asian Studies, University of California.
Harrell, Stevan & Erzi Mgebbu Lunze Ma. 1999. Folk theories of success: Where Han aren't always the best. In Gerald A. Postiglione (ed.), *China's national minority education*, 213–242. New York, NY: Falmer Press.
He, Baogang. 2014. The power of Chinese linguistic imperialism and its challenges to multicultural education. In James Leibold & Chen Yangbin (eds.), *Minority education in China: Balancing unity and diversity in an era of critical pluralism*, 27–64. Hong Kong: Hong Kong University Press.
Heller, Monica. 2002. Globalization and commodification of bilingualism in Canada. In David Block & Deborah Cameron (eds.), *Gloablization and language teaching*, 47–64. London: Routledge.
Heller, Monica. 2003. Globalization, the new economy, and the commodification of language and identity. *Journal of Sociolinguistics* 7 (4). 473–492.
Heller, Monica. 2004. Analysis and stance regarding language and social justice. In Jane Freeland & Donna Patrick (eds.), *Language rights and language survival*, 283–286. Manchester: St Jerome Publishing.
Heller, Monica. 2010. Language as a resource in the globalized new economy In Nikolas Coupland (ed.), *Handbook of language and globalization*, 349–365: Malden, MA: Wiley-Blackwell.
Heller, Monica, Joan Pujolar & Alexandre Duchêne. 2014. Linguistic commodification in tourism. *Journal of Sociolinguistics* 18 (4). 539–566.
Hirsch, Francine. 2000. Toward an empire of nations: Border-making and the formation of Soviet national identities. *The Russian review* 59 (2). 201–226.
Holm, David. 2008. The old Zhuang script. In Anthony V. N. Diller, Jerold A. Edmondson & Luo Yongxian (eds.), *The Tai-Kadai languages*, 415–428. London: Routledge.
Holm, David. 2013. *Mapping the old Zhuang character script: A vernacular writing system from southern China*. Leiden: Brill.

Hornberger, Nancy. 2005. Opening and filling up implementational and ideological spaces in heritage language education. *The Modern Language Journal* 89 (4). 605–609.

Hu, Angang. 2012. 第二代民族政策：促进民族交融一体和繁荣一体 [Second generation minzu policies: The promotion of national integration and prospering as one]. *中国民族宗教网* [The China minzu religion web] http://www.mzb.com.cn/html/report/293011-1.htm (12 May 2016).

Hu, Guangwei. 2012. Chinese-English bilingual education in the PRC: Implications for language education for autochthonous ethnic minorities. In Gulbahar H. Beckett & Gerard A. Postiglione (eds.), *China's assimilationist language policy*, 175–189. London & New York, NY: Routledge.

Hu, Guangwei & Lubna Alsagoff. 2010. A public policy perspective on English medium instruction in China. *Journal of Multilingual and Multicultural Development* 31 (4). 365–382.

Hu, Ying-Hsueh. 2018. Multilingual Audio Announcements: Power and Identity. In Martin Pütz and Neele Mundt (eds.), *Expanding the Linguistic Landscape: Linguistic Diversity, Multimodality and the Use of Space as a Semiotic Resource*, 132–149. Bristol: Multilingual Matters.

Hult, Francis M. 2014. Drive-thru linguistic landscaping: Constructing a linguistically dominant place in a bilingual space. *International Journal of Bilingualism* 18 (5). 507–523.

Hult, Francis M. 2018. Language Policy and Planning and Linguistic Landscapes. In James W. Tollefson & Miguel Pérez-Milans (eds.), *The Oxford Handbook of Language Policy and Planning*, 333–352. New York, NY: Oxford University Press.

Iredale, Robyn, Naran Bilik & Guo Fei (eds.). 2003. *China's minorities on the move: Selected case studies*. New York, NY: M. E. Sharpe.

Iredale, Robyn & Guo Fei. 2003. Overview of minority migration. In Robyn Iredale, Naran Bilik & Guo Fei (eds.), *China's minorities on the move: Selected case studies*, 3–31. New York, NY: M. E. Sharpe.

Irvine, Judith T. & Susan Gal. 2000. Language ideology and linguistic differentiation. In Paul V. Kroskrity (ed.), *Regimes of language: Ideologies, polities, and identities*, 35–83. Santa Fe, NM: School of American Research Press.

Jaffe, Alexandra. 2004. Language rights and wrongs. In Jane Freeland & Donna Patrick (eds.), *Language rights and language survival*, 273–282. Manchester: St Jerome Publishing.

Jaffe, Alexandra. 2007. Discourses of endangerment: Contexts and consequences of essentializing discourses. In Alexandre Duchêne & Monica Heller (eds.), *Discourses of endangerment*, 57–75. London: Continuum.

Jakobson, Linda & Ryan Manuel. 2016. How are foreign policy decisions made in China? *Asia & The Pacific Policy Studies* 3 (1). 101–110.

Jaworski, Adam. 2014. Mobile language in mobile places. *International Journal of Bilingualism* 18 (5). 524–533.

Jaworski, Adam. 2015. Globalese: A new visual-linguistic register. *Social Semiotics* 25 (2). 217–235.

Jaworski, Adam & Ingrid Piller. 2008. Linguascaping Switzerland: Language ideologies in tourism. In Jürg Strässler & Miriam A. Locher (eds.), *Standards and norms in the English language*, 301–321. Berlin: Mouton de Gruyter.

Jaworski, Adam & Crispin Thurlow. 2010. Introducing semiotic landscapes. In Adam Jaworski & Crispin Thurlow (eds.), *Semiotic landscapes: Language, image, space*, 1–40. London: Continuum.

Johnson, David Cassels & Thomas Ricento. 2013. Conceptual and theoretical perspectives in language planning and policy: Situating the ethnography of language policy. *International Journal of the Sociology of Language* 2013 (219). 7–21.
Johnstone, Barbara. 1990. *Stories, community and place: Narratives from middle America*. Bloomington, IN: Indiana University Press.
Kachru, B. B. 1985. Standards, codification and sociolinguistic realism: The English language in the outer circle. In R. Quirk & H. G. Widdowson (eds.) *English in the world: Teaching and learning the language and literatures*, 11–30. Cambridge: Cambridge University Press.
Kaup, Katherine Palmer. 2000. *Creating the Zhuang: Ethnic politics in China*. Boulder, CO: Lynne Rienner Publishers Inc.
Kawash, Samira. 1998. The homeless body. *Public Culture* 10 (2). 319–339.
Kipnis, Andrew. 2012. Constructing commonality: Standardization and modernization in chinese nation-building. *The Journal of Asian Studies* 71 (3). 731–755.
Kloss, Heinz. 1965. Territorialprinzip, bekenntnisprinzip, verfugungsprinzip: Uber die moglichkeiten der abgrenzung der volklichen zugehorigkeit. *Europa Ethnica* 22. 52–73.
Kramsch, Claire & Anne Whiteside. 2008. Toward a theory of symbolic competence. *Applied Linguistics* 29. 645–671.
Kress, Gunther & Theo van Leeuwen. 2006. *Reading images: The grammar of visual design* (2nd edn). London: Routledge.
Lafont, Robert. 1997. *Quarante ans de sociolinguistique a la peripherie*. Paris: L'Harmattan.
Lam, Agnes S. L. 2005. Language education in China: Policy and experience from 1949. Journal of Asian Pacific Communication 20 (2). 323–325.
Landry, Rodrigue & Richard Y. Bourhis. 1997. Linguistic landscape and ethnolinguistic vitality: An empirical study. *Journal of Language and Social Psychology* 16 (1). 23–49.
Lane, Pia, James Costa and Haley De Korne (eds.) *Standardizing Minority Languages Competing Ideologies of Authority and Authenticity in the Global Periphery*. New York, NY: Routledge.
Lanza, Elizabeth & Hirut Woldemariam. 2009. Language ideology and linguistic landscape: Language policy and globalization in a regional capital of Ethiopia. In Elana Shohamy & Dirk Gorter (eds.), *Linguistic landscape: Expanding the scenery*, 189–205. New York, NY: Routledge.
Lefebvre, Henri. 1991. *The production of space*. Oxford: Blackwell Publishing.
Leibold, James. 2007. *Reconfiguring Chinese nationalism*. New York, NY: Palgrave MacMillan.
Leibold, James. 2015. Performing ethnocultural identity on the Sinophone internet: Testing the limits of minzu. *Asian Ethnicity* 16 (3). 274–293.
Leibold, James 2012. Toward a second generation of ethnic policies? *China Brief* XII (13). 7–10.
Leibold, James & Chen Yangbin. 2014. Diversity in an era of critical pluralism. In James Leibold & Chen Yangbin (eds.), *Minority education in China: Balancing unity and diversity in an era of critical pluralism*, 1–26. Hong Kong: Hong Kong University Press.
Leibold, James & Chen Yangbin (eds.). 2014. *Minority education in China: Balancing unity and diversity in an era of critical pluralism*. Hong Kong: Hong Kong University Press.
Leibold, James & Timothy A. Grose. 2019. Cultural and political disciplining inside China's dislocated minority schooling system. *Asian Studies Review* 43 (1). 16–35.
Leung, Janny H. C. 2019. *Shallow equality and symbolic jurisprudence in multilingual legal orders*. New York, NY: Oxford University Press.

Li, Fenfei & Deng Jinting. 2016. The limits of the arbitrariness in anticorruption by China's local Party discipline inspection committees. *Journal of Contemporary China* 25 (97). 75–90.

Li, Hongjie & Anna Maria Lundberg (eds.). 2008. *Minority language use and cultural development: International comparison of policy and law* 少数民族语言使用与文化发展：政策和法律的国际比较. Beijing: Central University of Nationalities Press.

Li, Jia. 2017. *Social reproduction and migrant education: A critical sociolinguistic ethnography of burmese students' learning experiences at a border high school in China*. Sydney: Macquarie University PhD thesis.

Li, Lianjin. 2005. 广西各民族语言的形成与相互间的影响 [The influence of the forms and overlap of each language of guangxi's minzu]. In Chen Hailun & Li Lianjin (eds.), 广西语言文字使用问题调查与研究 [Investigation and research on the subject of the usage of Guangxi languages and scripts], 9–15. Nanning: Guangxi Education Press.

Li, Qiuhong & GZAR Areal Annals Compilation Committee (eds.). 2010. 广西照片志 [Guangxi photographic annals]. Nanning: Nanning Squared Software and New Technologies Corporation Ltd.

Li, Xulian & Huang Quanxi. 2004. The introduction and development of the Zhuang writing system. In Zhou Minglang & Sun Hongkai (eds.), *Language policy in the People's Republic of China: Theory and practice since 1949* (Language Policy 4), 239–256. Boston, MA: Kluwer Academic Publishers.

Li, Yuming. 2015. *Language planning in China*. Berlin & Beijing: De Gruyter & The Commercial Press.

Liang, Min, Zhang Junru, Wang Fushi & Mao Zungwu. 1988. Minority languages: Guangxi Zhuang Autonomous Region (notes to Map C12). In Liang Min & Zhang Junru (eds.), *Language atlas of China*. Hong Kong: Pacific Linguistics.

Lickorish, Michael G. 2008. *Tending the eternal tomb: Manchu identity after empire*. Canberra: The Australian National University PhD thesis.

Lifang (ed.) 2018. Urbanization rate of China's agricultural province exceeds 50 pct. *Xinhua Net News*. http://www.xinhuanet.com/english/2018-03/05/c_137017957.htm (2 September 2020).

Lin, Angel M. Y. & Jasmine C. M. Luk. 2005. Local creativity in the face of global domination: Insights of Bakhtin for teaching English for dialogic communication. In Joan Kelly Hall, Gergana Vitanova & Ludmila A. Marchenkova (eds.), *Dialogue with Bakhtin on second and foreign language learning: New perspectives*. 77–98. London: Lawrence Erlbaum Associates.

Liu, Cunhan. 2005. 丰富多彩的语言宝藏 [Hidden treasures of linguistic abundance]. In Chen Hailun & Li Lianjin (eds.), 广西语言文字使用问题调查与研究 [Investigation and research on the subject of the usage of Guangxi languages and scripts], 3–8. Nanning: Guangxi Education Press.

"*Liuzhou Laowai*". 2009. No direction home. *Liuzhou Laowai blog*, http://liuzhou.co.uk/wordpress/2009/06/06/no-direction-home/ (2017)

Lo Bianco, Joseph, Jane Orton & Gao Yihong (eds.). 2009. *China and English: Gloablisation and the dilemmas of identity*. Buffalo, NY & Bristol: Multilingual Matters.

Lou, Jackie. 2016. *The linguistic landscape of Chinatown: A sociolinguistic ethnography*. Clevedon: Multilingual Matters.

Lu, Hai & Li Fanglan. 2012. Contact-induced change in status planing: A case study of Zhuang Putonghua. *International Journal of the Sociology of Language* 2012 (215). 19–40.

Luo, Yongxian. 2008a. Sino-Tai and Tai-Kadai: Another look. In Anthony V. N. Diller, Jerold A. Edmondson & Luo Yongxian (eds.), *The Tai-Kadai languages*, 9–28. London: Routledge.
Luo, Yongxian. 2008b. Zhuang. In Anthony V. N. Diller, Jerold A. Edmondson & Luo Yongxian (eds.), *The Tai-Kadai languages*, 317–377. London: Routledge.
Luo, Yongxian. 2015. Evidentiality and epistemic modality in Zhuang. *Linguistics of the Tibeto-Burman Area* 38 (1), 3–25.
MacroPolo. 2020. The Committee. *Paulson Institute website* https://macropolo.org/digital-projects/the-committee/?fbclid=IwAR1UwyhVtgRTvrasWKsjpL9ud4VYAH6wZQWFxGmRL8H0J5JcOmioQnPpP2k (7 September 2020).
Mair, Victor. 2013. The languages on Chinese banknnotes. *Language Log* https://languagelog.ldc.upenn.edu/nll/?p=7013 (2 September 2020).
Malinowski, David. 2009. Authorship in the linguistic landscape: A multimodal-performative view. In Elana Shohamy & Dirk Gorter (eds.), *Linguistic landscapes*, 107–125. New York, NY: Routledge.
Manuel, Ryan. 2015. *Strong state, weak system: Social health insurance in rural China 1956–2007.* Oxford: University of Oxford DPhil thesis.
Maps Open Source. n. d. *China provinces outline map*. http://mapsopensource.com/China-provinces-outline-map.html (2 September 2020).
Martini, Martino. 1659. *Map of Qvangsi thirteenth province of China with relief shown pictorially [Plate 14]*. Amsterdam: J. van Blaeu.
May, Stephen 2005. Language rights: Moving the debate forward. *Journal of Sociolinguistics* 9 (3). 319–347.
McLelland, Nicola & Annette Hui Zhao (eds.). (in press). *Language standards, norms, and variation in Asia*. Bristol: Multilingual Matters.
McRae, Kenneth D. 1975. The principle of territoriality and the principle of personality in multilingual states. *International Journal of the Sociology of Language* 1975 (4). 33–54.
Ministry of Education of the PRC. 2010. *Outline of China's national plan for medium and long-term education reform and development (2010–2020)* https://internationaleducation.gov.au/International-network/China/publications/Documents/China_Education_Reform_pdf.pdf (2 September 2020).
Moody, Andrew, Hu Haiyan & Ma Wei. 2011. 'Go west' policy is an economic milestone for nation. *The China Daily (English language online edition)*. https://www.pressreader.com/hong-kong/china-daily/20111209/282613144610173 (2 September 2020).
Mortimer, Katherine S. 2016. A potentially heteroglossic policy becomes monoglossic in context: An ethnographic analysis of Paraguayan bilingual education policy. *Anthropology & Education Quarterly* 47 (4). 349–365.
Moseley, Christopher (ed.) 2010. *Atlas of the world's languages in danger* (3rd edn). Paris: UNESCO.
Mowbray, Jacqueline. 2012. *Linguistic justice: International law and language policy* Oxford: Oxford University Press.
Mufwene, Salikoko. 2002. Colonization, globalization and the plight of 'weak' languages. *Journal of Linguistics* 38 (2). 375–395.
Mullaney, Thomas. 2006. *Coming to terms with the nation: Ethnic classification and scientific statecraft in modern China, 1928–1954*. New York, NY: Columbia University PhD thesis.
Mullaney, Thomas. 2011. *Coming to terms with the nation: Ethnic classification in modern China* (Asia: Local Studies / Global Themes 18). Berkeley & Los Angeles, CA: University of California Press.

Nanning Municipal Minority Language Works Commission. 2019. 《南宁市壮文社会使用管理办法》实施评估报告发布时间 [Implementation Evaluation Report of " Management Measures for Social Usage of Zhuangwen in Nanning "]. *广西南宁市民族宗教事务委员会网站* [*Guangxi Nanning Municipal Ethnic and Religious Affairs Committee Website*] http://mw.nanning.gov.cn/ztlm/lszt/yfxzzl/t4128044.html (30 October 2020).

National Bureau of Statistics & Yunnan Bureau of Statistics. 2016 [2010]. Yunnan province: Administrative units. *Geohive*. http://www.geohive.com/cntry/cn-53.aspx (4 November 2016).

National Bureau of Statistics of China. 2011. Communiqué of the National Bureau of Statistics of People's Republic of China on major figures of the 2010 population census (no. 1). Beijing: National Bureau of Statistics.

National People's Congress. 2013. New nat'l legislature sees more diversity [Press release]. *National People's Congress website* http://www.npc.gov.cn/englishnpc/news/Focus/2013-02/27/content_1759084.htm (4 November 2016).

National People's Congress. 2016. National People's Congress. *National People's Congress website* http://www.npc.gov.cn/englishnpc/Organization/node_2846.htm (4 November 2016).

National People's Congress. 2020. About Congress. *National People's Congress website* http://www.npc.gov.cn/englishnpc/c2842/column.shtml (7 September 2020).

Noy, Chaim. 2007. Sampling knowledge: The hermeneutics of snowball sampling in qualitative research. *International Journal Of Social Research Methodology* 11 (4). 327–344.

NPC Observer. 2017. Explainer: China to Amend the Constitution for the Fifth Time (UPDATED). *NPC Observer blog* https://npcobserver.com/2017/12/27/explainer-china-to-amend-the-constitution-for-the-fifth-time/ (14 October 2020).

Ostapirat, Weera. (2000). Proto-Kra. *Linguistics of the Tibeto-Burman Area* 23 (1). 1–251.

Papen, Uta. 2015. Signs in cities: The discursive production and commodification of urban spaces. *Sociolinguistic Studies* 9 (1). 1–26.

Paulston, Christina Bratt. 1997. Language policies and language rights. *Annual Review of Anthropology* 26. 73–85.

Peck, Amiena & Christopher Stroud. 2015. Skinscapes. *Linguistic Landscape* 1 (2). 133–151.

Pennycook, Alistair. 2004. Performativity and language studies. *Critical Inquiry in Language Studies: An International Journal* 1 (1), 1–26.

Pennycook, Alistair and Emi Otsuji. 2011. Making scents of the landscape. *Linguistic Landscape* 1 (3). 191–212.

Piller, Ingrid. 2011. *Intercultural communication: A critical introduction*. Edinburgh: Edinburgh University Press.

Piller, Ingrid. 2015. Language ideologies. In Karen Tracy (ed.), *The International Encyclopedia of Language and Social Interaction*, 1–10. Boston, MA: John Wiley & Sons Inc.

Piller, Ingrid. 2016. *Linguistic Diversity and Social Justice: An Introduction to Applied Sociolinguistics*. New York, NY: Oxford University Press.

Piller, Ingrid. 2017. 2017 BAAL Book Prize. *Language on the Move blog* https://www.languageonthemove.com/2017-baal-book-prize/ (31 October 2020).

Piller, Ingrid & Alexandra Grey. 2019. Language and globalization: Mapping the field. In Ingrid Piller & Alexandra Grey (eds.), *Language and globalization*, 1–19. London: Routledge.

Population Reference Bureau. 2011. Population of provinces, municipalities, and autonomous regions, 2010 census of China, and change in the percent distribution by area,

2000–2010. *Population Reference Bureau* http://www.prb.org/pdf11/china-2010-census-results-table.pdf (3 September 2020).
Premaratne, Dilhara. 2015. Globalisation, language planning and language rights: The recent script policy measures adopted by Japan and the People's Republic of China. *Current Issues in Language Planning* 16 (4). 425–440.
"浪子天涯" [Prodigal Son]. 2016. *Bouxcuengh Raeuz [We Zhuang] blog*. http://gaisi144.blog.163.com/ (2 September 2020).
Pütz, Martin and Neele Mundt. 2018. Multilingualism, Multimodality and Methodology: Linguistic Landscape Research in the Context of Assemblages, Ideologies and (In)visibility: An Introduction. In M. Pütz, & N. Mundt (Eds.), *Expanding the Linguistic Landscape: Linguistic Diversity, Multimodality and the Use of Space as a Semiotic Resource*, 1–22. Bristol: Multilingual Matters.
Qian, Junxi. 2014. Performing the public man: Cultures and identities in China's grassroots leisure class. *City & Community* 13 (1). 26–48.
Qian, Junxi, Qian Liyun & Zhu Hong. 2012. Representing the imagined city: Place and the politics of difference during Guangzhou's 2010 language conflict. *Geoforum* 43 (5). 905–915.
Qin, Fengyu & Tian Chunlai. 2011. 广西汉壮语方言的 '曝 ' ['sak7' in the Zhuang and Han dialects of Huangxi]. 民族语文 [Minority Languages of China] 2011 (5). 26–36.
Qin, Fengyu & Wu Fuxiang. 2009. 南宁白话'过'的两种特殊用法[Two special usages of 'guo' in Nanning Baihua]. 民族语文 [Minority Languages of China] 2011 (3). 16–29.
Rampton, Ben & Costadina Charalambous. 2010. Crossing: A review of research. *Working Papers in Urban* Language *&* Literacies (Paper 58). London: King's College.
Ramsey, S. Robert. 1987. *The languages of China*. Princeton, NJ: Princeton University Press.
Razack, Sherene H. 2002. When place becomes race. In Sherene H. Razack (ed.), *Race, space and the law*, 1–20. Toronto: Between the Lines.
Reh, Mechthild. 2004. Multilingual writing: A reader-oriented topology – with examples for Lira Municipality (Uganda). *International Journal of the Sociology of Language* 2004 (170). 1–41.
Ricento, Thomas. 2000. Historical and Theoretical Perspectives in Language Policy and Planning. *Journal of Sociolinguistics* 4 (2): 196–213.
Ricento, Thomas (ed.) 2015. *Language policy and political economy: English in a global context*. New York, NY: Oxford University Press.
Ricento, Thomas & Nancy Hornberger. 1996. Unpeeling the onion: Language planning and policy and the ELT professional. *TESOL Quarterly* 30 (3). 401–427.
Roche, Gerald. 2017. The transformation of Tibet's language ecology in the 21st century. *International Journal of the Sociology of Language* 2017 (245). 1–35.
Roche, Gerald. 2019. Articulating language oppression: Colonialism, coloniality and the erasure of Tibet's minority languages. *Patterns of Prejudice*. 53. 48–514.
Roche, Gerald and James Leibold. 2020. China's Second-generation Ethnic Policies Are Already Here: What China's History of Paper Genocide Can Tell Us about the Future of Its 'Minority Nationalities'. *Made In China Journal* https://madeinchinajournal.com/2020/09/07/chinas-second-generation-ethnic-policies-are-already-here/ (online only, 7 October 2020).
Roche, Gerald, James Leibold and Ben Hillman. 2020. Urbanizing Tibet: Differential inclusion and colonial governance in the People's Republic of China. *Territory, Politics, Goverance*.
Rohsenow, John S. 2004. Fifty years of scrip and written language reform in the PRC. In Zhou Minglang & Sun Hongkai (eds.), *Language policy in the People's Republic of China: Theory*

and practice since 1949 (Language Policy 4), 21–44. Boston, MA: Kluwer Academic Publishers.
Ruiz, Richard. 1984. Orientation in language planning. *National Association of Bilingual Education Journal* 8 (2), 15–34.
Said, Edward W. 1978. *Orientalism* (1st edn). London: Routledge & Kegan Paul.
Sapio, Flora. 2009. Third five-year reform outline for the People's Courts (2009–2013). *Forgotten Archipelago* https://florasapio.blogspot.com/ (21 February 2016).
Sassatelli, Monica. 2017. 'Europe in your pocket': Narratives of identity in euro iconography. *Journal of Contemporary European Studies* 25 (3). 354–366.
Scally, Patrick. 2016. Yunnan's population by the numbers. *Go Kunming* http://www.gokunming.com/en/blog/item/3769/yunnans_population_by_the_numbers (2 September 2020).
Schein, Louisa. 2000. *Minority rules: The Miao and the feminine in China's cultural politics*. Durham, NC: Duke University Press.
Schiffman, Harold F. 1996. Typologies of multilingualism and typologies of language policy. In Harold F. Schiffman (ed.), *Linguistic culture and language policy*, 26–54. London: Routledge.
Schwandt, Thomas A. 1997. *Qualitative inquiry: A dictionary of terms*. Thousand Oaks, CA: Sage.
Scollon, Ron & Suzie Wong Scollon. 2003. *Discourses in place: Language in the material world*. Abingdon: Routledge.
Scott, James C. 1998. *Seeing like a state: How certain schemes to improve the human condition have failed*. New Haven, CT: Yale University Press.
Sebba, Mark. 2010. Discourses in transit In Adam Jaworski & Crispin Thurlow (eds.), *Semiotic landscapes: Language, image, space*, 59–76. London: Continuum.
Seth, Shobhit. 2019. Baidu vs. Google: What's the difference? *Investopedia* https://www.investopedia.com/articles/investing/051215/baidu-vs-google-how-are-they-different.asp (2 September 2020).
Shanghaiist. 2014. Shanghai pilot program encourages kids to speak Shanghainese in school. *Shanghaiist* http://shanghaiist.com/2014/01/25/shanghai-pilot-program-encourages-shanghainese-in-school.php (3 March 2016).
Sharma, Bal Krishna. 2019. The scarf, language, and other semiotic assemblages in the formation of a new Chinatown. *Applied Linguistics Review*. 0 (0) Ahead of Print. 1–27.
Sheller, Mimi & John Urry. 2006. The new mobilities paradigm. *Environment and Planning A* 38. 207–226.
Shen, Qi & Gao Xuesong. 2019. Multilingualism and policy making in greater China: Ideological and implementational spaces. *Language Policy* 18 (1). 1–16.
Shohamy, Elana. 2006. *Language policy: Hidden agendas and new approaches*. London & New York, NY: Routledge.
Shohamy, Elana & Dirk Gorter (eds.). 2009. *Linguistic landscape: Expanding the scenery*. Neew York, NY: Routledge.
Shohamy, Elana, Iair G. Or, Summer Haj Yehia, Sarah Naaman, Moraia Trijnes, Hanne Juel Solomon & Michal Tannenbaum. 2019. *Researching the use of linguistic landscape for enhancing multilingual awareness in schools*. Paper presented at the XIScape2019: 11th Linguistic Landscape Workshop, Chulalongkorn University, 4–6 June.
Simpson, Andrew. 2016. Chinese language and national identity. In Chan Sin-Wai (ed.), *The Routledge encyclopedia of the Chinese Language*, 90–103. Abingdon & New York, NY: Routledge.

Sina News. 2009. 独家]南宁路牌两种拼音 上为壮语下为汉语（图）[(Exclusive) Nanning Street Signs Two Kinds of Pinyin Zhuangyu Above Hanyu Below (picture)]. *Sina 新闻中心* [Sina News Centre] http://news.sina.com.cn/o/20090728/214716027776s.shtml. (6 October 2015)

Sina Property. 2014, O-Park通昊·创智天地[O-Park Tong Hao·K.I.C.]. *SINA* http://gx.house.sina.com.cn/scan/2014-06-16/11324218553.shtml (16 June 2014.)

Sinj, Bwzhaij & Lizmingz Loz. 2008. *900 gawq vahcuengh 壮语900句* [900 Zhuang language phrases]. Nanning: Guangxi Minzu Press.

Sloboda, Marián, Eszter Szabó-Gilinger, Dick Vigers & Lucija Šimičić. 2010. Carrying out a language policy change: Advocacy coalitions and the management of linguistic landscape. *Current Issues in Language Planning* 11 (2). 95–113.

Smith, Anthony D. 2005. The genealogy of nations: An ethno-symbolic approach. In Atsuko Ichijo & Gordana Uzelac (eds.), *When is the nation?* 95–112. London & New York, NY: Routledge.

Sonam, Lhundrop [Tunzhi], Hiroyuki Suzuki and Gerald Roche. 2019. Language contact and the politics of recognition amongst Tibetans in the People's Republic of China: The rTa'u-Speaking 'Horpa' of Khams. In Selma K. Sonntag (ed.) *The Politics of Language Contact in the Himalaya*. 17–48. Open Book Publishers.

Spolsky, Bernard. 2004. *Language policy*. New York, NY: Cambridge University Press.

Spolsky, Bernard & Elana Shohamy. 2004. Preface by the series editors. In Zhou Minglang & Sun Hongkai (eds.), *Language policy in the People's Republic of China: Theory and practice since 1949* (Language Policy 4), xvi. Boston, MA: Kluwer Academic Publishers.

State Council Information Office of the PRC. 1999. *White paper 1999: Regional autonomy for ethnic minorities in China [English]*. Beijing: Permanent Mission of the People's Republic of China to the UN.

State Council Information Office of the PRC. 2005a. *Basic facts about the 155 ethnic autonomous areas in China*. Beijing: Permanent Mission of the People's Republic of China to the UN.

State Council Information Office of the PRC. 2005b. *White paper 2005: Regional autonomy for ethnic minorities in China [English]*. Beijing: Permanent Mission of the People's Republic of China to the UN.

State Council Information Office of the PRC. 2016. Ethnic regions see economic growth. *State Council Information Office website* http://www.scio.gov.cn/32618/Document/1536017/1536017.htm (7 October 2020).

State Council Information Office of the PRC. 2017. China publishes first encyclopedia of ethnic groups. *State Council Information Office website* http://www.scio.gov.cn/32618/Document/1560391/1560391.htm (12 October 2020).

Stites, Regie. 1999. Writing cultural boundaries: National minority language policy, literacy planning, and bilingual education. In Gerard A. Postiglione (ed.), *China's national minority education: Culture, schooling and development*, 95–130. New York, NY: Falmer Press.

Stroud, Christopher & Dmitri Jegels. 2014. Semiotic landscapes and mobile narrations of place: Performing the local. *International Journal of the Sociology of Language* 2014 (228). 179–199.

Sun, Hongkai. 1992. Language recognition and nationality. *International Journal of the Sociology of Language* 1992 (97). 9–22.

Sun, Hongkai & Florian Coulmas. 1992. Preface. *International Journal of the Sociology of Language* 1992 (97). 5–7.

Szabó, Tamás Péter and Troyer, Robert A. 2017. Inclusive ethnographies: Beyond the binaries of observer and observed in linguistic landscape studies. *Linguistic Landscape. An international journal* 3 (3). 306–326.

Tam, Gina Anne. 2020a. *Dialect and Nationalism in China, 1860–1960*. Cambridge: Cambridge University Press.

Tam, Gina Anne. 2020b. What makes a language policy revolutionary? *Age of Revolutions blog* https://ageofrevolutions.com/2020/10/14/what-makes-a-language-policy-revolutionary/ (15 October 2020).

Tai, Chung Pui. 2005. *Literacy practices and functions of the Zhuang character writing system: Abstract*. Hong Kong: University of Hong Kong MPhil thesis.

Tapp, Nicholas & Don Cohn. 2003. *The tribal peoples of south west China*. Bangkok: White Lotus.

Te Yi Lan Lu. 2014. Yous ndei gwn van 如礼金万 dư đây kin van qyus ndil genl waanl [A gift of millions]; *Gij fwen angs cieng bi 2014 2014 年壮语布依语新春贺 岁歌曲(q-s) The Rau language songs for Spring Festival 2014* [CD]. Nanning: Ranz Sing Ngaeuz Daeg It.

Tenzin, Jinba. 2013. *In the land of the eastern queendom: The politics of gender and ethnicity on the Sino-Tibetan border*. Seattle, WA: University of Washington Press.

Terdiman, R. (1987). The force of law: toward a sociology of the juridical field by Pierre Bourdieu: translator's introduction. *The Hastings Law Journal* 38 (July). 805–813.

Thurlow, Crispin & Adam Jaworski. 2010. Silence is golden: The 'anti-communicational' linguascaping of super-elite mobility. In Adam Jaworski & Crispin Thurlow (eds.), *Semiotic landscapes: Language, image, space*, 187–218. London: Continuum.

Thurlow, Crispin & Adam Jaworski. 2011. Tourism discourse: Languages and banal globalization. *Applied Linguistics Review* 2 (2011). 285–312.

Thurlow, Crispin & Adam Jaworski. 2014. 'Two hundred ninety-four': Remediation and multimodal performance in tourist placemaking. *Journal of Sociolinguistics* 18 (4). 459–494.

Todd, Brett. 2013. Reparar el silencio: justicia para los daños lingüísticos causados por colonización y conflicto. *Revista de Derecho Público* 2013 (31). 1–39.

Todd, Brett. 2015. *Linguistic Reparative Justice for indigenous peoples: The case of language policy in Colombia*. Sydney: University of New South Wales PhD Thesis.

Tomba, Luigi. 2014. *The government next door: Neighbourhood politics in urban China*. Ithaca, NY & London: Cornell University Press.

Tsung, Linda T. H. 2014. *Language power and hierarchy: Multilingual education in China*. London & New York, NY: Bloomsbury Academic.

Turner, Jessica Anderson. 2010. *Cultural peformances in the Guangxi tourism commons: A study of music, place, and ethnicity in southern China*. Bloomington IN: Indiana University PhD thesis.

UNDP. (2020). China: Belt and Road Initiative. *United Nations Development Programme*. https://www.cn.undp.org/content/china/en/home/belt-and-road.html (2 October 2020).

UNESCO Institute for Lifelong Learning. 2010. China: Outline of China's national plan for medium- and long-term education reform and development (2010–2020): Abstract [Press release]. *UNESCO Institute for Lifelong Learning website* http://uil.unesco.org/fileadmin/keydocuments/LifelongLearning/en/China-2010-abstract-lll-strategy.pdf (4 October 2016)

United Nations Office of the High Commission for Human Rights. 2010. *Declaration on the rights of persons belonging to national or ethnic, religious and linguistic minorities [booklet]*. Geneva: United Nations OHCHR.

Van Parijs, Philippe. 2000. Must Europe be Belgian? On democratic citizenship in multilingual polities. In Catriona McKinnon & Iain Hampsher-Monk (eds.), *The demands of citizenship*, 235–253. London & New York, NY: Continuum.

Vertovec, Steven. 2007. Super-diversity and its implications. *Ethnic and Racial Studies* 30 (6). 1024–1054.

Wang, -. 2005. Enactment of regulations enforcement of law on regional autonomy for ethnic minorities. *China Law [Peking University Press]*, 2005 (4), 78.

Wang, Fahui, Guanxiong Wang, John Hartmann & Wei Luo. 2011. Sinification of Zhuang place names in Guangxi, China: A GIS-based spatial analysis approach. *Transactions of the Institute of British Geographers* 37 (2). 317–333.

Wang, Ge. 2016. *Pains and Gains of Ethnic Multilingual Learners in China: An Ethnographic Case Study*. Singapore: Springer.

Wang, Jun. 1979. 壮语 及壮汉人民怎样互学语言 [Zhuang language how Zhuang and Han peoples can study each other's language]. Beijing: Beijing Nationalities Press.

Wang, Jun. 1983. 壮侗语族语言简志 [Zhuang and Dong language groups language brief]. Beijing: Beijing Nationalities Press.

Wang, Jun. 1990. 推广普通话和贯彻落实民族语文政策 [Promote the common language and support the implementation of national minority language and script regulations]. In Chinese National Minority Bilingual Education Commitee (ed.), 中国民族双语研究论及 [Research Discussions on Chinese Bilingual Minorities], 31–38. Beijing: Beijing Nationalities Press.

Wang, Rachel. 2013. *China for kids*. USA: (self-published).

Wang, Yuxiang & JoAnn Phillion. 2009. Minority language policy and practice in China: The need for multicultural education. *International Journal of Multicultural Education* 11 (1), 1–14.

Wee, Lionel. 2011. *Language without rights* Oxford & New York, NY: Oxford University Press.

Wei, Changhao. 2018, Annotated translation: 2018 amendment to the PRC Constitution (version 2.0). *NPC Observer*. https://npcobserver.com/2018/03/11/translation-2018-amendment-to-the-p-r-c-constitution/ (2 September 2020).

Whaley, Lindsay. 2004. Can a language that never existed be saved? In Jane Freeland & Donna Patrick (eds.), *Language rights and language survival*, 139–149. Manchester: St Jerome Publishing.

Woolard, Kathryn A. & Bambi B. Schieffelin. 1994. Language ideology. *Annual Review of Anthropology* 23. 55–82.

Wurm, Stephen Adolphe (ed.). 1988. *Language atlas of China* (Pacific Linguistics Series C, 102). Hong Kong, China: Longman.

Xinhua. (2019). Thematic Forum on People-to-people Connectivity of 2nd Belt and Road Forum held in Beijing. *People's Daily Online*. http://en.people.cn/n3/2019/0426/c90000-9572632.html (2 October 2020).

Xu, Hao. 2019. Putonghua as 'admission ticket' to the linguistic market in minority regions in China. *Language Policy* 18 (1). 17–38.

Yabuki, Susumu & Stephen M. Harner. 1999. *China's new political economy: Revised edition*. Boulder, CO: Westview Press.

Yan, Sun. 2004. *Corruption and market in contemporary China*. Ithaca, NY: Cornell University Press.

Yang, Hongyan. 2012. *Naxi, Chinese and English: Multilingualism in Lijiang*. Sydney: Macquarie University PhD thesis.

Yang, Rui. 2014. China's removal of English from Gaokao. *International Higher Education* 75 (Spring). 12–13.

Yang, Y. G. 2006. 语言民族变体研究：夹壮普通话个案 [Study on ethnic varities of a language: A case study of Zhuang Putonghua]. Nanjing: Nanjing University DA thesis.

Yu, Xingzhong. 2009. Regulatory and institutional framework of regional autonomy for ethnic minorities in China. *China Law* 2009 (2). 56–60.

Yue, Xuying, Zhang Zongtang, Wu Jing & Zhao Chao. 2010. Blueprint for educational modernization. *People's Daily*. http://www.moe.edu.cn/publicfiles/business/htmlfiles/moe/s3501/201010/109029.html (4 October 2016).

Zabrodskaja, Anastassia. 2014. Tallinn: Monolingual from above and multilingual from below. *International Journal of the Sociology of Language* 2014 (228). 105–130.

Zenz, Adrian & James Leibold. 2019. Securitizing Xinjiang: Police recruitment, informal policing and ethnic minority co-optation. *The China Quarterly* July. 1–25.

Zhang, Junru. 1999. 壮语方言研究 [Zhuang dialects research]. Chengdu: Sichuan Minzu Press.

Zhang, Jie. 2011. *Language policy and planning for the 2008 Beijing Olympics: An investigation of the discursive construction of an Olympic city and a global population*. Sydney: Macquarie University PhD thesis.

Zhang, Qian. 2014. Feeling the beat of the bamboo dance. *Shanghai Daily*. https://archive.shine.cn/sunday/now-and-then/Feeling-the-beat-of-the-bamboo-dance/shdaily.shtml (2 September 2020).

Zhang, Shengzhen (ed.). 1997. 壮族通史 [General History of the Zhuangzu] (Volume 3). Beijng: Beijing Nationalities Press.

Zhou, Lingxia. 2016. *Hegemony and counter-hegemony in the language campaigns in China*. Paper presented at Language and Conflict: Politics of Language and Identity across Contexts, SOAS University, 20 May.

Zhou, Minglang. 2000. Language policy and illiteracy in ethnic minority communities in China. *Journal of Multilingual and Multicultural Development* 21 (2). 129–148.

Zhou, Minglang. 2001. Language policy and reforms of writing systems for minority languages in China. *Written Language & Literacy* 4 (1). 31–65.

Zhou, Minglang. 2003. The politics of vernacular writing systems. In Minglang Zhou (ed.), *Multilingualism in China: The politics of writing reforms for minority languages, 1949–2002*, 209–279. Berlin: Mouton de Gruyter.

Zhou, Minglang. 2004. Minority language policy in China: Equality in theory and inequality in practice. In Zhou Minglang & Sun Hongkai (eds.), *Language policy in the People's Republic of China theory and practice since 1949* (Language Policy 4), 71–95. Boston, MA: Kluwer Academic Publishers.

Zhou, Minglang. 2012a. Historical review of the PRC's minority/indigenous language policy and practice. In Gulbahar H. Beckett & Gerard A. Postiglione (eds.). *China's assimilationist language policy*, 18–30. London & New York, NY: Routledge.

Zhou, Minglang. 2012b. Introduction: The contact between Putonghua (modern standard Chinese) and minority languages in China. *International Journal of the Sociology of Language* 2012 (215). 1–17.

Zhou, Minglang & Heidi A. Ross. 2004. Introduction: The context of the theory and practice of China's language policy. In Zhou Minglang & Sun Hongkai (eds.), *Language policy in the*

People's Republic of China: Theory and practice since 1949 (Language Policy 4), 1–18. Boston, MA: Kluwer Academic Publishers.

Zhou, Qingsheng. 1992. Aspects of Chinese ethnosociolinguistic studies: A report on the literature. *International Journal of the Sociology of Language* 1992 (97). 59–73.

Zhou, Yun. 2013. *Question of ethnic group formulation in the Chinese census*. Paper presented at the XXVII International Union for the Scientific Study of Population International Population Conference, Korea Institute of Population Problems, 26–31 August.

Zhu, Guobin. 2014. The right to minority language instruction in schools: Negotiating competing claims in multinational China. *Human Rights Quarterly* 36 (4). 691–721.

Index

agency. See *habitus*: agency
ASEAN 26, 289
– China-ASEAN Expo 2015 155, 259, 262
autonomous regions 96, 107, 279
– five 46
– Guangxi Zhuangzu. See Guangxi Zhuangzu Autonomous Region (GZAR)
– Inner Mongolia 21, 27, 29, 72, 75, 84, 296
  – study sites 29
– lack of legal autonomy 111
– *Regional Autonomy Law.* See Regional Autonomy Law
– regulations on public language display 72
– Tibet (Xizang) 72, 85
– Xinjiang 20, 72

Baihua 'Nanning Vernacular' 50, 85
Basic Principles 99
Beijing
– study sites 28–29

Cantonese 52, 85, 109, 220
Chinese People's Political Consultative Conference 119
– Committee for Ethnic and Religious Affairs 120
– national, provincial and regional committees 120
Coloniality 294
Constitution
– 1954 6, 69, 93, 124
– 1975 6, 76, 124
– 1978 6, 124
– 1982 5, 68, 76, 86, 93, 96, 113, 120, 280–281, 295
  – Article 119 96
  – Article 121 124
  – Article 139 76
  – Article 36 116
  – Article 4 68, 95, 113
    – 2018 amendments 95
  – Article 5 71
  – Part III, structure of the state 120
  – Preamble 71, 93, 120

– unofficial re minority language varieties 86
– *Common Program* 6, 69
Constitution of the CPC 116–117
covert policy. See language rights:language policy:*de facto* policies
CPPCC Charter 120
Criminal Law
– Articles 250–251 79
Criminal Procedure Law
– Article 9 77
critical sociolinguistics 14
Cultural Revolution 4
– literacy 57

Dalian Intermediate People's Court 76, 89
danwei 'workplace unit' 3
– legal responsibility re languages 72
de facto policies
– linguistic landscapes 141
de jure policies
– linguistic landscapes 141
Declaration on the Rights of Persons Belonging to National or Ethnic, Religious and Linguistic Minorities 70
Detailed Implementation Rules for the Management of Place-Names Ordinance 261
difference-aware equality 296
double domination 9
– double assimilation 12
– double marginality 31
doxa (Bourdieu) 15
– public space 24

Education Law
– Article 10 130
– Article 12 73
– Article 57, 59 130
Electoral Law 119
English
– bilingual signage 151
– state-funded education 136
– up-scaling places 177

ethnosociolinguistics 14
European Charter for Regional or Minority Languages 279

formal policy. See language rights:language policy:*de jure* policies

Gaokao 'university entrance exam' 61
globalization
– Chinese characteristics 7
– global languages 4, 8, 114
  – English 4, 8
  – Putonghua 4
– international law on languages 113
– marketization 11
– modernization 4
– superdiversity 8
Guangdong Province 46, 48
Guangxi University (GU) 29, 143, 145
Guangxi University for Nationalities (GUN) 28, 143, 147, 154, 168
Guangxi Zhuangzu Autonomous Region (GZAR) 19, 45, 107
– Bureau of Translation 125
  – future operation 268
– corruption 46
– Engel coefficient 60
– GDP per person 60
– governing structure 117
– government circulars 123
– governor 120, 122
– Guangxi Province, historic 39, 109
– GZAR Ethnic Affairs Commission 121
– GZAR Minority Language Commission 122
– GZAR People's Congress 123
– *GZAR Regulations* 123, 254, 259, 268, 278, 285–286, 289, 294
  – future operation 268
  – right to languages in court 269
– national strategic importance 11
– non-Zhuangzu minority minzu 46, 52, 192, 216
– Open Up The West campaign 8
– state-funded mediamedia. See Zhuang language: state-funded media
– study sites 28–29
Guizhou Province X, 39

habitus (Bourdieu) 15
– agency 16
– linguistic landscape 142
– naturalization of public language norms 186
Hakka 52
Hanyu 'Han language' 6
Hanzi 'Han characters' 13
heteroglossia (Bakhtin) 184
Hong Kong 295
hukou 'household registration' 30

imagined community (Anderson) 39, 62, 154, 176, 180, 184, 302
informal policy. See language rights: language policy:*de facto* policies
Inner Mongolia Autonomous Region 24, 25, 71, 80, 125, 304,
Inner Mongolia University of Science & Technology (IMUST) 29
Interim Provisions 123, 254, 256, 285
International Covenant on Civil and Political Rights 70

language governance 24
language ideologies 82
– aspiring monolingualism 13
– developmentalism 15, 24, 83, 97, 100, 186, 281, 288
  – language equality 100
  – literacy 97
  – méconnaissance / misrecognition 15, 104, 186, 299
  – national security 97
  – normative state responsibility 100
  – standardization 100
  – Zhuang education 137
– iconization 179
– monolingual mindset 83
– nationalism 83
– nationalization of heritage 300
– one nation, one language 83, 291
– pluralism 12
– recursive 26, 104
  – developmentalism 104
  – nation-state 83
– securitization 4

- spatialized linguistic order 185
- standard language ideology 83
- standardization 299
- territorialization 83, 109, 281, 288
- visual 141, 282
- zero-sum 289
language policy
- behavioral change 303
- ideological or implementational space (Hornberger) 271
- orientations 300
- shaping bilingual culture (Coupland) 267, 269
language resources
- government identity and legitimacy 180
language resources (Heller) 18
language rights
- critical theory 18
- *de facto* language policy 22, 87, 276
  - courts 87
- *de jure* language policy 23, 276
- ethnography of language policy 18
- group rights 297
- international 115
- language policy 24, 138, 271
  - *de facto* policies 138
  - *de jure* policies 138
  - language planning 271
- language policy mechanisms 16, 21
- linguistic landscapes 23
- minority language freedom 5, 275, 277, 287–288, 297, 299
- positive and negative rights 69
- public space 21, 276
- Putonghua 282
- right to learn and use Putonghua 6
- situated / emic 17
- state-funded media 135
- trends in Chinese rights law 82
law as declamations of general policy principles 81
law as discourse 15, 23, 294, 297
- over-application of laws 263
- under-application of laws 261
law as specific, actionable rights 81
Legislative Interpretation Law 111

Lianshan Zhuangzu-Yaozu Autonomous County 46, 107, 113
- Zhuangzu population 49
linguascaping 16
linguistic justice 16, 82, 92, 294–295
- liberalism / illiberalism 298
- linguistic reparative justice 298
- Nancy Fraser 298
- social justice 298
linguistic landscape
- agency 268, 285
- commented / narrated walking 220
- denaturalizing (Kress and van Leeuwen) 251
- experiencing fixed texts as temporary / mobile 228
- government authorship 239
- linguascaping 218, 253, 266–267
  - (Grey) 252
  - (Jaworski and Piller) 253
  - government as author 266
  - government as co-author 267
  - government as regulator 267
- lived landscape 16, 304
- social actors 219
  - authors 219
  - viewers 221
- soicla actors 249, 266
- government heterogeneity 266
- subjective invisibility 302
- top-down and bottom-up analytic division 251
linguistic landscapes
- relationship to semiotic landscapes 187

Macau 295
Mandarin topolects 8
- GZAR 52
methods 26, 276
- accelerated / rapid ethnography 32
- language leader participants 30, 276
- lived landscape 16, 304
- pseudonyms 30
- student participants 29, 276
minzu 6
- barbarians, historic 4, 43
- English 4

- *Bouyeizu* 36, 51, 302
- derogatory names, historic 164, 194
- *Dongzu* 31, 129
- *Duoyuan Yiti* 'multiple cultures, one body' 45
- *Hanzu* 6, 31, 39, 46, 60–61, 292
  - education 61
  - *non-Hanzu* 202
  - poverty 60
- hidden / unofficial groups 31–32
Inner Mongolia Autonomous Region.
   See autonomous regions: Inner Mongolia
- Miao album 41, 196
- *Miaozu* 41, 129
- Mongolian (*Mengzu*) 10, 171
  - on banknotes 171
- nations / nationalities 10
- people of the Baiyue Basin, historic 193
- *peuples sauvages* 'wild peoples', historic 39
- reclassification 43
- Republican 'five nations' 39
- *Shuizu* 129
- specialist minzu universities 28, 128
- *Tchoang Kolao/Kelao*, historic 41
- Tibetan 19, 85, 171
  - on banknotes 171
- *una gente ruda* 'a crude race', historic 41
- Uyghur 19, 70, 171, 203
  - Arabic script 203
  - linguistic landscape representation 203
  - on banknotes 171
- Xinjiang Uyghur Autonomous Region.
   See autonomous regions:Xinjiang 20
- *Yaozu* 31, 50, 129
- *Zhongjia*, historic 42
- *Zhuangzu* 18, 38, 42–43, 179, 195, 199, 279
  - 'love ball' trope 196
  - anachronistic 43
  - costume trope 197
  - *Cuengh* 'Zhuang' / *Bouxcuengh* 'Zhuangzu' 42, 192
  - drum trope 195
  - education 61

- indexed in linguistic landscape 179
- poverty 60
- *rauz / raeuz* 192
- visual representation of women 199
- 多元一体Duoyuan Yiti 'multiple cultures, one body' 94
- 统一多民族国家 'unified multi-minzu country' 10
Minzu University of China (MUC) 28, 143, 172

Nanning Measures 80, 123, 254–260, 264, 267–268, 270, 277, 285, 287
National Outline for Medium and Long-term Educational Reform and Development (2010–2020) 75, 98
National People's Congress 117–118
- Ethnic Affairs Committee 119

Opening and Reform 3
overt policy. See language rights:language policy:*de jure* policies

Party Central Committee 117, 121
Party-State model 115
Pinghua 52
Pinyin IX
politics of recognition 297
production format (Goffman) 184
Putonghua IX
- bilingual signage 151
- introduction to the PRC 6
- linguistic landscape dominance 174
- literacy 58
- monolingual signage 144
- on banknotes 171
Putonghua Law 6, 253, 282
- Article 10 73
- Article 19 255
- Article 4 69
- Articles 11–15 255
- Articles 26–27 71

Reform Outlines for the People's Courts 78
Regional Autonomy Law
- Article 27 74
- incomplete devolution 111

– Regulations of the State Council on the Enforcement of the Law on Regional Autonomy for Ethnic Minorities 111
Renmin University of China (RUC) 29

second generation minzu policy 44, 63
securitized language policy. *See* language ideologies:securitization
semitotic affordances (Jaworksi and Thurlow) 247, 249
Shanghainese 72
Southwest Guiliuhua 51
Southwestern Mandarin 52
standardization. *See* language ideologies: standardization
State Council 121
– Ministry of Education 123, 133
  – Bureau of Minority Education 123
  – GZAR Department of Education 128, 133
  – minzu universities 128
– National Ethnic Affairs Commission 121
– Yunnan Ethnic Affairs Commission 121
State Language Commission 123
symbolic jurisprudence (Leung) 105
symbolic power 14
symbolic power (Bourdieu) 82, 92, 104, 109, 116, 141, 143, 183, 226, 240, 265

UN Declaration on the Rights of Persons Belonging to National or Ethnic, Religious and Linguistic Minorities 115
unified multi-minzu nation 193
United Front Work Department 117, 121
unity in diversity 115
urbanization 11, 291
– cultural 278
– cultural urbanization 26, 175, 214
– in GZAR 47
– internal migration 11
– *liudong* 'flow of people' 11
– mobilities paradigm 31, 144
– mobility 143, 287
– rural poverty 60
– rural Zhuang readers 245
– student mobility 30, 143
– urban *hukou* 'household registration' 31
– Zhuangzu 47

Vienna Convention 265
Vietnamese 170

Wenshan Zhuangzu-Miaozu Autonomous Prefecture 46, 107
– Zhuangzu population 48

yong-ti dichotomy 4
Yubao 'Language Protection' project 4, 300
Yunnan Minzu University (YMU) 28, 143, 154, 165, 172
Yunnan Ordinance 126
Yunnan Ordinance 254
Yunnan Province 46, 48, 117
– study sites 28

Zhuang language
– bilingual signage 151
– bilingualism / multilingualism 51
– commercial text 166, 170, 175, 181, 189, 210, 266
  – authorial agency 266
– court 76
– Cyrillic 37
– domains of use 54
– down-scaling places / localizing 177
– endangered language 36
– explicit linguistic landscape references to 188
– fragmentary / partial translation 175, 258, 260, 268, 283
– government authorship 174, 183, 214
– government identity and legitimacy 180
– grassroots text 183
– heritage discourses 174, 176, 216, 235
– International Phonetic Alphabet 37
– language corridor 45
– language shift 36
– literacy 36, 57, 59, 61, 132, 175, 178, 232, 244, 246, 248, 290
  – public lesson 246
– monolingual signage 150
– new scripts 87
– notional inheritors 3
– Pinched Zhuang 90, 296
– primary schooling 128, 131

- experimental schooling 131
- rural 129
- transitional schooling 128–129
- public representation of living language practices 215
- relationship to Bouyei language 36
- relationship to English 58, 61, 222
- relationship to Putonghua Pinyin 58, 222
- relationship to Tai languages 35
- Romanization 301
- Romanized 37, 57, 174, 201, 235, 243, 250, 294
  - linguistic landscape 174
  - not indexing Zhuang speakers 214
  - preserving culture 243
  - recognizability 222, 250, 302
  - second reform 57
- Sawndip 'uncooked characters' 37, 58, 163–164, 174, 235, 248, 290
- secondary schooling 128, 130
- speaker numbers 50
- speaker participants 31
- Square Characters 37, 58, 135
- Standard Zhuang 26, 36, 56, 301
  - marketability 26
- state-funded media 58, 135, 166, 204, 211
  - *Third of the Third* magazine 58, 132, 135, 166, 204, 290
- Wuming Zhuang 56, 159
- Zhuang Studies 28
- Zhuangness 187
- Zhuang-Putonghua 56
- Zhuang-speaking Han peoples 42
- *Zhuangwen* 'Zhuang writing'. *See* Zhuang language: Romanized

www.ingramcontent.com/pod-product-compliance
Lightning Source LLC
Chambersburg PA
CBHW071734150426
43191CB00010B/1573